Globalization and Empire

Globalization and Empire

*The U.S. Invasion of Iraq, Free Markets,
and the Twilight of Democracy*

Stephen John Hartnett and Laura Ann Stengrim

THE UNIVERSITY OF ALABAMA PRESS
Tuscaloosa

Copyright © 2006
The University of Alabama Press
Tuscaloosa, Alabama 35487-0380
All rights reserved
Manufactured in the United States of America

Typeface: ACaslon

∞

The paper on which this book is printed meets the minimum requirements of American National Standard for Information Sciences-Permanence of Paper for Printed Library Materials, ANSI Z39.48-1984.

Library of Congress Cataloging-in-Publication Data

Hartnett, Stephen J.
   Globalization and empire : the U.S. invasion of Iraq, free markets, and the twilight of democracy / Stephen John Hartnett and Laura Ann Stengrim.
      p. cm. — (Rhetoric, culture, and social critique)
   Includes bibliographical references and index.
   ISBN-13: 978-0-8173-1501-6 (cloth : alk. paper)
   ISBN-10: 0-8173-1501-2
   1. Iraq War, 2003–2. Rhetoric—Political aspects—United States—History—21st century. 3. Globalization—Political aspects—United States. I. Stengrim, Laura Ann. II. Title. III. Series.
   DS79.76.H3756 2006
   808.53′0973′090511—dc22

                                                                    2005024351

Contents

Acknowledgments

We offer this book from positions of deep sadness and unflagging hope, for although we are not proud of our nation's actions in Iraq, and although many of the stories and facts conveyed here can only be called shameful, we continue to believe in the promises and practices of American democracy. We have thus written this book not only to reveal the utter mendacity of the Bush administration and to explain the numbing complexities of globalization but also to try to embody a sense of informed citizenship, to demonstrate how dissent is a fundamental part of the democratic process, to practice what we refer to as *rhetorical integrity*. Indeed, although we argue that post-9/11 America has drifted toward a series of rhetorical, economic, political, and military positions that we find terrifying, we continue to believe that it is not too late to build a new sense of patriotism based less on provincial anger than on international solidarity, less on the unleashing of rage than on the search for understanding, less on nationalizing fear than on globalizing hope, less on the principles of empire than on renewed democracy. Our hopes in this regard reflect our immersion in multiple communities that provide insight and inspiration in these dangerous and heartbreaking times. These acknowledgments thus thank both the individuals who have shaped our thinking and the larger intellectual and activist communities that have made our work possible.

Materials from the introduction were presented before our colleagues at Eastern Illinois University, where special thanks are due to our host, Dagni Bredesen, and to our colleagues in the University of Illinois Institute of Communications Research brown-bag lunch series. A draft of chapter 1 was presented to the University of Illinois Working Group on Globalization and Empire, where we received helpful commentary from Zsuzsa Gille and Jan Nederveen Pieterse from the Department of Sociology, John McKay from the Department of History, Matti Bunzl from the Department of Anthropology, and Michael Rothberg from the Department of English. Materials from this chapter were also presented before the University of Illinois Program in Arms Control, Disarmament, and International Security; we want to thank the director, Cliff Singer; the associate director, Matt Rosenstein; and one of the center's 2003/2004 research fellows, Joshua Barbour. An early version of that chapter appeared in *Cultural Studies<=>Critical Methodologies* 4, no. 2 (2004); that material appears here courtesy of Sage Publications.

The bulk of chapters 2 and 3 were drafted in the 2003/2004 academic year, when Stephen served as a research fellow of the Illinois Program for Research in the Humanities (IPRH). Special thanks are due to the IPRH's director, Matti Bunzl, and associate director, Chris Catanzarite, who together have built an institutional space where interdisciplinary thought thrives. Various sections of this book have been presented before IPRH panels and workshops; special thanks are due to our colleagues in the IPRH Reading Group on Citizenship, Education, and the Globalizing World. Materials from chapter 3 were presented in three forms (an invited lecture on weapons of mass destruction, a panel on cultural destruction, and a roundtable on globalization) before the 2004 Crossroads in Cultural Studies International Conference, where we had the opportunity to discuss our work with scholars from around the world. We want to thank Norman Denzin for this opportunity and thank Sonia Ertekin for recording and airing our presentations on her radio show from Istanbul. An abbreviated version of chapter 2 was published in the *South Atlantic Quarterly* 105, no. 1 (2006) where we are especially grateful for the editorial genius of Dana Nelson and Christi Stanforth.

Sections of chapter 4 were discussed with Bob McChesney on his *Media Matters* radio show, a wonderful weekly exhibit of informed debate. Chapter 4 was also read carefully by Kirk Freudenberg. The conclusion was revised according to insightful commentary from Chuck Morris, Jed Esty, and Cara Finnegan; a conversation with Ruth Hoberman about Auden's poems; and following another mind-bending Wednesday night conversation with Adam Sutcliffe, who has provided years of argument-sharpening dialogue and inspiring friendship. His little Orlando was born in the final days of our writing this book, again reminding us of why we do what we do.

In addition to the help offered on specific chapters noted here, the entire book was read and edited by current and former University of Illinois colleagues, including Brett Kaplan from the Department of Comparative Literature; Norman Denzin from the Institute of Communications Research (ICR); Zohreh Sullivan, Jim Hurt, and Allan Borst from the Department of English; Donovan Conley (now at the University of Nevada at Las Vegas) and Jeremy Engels from the Department of Speech Communication; and Belden Fields from the Department of Political Science. Materials were also presented, and ideas tested, in graduate seminars and undergraduate courses, where students' concerns and comments were, as always, crucial in forming our arguments.

In terms of our political work, we have drawn insight and inspiration from our friends at the Urbana-Champaign Independent Media Center, especially the group that produces the *Public-i,* our local alternative newspaper. Thanks are due here to Belden Fields, Darrin Drda, Meghan Krausch, Paul Mueth, Linda Evans, and Scott Edwards. Since 9/11 the University of Illinois Teachers for Peace and Justice (TFPJ) have sponsored teach-ins, workshops, discussions, and other activities at which many of our ideas were first aired. Among our TFPJ friends and event participants, special thanks are due to Michael Weissman from the Department of Physics; Al Kagan from the School of Library Sciences; Zohreh Sullivan, Bill Maxwell, Julia Walker, and Michael Rothberg from the Department of English; Bob McChesney from the ICR; and Adam Sutcliffe and Maria Todorova from the Department of History. Champaign-Urbana's Anti-War Anti-Racism Effort (AWARE) has also been a major source of support; many thanks to Sunie Davis, Ricky Baldwin, Lisa Chason, Sandra Ahten, and Carol Inskeep and Matt Murrey, whose political picnics are joyous enactments of community. We have also drawn inspiration from and presented our ideas at the University YMCA, where the Friday Forum speaker series provides a model of informed civic engagement; thanks here are due to Steve Shoemaker and Becca Guyette.

Moving from local to national affiliations, we are grateful for the community of thinkers and activists who gather around the events of the National Communication Association (NCA). For example, our thoughts about globalization, empire, and post-9/11 U.S. foreign policy were aired in 2003 and 2004 at Dilip Gaonkar's Summer Rhetoric Institute at Northwestern University, where we had the opportunity to share our ideas with faculty and graduate students from around the nation. We are grateful for lengthy e-mail exchanges with Larry Frey; for conversations at conferences with Robert Ivie, Dana Cloud, John Sloop, Vanessa Beasley, Bryan Taylor, Bonnie Dow, James Arnt Aune, Christine Harold, and Gordon Mitchell; and to those NCA colleagues who marched with Stephen in Miami in November 2003 to protest the Free Trade of the Americas Agreement. Thus merging scholarship with activism, research with citizenship, our many friends and colleagues thanked here have encouraged us to think about the opportunities and obligations of pursuing rhetorical criticism as the practice of democratic integrity.

We would also like to thank our friends at the University of Alabama Press, including our editor, Daniel Waterman; our copyeditor, Kathy Swain; our visionary series editor, John Lucaites; and our most enjoyable critic, Robert Hariman. Despite our blockheaded resistance, Daniel, Kathy, John, and Bob have relentlessly prodded us toward clarity of expression and argument.

Finally, Stephen thanks Brett again for her unconditional love and support; Anya and Melia for delaying completion of this book as much as possible in their infinitely joyous ways; and Rod and Sandy for modeling humble commitment. Laura thanks her mom, dad, auntie, and grandparents for embodying consistency and honesty; her friends for their patience and kindness; and her fellow activists at the Independent Media Center for knowing that laughter makes it all worthwhile.

List of Abbreviations and Acronyms

ACTA: American Council of Trustees and Alumni
ADM: Archer Daniels Midland
AI: Amnesty International
BCI: Boots & Coots International Well Control
CAFTA: Central American Free Trade Agreement
CB: Custer Battles
CBO: Congressional Budget Office
CCP: Crisis Consulting Practice
CDI: Center for Defense Information
CEIP: Carnegie Endowment for International Peace
CEPR: Center for Economic and Policy Research
CFR: Council on Foreign Relations
CIA: Central Intelligence Agency
CNS: Center for Nonproliferation Studies
CPA: Coalition Provisional Authority
CPI: Center for Public Integrity
CRS: Congressional Research Service
CSIS: Center for Strategic and International Studies
DAC: Development Assistance Committee of the OECD
DIA: Defense Intelligence Agency
DOE: Department of Energy
DSB: Defense Science Board
EA: Elliott Associates
EPI: Economic Policy Institute
ETF: Vice President Cheney's Energy Task Force
EU: European Union
FCC: Federal Communications Commission
FOIA: Freedom of Information Act

FTAs: Free trade agreements (in general)

FTAA: Free Trade Area of the Americas

GAO: U.S. General Accounting Office; renamed in 2004 as the Government Accountability Office

GATT: Global Agreement on Tariffs and Trade

GDI: UN Gender-Related Development Index

GDP: Gross domestic product

GEM: UN Gender Empowerment Measure

GNP: Gross national product

GSP: Generalized System of Preferences

G-8: Group of nations that meet to discuss global issues (U.S, U.K., Canada, France, Germany, Italy, Russia, Japan)

G-20/23: Group of nations in solidarity with the global south

HB: Hebrew Bible

HDR: UN *Human Development Report,* 2002

HFI: UN Human Freedom Index

HP: Hewlett Packard

HPI: UN Human Poverty Index

HRW: Human Rights Watch

HSIC: Homeland-Security-Industrial-Complex

IADB: Inter-American Development Bank

IAEA: International Atomic Energy Agency

ICRC: International Committee of the Red Cross

ID/IQ: Indefinite Delivery/Indefinite Quantity Contracts

IGO: International governmental organization

IMF: International Monetary Fund

INR: Department of State's Bureau of Intelligence and Research

IPS: Institute for Policy Studies

IRS: Internal Revenue Service

JCT: Joint Committee on Taxation

JIC: British Joint Intelligence Committee

KA: Kissinger Associates

KBR: Kellogg Brown & Root

LogCAP: Logistics Civil Augmentation Program

MNCs: Multinational corporations

NAFTA: North American Free Trade Agreement

NASA: National Aeronautics and Space Administration

NATO: North Atlantic Treaty Organization

NBS: New Bridge Strategies
NGOs: Nongovernmental organizations
NIE: National Intelligence Estimate, 2002
NRDC: National Resource Defense Council
NSA: National Security Archive
NSSUS: *National Security Strategy of the United States,* 2002
OECD: Organization for Economic Cooperation and Development
OSP: Office of Special Plans
PCO: Project and Contracting Office
PDB: Presidential Daily Briefing
PFI: UN Political Freedom Index
PMFs: Private military firms
PNAC: Project for the New American Century
RTI: Research Triangle Institute
SEC: Securities and Exchange Commission
SEEN: Sustainable Energy and Economic Network
SRR: Gap Inc.'s *Social Responsibility Report,* 2003
TBI: Trade Bank of Iraq
TDF: Telecommunications Development Fund
TNCs: Transnational corporations
UAV: Unmanned aerial vehicle
UN: United Nations
UNESCO: UN Educational, Scientific and Cultural Organization
UNMOVIC: UN Monitoring, Verification, and Inspection Commission
UNSCOM: UN Special Commission
USAID: United States Agency for International Development
US-CFTA: U.S.–Chile Free Trade Agreement
US-SFTA: U.S.–Singapore Free Trade Agreement
WDR: World Bank *World Development Report,* 2004
WMDs: Weapons of mass destruction
WTO: World Trade Organization
WWC: Wild Well Control, Inc.

Globalization and Empire

Introduction

Globalization, Empire, and the Productions of Violence

The Bush administration and its allies have sought to portray the perpetrators of 9/11, the Taliban and al Qaeda, and Saddam Hussein's Iraq—
with North Korea and Iran thrown in for good measure—as irrational
yet deadly embodiments of an "axis of evil" sprung forth from bizarre,
inexplicable sources. In his 2002 State of the Union address, the axis-of-
evil speech delivered four months following 9/11, President Bush argued
that rogue states and their terrorist allies rely on "thousands of dangerous killers . . . spread throughout the world like ticking time bombs."
The president then pledged to "eliminate the terrorist parasites," thus
rhetorically turning inanimate, bomblike terrorists into a teeming pool of
subhuman leeches threatened with an open-ended death sentence. Two
and one-half years later, following yet another terrorist strike, this time
on the southern fringe of Russia, David Brooks wailed in the *New York
Times* that the world was under assault by a "cult of death" that thrives on
the "sheer pleasure of killing and dying. It's about massacring people. . . .
It's about experiencing the total freedom of barbarism. . . . It's about the
joy of sadism and suicide." Rather than seeing global terrorism in political
terms, Brooks diagnosed this cult of death as "pathological," thus turning
its members into disease-riddled deviants. Rendering terrorists as inanimate bombs, psychologically damaged, diseased, and subhuman—in all
cases portraying them as acting without forethought, provocation, or
reason—may edify those who wish to comprehend the world as if it were
a fairy-tale contest between Good and Evil, yet it clouds our abilities to
think about the historical, political, economic, and cultural causes of violence. In contrast to the president's, Brooks's, and others' attempts to render events since 9/11 in such moralistic, medical, psychological, and theological terms, we propose that 9/11, global terrorist strikes since then, and
the subsequent U.S.-led wars in Afghanistan and Iraq and against terror-

ism more generally can only be understood by examining how globalization, empire, and their accompanying rhetorical justifications have produced contexts ripe for violence.[1]

We therefore focus on the arguments used to sanction the U.S. war on Iraq (chapter 1), on the rhetoric explaining post-9/11 U.S. foreign policy more broadly (chapter 2), on both the deep economic agendas and rhetorical positions of the key international and U.S. institutions driving our moment of globalization (chapter 3), and, as a case study pulling these threads about war and globalization together, on the colonization of postwar Iraq under the rubric of economic reconstruction and democracy building (chapter 4). By focusing in each chapter on the relationship between the Bush administration's public arguments and its actual policies, we hope to illustrate the powerful bond between fraying and increasingly deceptive norms of public discourse and post-9/11 political and economic policies. Indeed, our case studies illustrate the remarkably complicated ways the Bush administration has used 9/11 as an elastic justification for waging wars of globalization and empire under the banner of free trade and democracy—hence fulfilling Herbert Marcuse's prescient 1964 warning that "liberty can be made into a powerful instrument of oppression."[2]

As long-time activists we are committed not only to critiquing the world but also to changing it; we accordingly include a lengthy appendix offering a guide to what we believe are the most productive action groups, think tanks, government sites, watchdog services, and other sources of information for scholars and empowerment for activists. If readers find our arguments persuasive, then we hope they will use this appendix to support their own scholarship and activism, hence joining the rising chorus of citizens trying to restore some sense of balance and decency—what we call below *rhetorical integrity*—to our public debates about foreign policy, international economics, and the fate of democracy. Less a definitive statement than an elaborate invitation to engage in debate and action, we offer the following chapters as prompts to future discussions about the fate of democracy in an age of globalization and empire.

~

Six days after 9/11, while the World Trade Center still smoldered, the *New Yorker* published a series of reflections from nine famous authors. The compassion and insight of those comments served as welcome reminders that the nation would survive, that violence could not silence creative and brave souls committed to thinking about the fate of democracy. But the *New Yorker's* offerings were exceptional in their tone and candor, for the mood in America at the time was somber and defiant, not critical—that is, the nation appeared to have coalesced around two responses: grieve for the dead and destroy those who committed the atrocities. As a rebuke to the second of these responses, which at the time many of us assumed would lead to terrible wars of retribution, and which still appears to drive U.S. foreign policy more than four years later, Susan Sontag wrote, "Let's by all means grieve together. But let's not be stupid together." Those two sentences earned Sontag entrance onto blacklists around the nation; callers to radio talk shows seethed her name as if it was synonymous with treason and cold-blooded inhumanity.[3]

But those of us who had been following the activities of neoconservatives since the close of the first Gulf War knew from the moment 9/11 unfolded before our stunned eyes that it would not be long before the Bush administration invaded Iraq. For from the mid-1990s onward, a group of prominent neoconservatives had been lobbying to finish the work of the first Gulf War by orchestrating regime change in Iraq. In 1996, the Study Group on a New Israeli Strategy, convened by the aggressive Israeli right-wing think tank, the Institute for Advanced Strategic and Political Studies, released "A Clean Break: A New Strategy for Securing the Realm." Cowritten by Richard Perle (the chair of the group), Douglas Feith, David Wurmser, and other neoconservatives who would assume key roles in George W. Bush's administration, "A Clean Break" calls for "removing Saddam Hussein from power." Startlingly belligerent and marked by what Middle East expert Rashid Khalidi describes as "enthusiastic ignorance and ideological blindness," the report envisions Israel and the United States as launching a Middle East–revising grand strategy based on military power, including "*striking at select targets in Syria proper.*" This strategy was updated in a 26 January 1998 letter to President Bill Clinton, when a group of neoconservatives associated with the Project for the New American Century (PNAC) urged the president to "remove Saddam Hussein's regime from power." Raising the specter of Iraq acquiring weapons of mass destruction (WMDs), the authors urged President Clinton to cultivate "a willingness to undertake military action" regardless of strong opposition within the UN Security Council. Thus illustrating an obsession with WMDs, a commitment to preemptive military force, and disregard for international diplomacy, the letter writers called for war on Iraq. Signed by Richard Armitage, John Bolton, Robert Kagan, Richard Perle, William Kristol, Donald Rumsfeld, Paul Wolfowitz, and other PNAC figures, the letter left little doubt that if its authors controlled U.S. foreign policy, then the United States would invade Iraq. The PNAC letter was followed by "Bombing Iraq Isn't Enough," a 30 January 1998 *New York Times* editorial by Robert Kagan, where he called on President Clinton to "order ground forces into the gulf," for "Saddam Hussein must go." Responding to this pressure, the Clinton administration made regime change a formal part of its foreign policy with the 7 October 1998 Iraq Liberation Act, which authorized U.S. intelligence agencies and the Pentagon to spend $97 million cultivating anti-Saddam rebellions in Iraq. The covert actions—critics might call them state-sponsored terrorism—carried out under the Iraq Liberation Act were failures. Nonetheless, when George W. Bush assumed the presidency in January 2001 and promptly appointed many of the 1996 "Clean Break" strategists, the 1998 PNAC letter's authors, the Liberation Act's supporters, and other neoconservative figures to positions of power, there could be little doubt that war with Iraq was imminent.[4]

In fact, Seymour Hersh learned in interviews conducted in Syria in December 2003 with Ahmad Sadik, a former brigadier general in the Iraqi Air Force, that "soon after George Bush's election brought into office many of the officials who had directed the 1991 Gulf War," Hussein assumed war was coming. He was so convinced the United States was about to attack that in early 2001, before 9/11, he began planning the postinvasion insurgency that has turned the U.S. occupation of Iraq into a bloody quagmire. Thus, from the earliest moments of the tragedies of 9/11, those of us—including Hussein—who had followed the arguments of PNAC-linked neoconservatives, feared that the Bush administration would use the terrorist attacks as the justification for pursuing regime change in Iraq. Sure enough, Bob Woodward's *Plan of Attack* reports that "at 2:40 P.M. that day [9/11] . . . Rumsfeld raised with his staff the possibility of going after Iraq as a response to the terrorist attacks." We know from Ron Suskind's *The Price of Loyalty*, another scathing account of the Bush White House based on conversations with Paul O'Neill, the former treasury secretary, that Defense Secretary Rumsfeld "had raised the question of Iraq" again at a National Security Council meeting on September 13, long before there was any evidence regarding alleged links between Iraq and the perpetrators of 9/11. Likewise, in *Against All Enemies*,

Richard Clarke recounts how, the morning following 9/11, he walked into the White House ready to tackle al Qaeda, only "to realize with almost a sharp physical pain that Rumsfeld and Wolfowitz were going to try to take advantage of this national tragedy to promote their agenda about Iraq." When Sontag asked her readers to "not be stupid together," then, she was clearly hoping to preempt the use of 9/11's tragedies as justifications for launching a war that was *already being planned before the towers fell.*[5]

In that same set of reflections on 9/11, published alongside Sontag's fury-prompting comments, John Updike observed how difficult it is when "suddenly summoned to witness something great and horrendous . . . not to reduce it to our own smallness." Like Sontag, although in a more measured tone, Updike was asking readers not to succumb to the numbing existential shock of the moment and instead to struggle to maintain their capacities for thinking historically and strategically about 9/11 and how the event would transform global politics. Following Sontag and Updike and the hundreds of other writers, scholars, and activists from whom we have drawn solace, inspiration, and guidance since 9/11, many of whom we rely on in the following chapters, this book strives to honor the "smallness" of personal experience while contextualizing it within some of the larger forces shaping our lives. Indeed, our task in this book is to offer readers the rhetorical tools, informational base, and historical background necessary for understanding how liberty, freedom, and democracy have been turned into powerful rhetorical instruments justifying globalization and empire.[6]

To help us comprehend our current moment of globalization and empire in historical terms, thus situating recent claims about freedom and democracy, free trade and globalization, within narratives that predate 9/11, we turn briefly to J. A. Hobson's 1902 exposé of the corruption and cronyism driving the British Empire. Working under the chapter heading of "Economic Parasites of Imperialism," Hobson offers this poignant observation:

Seeing that the imperialism of the last three decades is clearly condemned as a business policy, in that at enormous expense it has procured a small, bad, unsafe, increase of markets, and has jeopardized the entire wealth of the nation in rousing the strong resentment of other nations, we may ask, 'How is the British nation induced to embark upon such unsound business practices?' The only possible answer is that the business interests of the nation as a whole are subordinated to those of certain sectional interests that usurp control of the national resources and use them for their private gain.

The world of President Bush's wars in Afghanistan and Iraq is of course fundamentally different from the one that saw British forces circling the globe; nonetheless, Hobson's study rings true. In fact, in offering a critique as applicable to the crony capitalism driving the reconstruction of Iraq as to the British Empire, Hobson argues that the usurpation of national resources for private gain produces catastrophic consequences on both domestic and international levels.[7]

Domestically, the rise of imperialism's economic opportunists means that "certain definite business and professional interests feeding upon imperialistic expenditure, or upon the results of that expenditure, are set up in opposition to the common good." Because of imperialism, domestic programs languish, political accountability suffers, and, as elucidated so clearly in Eric Hobsbawm's *The Age of Empire*, norms of cosmopolitan internationalism slide toward chauvinism, exceptionalism, and xenophobia. As Hobsbawm observes of the decade preceding World War I, empire-hungry elites did not stress "glory and conquest, but that 'we' were the victims of aggression" by a foggy "they" that "represented a moral threat to the values of freedom and civilization which 'we' embodied." Internationally, the triumph of these same forces means "the use of the machinery of government by private interests . . . to secure for them economic gains outside their country." Hobson's usurpers therefore transform "the machinery of government" into a war-making, nation-conquering battering ram—justified at every step by claims to be defending civilization—used to topple foreign barriers to profitability. Taken together, these entwined domestic and international consequences point to an assault not only on the political sovereignty and market autonomy of foreign nations but also on the sense of representational government, decision-making transparency, and pursuit of the general welfare that render democracy (even the diluted British version of the early twentieth century) legitimate. For Hobson and Hobsbawm, then, imperialism is toxic: it compromises the state's ability to govern at home, drains the treasury, fuels racism and militarized versions of nationalism, and enriches a class of political and economic usurpers at the cost of the "common good."[8]

Most important for this book, Hobson and Hobsbawm demonstrate that the push for empire at the close of the nineteenth and opening of the twentieth centuries created a cascading series of foreign enemies, turning the emissaries of empire into walking targets for those who resented the political, economic, and cultural encroachments of foreigners. Peter Linebaugh and Marcus Rediker's *The Many-Headed Hydra* is especially powerful in this regard, for it demonstrates how the earliest thrusts of the British Empire into the New World, beginning with attempts to establish colonial/capitalist outposts in the late sixteenth and early seventeenth centuries, triggered waves of ship mutinies, slave rebellions, counterimperial insurgencies, and other forms of violence that would likely fall under today's heading of terrorism. Reading Hobson, Hobsbawm, Linebaugh and Rediker, and the many other critics of empire who appear in this study thus makes it painfully evident that 9/11, despite the stunning originality of the methods of and staggering death toll from the attacks, is not so much an inexplicable and random event as yet another in a long series of violent backlashes against a string of different empires.[9]

Indeed, the fact that the fury of 9/11 was directed at the World Trade Center and the Pentagon underscores our argument, for it demonstrates how the attacks were directed at the twin pillars of U.S. power: leadership of globalizing free markets and unrivalled military dominance. The symbolism of the targets is so obvious, and the powers they represent so ubiquitous yet mundane for many Americans, that a surprising number of observers have acted—following the rhetorical cues provided by President Bush, David Brooks, and many others—as if the attacks were not opening salvos in a strategic war against globalization (the towers) and empire (the Pentagon), but evidence of a battle over the future of civilization itself. As we demonstrate in chapter 2, this clash-of-civilizations thesis is politically, geographically, culturally, and historically vacuous at best, propagandistic at worst. To accept Sontag's controversial challenge to "not be stupid together" therefore entails situating 9/11 and the subsequent wars launches by the United States within the histories of globalizing capitalism, expanding empires, and the many forms of violence they inevitably produce.

As rhetorical critics we are particularly concerned with addressing how elites have sought to decouple the violence of war, economic domination, and cultural conquest from any sense of political, economic, or historical causality. We therefore examine how the chant of "free trade" has been remarkably persuasive for justifying globalization and forwarding empire. Indeed, while there are a dizzying number of theories, histories, and definitions bidding to explain the now-ubiquitous (yet deeply confusing) notions of globalization and empire, our research demonstrates that from the earliest moments of international trade, national conquest, and cultural exchange, capitalist elites and their political allies have used varying notions of free trade to justify their actions. For example, from as early as the Dutch commercial empire of the mid-seventeenth century, globe-trotting capitalists—sometimes acting as official servants of the state, sometimes as its hired mercenaries, and sometimes as adventurers whose initial forays would lead to later state intervention—have linked notions of free trade, international law, and domestic peace and prosperity to explain their right to exploit the raw materials and labor forces of foreign markets. According to David Armitage, the British initially did not have the manpower to invade the New World with formal armies, meaning that the state "led from behind and *allowed private enterprise to bear the burdens of conquest and settlement.*" And although their triumph in the Seven Years' War (begun in 1756) launched the British on an unprecedented course of globalizing colonialism, it would not be long before their defeat at the hands of revolutionary Americans (and their allies, the French, Dutch, and the Spanish, each of whom waged war against the British in far-flung colonies) demonstrated that profits would be better pursued not by setting up colonial administrations but by leveraging economic power via what Linda Colley calls the "cheap and indirect version of empire." In fact, P. J. Cain argues that by the nineteenth century "free trade imperialism" had become Britain's strategy for continued international domination. Cain notes, however, that "free trade was seen as a weapon . . . and when it did not seem to answer to their needs it was not supported." Indeed, the rapidity with which champions of free trade could become either ardent protectionists or aggressive colonizers suggests that the earliest proponents of free trade were less committed to building a unified and unfettered global market of economic opportunity—the supposed goals of globalization—than to continued enrichment and expanded political power—the reality of empire—under whatever rhetorical banner seemed most persuasive.[10]

As Harry Magdoff has noted, the instrumental use of free trade to justify certain imperialist actions and globalization more generally enabled the British and then Americans—both of whom eventually learned to dread the fury of anticolonial violence—to pursue "imperialism without colonies." That is, state military power would be used to open up and then protect the profitability of foreign markets, yet the conquering state and its capitalist elites—its "usurpers," to use Hobson's term—would not have to assume the economic, diplomatic, and cultural costs of governing their conquered territories. Thus, whereas earlier versions of colonialism sought to produce client regimes by imposing settler-dominated administrations capable of governing daily life down to the smallest detail (such as in the British colonies in the Americas before 1776 and then again in India and throughout Africa at the close of the nineteenth century), post–World War II free trade imperialism has increasingly been based on the understanding that expropriating profits need not be tied down by the burdens of actual governance.[11]

For example, at the height of the cold war the United States maintained as many as eight hundred facilities around the globe, thus managing the world's largest network of troops, weapons, communications, and intelligence agents, yet those eight hundred sites were run under tight scrutiny and served limited roles: they were military bases, not diplomatic or cultural outposts charged with extending U.S. values and administrative responsibilities to their host nations (although as Cynthia Enloe and Chalmers Johnson have demonstrated, they were and are painfully effective in spreading drugs, alcohol, pornography, sexual diseases, traffic accidents, environmental damage, and other detritus of U.S. consumer culture to the neighborhoods surrounding the bases). Anti-Communism was the driving justification for these facilities, hence rendering their purpose in explicitly market and military terms: they were armed to the teeth, ready to deter supposed Communist aggression anywhere and anytime, all the while protecting the trade routes, raw materials, and foreign markets that enabled postwar capitalism to flourish. Fighting Communism thus served as the rhetorical cover obscuring the fact that post–World War II free trade imperialism was deeply linked to a global military—*yet not traditionally colonial*—empire. Johnson thus argues in *The Sorrows of Empire* that the United States has been pursuing "a new form of imperialism" by "creating not an empire of colonies but an empire of bases." In this sense, then, we may think of the past half-century of globalization as an ever-expanding form of U.S.-led free trade imperialism, as the global pursuit of economic and political advantage in foreign lands policed by U.S. military power yet not ruled by it in any direct governing manner. Aijaz Ahmad thus describes the United States as pursuing "the first fully post-colonial imperialism."[12]

Perhaps reflecting the failures of that strategy (which we elucidate in chapter 3), recent events suggest that the United States may be shifting its energies back toward a form of globalization closer to the old empire-building model of colonialism decried by Hobson and Hobsbawm. Indeed, whereas the neoliberalism of the Clinton presidency was concerned with establishing transnational mechanisms for expanding free trade imperialism, with using state power to advance commercial interests on a global scale, President George W. Bush has embarked on a course of empire-building colonialism, complete with U.S. armed forces and companies stationed indefinitely in foreign lands—Afghanistan and Iraq for now, with more likely to come—ruled by governments that, as we demonstrate in chapter 4 and our conclusion, are mere puppets for U.S. power. The war against terrorism has thus replaced Communism as the overriding justification for continued U.S. military domination of the globe, with a chorus of figures arguing that we must fight foreign wars to keep the "homeland" safe. Yet the bulk of elite documents explaining the United States' aggressive merging of free trade-driven globalization and warmaking empire have relied on notions of historical obligation, market opportunity, and cultural advancement that echo the universal righteousness and moralizing fervor that drove Britain's earlier attempts to colonize much of the world under the banner of the "white man's burden." One of the many conceptual difficulties of thinking about post–9/11 U.S. economic and foreign policy, then, is trying to figure out how much of it is radically new, how much of it is a repackaged version of cold war mentalities, and how much of it is a return to earlier forms of empire.

For example, President Bush's preface to the 2002 *National Security Strategy of the United States,* the foreign-policy blueprint released roughly one year following 9/11, begins with the sweeping claim that the twentieth century concluded with a "decisive victory for the forces of freedom—and a single model of national success: freedom, democracy, and free enterprise. . . . These values of freedom are right and true for every person, in every society." Speaking both as an imperialist commander and an evangelical preacher, both as a warmaker and a saver of souls, President

Bush then promises that "we will actively work to bring the hope of democracy, development, free markets, and free trade to every corner of the world." The document's opening chapter echoes this claim, arguing that U.S. values "are right and true for all people everywhere." Such startling moments of hubris indicate how under the Bush administration globalization will not follow the cold war model of free trade imperialism but the model of empire-building, world-homogenizing colonialism where U.S. forces seek not to contain enemies but to reform and liberate—by force if necessary—those who do not yet share U.S. values. By proclaiming that his administration will strive to extend these values "to every corner of the world," President Bush indicates his commitment to a new imperialism that knows no bounds. Although rendered in a tone that we characterize in chapter 2 as "benign universalism," such sanctimonious claims indicate how, following 9/11 and the fall of Communism, the economic and cultural processes often discussed under the rubric of globalization have become enmeshed in the military and political processes often discussed under the rubric of imperialism, with both globalization and empire now justified under the banner of "democracy, development, free markets, and free trade."[13]

This remarkable turn of events, with empire cloaked by chants of freedom and democracy, is only possible because of the vast and stupefying ability of certain powers to control the meaning of language itself. As Theodor Adorno lamented in 1945 in *Minima Moralia: Reflections from Damaged Life*, his beautiful yet melancholy collection of ruminations on the Holocaust and the rise of what he called "the culture industry": "Things have come to pass where lying sounds like truth, truth like lying. . . . The confounding of truth and lies, making it almost impossible to maintain a distinction, and a labor of Sisyphus to hold on to the simplest piece of knowledge, . . . [marks] the conversion of all questions of truth into questions of power." On the one hand, Adorno's biting observation that truth and lying have become little more than playthings of those in power, conceptual tools wielded to justify the genocidal warmaking that turned Europe into the world's largest mass grave, may strike twenty-first-century readers as either overblown or outdated. On the other hand, those of us who watched President Bush drag the United States into a needless war in Iraq over mythical weapons of mass destruction and equally mythical Iraq/al Qaeda connections, and those of us who watched as the world's supposedly most free press turned in the months leading up to and through the first phase of the war into a genuflecting body of embedded supplicants, dazed by the allure of power, cannot help but recognize the chilling accuracy and current applicability of Adorno's claim.[14]

The question, of course, is, how did we arrive at yet another situation where "lying sounds like truth, truth like lying"? It may prove helpful to try to answer that question not so much in terms of truth and lying—words corrupted to the point of permanent uncertainty by power—as in terms of *integrity* and *hypocrisy.* As described by Thomas Farrell in *Norms of Rhetorical Culture,* "Integrity is less an attribute specifically applicable to persons and their character than an emergent, acquired trait of messages that are presented and upheld in public life." For those of us who practice rhetorical criticism in the hope that it enriches the civic life of our democracy, the "acquired traits" that fill public discourse with integrity include the presentation of verifiable evidence, consideration of ethical norms that transcend the instrumental, the careful consideration of counterarguments, and the ability to transform one's positions based on ethical considerations, emergent counterevidence, and persuasive counterarguments. Integrity therefore requires the give-and-take of information and ideals, striving not so much for some absolute truth as for the best-available understanding of a given situation. In this sense, then, whereas hypocrisy pollutes the means of persuasion to achieve certain private or corporate ends, practicing integrity means privileging the norms of fair and democratic deliberation to achieve what Hobson called "the common good."[15]

Indeed, we argue that rhetorical criticism is a necessary tool of democracy, because each citizen's capacity to fathom the complexities of our political life hinges on the abilities to listen, read, write, view, and speak critically, hence enabling her or him not only to consume political rhetoric but to produce it, thus contributing to national dialogue. This is in many ways an ancient belief, for as Gerard Hauser reminds us in his opening essay in *Rhetorical Democracy,* "instruction in rhetoric rose to prominence in antiquity from the understanding that oratorical competence was inherent to participation in the Athenian democracy and the Roman republic. . . . Skillful expression resulted in public decisions based on public deliberation rather than private arrangements. As such, rhetoric lay at the heart of citizenship." Linking Hauser's thoughts on ancient Athens to Farrell's account of integrity, we argue that rhetorical criticism, informed citizenship, and integrity-driven public deliberation go hand in hand—they are among the first principles of democratic life. We therefore hope this book reaffirms the relationship between good public discourse and good public policy, between rhetorical analysis and public judgment, between a rhetorically skilled public and sustainable democracy.[16]

Given the disconcerting ways so much of U.S. public discourse has slid into shrill and hysterical stupidity—with mudslinging, jingoistic cheerleading, apocalyptic fantasies, chest-thumping warmongering, absurd color-coded threat warnings, and the production of factual distortions all so rampant that one is hard pressed to find informed, balanced, historically inflected, and fair-minded deliberation anywhere in the corporate mass media—calling for the practicing of integrity in public life amounts to nothing less than a radical demand to salvage democracy itself. Our notion of *rhetorical-criticism-as-the-practice-of-democratic-integrity* therefore eludes the snares of power-defined truth described above by Adorno, instead aspiring not to a fixed place (either Truth or Lying) but to an unfolding and pragmatic process of fair-minded public deliberation.[17]

To demonstrate how pursuing this notion of *rhetorical-criticism-as-the-practice-of-democratic-integrity* would entail fundamental transformations in U.S. political life, we turn briefly to three representative examples of how communicative hypocrisy hamstrings public deliberation about the crises of our age. First, consider one of the actions of House Republicans in the flush days following the November 2004 reelection of President Bush. Emboldened by their increased House majority and fearing impending indictments for a mountain of illegalities allegedly committed by majority leader Tom DeLay, the Republicans waited but two weeks after the election to revoke a long-standing rule that required party leaders to step aside when indicted. Hence throwing ethics out the window to protect DeLay's continued mastery of the House, the Republicans made it clear that they would put party power above the national interest. (This maneuver produced a firestorm of criticism, eventually forcing House Republicans to annul the order.) Second, consider the work of Porter J. Goss, President Bush's post-Tenet head of the CIA, who responded to the president's reelection by advising CIA employees that their job is to "support the administration and its policies in our work." Goss warned that "as agency employees we do not identify with, support, or champion opposition to the administration or its policies." Goss was telling his CIA employees that they were no longer independent providers of impartial intelligence but hired propagandists, what Thomas Powers describes as "an operational arm of the White House." Third, consider the September 2004 *Report of the Defense Science Board* (DSB) *Task Force on Strategic Communication,* which describes in painful detail how the United States is losing "a generational and global struggle about ideas." The problem of plummeting U.S. international credibility is immense, as the report noted that following the U.S. invasion of Iraq, "Arab/Muslim anger has intensified. . . . The U.S. is viewed unfavorably by overwhelming majorities in Egypt (98 percent), Morocco (88 percent), and Jordan (78 percent). The war has increased mistrust of America in Europe, weakened support for the war on terrorism, and undermined U.S. credibility worldwide." Hence offering a stunning moment of elite truth telling, the report depicts post-9/11 U.S. foreign policy as an unmitigated disaster. But rather than addressing the deep historical, economic, and political reasons why the United States is losing the global war of ideas, the report offers bureaucratically thick, labyrinthine recipes for making current U.S. "messages" more effective. For example, offered under the heading of "The Case for a New Vision," the report argues that "strategic communication can help to shape context and build relationships that enhance the achievement of political, economic, and military objectives. It can be used to mobilize publics in support of major policy initiatives." So rather than addressing the root causes of the United States' precipitous nosedive in international legitimacy, the DSB report calls for improved "strategic communication"—what it later calls "managed information dissemination" —that is, for "mobilizing publics" via better propaganda.[18]

Ethics be damned; dissent be silent; propaganda be better—these are the chilling communicative lessons taught by the DeLay, CIA, and DSB examples. Taken together, they suggest why Russell Baker would characterize Washington, D.C., as sinking, under the Bush White House's leadership, into "an age of moral and philosophical sterility." Expanding from Washington to the nation as a whole, Wendell Berry has argued that post-9/11 America is sliding toward a "new strategy" of politics that "depends on the acquiescence of a public kept fearful and ignorant, subject to manipulation by the executive power, and on the compliance of an intimidated and office-dependent legislature." Joan Didion has diagnosed the nation as suffering from a warmongering "enthusiasm for bellicose fantasy." For Baker, Berry, and Didion, respected long-time observers of our national scene, post-9/11 America has lost its habit of reveling in the wonderfully messy and sometimes ennobling elegance of public debate, instead succumbing to the numbing communication nightmares noted above. Indeed, losing our sense of what it means to celebrate and engage in legitimate public deliberation leaves the nation with a government that, according to Berry, "cannot be democratic" and a citizenry that cannot be free.[19]

The DeLay, CIA, and DSB examples are therefore alarming indicators of how desperately we need to reclaim a notion of informed criticism and political participation that foregrounds fair and open deliberation on the day's most pressing topics. As part of our effort to model a form of *rhetorical-criticism-as-the-practice-of-democratic-integrity*—that is, a form of public thought that honors ethics, celebrates dissent, and debunks propaganda—we attempt to enliven public discourse about globalization, empire, and the U.S. invasion of Iraq by engaging in a rigorous, four-step analysis:

1. We consider the public statements of elite players from September 2001 to May 2005 in terms of their persuasive components: What stories do they tell? What visual images do they deploy? What is their evidence? What are their dominant metaphors, symbols, and other aesthetic forms of persuasion? What assumed ethical considerations, unstated stereotypes, implied narratives, or other submerged yet powerful tools of persuasion are employed?

2. We then ask what competing actors say about these claims. That is, what counterarguments are provided by critics, other political actors, scholars, journalists, activists, and so on to help us think more critically and creatively about the claims of those in power?

3. Whereas these first two steps fall comfortably within the bounds of traditional rhetorical scholarship and amount to a form of comparative textual criticism, we also strive to tackle each specific question addressed herein by looking to the best-available evidence provided by experts. More than just a series of critical readings of select public arguments, the book offers substantial and original arguments regarding the topics at hand. For example, along with placing the words of President Bush and his critics in tension regarding weapons of mass destruction, we offer evidence from weapons experts from a variety of perspec-

tives. We offer an empirically rich, evidence-saturated book providing readers the information necessary to reach their own conclusions about weapons of mass destruction, post-9/11 U.S. foreign policy, the economics of globalization, and the occupation and reconstruction of Iraq.

4. Finally, because many of the arguments addressed here draw so heavily on shared cultural assumptions about race, class, religion, modernity, technology, and U.S. national exceptionalism, we supplement our rhetorical analyses of primary documents and our evidence-rich counterarguments with a sense of theoretical complexity and historical depth. As demonstrated above in our opening comments on Hobson, Hobsbawm, Linebaugh and Rediker, Colley, and others, we hope to offer readers glimpses into the ways our current moment has evolved from earlier stages of international capitalism and various models of empire. Furthermore, given the skill with which the Bush administration has revised history to fit propagandistic needs, we hope to demonstrate how history itself functions as an inventional resource, a rhetorical grab bag of references, stories, and images to be used to one's advantage in making public arguments.

Considered as a whole, this four-step method of analysis enables us to perform the pedagogical task of cutting through confusion and the muckraking task of cutting through propaganda. As David Harvey argues in *The Condition of Postmodernity*, referring to the deluge of signs produced by the mass media, "excessive information is one of the best inducements to forgetting." Indeed, given the remarkable flood of information washing over citizens, much of it fragmentary and some of it simply wrong, our goal is to pull together stray threads, to connect the dots between disparate events, to counter mythmaking and forgetting with sound evidence offered in an explanatory narrative. We therefore engage in the rhetorical criticism of important public arguments about globalization and empire while also providing readers the information that will enable them to contribute to the production of informed civic discourse. The book therefore moves beyond static notions of truth and lying, partisan bickering and hysterical posturing, to offer a case study of how undertaking painstaking scholarship, practicing political commitment, thinking historically, and honoring a sense of obligation to what we saw Hobson call "the common good" may lead to a form of rhetorical criticism that models democracy-enhancing integrity.[20]

To foreshadow how this method of criticism enables us to think critically about the relationships among globalization, empire, and the productions—both physical and rhetorical—of violence, we offer the following case studies. The first, addressing what we call "just following orders and shouldering burdens," argues that the atrocities committed at the Abu Ghraib prison in Baghdad reveal the horrible contradictions of fighting wars of empire in the name of spreading democracy. The second, illustrating what we call "capitalist truth telling," shows how the rhetorical analysis of speeches and writings by elites reveals the relationships among globalization, empire, and violence. The third, arguing that "free trade is a lie," examines the ways globalizing neoliberalism cannot practice what it preaches, instead using free trade as a rhetorical justification for pursuing capitalist empire. Taken together, these opening studies frame the key concerns of *Globalization and Empire*.

Just Following Orders and Shouldering Burdens: How Abu Ghraib Reveals the Relationships among Globalization, Empire, and the Productions of Violence

We spend considerable time in this book chronicling and analyzing the terribly botched reconstruction of Iraq; as an opening contribution to that argument we turn our attention below to the abuses in Iraq's notorious Abu Ghraib prison. The scandal erupted into global consciousness in the spring of 2004, when hundreds of graphic photographs entered the ever-expanding web of international media. In one image an Iraqi prisoner stands on a cardboard box, his head covered in a hood, his body draped in a dark brown shawl revealing a glimpse of collarbone. The prisoner's arms are outstretched as if he were pinned to a cross, with wires attached to the tips of fingers on both hands; some observers claimed the wires were also attached to his penis. Perhaps the product of the disorientation caused by his hooding, or of fatigue from enduring such torture, the prisoner tilts slightly to his left with his palms facing outward, in what looks like an appeal for mercy. The room is gray and featureless; small wiring tracts or pipes climb the wall behind the victim; it could be a dungeon in almost any prison in the world. Numerous reports suggested that the prisoner was warned that if he slipped off the box he would be electro- cuted by the wires strung about his body.

In another image six or seven prisoners are piled on top of each other in what looks like a bungled attempt to reproduce the old cheerleading or beach-crowd-pleasing human pyramid, except in this pyramid the prisoners are naked, save for what appear to be green canvas bags slipped over their heads. It is not clear whether the ragged pyramid of bodies is collapsing or has been prodded into motion by guards, perhaps to initiate some mock sexual activity in the pile. Two U.S. soldiers stand behind the pile of naked Iraqi prisoners, happily facing the camera. One leans mis- chievously close to the pile, her face at roughly the height of the genitalia of the man on top of the pyramid; she is grinning in a performative way, hinting that she might dive into the pile for a bit of fun. The second soldier is standing behind her, his bulky arms crossed, a broad smile across his face. His hands are encased in green gloves, a precaution pro- tecting him from potential diseases carried by his captives; his right hand gives the thumbs-up gesture, suggesting *project accomplished, task fulfilled, job well done.*

In yet another image a dead Iraqi is wrapped in an unzipped body bag lying amid melting ice; his teeth are either missing or chipped, his nose is broken, his right eye is swollen shut, and his cheek is bandaged—he has clearly been beaten to death. Comments from Staff Sergeant Ivan Frederick's diary indicate that after the prisoner was killed, U.S. troops tried to hide their brutality by placing the victim on a gurney and insert- ing "a fake IV," making it look like the prisoner had died while receiving intravenous fluids during a medical procedure. Record keeping at Abu Ghraib prison was so intentionally vague, as dictated by the CIA's prac- tice of holding what it calls "ghost detainees," that the prisoner "was never processed and never had a number"—he is an anonymous cadaver, a nameless murder victim, an Iraqi arrested, sentenced, and punished without benefit of counsel or trial, and hence a stark representative of the horrors committed at Abu Ghraib by U.S. soldiers, intelligence officers, and their contracted colleagues.[21]

Anyone anywhere with a sense of decency would see these pictures and be revolted, for here are images of hell, where prison guards engage in institutionally sanctioned dehumanization, where ends justify means, where democratic checks and balances and the rule of law are tossed aside in a frenzy of retribution. Worse yet, most of the prisoners at Abu Ghraib are innocent. In fact, the devastating February 2004 *Report on the Treatment by the Coalition Forces of Prisoners of War* by the International Committee of the Red Cross (ICRC) reveals that "military intelligence officers told the ICRC that in their estimate between 70 percent and 90 percent of the persons deprived of their liberty in Iraq had been arrested by mistake." *The Final Report of the Independent Panel to Review DOD Detention Operations,* the August 2004 study chaired by James R. Schlesinger, formerly President Richard Nixon's secretary of defense, likewise noted that "the Army Inspector General estimated that up to 80 percent of the detainees being held for security and intelligence reasons might be eligible for release upon proper review of their cases." Decoded from bureaucratic prose, this means that even the U.S. Army agrees that 80 percent of the detainees at Abu Ghraib were mistakenly arrested. So many innocent Iraqis were thrown into Abu Ghraib prison because, as the Schlesinger report admits, the "line units conducting raids" in Baghdad were not trained for such tasks: "lacking interrogators and interpreters to make precise distinctions in an alien culture and hostile neighborhoods, *they reverted to rounding up any and all suspicious-looking persons*—all too often including women and children." The U.S. forces supposedly bringing the protection of law and order to Iraq thus resorted to indiscriminate group arrests, acting less like ambassadors of democracy than imperial disappearance squads.[22]

Confirming widespread revulsion at the excesses of certain parts of American culture, the Abu Ghraib torture scandal thus illustrates institutionalized debauchery, sexual perversion, casual brutality, and a justice system gone horribly wrong, where between 70 to 90 percent of prisoners suffer wrongful arrest. The hundreds of images of abuse from Abu Ghraib—of dogs attacking prisoners, of men raping women, of men raping men, of beatings taking place, of post-beating gloating, many of them merging the shadowy world of torture and pornography—have electrified the world, prompting yet another wave of ferocious backlash against the United States. Consider Iraqi artist Salah Edine Sallat's mural in Sadr City, Baghdad. On the right side of the painting we see a rendition of the first image described above, of the torture victim standing hooded on a box; the electrical wires attached to his hands and penis trace across the wall, leading to the left side of the painting, where the Statue of Liberty, hooded as if in the Ku Klux Klan, reaches up to throw the switch on a fuse box. The mural argues that Lady Liberty has become a racist torturer, holding a book of laws in one hand while jolting a prisoner with electricity with the other. In a pseudonymous blog entry of 7 May 2004, one Iraqi woman observed that "people are seething with anger—the pictures of Abu Ghraib are everywhere. Every newspaper you pick up has pictures of some atrocity or another. It's like a nightmare that has come to life." Such outrage is common in Europe as well, as Julio Godoy reported from Paris for the Inter Press Service that the Europeans he had interviewed were seeing Abu Ghraib as further confirmation of the excesses and brutality driving U.S. policy in Iraq. For example, Hans-Ulrich Klose of the German Social Democratic Party, which originally supported the U.S. invasion, observed that "I am not sure that the U.S. will ever again be capable of acting internationally as a superpower that commands respect."[23]

As if to confirm the worst fears expressed in Sallat's mural, the anonymous blog, and Klose's warning, right-wing commentators responded to the scandal by rushing to defend the righteousness of the U.S. occupation in general and the treatment of Iraqi prisoners in particular. Rejecting the claim that the abuses indicate the logical outcome of empire, the inevitable brutality of occupying a foreign country, Zhi Hamby, director of administration for the National Military Intelligence Association, said instead that the images simply prove that "we've got six rotten soldiers." Assuming that torture should be an accepted weapon in the war on terrorism, Senator James Inhofe (R-OK) responded, "I'm probably not the only one . . . [who] is more outraged by the outrage than by the treatment." Whitewashing the abuses while reinforcing the Bush administration's deceptive claim that invading Iraq was tied to the hunt for al Qaeda, the conservative journalist William Safire argued that "we need not let our dismay at the predations of some self-photographing creeps overwhelm the morally sound purpose of our anti-terror campaign." While denying that the images amounted to torture, Defense Secretary Donald Rumsfeld argued on 7 May 2004 that the atrocities were the result of mismanagement and are "inconsistent with the values of our nation . . . with the teachings of the military . . . [and are] fundamentally un-American." Four days later Rumsfeld returned to the "rotten soldiers" thesis, suggesting that the atrocities were carried out by "a few who have betrayed our values." Taking such denials and evasions to a startling low, talk show celebrity Rush Limbaugh argued that "this is no different than what happens at the Skull and Bones initiation. . . . And we're going to ruin people's lives over it and we're going to hamper our military effort. . . . You ever heard of emotional release? You heard of the need to blow some steam off?"[24]

From these perspectives, the atrocities at Abu Ghraib are either unfortunate glitches in an otherwise well-ordered machine (Hamby, Safire, Rumsfeld), the deserved consequence of opposing or threatening U.S. empire (Inhofe), or not glitches at all, simply troops "blow[ing] some steam off" like drunken fraternity boys (Limbaugh). While expressed in differing tones and focused on different details, these five arguments share the assumption that the *system works*. In fact, President Bush argued before the American Conservative Union in Washington, D.C., on 13 May 2004 that "the conduct of a few inside Iraqi prisons was disgraceful" but that "their conduct does not represent the character of the men and women who wear our uniform." According to the president, the U.S. armed forces are not torturers but saviors, bringing "great decency and unselfish courage" to the world. In perhaps the strangest response to the scandal, Secretary of Defense Rumsfeld, while on a speaking tour in Arizona in late August 2004, months after graphic and irrefutable evidence of interrogation-driven tortures at Abu Ghraib had circulated around the globe, argued in an interview on the radio that "I have not seen anything thus far that says that the people abused were abused in the process of interrogating them." At a news conference later that same day in Phoenix, Secretary Rumsfeld claimed that "all of the press, all of the television thus far that tried to link the abuse that took place to interrogation techniques in Iraq has not been demonstrated." Thus, while the president sought to diffuse the scandal by cordoning it off as an unfortunate aberration overshadowed by the heroism of democracy-spreading U.S. troops, Secretary Rumsfeld took the more boorish route of simply denying any connection between prison torture and military interrogations.[25]

Rejecting the "rotten soldiers" thesis, refusing to see torture as evidence either of "blow[ing] some steam off" or "great decency," and understandably outraged by Secretary Rumsfeld's clueless denials, critics of the Bush administration have countered that the tortures at Abu Ghraib epitomize the injustice of waging war on the basis of lies. For as we demonstrate in chapter 1, it was widely understood before the war that Iraq had no WMDs and no direct links to al Qaeda or 9/11, meaning the war was fought under false pretenses produced by what we call "the whole operation of deception." From this perspective, the abuses at Abu Ghraib are not exceptional but representative, not aberrations within an otherwise functional system but revelations of the depravity and violence that lie at the heart of empire. As Al Gore argued in a fiery speech at New York University on 26 May 2004, "The abuse of the prisoners at Abu Ghraib flowed directly from the abuse of the truth that characterized the administration's march to war and the abuse of the trust that has been placed in President Bush by the American people in the aftermath of September 11th." In the same vein, Susan Sontag observes in "Regarding the Torture of Others" that when "considered in this light, *the photographs are us*. That is, they are representative of the fundamental corruptions of any foreign occupation together with the Bush administration's distinctive policies."[26]

Strong support for Sontag's outrage has been provided by an internal army report completed by Major General Antonio Taguba in February 2004, roughly two months before the images were leaked to the press in late April and first aired on CBS's *60 Minutes II* on 28 April. According to Taguba, U.S. troops serving as prison guards at Abu Ghraib had been engaging since at least October 2003 in repeated instances of "egregious acts and grave breaches of international law." The list of crimes chronicled in Taguba's report amounts to a handbook of unlawful, sexually tinged torture. Moreover, many of the worst acts of abuse took place not in the course of high-stakes intelligence-gathering interrogations—which for hardliners serve as military situations that transcend the law—but during the processing of new prisoners, when, in a scenario repeated in U.S. prisons with shocking frequency, guards initiated new prisoners by erupting in what the *New York Times,* relying on testimony from the perpetrators, has characterized as "a night of gratuitous and random violence" marked by "twisted joviality."[27]

The perpetrators of this twisted joviality were well practiced in such violent prison initiation ceremonies, for many of them were trained in U.S. prisons before venturing to Iraq. Staff Sergeant Ivan Frederick II, nicknamed Chip, who was sentenced in October 2004 to eight years in prison for his role as one of the ringleaders of the abuse, had six years of experience as a prison guard in the Virginia Department of Corrections. Lane McCotter, an independent contractor who worked at Abu Ghraib prior to the scandal breaking, brought to Iraq a trail of alleged human rights abuses, including a well-publicized 1997 death that took place under his watch as director of the Utah Department of Corrections. Critics charge that other violations took place when his Management and Training Corporation worked as a contractor in New Mexico prisons. Army Specialist Charles Graner Jr., the strongman in the naked pyramid scenario described above, brought to Abu Ghraib his violence-laced experiences as a guard from a county jail and state prison in Pennsylvania. John Armstrong, hired by the State Department to consult on Iraqi prisons, led the Connecticut Department of Corrections when it was hit in 2003 with a lawsuit about wrongful deaths and an investigation of sexual harassment. Terry Stewart and Chuck Ryan, additional prison consultants in Iraq, were implicated in abuse scandals in Arizona prisons; their disciplinary practices while running Arizona prisons were described by the Arizona chapter of the American Friends Service Committee as entailing "absolute brutality." Rather than aberrant "rotten soldiers," the presence of Frederick, McCotter, Graner, Armstrong, Stewart, and Ryan illustrate how the tortures in Abu Ghraib amount to exported versions, colonial outsourcing—globalization in the worst sense of the word—of the excesses of the U.S. prison-industrial complex.[28]

Seen in this light we may think of Abu Ghraib as a harbinger of things to come, as early warning that the abuses and atrocities of the U.S. prison system—bursting now with more than two million prisoners and another five million parolees; housing more than thirty-five hundred prisoners scheduled for execution; home to routine sexual abuse and other human rights violations—will likely be a central part of the expanding U.S. empire. In fact, based on his analysis of the rise of post-9/11 secret detention centers around the world, where suspects are interrogated by U.S. intelligence agents, their contracted help, and foreign security experts, Stephen Grey has argued in the *New Statesmen* that we are witnessing the construction of "a vast archipelago of prison camps and centers where America can carry out torture by proxy." Jason Burke reports in the *Observer* that this torture by proxy is taking place not only in Guantánamo Bay and detention facilities in Afghanistan and Iraq, but also in Morocco, Syria, Egypt, Azerbaijan, Thailand, Qatar, and Saudi Arabia. The tortures at Abu Ghraib therefore point to the globalization of the worst aspects of the U.S. prison-industrial complex, to the construction of what Tom Engelhardt calls "our imperial mini-gulag."[29]

As demonstrated in the last of the three images discussed above, this emergent "archipelago of prison camps" is deadly; in fact, thirty-seven prisoners died in Afghanistan and Iraq between 2002 and the summer of 2004. While Hamby, Inhofe, Rumsfeld, Limbaugh, and President Bush try to portray the images from Abu Ghraib as examples of aberrant behavior in an otherwise fair and functional system, the combination of the links between Frederick, McCotter, Graner, Armstrong, Stewart, Ryan and the prison-industrial complex, the sheer terror of the images of torture, Grey's and Burke's chilling theses, and the scandal of thirty-seven dead prisoners make this point painfully clear: wherever the U.S. military goes—and it increasingly goes almost everywhere—so go sexual perversion, torture, human-rights-violating prison guards, and suspicious deaths.[30]

And just as prison guards in the United States have argued when caught committing abuses that they were just following orders, so Frederick and his fellow brutalizers have claimed that they were following orders given by military intelligence and CIA agents to soften up prisoners for interrogations. In fact, attempting to locate (or deflect) blame for the atrocities has sent Bush administration officials scurrying for explanations, pointing fingers at rival agencies, thus reproducing a scenario we describe in chapter 1 as the "intelligence turf wars" that erupted following the president's repeated deceptions regarding Iraqi WMDs. The first layer of responsibility thus hinges on who gave the order to engage in torture. Defense Secretary Rumsfeld has implicated the intelligence community, for under intense questioning in the Senate Armed Service Committee from Senator John McCain (R-AZ), he noted that "military intelligence people . . . were in charge of the interrogation part of the process." Indeed, John Barry, Michael Hirsh, and Michael Isikoff have reported in *Newsweek* that the torture pose caught in the first image discussed above is known to intelligence personnel as "the Vietnam." Whereas many of the images depict thuggish brutality mimicking any number of stock pornographic poses, "the Vietnam" is "a standard torture" device that enlistees would not be likely to know; rather, according to the *Newsweek* source, "ordinary American soldiers did this, *but someone taught them.*" "The Vietnam" thus indicates the presence of intelligence personnel, meaning that at least some of the torture was the product of forethought, the vicious result of orders from intelligence commanders. As the Schlesinger report acknowledges, referring here to the circumvention of both the Geneva Conventions and standard U.S. operating procedures, "the CIA was allowed to operate under different rules."[31]

Moving from on-site intelligence personnel to their superiors in Washington, and basing his conclusions on interviews with both retired and currently serving intelligence specialists, Seymour Hersh has argued that "the roots of the Abu Ghraib prison scandal lie . . . in a decision, approved by Defense Secretary Donald Rumsfeld, to expand a highly secret operation, which had been focused on the hunt for al Qaeda, to the interrogation of prisoners in Iraq." Known as "Copper Green," the operation was meant to extract intelligence about the escalating Iraqi insurgency by using the same torture devices employed in Afghanistan and Guantánamo Bay in Iraqi prisons. Hersh's thesis is confirmed in Lieutenant General Anthony Jones's *Investigation of the Abu Ghraib Prison and 205th Military Intelligence Brigade,* an August 2004 army study of the crisis, which states that as the security situation in Iraq deteriorated, so "pressure increased to obtain operational intelligence. . . . about the counter-insurgency." According to Hersh's source, Copper Green arrests and interrogations were driven by the understanding that, post-9/11, "the rules are grab who you must. Do what you want." Fighting the war on terrorism in general and the Iraqi insurgency in particular thus meant the end of the tenuous adherence by the United States to both the Geneva Conventions and the nation's own laws regarding the treatment of prisoners. Rather than isolated incidents of criminal behavior or the work of overzealous intelligence agents, then, the revelations from Abu Ghraib point to systemic torture, authorized at the highest levels, amounting to what the *New York Times* calls "a widespread pattern of abuse." Indeed, as the editors of the *Nation* claimed succinctly, "ultimate responsibility lies in Washington."[32]

In fact, the Schlesinger report reveals that the abuses in Abu Ghraib flowed directly from a series of White House decisions about how to prosecute the global war on terrorism. In one particularly revealing memo signed on 7 February 2002, President Bush announced that "none of the provisions of Geneva apply to our conflict with al Qaeda in Afghanistan or elsewhere in the world." This is the same memo where President Bush designated Taliban detainees as "unlawful combatants." The president makes it clear, however, that his law-revising memo is based on "the opinion of the Department of Justice dated January 22, 2002, and on the legal opinion rendered by the Attorney General in his letter of February 1, 2002." In other words, the president's memo reflected a drawn-out process of legal negotiation between a series of high-ranking U.S. officials—

including Alberto Gonzalez, who was appointed to replace John Ashcroft as attorney general in November 2004—who were committed to rewriting international law to fit the perceived needs of the United States. Anthony Lewis has studied these memos, concluding that "they read like the advice of a mob lawyer to a mafia don on how to skirt the law and stay out of prison." Internationally renowned human rights lawyer Francis Boyle has gone further, arguing that because White House Counsel Alberto Gonzales "originated, authorized, approved, and aided and abetted grave breaches of the Third and Fourth Geneva Conventions of 1949," he is "a prima facie war criminal."[33]

Whether the legal strategists at the White House should be considered mob lawyers or war criminals, we should note that the phrase "or elsewhere in the world" serves notice that the legal neologism of "unlawful combatants" will be applied in a global manner, again indicating how the spread of U.S. empire means the globalization of its profound disrespect for international law. Indeed, the logic of globalization means that nothing stays in one place for long: new transportation flows and information networks enable consumer goods, finance capital, technology, drugs, weapons, diseases, immigrants, pop songs, and the advice of mob lawyers to migrate across borders, seeping into unexpected spaces. Thus, although the White House's law-skirting memos were originally drafted to allow rough treatment of captured Taliban and al Qaeda fighters in Afghanistan and Guantánamo Bay, the Schlesinger report tracks how torture practices "migrated" to Abu Ghraib. There was "a store of common lore and practice within the interrogator community," the report says, meaning that troops taught to torture prisoners in Afghanistan and Guantánamo Bay brought their training with them to Baghdad. This migration of "common lore and practice" explains how Washington's approved Geneva Conventions–skirting treatments for "unlawful combatants" "migrated" from one prison to another, leading to innocent Iraqi civilians being tortured as if they were guilty al Qaeda terrorists. Major General George R. Fay's *Investigation of the Abu Ghraib Detention Facility and 205th Military Intelligence Brigade,* an August 2004 army report on the scandal, even mimicked the rhetoric of global economics, noting that one of the tortures depicted in the infamous photographs was "a technique which was *imported* [to Abu Ghraib] and can be traced through Afghanistan and GTMO [Guantánamo Bay]." Unable to contain approved torture techniques to appointed prisons, the White House must bear responsibility for the migration and importation of its shameful tactics to Baghdad.[34]

A third layer of responsibility rests with those officials who oversaw the contracting of prison duties, for although Frederick, McCotter, Graner, Armstrong, Stewart, and Ryan brought with them a sense of the abuses common in U.S. prisons, we also know that some of the perpetrators were working for CACI International and Titan, two companies with contracts to help run detention centers in Iraq. Given what we know about the poor training and lax oversight that allegedly mark many of the jobs performed by these postwar contractors (to whom we turn in chapter 4), responsibility for the atrocities rests not only with the intelligence officers who gave explicit orders to engage in torture, and not only with the president's legal advisors who devised the "unlawful combatants" strategy in the first place, but with those midlevel managers who unleashed untrained contracted personnel in such a volatile situation. In fact, Torin Nelson told the *Guardian* that he witnessed "cooks and drivers working as interrogators." The Schlesinger report confirmed that "35 percent of the contractors employed did not receive formal training in military interrogation techniques, policy, or doctrine." Linking transformations in the U.S. economy to job-seeking mercenaries in Iraq, Naomi Klein refers to abusive and untrained contractors freelancing their way through torture-laced interrogations as "McWorkers." From this perspective, many of the tortures committed at Abu Ghraib stand as foreshadowing of a privatized empire where excellence and experience give way to the unskilled and the untrained. Moreover, in a stunning example of what we refer to in chapter 4 as crony capitalism, CACI's alleged role in the Abu Ghraib tortures has not prevented the U.S. government from renewing its contracts with the company, which, in August 2004, received new contracts for work in Iraq valued at $23 million.[35]

A fourth layer of responsibility, the one that may prove most damning to U.S. credibility worldwide, points to a culture veering ever closer to cheerful brutality, to a form of mundane barbarism. How else can we explain the fact that U.S. soldiers in Abu Ghraib prison had taken pictures of their tortured prisoners and converted them into images appearing as screen savers on their computers? As Sontag observes, "It is hard to measure the increasing acceptance of brutality in American life, but its evidence is everywhere. . . . America has become a country in which the fantasies and the practices of violence are seen as good entertainment and fun. . . . What is illustrated in these photographs is as much the culture of shamelessness as the reigning admiration for unapologetic brutality."[36]

Seen in this light, any attempt to win the hearts and minds of Iraqis—let alone hundreds of millions of Muslims worldwide—is doomed to failure because large chunks of American culture, the very source of what we saw President Bush call above "great decency and unselfish courage," have slid into a rotten funk of pornography and gratuitous violence, with casual brutality filtering through daily life, with young men and women taking trophy photographs and videos of their sexually tinged spoils of war, with beatings and rapes and humiliations amounting, in Limbaugh's typically boorish prose, to "blow[ing] some steam off."

If the first explanation, the ordered-by-intelligence thesis, is considered paramount, then it indicates that the United States has embarked on a radical venture toward an empire where ends justify means, where the Geneva Conventions apply to others but not to the United States, where the United States fights its endless war on terrorism by employing the same brutal tactics as al Qaeda. If the second argument, the Washington-used-the-law-to-produce-"legal"-torture thesis, is paramount, then it indicates how far U.S. elites will go to win the war on terror, even if it means ruining international law in the process, even if it means torturing innocent civilians. If the third explanation, the mismanaged-contractors thesis, is paramount, then it portrays the United States as a bumbling yet deadly behemoth, one to be feared as much for its mass-produced incompetence as its firepower. If the fourth explanation, the culture-of-barbarism thesis, is paramount, then the United States appears not as a source of decency and courage but of globalizing pornographic brutality. Our rhetorical analyses in chapter 2 of the *National Security Strategy of the United States* and President Bush's post-9/11 speeches demonstrate these first two theses clearly: the abuses at Abu Ghraib stand not so much as exceptional crimes as clear illustrations of post-9/11 U.S. foreign policy, where the war on terror provides the justifying excuse for swaggering, law-breaking, torture-producing imperialism. We will save our readings of the *NSSUS* and President Bush's speeches for chapter 2, but in order to prove our point will turn here briefly to two public intellectuals whose arguments illustrate how the Abu Ghraib scandal embodies some of the core values of the Bush administration's post-9/11 foreign policy.

Consider Robert Kaplan's 2003 essay, "Supremacy by Stealth," where he offers ten rules for maintaining global U.S. supremacy. For our purposes here two rules stand out. "Rule no. 6: Bring Back the Old Rules" argues that U.S. foreign policy is better served by "covert means" than by "large-scale mobilizations." Because wars are sloppy and expensive and draw too much attention, Kaplan prefers surgical strikes against enemy leaders; he accordingly argues that the United States should embrace new technologies that "make assassinations more feasible." Recognizing that the United Nations is a cumbersome organization, Kaplan suggests the United States should avoid getting bogged down in debates with it and instead employ deadly covert means "to manage most problems long before they get to the Security Council." For this reason Kaplan supports "the increasing use of security-consulting firms and defense contractors" that can work under the public radar, getting jobs done quickly and discreetly, free from the entangling encumbrances of both international law and congressional oversight. The implications of these claims are made explicit in "Rule no. 8: The Mission is Everything," where Kaplan urges that "no mission should ever be compromised by diplomatic punctilio." Rather than the military serving as the tightly controlled stick behind the carrot of diplomacy run by democratically elected and publicly responsible representatives, Kaplan envisions a secret and privatized military conducting its own foreign policy—this is not so much democracy as democracy-as-the-justifying-excuse for an expansionist military empire. Combining Kaplan's rules 6 and 8 thus produces an environment conducive to the atrocities at Abu Ghraib, where human rights are inconveniences standing in the way of intelligence gathering, where a little torture in the grand cause of empire is not only acceptable but even heroic. Kaplan's message is clear: *get the job done by any means necessary, obey international law only when convenient.*[37]

For those horrified by the abuses committed at Abu Ghraib, one of Kaplan's more alarming arguments is that the duty to use violence to support the empire has in fact been thrust on an unwilling United States by an outbreak of global cowardice and incompetence on the part of other international players, whose lack of gumption has left the United States little choice but to act as global enforcer. In Kaplan's view, the United States has not chosen to engage Iraq, it has not chosen to be in Abu Ghraib; rather, its fundamentally moral leadership recognized an imposed yet pressing contingency, a situation not of its making but of such seriousness that it became the duty of the United States to respond. As Kaplan put it in an interview following on the heels of his "Supremacy by Stealth" essay, the United States has become an empire "as sort of an accidental consequence." Less the result of fifty years of post–World War II planning than a bold response to crises launched by others, the United States' rise to empire "was not part of a thought-out process." Atrocities like those committed in Abu Ghraib, Guantánamo Bay, and throughout Afghanistan, then, are the unfortunate yet acceptable consequence of the United States choosing to shoulder the burden of righting a world lurching toward anarchy.[38]

Kaplan is not alone in this view. Michael Ignatieff, a one-time liberal intellectual who has taken a hard turn to the right following 9/11, has argued in the *New York Times Magazine* that "into the resulting vacuum of chaos and massacre a new imperialism has reluctantly stepped." Like Kaplan, Ignatieff does not see recent events as the outcome of a half-century of botched U.S. leadership so much as the unfortunate result of the failures of others; less the agent of history than its chosen clean-up crew, Ignatieff suggests that "America has inherited a world" not of its own making. Empire, then, is not a choice but a "burden," an obligation, a dirty but honorable task calling for reluctant yet righteous U.S. action. President Bush has pursued this same argument, claiming in a May 2004 speech before the United State Army War College that post-9/11 U.S. actions simply reflect "the world as we find it." This line of reasoning has been marshaled by apologists for empire for at least the past hundred years. For example, Hannah Arendt reminds us in *The Origins of Totalitarianism*, writing in a caustic tone, that "it has often been said that the British acquired their empire in a fit of absent-mindedness, as consequence of automatic trends, yielding to what seemed possible and tempting, rather than as a result of deliberate policy. If this is true, then the road to hell may just as well be paved with no intentions as with proverbial good ones."[39]

Whereas Ignatieff reprises the responsibility-denying premise that U.S. empire, like the British, has evolved in what Arendt lambastes as "a fit of absent-mindedness," Kaplan brazenly implies that a few human rights violations in a rotting Iraqi dungeon are a small price to pay for the United States protecting the stability of the world. Hence embodying twenty-first-century versions of the late-nineteenth- and early-twentieth-century variations of such claims, Kaplan's unabashed *by any means necessary* argument and Ignatieff's *gosh somebody has to do this stuff* argument combine to illustrate the intellectual road that leads to Abu Ghraib and other imperial atrocities.

Capitalist Truth Telling: How Paul Bremer Admits that Globalization Produces Violence

Ambassador Lewis Paul Bremer III, who served as administrator of the Coalition Provisional Authority (CPA) in Iraq prior to the assumption of Iraqi sovereignty on 28 June 2004, previously served the U.S. government as Secretary of State Henry Kissinger's executive assistant in the 1970s, as ambassador to the Netherlands from 1983 to 1986, and as President Ronald Reagan's ambassador at large for counterterrorism from 1986 to 1989. When he retired from public service in 1989 he became managing director of Kissinger Associates (KA), the international consulting firm linking Kissinger's political contacts with business elites across the globe. The complicated and perhaps criminal dealings of KA became front-page news following 9/11, when President Bush nominated Kissinger to head the independent committee investigating the catastrophe. Rebuking charges that his intimate relationships with KA clients would compromise his ability to conduct an impartial investigation, Kissinger announced that he would not disclose his client roster, which in the past included major arms dealers, transnational energy corporations, multinational banks, and a coterie of other high-powered firms engaging in international political intrigues and economic transactions. Kissinger's reluctance to reveal his client list, when added to prior questions regarding both his and KA's connections with Saudi Arabian, Kuwaiti, Afghani, and Iraqi firms and figures, fueled widespread anger regarding the nomination. Whereas public furor eventually forced Kissinger to withdraw his nomination, his long-time colleague Bremer responded to 9/11 by launching his own KA-like firm providing global elites with logistical advice, insurance coverage, and financial support for doing business in the face of international terrorism. Bremer had demonstrated that he was a product of the Kissingerian school of realpolitik before his opportunistic response to 9/11, however, for when serving as chairman of the National Commission on Terrorism in 2000 he argued that the CIA should be allowed, counter to the law, to recruit assets who had committed human rights violations. Like his mentor, Kissinger, and like many officials in the

Bush administration following 9/11, Bremer understood that national security should trump human rights, that ends justify means.[40]

We turn to Bremer's comments and actions as administrator of the CPA in chapter 4, where we examine the ways crony capitalism is compromising U.S. attempts to reconstruct postwar Iraq, but we focus here on his work as chairman of Marsh & McLennan's Crisis Consulting Practice (CCP). Launched in October 2001, just one month following 9/11, CCP offers globe-straddling corporations "integrated and comprehensive crisis solutions covering all aspects of a business's operation." The *Insurance Journal* characterized CCP as focusing on "catastrophic risks" and as one of the industry leaders trying "to take advantage of the higher insurance prices and increased demand for insurance that have resulted from the attacks." Although initiating a capitalist venture to profit from the horrors of 9/11 may appear to be the high point of crass opportunism, it is also starkly revealing. For given the obvious connections between the terror strikes of 9/11, certain aspects of U.S. foreign policy, and some of the more brutal economic practices of the globalizing corporations likely to contract its services, CCP's founding illustrates how for the world's business and political elites, the intricate entwining of globalization, empire, and violence is not the stuff of conspiracy theories but a daily reality to be addressed as part of the inevitable result of global capitalism. Indeed, whereas Kissinger and KA have spent the past decades denying an avalanche of allegations regarding wrongdoings, Bremer's work for CCP amounts instead to a stunning act of capitalist truth telling, for it begins with the understanding that globalizing neoliberalism produces violence.[41]

For example, in a post-9/11 essay posted on the CCP Web site, titled "New Risks in International Business," Bremer acknowledges that the "rapid expansion of the Western economic model, the relatively free flow of capital, goods, and services, and the explosion of information technology have contributed to political and social tensions in some countries." Noting that deregulated capital markets have destabilized many developing nations, Bremer admits that "these trends and other features of globalization also create real tension in emerging markets." Bremer is especially frank when addressing the ways globalizing neoliberalism has accelerated both domestic and international wealth gaps. The Philippines, for example, a nation hit especially hard by the 1997 financial crash, had an elite class that made "20 times as much as the bottom ten percent in 1994," yet following the crisis "the top group earned 24 times as much as the bottom group." Likewise, the 18 percent poverty rate in 1998 in Pakistan leapt to 32 percent in 1999. Bremer observes that the shock therapies imposed on the Philippines and Pakistan, leading to what he calls the "painful consequences of globalization," "put enormous pressure on traditional retailers and trade monopolies." Given the ways U.S. corporate interests are seen—whether accurately or not—as driving these "painful consequences," it comes as no surprise to learn that "over the past 30 years, 80 percent of terrorist attacks against the United States have been aimed at American businesses." Moreover, given the widespread belief that the United States was largely responsible for the economic devastation wrought in the Philippines and Pakistan, there can be little wonder that both nations are hotbeds for anti-U.S. terrorism.[42]

As Naomi Klein has observed, when progressive scholars and activists "make the kinds of frank links between terrorism and the failing global economy" as made in Bremer's CCP essay, they "are called lunatics." But writing as an advice-spewing corporate executive, not as an ideological warrior, and hence writing as someone more concerned with accurately analyzing the current moment than with mystifying it for political purposes, Bremer makes it clear that globalizing capitalists and empire-building U.S. political actions create logical results: economic resentment, political rage, and terrorist violence. When critics of the Bush administration level such charges they are dismissed as traitors and trouble-makers, yet when Wall Street kingpins and Beltway insiders like Bremer make such charges they reflect the shrewd understanding of global capitalist elites, hence largely confirming the same charges the Bush administration and its allies would like to dismiss as insane. Bremer thus illustrates how we use such instances of capitalist truth telling as insider accounts that unravel the web of mystifications elites use to decouple economics, politics, and violence.[43]

For another example of capitalist truth telling we turn to Thomas Friedman, the Pulitzer Prize–winning journalist who has made a career out of celebrating globalizing neoliberalism. Friedman's 1999 *The Lexus and the Olive Tree* forwards his "Golden Arches Theory of Conflict Resolution," claiming that "when a country reaches the level of economic development where it has a middle class big enough to support a McDonald's network, it becomes a McDonald's country. And people in McDonald's countries don't like to fight wars any more, they prefer to wait in line for hamburgers." Friedman bases this theory on his observation that "no two countries that both had McDonald's had fought a war against each other since each got its McDonald's." The presence of McDonald's amounts, for Friedman, to a surefire marker of a country's civilizing integration into the world of globalizing capitalism. Indeed, from this perspective, globalizing neoliberalism teaches the world how to live in peace, enjoying infinite consumer choices rather than waging endless wars.[44]

The notion that the kinds of individual decision making and personal agency informing consumer choices about hamburgers may be compared to the kinds of governmental decision making and group agency that produce wars is of course absurd. But we need not criticize Friedman's theory for its remarkable naiveté, for his corporate cheerleading is compromised by two moments of capitalist truth telling. First, he acknowledges that in his theory "civil wars and border skirmishes don't count." But according to the United Nations' 2002 *Human Development Report* (*HDR*), "since 1990 an estimated 220,000 people have died in wars between states, compared with nearly 3.6 million in wars within states." Rather than happily interpreting the presence of McDonald's as an indicator of how globalization is spreading stable civil societies and prospering middle classes, then, the *HDR* demonstrates that Friedman's *civil-wars-don't-count* caveat renders his theory trivial, for aside from the recent invasions by the United States of Afghanistan and Iraq, our current moment of globalization is marked largely by civil wars. Less a comment on the successes of globalization than on the prudent investment strategies of McDonald's, Friedman's "Golden Arches Theory of Conflict Resolution" actually demonstrates that globalization produces armed enclaves surrounded by warring hinterlands. In fact, in a telling moment in his closing chapter, Friedman acknowledges that "the hidden hand of the market will never work without a hidden fist. McDonald's cannot flourish without McDonnell Douglas, the designer of the U.S. Air Force F-15."[45]

Despite its remarkable banality, then, Friedman's theory offers two crucial, Bremerian realizations. First, globalization's benefits, like McDonald's products, accrue only in protected enclaves distanced from the genocidal civil wars and border skirmishes that "don't count"—even while producing the vast majority of military deaths worldwide—in the eyes of neoliberalism's proponents. Second, these safe havens of transnational capitalism depend on the military-industrial complex, on the policing power of U.S. empire. The capitalist truth tellings of Bremer and Friedman thus make it clear that globalization and empire, McDonald's and McDonnell Douglas, go hand in hand, bringing consumer choice and political freedom to the few only by managing the various forms of economic, political, and military violence experienced by the many.

Free Trade Is a Lie: How the Rigged Trade Game Produces Resentment

Whereas the term "free trade" implies a world without economic borders, where goods fly unimpeded by tariffs across national boundaries to compete on level playing fields cleared of trade-skewing subsidies and price controls, the fact is that the global economy is rigged in complex ways to favor the interests of traditional elites. For example, the *New York Times* remarked in a scathing editorial titled "The Rigged Trade Game" that "while nearly one billion people struggle to live on $1 a day, European Union cows net an average of $2 apiece in government subsidies." So European cows have higher incomes than almost a billion people around the globe—that is not a recipe for happy and productive integration into the neoliberal world of free markets. Worse yet, while the United States and other traditionally wealthy states boast of attempts to salvage the hopes and economies of less-developed nations, the fact is that "the developed world's $320 billion in farm subsidies last year [2002] dwarfed its $50 billion in development assistance." Responding to pressure from the World Trade Organization, the United States announced in July 2004 that it would cut its domestic farm subsidies by 20 percent. Cementing this reduction depended, however, on developing nations agreeing to lower tariffs on imported manufactured goods, meaning that gains made by agricultural workers in developing nations may be balanced by losses by their counterparts in manufacturing. Fully aware of the complicated economics at play here, yet still reproducing a popular critique of globalization as little more than an accelerated version of elite privilege, the *Times* concluded that globalization as practiced by the United States and its G8 allies (the G8 consists of the United States, United Kingdom, France, Germany, Canada, Italy, Japan, and Russia) is a rigged game, "a one-way street" where foreign markets are forced to open up to U.S. and G8 goods and capital while subsidies and other advantages enjoyed by elite nations render such practices patently unfair to less-developed nations. Given this premise, it comes as no surprise to learn that following the brutal economic crisis that hammered the Philippines in 1997, many Filipinos have come to "view the much-promoted globalization as a new imperialism."[46]

Like the editors of the *Times* and neoimperialism-fearing Filipinos, many of the critics we rely on in this book—including Joseph Stiglitz, David Harvey, Ellen Meiksins Woods, William Greider, Ernst Mandel, Tariq Ali, and dozens of others—argue that *free trade is a lie,* a convenient rhetorical term used to justify the ways G8 nations continue to exploit the natural resources, human labor, collective finances, and consumer markets of developing nations. As William Finnegan summarizes these claims, "The U.S. shoves free-trade doctrine down the throat of every country it meets while practicing, when it pleases, protectionism." One of the troubling questions we address in chapter 3 and our conclusion, however, is if globalization is "rigged" to favor G8 states in general and the United States in particular, then why does the U.S. trade deficit continue to soar? The Economic Policy Institute reported in February 2004 that the U.S. "merchandise trade deficit reached a record level of $549 billion in 2003"; when adjusted for services the deficit went down to $489 billion, still a 17 percent increase over 2002. So while free trade may be a misnomer—for it clearly aids a small coterie of G8-based multinational corporations by "rigging" international trade—there is little doubt that over the past decades globalizing free trade has encouraged a steady decline in the relative economic power of the United States, turning it into a debtor nation. One of the key interpretive dilemmas, then, is trying to figure out who actually benefits from globalization and who suffers from it, hence forcing us to counter corporate cheerleaders and provincial patriots by disentangling corporate agendas from national interests, economic actions from political claims, the promises of elites from the lived realities of daily life.[47]

Thinking critically about globalization therefore entails two clear moves: first, demystifying its actual economic impacts on Americans and our international neighbors and, second, tracing how economic situations bleed into political arguments. For example, writing from Hyderabad, India, Amy Waldman chronicles the lives of impoverished street sweepers: "they bend to clear errant flotsam from the curbs, and straighten to see the immaculate imagery of the new India: hundreds of billboards advertising cars, mobile phones, and Louis Phillipe shirts." Earning the equivalent of but $40 per month, these street sweepers must live the daily humiliation of knowing that such "temptations are forever out of reach." Following the Washington Consensus norms of development (which we address in detail in chapter 3), including slashing public expenditures and lowering wages, all in the name of triggering unfettered capitalist competition, India has largely dismantled its once sprawling public sector. For Hyderabad's street sweepers, who were once public employees with better wages, job protection, and some benefits, this combination of globalizing neoliberalism and local structural adjustments has created "a trickle down of raised expectations and lowered opportunity." If we assume that the fate of the street sweepers of Hyderabad is partially representative of similar scenarios for workers around the globe, then it is safe to assume that in many places free trade will not introduce high-octane entrepreneurial capitalism so much as resentment, a burning taste of injustice and inequality. Indeed, as the UN's *HDR* observes, "in a globalizing world the increasing interconnectedness of nations and peoples has made the [economic] differences between them more glaring."[48]

In this sense, free trade is not only an economic lie but a particularly provocative and politically dangerous lie likely to produce resentment among those who suffer the consequences of the "rigged" trade game. In fact, in a fiery speech delivered as part of the opening ceremony of the G-15 summit held in Venezuela in March 2004, Hugo Chávez, the president of Venezuela, linked the rigged trade game to neocolonialism and urged the global "South" to rise up against globalizing neoliberalism. In a stark reminder to U.S. elites of the links between economic despair and political violence—hence echoing Bremer's comments from above—Chávez warned that "this exploitation model has turned Latin America and the Caribbean into a social bomb ready to explode."[49]

Similar claims are offered in Arundhati Roy's *Power Politics*. Roy is an acute observer of how globalizing free markets have fueled India's (re)fracturing into a nation of warring political factions, rival religious sects, and the lucky few lording over the destitute millions. For Roy, the promises of a golden free trade–fueled future of wealth and prosperity crash against the reality of mass poverty and provincial traditionalism, producing a dizzying world of contradictions:

As Indian citizens we subsist on a regular diet of caste massacres and nuclear tests, mosque breakings and fashion shows, church burnings and expanding cell phone networks, bonded labor and the digital revolution, female infanticide and the NASDAQ crash, husbands who continue to burn their wives for dowry and our delectable stockpile of Miss Worlds. I don't mean to put a simplistic value judgment on this peculiar form of "progress" by suggesting that Modern is Good and Tradition is Bad—or vice versa. What's hard to reconcile oneself to, both personally and politically, is *the schizophrenic nature of it.*

Much like Fredric Jameson's literary (and explicitly not medical) discussion of schizophrenia in *Postmodernism; or, The Cultural Logic of Late Capitalism,* Roy sees the flooding of India with globalization's new goods and technologies as creating a jarring world where the ancient and the futuristic stand side by side, where immense wealth and crushing poverty populate the same space, where utopian hopes and deadening angers commingle in an exciting and alienating wash of confusion.[50]

Such descriptions strike us as *existentially true*—they feel right, they approximate the chaos and cacophony of lived experience. But as we demonstrate in chapters 3 and 4, this sense of confusion and alienation, prompting both Roy and Jameson to think of schizophrenia, should not be turned into a mantra of disempowerment, for there are relatively straightforward means of explaining the mechanics of globalizing free markets. We thus refer in chapter 3 to the institutional architecture of globalization and focus on the ways the World Bank, International Monetary Fund (IMF), and World Trade Organization (WTO) structure the flows of power and privilege that drive our age of globalization. Likewise, in chapter 4 we show how the U.S. reliance on crony capitalism in postwar Iraq, which is indeed suffering a sense of cultural schizophrenia, may be analyzed as the product of an elaborate system of corruption and favoritism. While we agree with many commentators that free trade is a useful lie, globalizing neoliberalism is a historical fact, one that must be analyzed and understood from the rhetorical perspectives of its supporters and its critics as well as from the analysis of its material consequences. We therefore share Roy's and Jameson's awestruck sense of existential confusion before what they call the schizophrenia of globalization, yet we are also concerned with locating the causal structures of power that facilitate globalizing free markets and their attendant whirl of economic change, cultural transformation, and political upheaval.

Finally, we should acknowledge that critics and strategists also refer to globalization when talking about economies that transcend the normal bounds of trade and capital, including the legal and illegal exchange of drugs, ideas, information, goods, services, citizens, tourists, sex, diseases, medications, weapons, music, art, and tradition. As Arjun Appadurai has argued, globalization is a remarkably complicated process occurring on many "scapes," including ethnoscapes, mediascapes, technoscapes, financescapes, and ideoscapes. Although we want to honor the complexity of these scapes, and although we often find ourselves awed before the sense of schizophrenia they produce, our concern here is to locate the ways new forms of capitalism link to empire, and vice versa, hence searching for the mechanisms that produce violence in its rhetorical, economic, and military versions. We do not intend to offer a determinist model where economics drives all cultural and political transformations, nor do we want to suggest that other "scapes" are less important than the ones we address here; rather, we hope to demystify one small part of globalization by revealing the relationships among its proponents' claims and the institutional architecture of their power and privilege. As suggested by the title of this introduction, then, we hope to use the tools of interdisciplinary rhetorical criticism to reveal how globalization and empire produce violence.[51]

"The Whole Operation of Deception"

Reconstructing President Bush's Rhetoric of Weapons of Mass Destruction

War is a grisly business: bodies are ripped asunder; cities are leveled; families are broken; lives, nations, and entire cultures are shattered; yet wars are fought, over and over and over, each time for reasons that some set of leaders argue are pressing, nation threatening, unavoidable. Although the post-9/11 war against terrorism can plausibly be seen as an act of self-defense, we argue here that the war on Iraq is a war of choice. To demonstrate how terribly wrong that choice is, we offer a reconstruction and critique of the publicly stated reasons for choosing war, focusing on President Bush's rhetoric regarding Iraq's weapons of mass destruction. We conclude that the president's arguments were fabrications spun from evidence that was shaky at best, outright nonsense at worst, and that the labyrinthine cover-ups following these initial fabrications amount to a second, equally dangerous series of lies. Although it is not the first time deceptions have been foisted on the world by a dissembling president, we demonstrate that President Bush's WMD rhetoric amounts to a pattern of lying that poses a serious threat to the foundational principles of democracy.

Furthermore, the president's operation of deception, ostensibly launched to try to prevent the mass violence that *might be* caused by Iraq's alleged WMDs, has lead to mass deaths. For example, we know of 139 American soldiers lost in the initial invasion of Iraq; that death toll has skyrocketed during the course of occupation, with the total of dead U.S. troops as of 9 June 2005 standing at 1,671; another 185 coalition forces have been killed thus far, bringing the total of coalition dead to 1,856. Another 12,348 U.S. soldiers have been wounded in the operation; 154 civilian contractors have been killed, and there is no end in sight to the violence.[1]

No one knows how many Iraqi soldiers died during the war, with estimates ranging from a low of 13,500 to a high of 45,000. Iraq Body

Count's estimate of Iraqi civilians killed either in the war or during the occupation stands between a low of 22,047 and a high of 25,010. Furthermore, as many as twenty thousand Iraqi civilians were injured in the war, including eight thousand in Baghdad alone. These numbers pale in comparison, however, to those released in November 2004 by Britain's *Lancet*, which published results from a survey done on the ground in Iraq, where investigators interviewed Iraqis throughout the country to develop a comprehensive summary of civilian deaths between January 2002 and November 2004. The researchers estimated at least one hundred thousand civilian deaths resulting from the invasion and occupation of Iraq, most of them the result of coalition air strikes on civilian areas.[2]

The war on Iraq has also proved deadly to the journalists attempting to report its horrors to the world. For example, in September 2003 Mazen Dana was shot by a U.S. soldier who mistook Dana's camera for a rocket-propelled grenade launcher. In April 2004 a U.S. attack on the offices of Al-Jazeera killed journalist Tareq Ayoub; an unknown assassin shot another Al-Jazeera correspondent in May 2004. Coupled with the insurgents' escalating targeting of journalists, the Institute for Policy Studies reports that as of late September 2004, as many as forty-four media workers have been killed in Iraq. The president's war to preempt the use of WMDs has thus caused many deaths of and injuries to U.S. and coalition troops, Iraqi troops and civilians, and international reporters.[3]

Moreover, the president's war against supposed WMDs has left Iraq devastated and lawless. Assaults on U.S. troops and international aid workers, estimated in September 2004 to total *eighty-seven attacks a day*, demonstrate that the phrase "postwar" is deeply misleading. For example, in Baghdad on 11 February 2004, car bombings outside army and police recruitment centers killed between thirty-six and forty-seven people, only one day after a truck bombing in Iskandariya, just south of Baghdad, killed at least fifty people. On 1 February 2004, more than one hundred people in Irbil, a Kurdish town, were killed when two suicide bombs exploded. In addition to attacks against Iraqis suspected of collaborating with the occupiers, a conflict between Kurds and Shiite and Sunni Muslims has flared up. The *Los Angeles Times* reported that during the Ashura feast in early March 2004, twin suicide bombings in Karbala and Baghdad "tore into throngs of Shiite pilgrims, splattering the walls of venerated shrines with blood and body parts." In Baghdad, the article goes on to detail, three men "set off explosives-laden vests, thus shredding the crowd with shrapnel, blowing a massive wooden door off its hinges, and littering a courtyard with mangled corpses and bloodied shoes that the faithful had stored on shelves at the entrance of the prayer area." Then, in Basra on 21 April 2004, at least sixty-eight people were killed in bomb attacks on a school bus and Iraqi police recruits at three city police stations.[4]

The miseries of postwar Iraq have been acute in Falluja, where, in April 2004 alone, more than six hundred Iraqis were killed by U.S. troops and the militants battling them from street corner to street corner. The U.S. military does not keep track of civilian deaths, however, so journalists, doctors, and volunteers make their best estimates, suggesting that as of April 2004, the civilian death toll in Falluja, a city of three hundred thousand, was approximately eight hundred. The death toll was so high that a makeshift cemetery for dead Iraqis was hastily set up amid what used to be a soccer stadium. A gravedigger called Nasser was quoted in the *New York Times* as saying, "We have stacked the bodies one on top of the other"; the same report claims that some graves are simply labeled as "hands," "fingers," and "child," as the anonymous bodies and parts of bodies pulled from bombed homes are impossible to identify. We return to the disaster of "postwar" Iraq in more detail in chapter 4 and our conclusion, but these opening comments make the point clearly: President Bush's war to preempt possible catastrophe has in fact created one—he has needlessly plunged the United States, its allies, and Iraq into a deadly quagmire.[5]

In order to understand how the president dragged the United States, its allies, and Iraq toward this disaster, we reconstruct the WMD arguments he used to justify waging war. In so doing we echo the anger Senator Robert Byrd voiced in his speech in the Senate on 21 May 2003, when he warned that "the American people unfortunately are used to political shading, spin, and the usual chicanery. . . . But there is a line. . . . When it comes to shedding American blood—when it comes to wreaking havoc on civilians, on innocent men, women, and children, callous dissembling is not acceptable. Nothing is worth that kind of lie. . . . [But] mark my words . . . the truth will emerge. And when it does, this house of cards, built of deceit, will fall."[6]

Indeed, we hope this book hastens the collapse of the Bush administration's house of cards. To explicate and contextualize the president's WMD rhetoric we proceed in this chapter via four steps. First, to demonstrate to readers the complexity of the prewar intelligence regarding

Iraq's alleged WMDs, we review seven representative texts from establishment sources. Second, to illustrate how the president warped this intelligence, we offer both a chronological catalogue and a rhetorical critique of his (and many of his administration's key spokespersons') arguments about WMDs. Third, we examine the available counterevidence to this WMD rhetoric by analyzing Secretary of State Colin Powell's UN testimony of 5 February 2003. And fourth, by focusing on the administration's pattern of lies regarding Iraq's alleged attempt to purchase African uranium, and especially its brutal (and apparently criminal) response to Joseph Wilson's revelations that such charges were known to be false, we examine the turf wars that have surfaced between competing U.S. intelligence agencies, the public controversy regarding the president's WMD rhetoric, and the administration's bungled postwar cover-ups. The chapter closes with an epilogue in which we situate WMD discourse within larger questions regarding the production of violence and the backlash of terrorism caused by the pursuit of U.S. empire.[7]

In addition to reconstructing the arc of events and claims that led the United States into war in Iraq, our analysis demonstrates three key findings:

- First, whereas the intelligence community presented the president with a debate in flux, with materials steeped in cautionary prudence, President Bush translated this information into hyperbolic and frequently terrifying public pronouncements ringing with certainty.
- Second, by claiming utter certainty, regardless of both countervailing and missing evidence, the president's urgent pronouncements about the imminent threat posed by Iraqi WMDs amount to fiction, not fact. We therefore show that President Bush is a skilled practitioner of what Wayne Booth has called "rhetrickery." Indeed, by studying his major public speeches since 9/11, we conclude that President Bush has grown beyond his standing as a bumbling oaf, a rhetorically challenged buffoon, to function instead as a cunning master of the rhetorical arts of *argumentum ad ignorantiam*, prolepsis, hyperbole, and the logical fallacy of "position-to-know."[8]
- Third, the president's WMD rhetrickery has been so controversial that it has both triggered a bitter public outcry about lying in politics and revealed a simmering turf war within his administra-

tion's many intelligence agencies. Studying the administration's responses to this public outcry and its handling of these intelligence turf wars reveals some of the troubling political machinations that lay behind this presidency's modes of rhetorical production and, more important, expose an administration committed to circumventing the checks and balances that keep American democracy from sliding into tyranny.[9]

Cynics will respond that lying and politics go hand in hand, that Presidents Johnson, Nixon, Ford, Reagan, Carter, Bush, and Clinton, for example, have bequeathed to the nation a rich tradition of White House lying. But as we demonstrate here, President Bush's WMD lies are in a class of their own, for they not only have dragged the nation into deadly messes in Afghanistan and Iraq but also serve as the justifications for the implied future wars described by the 2002 *National Security Strategy of the United States* as necessary to "rid the world of evil." Following Hannah Arendt's classic analysis of *The Pentagon Papers,* we conclude—as foreshadowed in our title—that President Bush's rhetrickery is not the result of loose talk but of an administration-wide campaign, of what Arendt calls the "whole operation of deception." Considering the shameful status of reconstruction in Afghanistan, the escalating violence in Iraq, and the president's open-ended strategy of waging unilateral war, we conclude that the whole operation of deception has already produced, is currently fueling, and will continue to create violence on a global scale—for as we demonstrate here, *speech kills.*[10]

The Intelligence Community's Prewar Analysis of Iraq's Alleged WMD Programs

We review below seven of the key documents the president and his administration are likely to have relied on for forming their arguments regarding Iraq's alleged WMD programs. This first section of the chapter provides readers with a sense of the factual and rhetorical resources available to the president, thus supplying the necessary foreground for the rhetorical analyses that follow. This first section also counters the still-prevalent assumption that President Bush was acting on irrefutable evidence. For example, in an article in *Time* magazine in September 2003, Charles Krauthammer blustered that "it is hard to credit the deception charge when every intelligence agency on the planet thought Iraq had these weapons and, indeed, when the weapons there still remain un-accounted for." Like so many of his fellow reporters, Krauthammer has not only accepted the president's allegations as facts, but is so committed to defending them that he engages in both the whopping exaggeration that "every intelligence agency on the planet" agreed on the prewar intel-ligence regarding Iraqi WMDs and in the counterfactual prophesy that even though no WMDs have been found, *they must be there somewhere.* We make no claim to have studied every document produced by every intelligence agency on the planet, and we make no claim to know what may or may not be uncovered someday in Iraq, but we do show below that seven elite sources of intelligence—including the Central Intelli-gence Agency (CIA), the State Department, the Department of Energy (DOE), and the British Joint Intelligence Committee (JIC)—were in fact internally conflicted regarding the status of Iraqi WMDs.[11]

Because most of the October 2002 *National Intelligence Estimate* (*NIE*) remains classified, we turn to the CIA's October 2002 report, *Iraq's Weap-ons of Mass Destruction Programs.* The CIA's report argues that Iraq is attempting to produce ballistic missiles and unmanned aerial vehicles (UAVs); it claims that Iraq is "seeking nuclear weapons"; and it demon-strates in grisly detail that Hussein used chemical weapons to "kill or injure more than 20,000 people" between 1983 and 1988. The CIA's report also contains, however, some cautionary moments that merit closer rhe-torical attention. For example, when discussing Iraq's chemical weapons and their possible delivery systems, the report qualifies its claims in two places with the word "probably"—so the charges are not certainties, just probabilities. When discussing biological weapons, the report refers not to existing weapons but to Iraq's being "capable" of producing them—so they do not actually have the weapons, they might be capable of making them. In these two examples, as well as the two additional examples of-fered below, the CIA qualifies its arguments with subtle language that falls short of claiming certainty. The CIA is forced into this prudent po-sition because it has little hard information. In fact, in a telling statement that is bolded in the report, the CIA acknowledges that "Baghdad's vig-orous concealment efforts have meant that specific information on many aspects of Iraq's WMD programs is yet to be uncovered." Although these concealments violate a series of UN sanctions (including Resolutions 687, 707, 715, 1051, 1060, 1154, and 1284), notice that the CIA admits that *it has little specific information.*[12]

The fact that the CIA has little specific information leads to a series of rhetorically twisted passages revealing uncertainty regarding the main claims of *Iraq's Weapons of Mass Destruction Programs*. For example, consider the report's language concerning Iraq's nuclear weapons program and its alleged purchase of high-strength aluminum tubes for use in that program. "All intelligence experts agree that Iraq is seeking nuclear weapons and that these tubes could be used in a centrifuge enrichment program," the report claims categorically. But the CIA follows this sentence with the qualifying confession that "most intelligence specialists assess this to be the intended use, but some believe that these tubes are probably intended for conventional weapons use." So in the course of two sentences the claim moves from *all* intelligence experts agreeing on the charge to *most* intelligence specialists agreeing on the charge to a qualifying and therefore doubt-raising *but*. And note that this slide from certainty to uncertainty follows the charge not that Hussein *is using* aluminum tubes to enrich uranium, but that the tubes *could possibly be used* in this manner. These qualifying passages—exemplifying what Thomas Powers calls "that special verb form we might call the intelligence conditional"— wave before the careful reader warning signs indicating that these are assertions, strong assertions to be sure, but that they carry with them modifying buts, probablies, and other marks of uncertainty.[13]

The Bush White House was apparently not reading the CIA's documents as carefully as we are, however, at least partly because interpersonal communications between the CIA and White House were based on a gruff male bravado that privileged manly certainty over patient textual interpretation. For example, Bob Woodward reports in *Plan of Attack* that on 21 December 2002, CIA Director George Tenet and Deputy CIA Director John McLaughlin ventured to the Oval Office to present evidence of Iraqi WMDs to President Bush, Vice President Cheney, National Security Adviser Rice, and White House Chief of Staff Andrew Card. As noted in our discussion above, the CIA's information was sparse, largely outdated, and highly circumstantial. Thus, at the close of McLaughlin's presentation President Bush turned to Tenet, asking with incredulity, "This is the best we've got?" Overstating the CIA's case with one of the ubiquitous sporting clichés that seem to substitute for reasoned argument in contemporary American culture, Tenet responded, "It's a slam dunk case! . . . Don't worry, it's a slam dunk!" It will take years of investigative reporting to figure out whether Tenet had badly misread his agency's own nuanced warnings or whether he was simply telling the president what he thought the president wanted to hear. In either case, it is clear that Tenet's "slam dunk" assurance served as interpersonal assurance in the face of dubious evidence.[14]

Tenet was apparently not the only intelligence official overstating the case for Iraqi WMDs, however, as the British were engaged in their own forms of deception. Indeed, considering the deeply entwined arguments of President Bush and Prime Minister Tony Blair regarding the reasons for waging war in Iraq, it is important to consider the WMD evidence provided by British intelligence in two key documents. The first is the 24 September 2002 *Iraq's Weapons of Mass Destruction: The Assessment of the British Government;* the dossier is the work of the JIC, a blue-ribbon group of officials from a wide variety of British agencies. Originally drafted in March 2002, the first draft of the text reported that there was "no evidence that Saddam Hussein posed a significantly greater threat than in 1991 after the Gulf War." Six months of politically motivated revising led to the removal of that conclusion. Instead, the version of the text released in September argued that "uranium [amounting to "significant quantities" later in the text] has been sought from Africa." The most contested claim from the dossier is that "the Iraqi military are able to deploy these weapons [chemical and biological WMDs] within 45 minutes of a decision to do so." Relying in many cases on the same information found in the CIA's October report—including an identical photograph in both documents of an L-29 fighter jet supposedly converted into a UAV capable of spreading chemical and biological weapons—the dossier makes an unqualified case that Iraq possesses vast amounts of ready-to-use chemical and biological WMDs and is aggressively pursuing nuclear WMDs. Scrubbed of any sense of caution or doubt, the dossier's aggressive tone of certainty perhaps explains Prime Minister Blair's unflagging support for war in Iraq.[15]

The second important British document is the January 2003 report titled *Iraq—Its Infrastructure of Concealment, Deception and Intimidation,* a nineteen-page indictment of Hussein's strategies for terrorizing his own people, hiding WMDs, and complicating weapons inspections. We know the information in this document was considered persuasive—and perhaps even influential in shaping U.S. thinking regarding Iraq—for in his February 2003 testimony before the United Nations Secretary of State Colin Powell said, "I would call my colleagues' attention to the fine paper that the United Kingdom distributed yesterday." It turns out that this fine paper consists largely of plagiarized passages from outdated sources. Touted on its cover page as information based on "intelligence material," four pages of the document were not only plagiarized from an article by Ibrahim al-Marashi, a research associate of the Center for Nonproliferation Studies in Monterey, California, but al-Marashi's conclusions in the article—and hence the second British dossier's conclusions—are based on outdated information. Moreover, other parts of the second dossier were plagiarized from articles in *Jane's Intelligence Review,* including one essay from 1997. Because this second dossier amounts to little more than a crude cut-and-paste job relying on outdated information, it casts serious doubts on the legitimacy of the claims found in the first dossier.[16]

In fact, in September 2003 the *New York Times* reported that the claim that Hussein could deploy WMDs within forty-five minutes "applied only to short-range battlefield munitions," not long-range weapons and certainly not WMDs. But this postwar revelation should come as little surprise, for given our comments here it is clear that prudent reasoning would have found it difficult to locate pressing needs for war in either of these documents. Indeed, the web of fabrications and exaggerations is so dense in these texts, and the obfuscations used to explain them so devious, that the *London Times* reported on 28 July 2003 that "trust in Britain's political leaders has almost vanished."[17]

Given the compromised and outright bungled nature of these British documents, yet still hoping to convey the complexity of elite-establishment arguments regarding Iraq's alleged WMD programs, we consider below four additional sources of prewar information. For example, consider "Iraq: Nuclear, Biological, Chemical, and Missile Capabilities and Programs," a 2001 research brief posted under the heading of "Weapons of Mass Destruction in the Middle East" on the home page of the Center for Nonproliferation Studies (CNS) at the Monterey Institute of International Studies. Throughout this report, the CNS appears to lend support to President Bush's claim that regime change in Iraq is necessary to prevent its imminent use of WMDs to destabilize the Middle East and perhaps blackmail or even attack the United States. But careful readers will note that the CNS report is also laced with cautionary language, including the claims that Iraq "may retain" biological weapons, "may retain" and is "believed to possess" chemical weapons, and "may retain" long-range missiles. Like the CIA report discussed above, the CNS report foregrounds the fact that "precise assessment of Iraq's capabilities is difficult because most WMD programs remain secret and *cannot be verified* independently."[18]

In a similar vein, the Carnegie Endowment for International Peace (CEIP) begins its "Iraq Biological and Chemical Weapons Fact Sheet" with the cautionary reminder that "no one knows for certain how many, if any, chemical or biological weapons Iraq still has." In a statement that accords with our argument in the final section of this chapter, the CEIP notes that "some of the intelligence cited by officials before the war seems to have been based on defector information that so far has not proven accurate." And even if that information about alleged Iraqi WMDs was accurate, the CEIP reports that chemical and biological weapons "have limited military utility, particularly against mechanized forces." Furthermore, whereas previous Iraqi uses of chemical and biological WMDs relied on air delivery, the CEIP notes that "air delivery is all but impossible with manned aircraft given the U.S.-British air superiority." In short, the CEIP argues that Iraqi WMDs, regardless of their contested amounts, pose little threat to regional stability and therefore serve poorly as a cause for war.[19]

Similar conclusions were reached by Anthony Cordesman in *If We Fight Iraq: Iraq and Its Weapons of Mass Destruction,* a June 2002 report for the Center for Strategic and International Studies (CSIS). Cordesman is the Arleigh A. Burke Chair for Strategy at the CSIS and a respected expert on the questions addressed here. Cordesman essentially repeats the CEIP claim cited above, arguing that "Iraq's present holdings of delivery systems and chemical and biological weapons seem most likely to be so limited in technology and operational lethality that they do not constrain U.S. freedom of action or do much to intimidate Iraq's neighbors." Cordesman catalogues Hussein's many previous uses of WMDs, so like everyone cited here he agrees that the Iraqi regime has a brutal past, yet like the CEIP, Cordesman notes that much of the prewar hysteria regarding Iraqi WMDs was based on information provided by Iraqi exiles who "have little credibility." The CSIS report is exhausting, offering page after page of frequently contradictory information, yet it clearly lends credence to the conclusion that Iraq's alleged WMD capacities offered little immediate threat to U.S interests and therefore thin reasons for waging war.[20]

Finally, another example of ambivalent prewar intelligence is *Iraq: U.S. Efforts to Change the Regime,* an October 2002 report for Congress prepared by Kenneth Katzman, a specialist in Middle Eastern Affairs for the Congressional Research Service (CRS). Like his other work on the subject, Katzman's report is well researched and diligently balanced. One section of text, under the heading of "WMD Threat Perception," notes,

> Even if UN weapons inspectors return to Iraq . . . inspections alone will not likely ensure that Iraq is free of WMD. . . . [But] some outside experts, including former UNSCOM Chairman Rolf Ekeus, counter that inspections, even if not fully unfettered, would suppress Iraq's ability to reconstitute its WMD. Those taking this position maintain that the inspections (1991–1998) accounted for and dismantled a large portion of Iraq's WMD programs, although *substantial uncertainties remain* about Iraq's production of VX nerve agents, remaining chemical munitions, and the biological weapons Iraq produced.[21]

Katzman thus portrays a debate in flux, complete with *substantial uncertainties* about the central aspects of Iraq's alleged WMD programs. Like the CIA, CNS, CEIP, and CSIS reports cited above, then, Katzman understands that the possible threat of WMDs is serious, but also that the situation is filled with uncertainty.

Many observers agree that such uncertainty is inherent to the intelligence-gathering process. A brief digression back to the cold war illustrates this point nicely. In 1977, at the height of U.S./Soviet tensions over nuclear weapons, President Jimmy Carter was presented with a CIA report regarding the accuracy of Soviet missiles. One passage in the report noted that "the uncertainty band would cover the entire range of happiness." As interpreted by Thomas Powers, this phrase means that "you could read the figures any way you liked." This chilling story indicates that much of what passes for intelligence analysis is an inherently contested process of interpretation—it is not truth telling, not the collection of certainties, but the gathering of clues and hunches, the collection of shards that need careful sifting and cautious reading.[22]

In addition to the complexities of this hermeneutic process, experts note that the intelligence community is hampered by severe organizational problems as well. For example, in *Fixing Intelligence*, William Odom, the former director of the National Security Agency, argues that one of the "major deficiencies" of the U.S. intelligence community is "miscommunication" between agencies and even within agencies. Although Odom offers a series of suggestions intended to produce "a common understanding of community resource management," he nonetheless portrays the intelligence community as one—like most other vast organizational networks—riven with intellectual, political, and bureaucratic conflicts.[23]

As we shall see below, President Bush presented this complex intelligence community and its contested, interpretively dense field of intelligence as if it was univocal and steeped in certainty, thereby justifying war on Iraq by manipulating the available evidence to produce a simplistic tale of Good versus Evil. The most obvious reason for engaging in this rhetrickery is that being wrong about WMDs could have catastrophic consequences. From this perspective, it is better to err on the side of preemption than on the side of letting a rogue nation or terrorist group wreak havoc with WMDs. To make this argument publicly would have entailed describing to the American public a situation based largely on a fearful hunch, a dangerous gamble where the president chose to act with uncertainty rather than waiting until it might be too late. But President Bush did not choose this route of argument; instead, he claimed to know for sure that Iraq possessed WMDs. This unfortunate rhetorical decision not only led the nation into an unnecessary war but left the Bush White House open to charges of intentionally misleading the world.

"The Mother of All Misjudgments": A Catalogue and Critique of President Bush's WMD Rhetoric

The president's claims regarding Iraq's supposed WMDs have been characterized by Hans Blix, the executive director of the UN Monitoring, Verification, and Inspection Commission (UNMOVIC) during the years leading up to the U.S. invasion of Iraq, as "the mother of all misjudgments." Indeed, despite the CIA's, CNS's, CEIP's, CSIS's, and CRS's cautionary and often contradictory thinking—to say nothing of UNMOVIC's equally ambiguous reports—the president voiced his WMD charges in terms of certainty, of categorical knowledge beyond doubt. The president's WMD charges were first aired in his 29 January 2002 State of the Union address. Delivered in the midst of the war in Afghanistan and only four and one-half months after the trauma of 9/11, the president spoke that night to an angry nation, to an audience of recently terrorized citizens, many of whom were clamoring for retribution. The president thus received loud and sustained applause throughout his address, particularly when he claimed that Iran, Iraq, and North Korea constitute an "axis of evil." Few details were provided regarding either the axis of evil's various WMD programs or their links to terrorists, yet the threat of rogue states and terrorists using WMDs was portrayed as clear and chilling. Conflating terrorists and unnamed rogue states, and relying on the nation's still-fresh memory of 9/11, the president warned that such "dangerous killers, schooled in the methods of murder, . . . are now spread throughout the world like ticking time bombs, set to go off without warning." From as early as January 2002, then, the Bush administration began preparing the U.S. population for war in Iraq by producing hysterical portrayals of imminent WMD attacks.[24]

The following months saw the president occupied with the war in Afghanistan and buttressing what has become known as homeland security. It was therefore not until 7 October 2002 that the president returned to the task of portraying Iraq as a major purveyor of WMDs. Speaking from Cincinnati to a live television audience on the one-year anniversary of America's initiating military actions in Afghanistan, President Bush warned that Iraq "possesses and produces chemical and biological weapons. It is seeking nuclear weapons." These "horrible poisons and diseases and gases and atomic weapons," he claimed, "are controlled by a murderous tyrant." President Bush then warned listeners that Hussein's WMDs are "capable of killing millions" and of sowing "mass death and destruction." Repeating one of the more dubious claims from both the CIA and JIC texts discussed above, President Bush argued that "Iraq possesses ballistic missiles with a likely range of hundreds of miles. . . . [And] a growing fleet of manned and unmanned aerial vehicles that could be used to disperse chemical or biological weapons." The combination of these claims built the foundation for the president's theory of the need for pre-emptive U.S. military action against Iraq. Indeed, in a comment that encapsulates many of the president's post-9/11 themes, he warned that "facing clear evidence of peril, we cannot wait for the final proof—the smoking gun—that could come in the form of a mushroom cloud."[25]

Apparently swayed by such terrifying images, it took Congress but four days following President Bush's Cincinnati speech to pass House Joint Resolution 114 (H. J. Res. 114) late on the night of 11 October 2002.

Titled "Joint Resolution to Authorize the Use of United States Armed Forces against Iraq," H. J. Res. 114 granted the president sweeping powers to "use the Armed Forces of the United States as he determines to be necessary and appropriate in order to defend the national security of the United States against the continuing threat posed by Iraq." By granting the president the power to use military force without consulting Congress on a formal declaration of war—as mandated by section 8 of article I of the Constitution—H. J. Res. 114 sidestepped the Constitution and handed the president a blank check for waging war in Iraq. This frightening abdication by Congress of its traditional role of enforcing checks and balances on executive power was made doubly shameful by the fact that H. J. Res. 114 included in its prologue a veritable catalogue of the president's unsubstantiated claims. In fact, paragraphs 8, 9, and 10 of H. J. Res. 114 reproduce President Bush's assertions regarding Iraq's "capability and willingness to use weapons of mass destruction," its "willingness to attack the United States," and its links to both al Qaeda in general and 9/11 in particular. We address these charges in detail in the third and fourth sections of this chapter and show that they are false, thus demonstrating that H. J. Res. 114 amounts to the legal embodiment of the Bush administration's operation of deception.[26]

Armed with unlimited war powers by a compliant Congress, President Bush nonetheless still needed to persuade doubtful national and international audiences of the need for waging war on Iraq. He thus expanded his existing claims about WMDs in his 28 January 2003 State of the Union address, where he reported that "the United Nations concluded in 1999 that Saddam Hussein had biological weapons sufficient to produce over 25,000 litres of anthrax—enough to kill several million people." Hussein was also charged with the capacity of producing "38,000 litres of botulinum toxin—enough to subject millions of people to death." Iraq's supposed cache of "500 tons of sarin, mustard and VX nerve agent" were portrayed as capable of killing "untold thousands." Perhaps the most terrifying aspect of the president's speech that night was his portrayal of Iraq as a budding nuclear power. "The International Atomic Energy Agency confirmed in the 1990s," President Bush reported, "that Saddam Hussein had an advanced nuclear weapons development program, had a design for a nuclear weapon, and was working on five different methods of enriching uranium for a bomb." This sentence was followed by the one that has subsequently received much critical attention: "The British government has learned that Saddam Hussein recently sought significant quantities of uranium from Africa."[27]

To make sure that the nation and the world understood that invading Iraq was necessary to prevent its imminent use of WMDs, including nuclear weapons, President Bush repeated many of these charges in his eve-of-war speech on Monday night, 17 March 2003, when he delivered an ultimatum to Saddam Hussein, ordering him to leave Iraq within forty-eight hours or face invasion. The president claimed that "the Iraq regime continues to possess and conceal some of the most lethal weapons ever devised." The function of the imminent U.S. invasion, then, the president claimed, was "to eliminate weapons of mass destruction." Air strikes against Baghdad began that Wednesday night, 19 March 2003, with U.S. ground forces entering Iraq later that week. Thus, roughly eighteen months following 9/11, President Bush launched his preemptive war to eliminate WMDs.[28]

Having reconstructed the president's main WMD arguments leading up to the start of the war in Iraq, we now examine the rhetorical devices that structure his arguments and compare his WMD claims to the available evidence. Both forms of criticism are important, for although offering counterfactual evidence enables us to prove where, when, and how the president and his supporters lied, studying the overarching rhetorical strategies driving the president's WMD arguments enables readers to flag his lying not only in this instance but in the future as well.

In *A Handlist of Rhetorical Terms*, Richard Lanham defines *argumentum ad ignorantiam* as a logical fallacy by which one "argues that a proposition is true because it has never been proved false." In *A Pragmatic Theory of Fallacy*, Douglas Walton observes that "a seriously mischievous" version of this argument tactic occurs when one relies on "charges made purely on the basis of innuendo and suspicion." What makes *argumentum ad ignorantiam* so tricky, then, is the question of how one's evidence—or lack thereof—links thesis and conclusion. For example, because there is no definitive proof of Iraqi WMDs, may one conclude that they cannot possibly exist? Alternatively, because there is no definitive proof of their nonexistence, does this sanction one concluding that they must exist? In both cases the rhetorical/argumentative problem concerns the relationship between evidence and conclusion. Simply foregrounding the tenuousness or contingency of one's argument therefore enables any speaker to circumvent the charge of creating mischief by arguing falsely for a conclusion based on the absence of evidence. President Bush, however, is a speaker who uses few qualifiers; instead, he pronounces, he proclaims, he preaches with certainty, even when he has little or no evidence to support his claims. The president therefore offers a case study of how *argumentum ad ignorantiam* enables one to move from having no evidence to proclaiming certainty.[29]

In fact, as the president's WMD rhetoric slowly garnered more scrutiny in the summer following the invasion, one response of his appointees was to downplay the importance of evidence in the president's arguments. In a remarkable revelation of hubris, when confronted with the increasingly apparent gap between the president's rhetoric regarding Iraq's supposed WMDs and the available facts, Assistant White House Press Secretary Scott McClellan (who has since succeeded Ari Fleischer in that post) declared on 18 July 2003 that "the President of the United States is not a fact-checker."[30]

The claim was clearly intended to deflect blame for any erroneous WMD charges from the president, placing guilt instead on his speechwriters and intelligence agencies. But the president is apparently not alone in not checking his facts, for many of the president's appointees were equally categorical in their rhetoric, thus demonstrating that the use of *argumentum ad ignorantiam* was not merely the result of the president's sloppy speaking but the product of an entire administration's forethought. For example, in the following list of quotations we have highlighted those phrases that refuse any possibility of doubt regarding Iraq's WMDs:

- Speaking before the national convention of the Veterans of Foreign Wars in Nashville on 26 August 2002, Vice President Cheney claimed that "*we now know* that Saddam has resumed his efforts to acquire nuclear weapons. . . . Simply stated, *there is no doubt* that Saddam Hussein now has weapons of mass destruction."[31]
- During his press briefing of 9 January 2003, when questioned about the evidence supporting the president's claims regarding Iraq's WMDs, Press Secretary Ari Fleischer claimed that "*we know for a fact* that there are weapons there. . . . *We know* they have weapons of mass destruction of a chemical nature."[32]
- Following the initiation of the U.S. invasion of Iraq, at the White House press briefing of 21 March 2003, Fleischer said that "*there*

is no question that we have evidence and information that Iraq has weapons of mass destruction."[33]

- The next day, speaking at the daily press briefing at the U.S. Central Command in Doha, Qatar, Brigadier General Vince Brooks claimed that "*there is no doubt* that the regime of Saddam Hussein possesses weapons of mass destruction."[34]

- At that same press briefing, General Tommy Franks repeated Brooks's claim, arguing that "*there is no doubt* that the regime of Saddam Hussein possesses weapons of mass destruction." When pressed on the nature of U.S. intelligence supporting this claim, Franks refused to offer details, instead saying that his forces were moving to control "weapons of mass destruction, which *for certain, sure* exist within Iraq."[35]

- The following day, 23 March 2003, Kenneth Adelman, a member of the Pentagon Advisory Board, told the *Washington Post*, "*I have no doubt* we're going to find big stores of weapons of mass destruction."[36]

- Following the war, despite no new evidence supporting any of the claims listed above, Secretary Powell said on NBC's *Meet the Press* on 4 May 2003, "*I'm absolutely sure* that there are weapons of mass destruction there and the evidence will be forthcoming."[37]

We now know . . . there is no doubt; we know for a fact . . . we know; there is no question; there is no doubt; there is no doubt; for certain, [for] sure; I have no doubt; I'm absolutely sure—these are but eleven phrases among hundreds of examples of Bush administration officials, appointees, or supporters speaking with certainty regarding what the president referred to in his Cincinnati speech as the "clear evidence of peril" from Iraq's WMDs. But in not one instance was any hard evidence offered. These examples make it clear, then, that relying on *argumentum ad ignorantiam* was the driving rhetorical strategy not only of President Bush but of his entire administration.

In addition to *argumentum ad ignorantiam,* the president's WMD rhetoric relies heavily on prolepsis, hyperbole, and the logical fallacy of "position to know." For example, recall how in his Cincinnati speech the president slipped from the claim that Hussein was "seeking nuclear weapons" to the unqualified claim that he possessed "atomic weapons." Likewise, in his 2003 State of the Union address, notice how in his long catalogue of charges against Hussein, the president moved from arguing that Hussein possessed materials "sufficient to produce" WMDs to the conclusion that he had produced such weapons, thus gaining the ability "to kill several million people." Here and throughout his WMD rhetoric we see President Bush turning conditional claims (Hussein is seeking, might have, or might be able to produce WMDs) into unqualified certainties complete with grisly images of imminent massive deaths. The president therefore relies heavily throughout his WMD rhetoric on prolepsis, the rhetorical act of shifting time frames within the same argument. Indeed, moving regularly from future conditional claims, in which an act might happen given the right circumstances, to present certainties, in which an act is described as imminent, the president uses prolepsis to collapse speculative claims into descriptive claims, turning what might be into what is. Consider the president's Cincinnati speech, where he offered dreadful speculation regarding the possible appearance of a mushroom cloud over a nameless American city. Using prolepsis to collapse distinctions between past, present, and future, the president's terrifying image of a future nuclear death drew on cold war terrors to serve as an assumedly factual statement regarding present threats.[38]

These uses of *argumentum ad ignorantiam* and prolepsis are supplemented by heavy doses of hyperbole. Lanham defines hyperbole as "exaggerated or extravagant terms used for emphasis and not intended to be understood literally" and thus as a form of "self-conscious exaggeration." President Bush offers a startling variation on this definition, for it appears from his many WMD statements that although he regularly uses exaggerated and extravagant terms, he assumes that his charges will be taken literally, as actual statements of fact. Most of the president's hyperbolic WMD charges take the time-bending form described in the paragraph above and therefore are difficult to counter with hard evidence. But some of the president's hyperbolic statements invite simple factual rejoinders. For example, while we have shown above how President Bush portrayed Iraq as a threatening military juggernaut, the U.S. General Accounting Office reported in 2002 that whereas Iraq spent almost $19 billion per year on military expenditures between 1980 and 1990, by 1995 it was spending only $1.5 billion. According to a report published by the American Academy of Arts and Sciences, Iraq's military budget of $1.4 billion in 2001 placed it behind Saudi Arabia ($24.7 billion), Israel ($10.6 billion), Turkey ($7.4 billion), Kuwait ($5.1 billion), and Iran ($4.8 billion). These figures demonstrate that Iraq's military has been in a state of precipitous decline since 1995, thus placing it at a significant military disadvantage compared to many of its neighbors. Nonetheless, in an example of literalist hyperbole, where extravagant exaggerations are used not for ironic literary purposes but as a substitute for evidence, the president repeatedly portrayed Hussein's feeble army as a regional and even global threat capable of killing millions of innocents.[39]

While the Iraqi WMDs supposedly capable of delivering Armageddon to American doorsteps have yet to be found, the president hinted repeatedly (both before and after the war) that secret U.S. intelligence confirmed that Hussein possessed such weapons. The American public was thus asked to believe that there was evidence but that the president could not make it public for security purposes. This line of argumentative fallacy, known as "position-to-know reasoning," relies on a speaker calling on his or her expertise or authority to sanction a claim that would otherwise not be believable. For example, in his testimony before the United Nations on 5 February 2003, Secretary of State Colin Powell, while ostensibly presenting to the world the best intelligence the United States possessed, cautioned his audience that "I cannot tell you everything that we know" ("RUN," 2). Likewise, in his foreword to the British JIC's dossier on Iraq's WMDs, Prime Minister Tony Blair stated that "we cannot publish everything we know." When challenged in Parliament on 30 May 2003 regarding his repeated Bush-like arguments regarding WMDs, Blair responded that he had information that could "not yet [be] public" but that he would "assemble that evidence and present it properly." In President Bush and Secretary Powell's cases, using position-to-know amounts to abusing the authority of their office to demand compliance with an argument that lacks evidence; in Prime Minister Blair's case, position-to-know serves as a delaying tactic promising that in-hand evidence is too sensitive and can only be released at a later date. For Bush, Powell, and Blair, then, the fallacy of position-to-know enables them to marshal the massive prestige and power of their access to classified information to turn possibilities into certainties, a lack of information into purported evidence, dubious assertions into assumed facts.[40]

This use of the position-to-know fallacy reached its apogee in the 2003 State of the Union address, where President Bush cited the International Atomic Energy Agency (IAEA)—a group deeply opposed to the president's war in Iraq—as supplying evidence supporting his claims about Iraqi WMDs. President Bush did not name the report (referenced vaguely as from the 1990s), so we have no way of knowing to which one of the IAEA's hundreds of reports he was referring. But we do know that many of the IAEA's reports from that period were concerned with Iraqi WMD capabilities *prior to the first Gulf War,* which observers agree destroyed many of the WMD facilities in question. As the *Washington Post* reported, President Bush thus "cast as present evidence the contents of a report from 1996, updated in 1998 and 1999. In those accounts, the IAEA described the history of an Iraqi nuclear weapons program that arms inspectors systematically destroyed." Indeed, those WMD-producing facilities that survived the first Gulf War came under intense scrutiny between 1991 and 1998 by the United Nations Special Commission (UNSCOM), which according to a 2003 Issue Brief for Congress "destroyed all chemical weapons material uncovered—38,500 munitions, 480,000 liters of chemical agents, 1.8 million liters of precursor chemicals, and 426 pieces of production equipment items." In fact, Blix reports in *Disarming Iraq* that on 8 October 1997 he submitted to the UN Security Council an UNSCOM document that reflected "a general agreement among governments at the time that there were no significant further disarmament matters to clear up in [Iraq's] nuclear dossier, only some questions to clarify." Despite the president's rhetrickery, then, the IAEA and UNSCOM positions were clear: the combination of Gulf War I bombardments and postwar inspections left Iraq with no WMDs.[41]

UNSCOM concluded in 1995, however, that Iraq might possess additional post–Gulf War I stockpiles of up to four tons of VX (a nerve gas). This unaccounted-for VX is the most credible WMD charge critics have found, but given both the rapid decay of nerve agents and the difficulty of weaponizing them, this claim points not to a direct and imminent threat but to old, no-longer dangerous information. Moreover, Seymour Hersh has concluded from his analysis of CIA transcripts of interviews with Jafar Dhia Jafar, who worked on Iraq's nuclear weapons program in the 1980s, that the discrepancy between Iraq's, UNSCOM's, and the United States' estimates of "missing" WMD can be explained in this way: "The Iraqi government had simply lied to the United Nations about the number of chemical weapons used against Iran during the brutal Iran-Iraq war." The nine-hundred-page Duelfer report, titled *Comprehensive Report of the Special Advisor to the DCI on Iraq's WMD,* released 30 September 2004, confirms Hersh's thesis, noting that Hussein "sought to maintain ambiguity about whether he had illicit weapons mainly as a deterrent to Iran." If true, this would amount to a deadly irony: in attempting to "maintain ambiguity" regarding WMDs, Hussein gave President Bush just enough of the appearance of WMD impropriety to argue for a war to destroy weapons that had already been used. Intrigue aside, note that the UNSCOM report pointed to "up to four tons" of missing VX, not to the massive quantity of five hundred tons claimed in President Bush's 2003 State of the Union address. Apparently the president believed that he could rely on the power of the position-to-know argument not only to play fast and loose with the relevant dates and findings of these IAEA and UNSCOM reports, but to exaggerate their findings to almost comic book proportions.[42]

We return below to more recent IAEA reports on the status of Iraqi WMDs, but close this section by noting how the president's use of impossible-to-track-down information illustrates his abusing the authority of his office, its historically venerable "position-to-know" status, to awe listeners into taking old and therefore irrelevant evidence as fresh and imminently pressing evidence. In fact, in a blistering letter sent to CIA Director Tenet on 27 September 2003, Congressman Porter Goss (R-FL) and Congresswoman Jane Harman (D-CA), the ranking members of the House Permanent Select Committee on Intelligence, questioned the administration's use of the "position-to-know" fallacy. Referring to the administration's repeated claims that solid information about Iraq's alleged WMDs could not be divulged because of security reasons, Goss and Harman wrote that "we have not found any information in the assessments that are still classified that was any more definitive" than those cited publicly before the war. In short, Goss and Harman argued that the "position-to-know" fallacy was abused by the Bush administration to create the appearance of secret evidence that did not exist. (The letter apparently did not hurt Goss's relationship with the president, as he was picked to replace Tenet as head of the CIA in August 2004.)[43]

In each of the instances noted here, the president's, secretary of state's, administration officials', and prime minister's slippage from *may be* to *must be*, greased at each step by prolepsis, their authority of position-to-know, and literalist versions of hyperbole, amount to classic examples of *argumentum ad ignorantiam,* to the rhetorical trick of manufacturing certainty out of uncertainty. Having established the rhetorical devices structuring the Bush administration's WMD rhetoric, we turn now to the question of how it stands under the scrutiny of counterfactual criticism.

Secretary of State Colin Powell's UN Testimony and the Available Counterevidence

As demonstrated above, the president's claims regarding Iraqi WMDs take the form of assertions based not so much on hard evidence as on a suggestive lack of evidence. It is therefore difficult to argue with the president's claims, for without his providing details there is little data to study, little evidence to examine. To apply the force of counterfactual criticism to the president's WMD rhetoric means, then, that we must look to other examples in which the speaker attempted to persuade not only by means of prolepsis, literalist hyperbole, position-to-know, and *argumentum ad ignorantiam*, but by marshalling evidence. Considering that it was by far the most extensive effort on behalf of the Bush administration to present an evidence-based argument for war, we turn to Secretary of State Colin Powell's testimony before the United Nations on 5 February 2003. The testimony was given before the United States had declared that it would wage a unilateral war, back when the UN was still being courted as an international stamp of approval for U.S. plans in Iraq, hence making Powell's testimony an important moment both for winning UN support by sharing evidence for war and, just as important, for demonstrating to a wary world audience the mechanics of transparent, reasoned political debate supposedly championed by the United States.

To his credit, Secretary Powell offered a presentation that in many places was passionately delivered and powerfully persuasive. It was hard to hear his words and see his supporting images and not agree that war on Iraq would make the world a safer place—hence the rush by many reporters to depict the speech as a devastating, case-closing performance of truth telling. But hearing a frightening presentation and studying its transcript are two different tasks; indeed, examining the transcript of Secretary Powell's speech points to a series of claims that merit closer attention. One aspect of the speech that stands out is Powell's awareness that his administration is perceived as evidence challenged. For example, in classic demonstrations of protesting too much, the secretary emphasizes that his claims regarding WMDs are factual. Early in his testimony

Powell says, "My colleagues, every statement that I make today is backed up by sources, solid sources. These are not assertions. What we are giving you are facts and conclusions based on solid intelligence" ("RUN," 4). Later in his testimony Powell again promises his audience that "these are not assertions. These are facts corroborated by many sources" ("RUN," 7). Such insistence on the soundness of his evidence indicates Powell's unpleasant realization that by February 2003 his president's loose talk had created the perception that U.S. policy regarding Iraq was based on fiction, not fact.[44]

Nonetheless proceeding in the face of widespread doubt regarding the veracity of U.S. claims, Powell outlined seven main charges: (1) that the UN's weapons inspections teams had been compromised by spies; (2) that even in the face of UN inspections, Iraq was producing chemical and biological WMDs; (3) that Iraq was making significant progress toward producing a nuclear bomb; (4) that Iraq was developing UAVs to deliver chemical, biological, and nuclear WMDs; (5) that Iraq had deep connections with al Qaeda; (6) that Hussein's regime was a humanitarian disaster; and (7) that the combination of points one through six prove the United States' charge that Iraq poses an immediate threat to regional and even global security, thus sanctioning a preemptive military attack.

Before turning to our critique of Secretary Powell's arguments regarding WMDs, it is important to acknowledge the truth of his sixth point. Indeed, one would have to be obtuse not to cheer the fall of Hussein's rotten, murderous regime, where we know that dissidents were tortured, innocents were imprisoned, tens of thousands were executed, and large segments of the population were terrorized. In fact, the record of humanitarian abuse in Iraq is so damning that it leads us to a troubling conclusion: the only reason the Bush administration did not argue more forcefully for intervention on the basis of humanitarian reasons was because it was wary of establishing a precedent for military actions in the name of human rights. For if ridding the world of humanitarian disasters was the business of the United States in Iraq, then why would it not apply as well to the horrors under way in Burundi, or Liberia, or Colombia, or China, or the territories occupied by Israel? Instead, seeking a more proscribed set of reasons for waging war, the administration portrayed Iraqi WMDs as an imminent threat to civilization. But as we shall see below, eschewing the humanitarian argument in favor of WMD claims led the administration into a troubling thicket of questions regarding the reliability of its evidence.[45]

Secretary Powell's first charge, that UN weapons inspections teams had been neutralized by Iraqi spies, was supported first by Powell analyzing taped phone conversations between Iraqi scientists and satellite images of the Taji facility. Then, in one of the moments of his presentation that gathered much media attention—with some pundits breathlessly recalling a similar use of aerial photographs by Adlai Stevenson during the Cuban missile crisis—Powell mustered two photographs of a facility in Taji. In the first image Powell identified what he called "a signature item" of WMD production, pointing to a "decontamination vehicle," charging that such a vehicle indicated the presence of chemical and/or biological weapons production. In the second image the vehicle is gone. "The sequence of events," Powell concludes, "raises the worrisome suspicion that Iraq had been tipped off to the forthcoming inspections" ("RUN," 5–6). This charge was then expanded the following day in a scathing editorial by William Safire in which he argued that the UN inspections process had been "penetrated by Iraqi wiretaps and bugs," thus fatally compromising the search for WMDs. As a closing flourish, Safire concluded by claiming that "the Zarqawi poison works in northern Iraq" held both chemical weapons and al Qaeda members; in full war-hawk fury, and clearly supporting the course of action implied in Secretary Powell's testimony, Safire asked incredulously, "Why haven't we obliterated it?"[46]

Powell's and Safire's entwined comments require two rejoinders. First, Safire was wrong to name the supposed camp "the Zarqawi poison works," for Abu Musab al-Zarqawi was the operative supposedly linked to this site, not the name of the site itself. Furthermore, Zarqawi's alleged ties to al Qaeda, which Powell dwelled on in his testimony (see "RUN," 16–18), were known at the time to be tenuous at best. In fact, the *Observer* reported on 2 February 2003, three days before Powell's testimony, that Zarqawi "has never been mentioned in the list of senior Al-Qaeda men in bin Laden's entourage in Afghanistan." Following Powell's claims before the UN, the *Wall Street Journal, Washington Post,* and *New York Times,* among others, noted that while Zarqawi was indeed a dangerous fanatic with ties to anti-Semitic groups and a long record of terrorism—he is now widely attributed as a leader of the anti-U.S. insurgency in postwar Iraq—there was no evidence linking him to either al Qaeda or Hussein's regime. Like so much of the administration's case for war, then, the claim that Zarqawi somehow cemented a war-worthy link between al Qaeda and Hussein was circumstantial at best.[47]

Second, Powell's analysis of the photos appears to have been based on deception regarding both the status of the vehicle in question and the assumed cause of its movement. For nine days after Powell's testimony before the UN, Hans Blix briefed the UN Security Council on the status of his inspections teams' progress. During that briefing Blix said, "The presentation of intelligence information by the U.S. Secretary of State suggested that Iraq had prepared for inspections by cleaning up the sites and removing evidence of proscribed weapons programs. I would like to comment . . . that the two satellite images of the site were taken several weeks apart. The report of movement of munitions at the site could just as easily have been a routine activity as a movement of proscribed munitions in anticipation of imminent inspections." In his postwar memoir, *Disarming Iraq,* Blix went further, suggesting that at the time "our [UNMOVIC] experts" believed the supposed decontamination trucks could "just as well have been water trucks." Furthermore, Blix revealed that the alleged WMD plant, misnamed by Safire as "the Zarqawi poison works," in fact "had not in the past been associated with the production of biological weapons agents but with the storage of seed stock."[48]

Powell thus took what was most likely the routine movement of vehicles over "several weeks" as unquestionable evidence—*these are not assertions. What we are giving you are facts*—of infiltration of the weapons inspection program. But a retired CIA officer trained in photographic analysis has suggested that the vehicle in question appears not to be a "decontamination vehicle" but *a fire truck.* Whether the vehicles in question were fire or water trucks, it is clear that the Bush administration had no hard evidence of functioning WMD programs in Iraq; instead, it prodded Secretary Powell to mislead the UN by misreading the photographs.[49]

Secretary Powell's third main point, that Iraq was making significant progress toward producing a nuclear bomb, hinged in large part on evidence regarding "high-specification aluminum tubes," which, if modified in certain ways, could be used in "centrifuges for enriching uranium." To his credit, Powell noted that "there is controversy about what these tubes are for," but he followed this qualified statement with the firm claim that "most U.S. experts think they are intended to serve as rotors in centrifuges to enrich uranium." According to Secretary Powell, then, the tubes prove that Hussein "is determined to acquire nuclear weapons" ("RUN," 13). We now know that Powell made this same claim in his 26 September 2002 testimony before the Senate Foreign Relations Committee; this was the crucial meeting, preceded two days earlier by similar testimony by CIA director Tenet, at which Powell persuaded the committee to support the president's war powers act. From as early as September 2002, then, Powell was using the alleged weapons-grade tubes as a major reason for waging war against Iraq.[50]

But nine days following Powell's UN speech, on 14 February 2003, Dr. Mohamed ElBaradei, director general of the IAEA, testified before the UN Security Council on the status of the agency's investigations in Iraq. In his closing remarks ElBaradei stated that "the IAEA concluded, by December 1998, that it had neutralized Iraq's past nuclear program and that, therefore, there were no unresolved disarmament issues left at that time." Since the IAEA resumed its inspections in Iraq on 27 November 2002—following the 8 November 2002 UN Resolution 1441—ElBaradei reported that through the IAEA's 177 inspections at 125 sites, "Iraq has continued to provide immediate access to all locations" and that "we have to date found *no evidence of ongoing prohibited nuclear or nuclear-related activities in Iraq.*"[51]

Furthermore, in a remarkable postwar revelation, McClellan disclosed in a press conference at the White House on 18 July 2003 that the State Department's Bureau of Intelligence and Research (INR) never believed Iraq was pursuing an "integrated and comprehensive approach to acquire nuclear weapons." In discussing the presence of dissent within the classified *NIE* of October 2002, particularly regarding claims that Iraq was successfully reconstituting its nuclear weapons program, McClellan revealed that the INR had argued that "the available evidence [was] inadequate to support such a judgment." McClellan also revealed that the *NIE* contains a passage, referring to the aluminum tubes in question, in which the DOE "assesses that the tubes probably are not part of the [nuclear] program." This is a particularly important revelation, for as David Albright of the Institute for Science and International Security notes, "the DOE has virtually the only expertise on gas centrifuges and nuclear weapons programs in the U.S. government." In fact, the *Washington Post* revealed in August 2003 that when the DOE's leading experts from the Oak Ridge National Laboratory examined the evidence in late 2001, they "unanimously regarded this possibility [of using the tubes to make weapons grade uranium] as implausible." One of those experts, Houston G. Wood, told the *Post*'s Barton Gellman and Walter Pincus that "it would have been extremely difficult to make these tubes into centrifuges. It stretches the imagination to come up with a way. I do not know any real centrifuge experts that feel differently."[52]

Hence, despite overwhelmingly positive coverage in the U.S. mass media, much of Secretary Powell's February 2003 testimony regarding Iraq's WMD programs was refuted within one week by the IAEA and, more damning, was based on information discounted as early as October 2002 by the State Department's INR and as early as 2001 by the Department of Energy's nuclear experts. In sum, many of President Bush's and Secretary Powell's arguments for going to war were based on exaggerations, outright lies, or dubious interpretations of contested evidence. But possessing little evidence did not deter the Bush administration from making false assertions, for the logic of *argumentum ad ignorantiam* enabled it to base conclusions not on evidence but on the absence of evidence. Indeed, to be rhetorically accurate and ethically fair—to practice what we call rhetorical integrity—Powell and Bush should have couched their charges as allegations, as hunches, as probabilities, as suspicions yet to be confirmed. But instead, in each of the instances examined above, Bush and Powell took questionable evidence and spun it into incontrovertible evidence, making a case that was open for debate into a case that was supposedly shut and closed. For all intents and purposes, then, this is lying, attempting to manufacture evidence to support one's policy, conducting what can only be called an operation of deception.

The African Uranium Claim Debunked and the Fallout from Intelligence Turf Wars

As we have noted above, the administration's rhetorical choices regarding waging war on Iraq were complicated by political infighting among the White House, CIA, DOE, INR, and other key government intelligence agencies. In fact, documents that began to surface in the spring of 2003 point to a bitter struggle within competing government agencies regarding the meaning of the available information about Iraq's supposed WMD capacities in general and its pursuit of African uranium in particular. Tracking the intelligence turf wars that lay behind the president's WMD rhetoric enables us to study how institutional imperatives regarding power and prestige in Washington drove the administration's claims about Iraq. More important, by studying the elaborate cover-ups surrounding both the administration's arguments for war and these intelligence turf battles, we demonstrate how President Bush's operation of deception has subverted the checks and balances that guarantee the legitimacy of the democratic process. The irony here is bitter, for we show that President Bush has argued for a war ostensibly to protect democracy by besmirching democracy.

Before addressing the institutional turf wars regarding supposed Iraqi WMDs, however, let us first examine the controversial claim that drew attention to their existence. The contested line comes from the 2003 State of the Union address where President Bush declared that "the British government has learned that Saddam Hussein recently sought significant quantities of uranium from Africa." That statement may be considered legally sound, for as we demonstrated above, the British JIC had released a dossier in September 2002 with this claim. Thus, when pressed on the question, the Bush administration resorted to legalistic sophistry, with Condoleezza Rice chiming that the statement "was indeed accurate." By hiding behind the accurate claim that the British had made such a statement, Rice sidestepped the more pressing point that the content of that claim was known at the time to be false.[53]

In fact, it was widely known as early as the spring of 2002—ten months prior to the 2003 State of the Union address—that the claims about Iraq seeking African uranium were based on documents that were forgeries. The public became aware of the forgeries in the week following the president's 2003 State of the Union address, when, in testimony delivered to the UN, ElBaradei reported that "based on thorough analysis, the IAEA has concluded . . . that these documents . . . are not authentic." But it should not have taken ElBaradei and the IAEA to reach this conclusion, for the two documents contained four obvious errors: (1) the first letter referred to a 1965 Niger constitution that had been superseded by a constitution ratified in 1999; (2) on the first letter, the signature of President Tandja Mamadou was clearly botched; (3) the letterhead used for the second document was from the previous military regime, which had been replaced by a new government (with new letterhead) in 1999; and (4) the signature on the second letter, dated 1999, was for Allele Habibou, a minister of foreign affairs who had left the post in 1989.[54]

Moreover, it is widely known that the entire yearly output of Niger's "yellow cake," the form of uranium in question here, is contracted to French, Japanese, and Spanish corporations, so siphoning off massive amounts of material for illegal shipment to Iraq would have required the complicity of major U.S. allies. Accepting these documents as evidence of Iraq's nuclear weapons ambitions would thus have required either shamefully sloppy spy work or, perhaps worse, turning a blind eye to their status as forgeries because they satisfied the president's desperate need to produce reasons for war. In fact, a former CIA official told Seymour Hersh that "everybody knew at every step of the way that they were false—until they got to the Pentagon, where they were believed." Rice's retort that the line from the president's address was factually accurate was therefore mere quibbling, for a president who cites false information without marking it as such engages in unethical deception—this is lying.[55]

Defenders of the president have claimed that it was not known at the time that the Iraq/Niger claim was false, but this too is a lie. In fact, prior to the president endorsing the bogus British claim in his January 2003 State of the Union address, Vice President Dick Cheney asked the CIA to dispatch Joseph Wilson, a twenty-three-year career diplomat, to Africa to research the charges that Iraq was purchasing enriched uranium in Africa. In March 2002 Wilson reported to the CIA and State Department that the documents prompting such fears were forgeries. The *New York Times*'s Nicholas Kristof reported on 13 June 2003 that he had interviewed CIA officials confirming that "lower CIA officials did tell both the vice president's office and National Security Council staff members" that the charges were false. The *Washington Post*'s Dana Priest confirmed one week later that Wilson had conveyed his dismissal of the false claims to the National Security Council on 9 March 2002, seven months before the president's "mushroom cloud" Cincinnati speech and ten months before the president's January 2003 State of the Union address.[56]

Despite Kristof's and Priest's strong reporting, the White House continued to deny that it had been warned about the erroneous uranium charges. These denials prompted Wilson to expose the White House's lies in an editorial published in the *New York Times* on Sunday, 6 July 2003. In "What I Didn't Find in Africa," Wilson explained that he had flown to Niamey, the capital of Niger, in late February 2002. His first contact in Niamey was with U.S. Ambassador Babro Owens-Kirkpatrick, who was puzzled by Wilson's arrival, for the ambassador told Wilson that "she felt she had already debunked them [the claims about Iraq purchasing Niger uranium] in her reports to Washington." In his "diplomat's memoir" published following the scandal, titled *The Politics of Truth*, Wilson claimed that Owens-Kirkpatrick's report had been seconded by the research of Marine Corps General Carleton Fulford and that both figures had "definitively discredited the yellowcake rumor." This means that even before sending Wilson to Niger, Washington's war hawks had already disregarded two reports debunking the claim. Wilson conducted his research nonetheless, and "it did not take long to conclude that it was highly doubtful that any such transaction had ever taken place," for "there's simply too much oversight [by the IAEA] over too small an industry for a sale to have transpired." Wilson returned to the United States, where on 9 March 2002 he filed a detailed report with the CIA and the State Department's African Affairs Bureau. Wilson was therefore stunned to hear the president use information that both men knew was false in the 2003 State of the Union address.[57]

Appalled by his nation being dragged into war on the strength of lies, Wilson wrote his editorial in an attempt to set the record straight. Supporting his written editorial of 6 July with other media appearances, Wilson argued on NBC's *Meet the Press* that the information underlying the president's repeated assertions about Iraq purchasing African uranium was "erroneous, and that they knew about it well ahead of both the publication of the British white paper and the president's State of the Union address." Wilson's testimony thus provided the smoking gun proving three points: first, the Bush administration knew its claims about Iraq purchasing African uranium were incorrect; second, it knew so well in advance of the president's key speeches utilizing the false claim; and third, the White House's denial of this knowledge amounts to a shameful cover-up, and hence a second layer of lying.[58]

In fact, the Bush administration's response to these revelations was doubly dishonorable—demonstrating what Eric Alterman has called "the Nixonian depths" of its "moral depravity"—for not only did it deny the facts as provided by Wilson, Kristof, Priest, and others, but it attacked Wilson's family by "outing" his wife, Valerie Plame, as a CIA agent. Roughly one week following Wilson's truth-telling editorial, anonymous White House officials told as many as six prominent reporters that Plame was an undercover CIA agent specializing in WMDs. Of the six reporters who received the leak (including *Time* magazine's Matthew Cooper; the *Washington Post*'s Walter Pincus and Glenn Kessler; NBC's Tim

Russert; and the *New York Times*'s Judith Miller), only Robert Novak, the syndicated conservative columnist and ubiquitous CNN talking head, printed a story with the information. Leaking Bush administration officials and an irresponsible journalist thus teamed up to jeopardize Plame's career and to send a warning to other potential whistleblowers that the White House would punish those who brought its lies to public attention.[59]

As numerous observers have noted, revealing the name of a covert agent is a federal crime, punishable with a $50,000 fine and/or up to ten years in prison. Worse yet, outing Plame likely jeopardized the safety of some of her contacts, surely leading to the loss of intelligence assets that would have aided the war on terrorism. As summarized by Joseph Wilson, "the exposure of a clandestine operative is a reprehensible breach of trust between our political leadership and those who risk their lives to keep America safe. It is a profound betrayal of our country." Facing the urgings of Senator Charles Schumer (D-NY), Congresswoman Alcee Hastings (D-FL), and CIA director Tenet, and clearly recognizing that it had to respond to the scandal, the Justice Department announced at the close of September 2003 that it would investigate the crime. In March 2004 *Newsday* reported that "the federal grand jury probing the leak . . . has subpoenaed records of Air Force One telephone calls in the weeks before" the release of Plame's identity. Indeed, there is little doubt that the leak came from high-level White House officials. It will be some time before this issue is brought to conclusion, but for our purposes it demonstrates a chilling fact: that the Bush administration's operation of deception will deny the facts when it is confronted with them and will do everything in its power, including breaking the law and endangering the security of its own agents, to punish those who help produce evidence debunking its lies.[60]

In addition to Wilson's memos of March 2002, the White House also disregarded a second set of reports warning that its claims about African uranium were false. In fact, in preparation for President Bush's 7 October 2002 Cincinnati speech—still four months prior to the January 2003 State of the Union address—the White House contacted the CIA seeking intelligence to support the president's claims regarding Iraq's search for nuclear weapons. Apparently aware that the president might use the bogus charges regarding Niger, and clearly afraid that his using such information would tarnish its own professional integrity, the CIA told the White House of its doubts about the Iraq/Africa uranium charges. The

Los Angeles Times, New York Times, Washington Post, and numerous government officials have all verified that the CIA sent two cautionary memos, one on 5 October to Deputy National Security Adviser Stephen Hadley and another on 6 October to Hadley and National Security Adviser Condoleezza Rice. To make sure the memos were not lost in the shuffle, CIA Director Tenet called Hadley as well. No dashed-off response, Bob Woodward reports in *Plan of Attack* that the CIA's "three-and-a-half-page memo to Hadley" of 5 October "recommended twenty-two changes in Draft #6" of the Cincinnati speech. For the president to rely on the British claim thus points either to rank incompetence at the office of the national security adviser—*Hadley lost a memo and forgot a phone call? Rice missed a memo?*—or, again, to the fact that the president chose to disregard the CIA's analysis because it did not support his agenda. Congressman Henry Waxman (D-CA) summarizes this embarrassment as pointing either to "knowing deception or unfathomable incompetence."[61]

In a damning confession, an anonymous White House official admitted on 18 July 2003 that "the decision to mention uranium came from White House speech writers, not from senior White House officials"—meaning that fact was trumped by fiction, that the concerns of career CIA and State Department intelligence specialists were overridden by eager speechwriters working to appease a war-hungry president. This revelation was forced into the public largely because of comments made following a closed hearing of the Senate Intelligence Committee on 16 July. At this hearing the participants debated the origin of the false claim; following the hearing Senator Richard Durbin (D-IL) spoke bitterly, lamenting that "the president has within his ranks on staff some person who was willing to spin and hype and exaggerate and cut corners."[62]

But the lie was not the work of just a few fact-denying speechwriters, for following the Senate hearings of the sixteenth it was widely reported that the White House and the CIA had in fact engaged in intense pre–State of the Union "negotiations" during which the White House sought to circumvent the CIA's warnings by fiddling with the language—but not the content—of the false charge about African uranium. To make matters worse, in the 18 July press briefing following the Senate hearings of the sixteenth, McClellan lied about the timeline of events, claiming despite all the evidence that the White House had not been contacted about the contested claims before the speeches in question. Instead, McClellan claimed that "the first time many people here in the White House were aware of the forged documents" was "when you [the reporters to whom he was speaking] read it publicly" in the summer of 2003. And so denials were wielded to cover up original lies, creating an increasingly dense labyrinth of deception.[63]

In a telling moment that foreshadows our discussion below regarding how President Bush's rhetorical production was entwined in institutional turf wars, one of his responses to this escalating crisis of legitimacy was to blame the CIA. In a performance of what many pundits smirkingly referred to as "falling on his sword," the then CIA director Tenet was forced on 11 July 2003 to take the blame for the president citing the false uranium claim in his State of the Union address. But Tenet did not fall quietly, for in his intricate statement accepting blame for the president's lying he reminded listeners that "in September and October 2002 before Senate Committees, senior intelligence officials . . . told members of Congress that we differed with the British dossier on the reliability of the uranium reporting." Two paragraphs later, Tenet confirmed that the classified October 2002 *NIE* included a sentence written by the INR noting that "the claims of Iraqi pursuit of natural uranium in Africa are, in INR's assessment, highly dubious." Thus, in a high-stakes performance of irony, Tenet took responsibility for the faulty uranium claim in his opening paragraph only to spend the following two pages detailing how the presence of the claim in the president's speech could only be seen as the result of the White House disregarding congressional hearings, its own secret briefings, and the memos and phone calls described above.[64]

Tenet's ironic (non)admission of guilt apparently did not sit well with the White House, for it took but twelve days for the White House to shift the blame again, this time naming Stephen Hadley as the culprit behind the false claims about African uranium. Speaking on 23 July, twelve days after Tenet's performance on the eleventh, Hadley, described in one article as possessing "a reputation for fanatical attention to detail," confessed that he had misplaced the October 2002 memos and had found them only in late July 2003. Although Hadley's fall taking was free of Tenet's irony, it was difficult to imagine the fanatically detailed deputy national security adviser committing such an act of organizational ineptitude without a little nudge from his superiors. Indeed, despite his straight face, Hadley's dubious confession could not help but feel like a comic rejoinder to Tenet's ironic confession.[65]

But Hadley's confession did not need to be persuasive, for in yet another example of how the legislative branch is complicit with the White House's operation of deception, on 16 July 2003 the Senate rejected by a party-line vote of 51-45 Jon Corzine's (D-NJ) proposal to convene an independent twelve-member commission to study the scandal. Instead of this proposed independent commission (like the ones used to hunt President Clinton), the Republican-controlled Senate Select Committee on Intelligence took up the issue, seeking to lay the blame for these intelligence scandals on faulty CIA information instead of on Bush administration lying. Indeed, in the first part of its findings, released on 9 July 2004, the committee offered a stinging rebuke to the CIA while ignoring the larger question addressed here. Shielding the president, the committee's senators, as reported in an unusually large headline in the *New York Times*, "Assail CIA Judgments on Iraq's Arms as Deeply Flawed." Although we support that claim, it also means, at least for now, that the president's rhetorical trickery, Tenet's ironic fall taking, Hadley's unbelievable confession, and the intelligence community's crippling turf wars have been turned into a partisan charade shielding President Bush from independent scrutiny.[66]

But we need not wait for a Senate committee to fathom the depth of the bureaucratic turf wars that lay behind this controversy regarding President Bush's using evidence widely known to be false in his State of the Union address. As early as 16 December 2002, six weeks prior to the president's contested speech, Robert Dreyfuss reported in the *American Prospect* that "the Pentagon is bringing relentless pressure to bear on the agency [CIA] to produce intelligence reports more supportive of war with Iraq." The Pentagon engaged in such arm-twisting because, according to Dreyfuss, "inside the foreign-policy, defense, and intelligence agencies, nearly the whole rank and file, along with many senior officials, are opposed to invading Iraq."[67]

Apparently unable to intimidate the CIA into providing information more to its liking, the Pentagon created its own intelligence unit, The Office of Special Plans (OSP), to analyze materials regarding Iraq. Chaired by Abram Shulsky, a neoconservative hawk, the OSP reported directly to Undersecretary of Defense Feith, who in turn brought the OSP's briefs to Rumsfeld, thus circumventing the usual intelligence gathering and analyzing framework. Bypassing the usual vetting procedures enabled a war-hungry White House to turn dubious and fragmentary intelligence into the "evidence" necessary for arguing for war. In an interview with Seymour Hersh, the former National Security Council expert on Iraq, Kenneth Pollack, described the OSP as an attempt to "dismantle the existing filtering process that for fifty years had been preventing the policymakers from getting bad information." The OSP thus selectively chose information that supported the administration's war agenda and fed it directly to the White House regardless of doubts and warnings from the traditional intelligence community. Hersh reports that intelligence professionals refer to this dangerous process as "stovepiping." The metaphor is apt, for it suggests not only the rapid elevation of materials from the kitchen of intelligence gathering to the higher regions of policy making, but also the fact that what comes out of the stovepipe is smoke—not hard data and carefully processed analyses, but smoke, propaganda, informational pollution.[68]

Reflecting widespread dismay over news of the OSP's formation, the *Observer* referred to it as "a shadow, parallel intelligence network staffed not by espionage professionals but by favored political appointees." These appointees apparently flooded the CIA and State Department with "intelligence" gathered from exiled Iraqis, especially those associated with Ahmed Chalabi's Iraqi National Congress, thus suggesting that Shulsky's OSP was not getting hard data so much as rumors and wish lists from Chalabi's would-be post-Saddam rulers of the new Iraq. Putting this stovepiping process in perspective, Gordon Mitchell asks readers to "imagine ignoring the advice of an established investment counselor and instead basing your whole retirement strategy on stock tips you overhear at the bus stop." In fact, even while it was "stovepiped" to the White House without careful scrutiny, the validity of the information provided by Chalabi-linked exiles—like a cannot-miss stock tip overheard at the bus stop—was widely doubted by intelligence professionals. According to a postwar article in the *New York Times*, the Defense Intelligence Agency (DIA) concluded that "most of the information provided by Iraqi defectors who were made available by the Iraqi National Congress was of little or no value." Chalabi admitted as much in a March 2004 interview with the British *Telegraph*, where he chirped that "what was said before [the war] is not important . . . [for now] *we are heroes in error.*"[69]

Chalabi has been in error for a long time, however, for in 1992 he was convicted by the State Security Court in Ammam, Jordan, of what Jane Mayer reports were "thirty one charges, including embezzlement, theft, forgery, currency speculation, making false statements, and making bad loans to himself, to his friends, and to his family's other financial enterprises." The acts were allegedly committed while he ran the Petra Bank in Ammam, but Chalabi was not convicted until years later, after he was safely ensconced in London. He reportedly pocketed anywhere from $70 million to $158 million via the transactions in question. In 1993, Chalabi's Iraqi National Congress presented President Clinton with a plan for regime change in Iraq titled "The End Game." The plan was based largely on the wishful theory that a small military uprising would trigger a massive outpouring of anti-Saddam activism. The Clinton administration responded to the plan by funding joint Chalabi/CIA operations, which culminated in a failed insurrection in March 1995. Despite his trail of failures, the passage of the Iraq Liberation Act in October 1998, which Mayer argues he had a hand in drafting, meant that Chalabi was soon receiving as much as $10 million a year from the State Department for planning anti-Saddam activities. To cement his status in Washington, Chalabi cultivated close relationships not only with archconservative think tanks and lobby groups, including the American Enterprise Institute and the American-Israeli Public Affairs Committee, but also with U.S. oil companies, with whom he plotted post-Saddam scenarios of lucrative U.S./Iraq commercial ties. For more than a decade, then, Chalabi was running high-flying and allegedly illegal banking operations and milking Washington for millions of dollars worth of covert support while producing little noticeable change in Iraqi politics. Serving "in error" would thus appear to be Chalabi's trademark.[70]

Although the DIA's damning conclusions about the quality of Chalabi's intelligence were not made public until September 2003, six months after the war on Iraq began, reports indicate that the conflict between the OSP, CIA, DIA, and other intelligence experts came to a head in the days leading up to Secretary of State Powell's 5 February 2003 testimony before the UN. Powell and a team of intelligence officials gathered at the CIA on 1 February to begin piecing together the evidence. A dismayed Powell is reported at one point to have tossed a sheaf of papers into the air, exclaiming, "I'm not reading this, this is bullshit." Powell knew that much of the intelligence he had been given was bogus because a September 2002 DIA report had previously concluded that "there is no reliable information on whether Iraq is producing and stockpiling chemical weapons." So while the CIA couched its reports in terms of possibilities, while the DIA offered "no reliable information," and while the INR and DOE offered strong warnings, one can imagine the exile-fed OSP arguing for certainty, thus leaving Powell squeezed between prudent and professional intelligence officials and OSP's gung-ho war hawks. The fact that this intelligence turf war led to botched information comes as no surprise, for as Odom reports in *Fixing Intelligence*, "competitive analysis has seldom produced better analysis, but it has frequently inspired intense parochialism. As a rule, it creates more heat than light."[71]

These heat-but-not-light-producing intelligence turf wars were so apparent and so important in terms of figuring out who was driving U.S. foreign policy that in the first week of June 2003 Douglas Feith, undersecretary of defense, called a press conference to try to dismiss charges that the OSP had politicized questionable intelligence to fit President Bush's preformed imperatives. Despite Feith's efforts, by July 2003 the *New York Times* was referring to "the feud between the CIA and White House." By late May 2004 the intelligence turf wars between the Pentagon, CIA, and State Department had become so heated that even conservative columnist William Safire observed that the agencies were engaging in "tribal warfare." These turf battles resurfaced in March 2004, when Karen Kwiatkowski, a lieutenant colonel in the air force who worked on sensitive intelligence matters, retired from twenty years of service in disgust because of OSP's actions. In a scathing exposé published in *Salon*, she wrote that "I observed firsthand the formation of the Pentagon's Office of Special Plans and watched . . . neoconservative agenda bearers within OSP usurp measured and carefully considered assessments, and through suppression and distortion of intelligence analysis promulgate what were in fact falsehoods to both Congress and the executive office." Kwiatkowski's damning charges have been corroborated not only by the numerous sources cited above, but by Senator Carl M. Levin, the senior Democrat on the Armed Services Committee, who argued in October 2004 that OSP leader Feith had been practicing "continuing deception" in his testimonies before Congress regarding alleged Iraqi WMDs and ties to al Qaeda. Levin charged that Feith's statements "did not reflect accurately the intelligence agencies' assessment." More than just institutional wrangling over power and prestige, these confrontations revolved around foreign-policy–shaping disagreements over who was providing intelligence and analysis to the White House.[72]

Indeed, Seymour Hersh reported in the *New Yorker* as early as July 2003 that the OSP had taken over the intelligence functions once played by the CIA, DIA, FBI, and INR and that the OSP was relying for much of its intelligence on less-than-credible Chalabi allies. The Steering Group of Veteran Intelligence Professionals for Sanity was so dismayed by the growing cascade of information pointing to the OSP cooking intelligence that on 2 May 2003 it sent a bristling letter of complaint to the president. The letter charged that "while there have been occasions in the past when intelligence has been deliberately warped for political purposes, *never before has such warping been used in such a systematic way* to mislead our elected representatives into voting to authorize launching a war."[73]

While the Veteran Intelligence Professionals for Sanity's letter seethes with rage at the compromising of their profession for the president's warmongering, the fact is that intelligence has been systematically warped on prior occasions to fit political needs. Whereas prudent foreign policy uses intelligence to inform strategy, numerous administrations have reversed this relationship and fabricated evidence to conform to policy. For example, the *Pentagon Papers* proved that over the course of many presidencies, the executive branch systematically ignored intelligence and then systematically produced false intelligence to support its disastrous policies in Vietnam. Hannah Arendt's 1969 essay about the *Pentagon Papers,* titled "Lying in Politics," serves as a cautionary tale of the ramifications of such long-term, systemic lying. Arendt argues that "if the mysteries of government have so befogged the minds of the actors themselves that they no longer know or remember the truth behind their concealments and their lies, the whole operation of deception . . . will run aground or become counterproductive." The push to manufacture evidence, then, to rely on *argumentum ad ignorantiam,* prolepsis, hyperbole, and "position-to-know" to lie about what one knows or does not know, becomes a self-fulfilling and ultimately devastating feedback loop in which one loses the ability to recognize reality as anything other than one's own production, one's own lie.[74]

The damage this systematic lying does to democracy is immeasurable. As Paul Krugman lamented in an ominous editorial titled "Things to Come," in the days leading up to waging war on Iraq "we got assertions about a nuclear program that turned out to be based on flawed or faked evidence; we got assertions about a link to al Qaeda that people inside the intelligence services regard as nonsense. Yet those serial embarrassments went almost unreported by our domestic news media. . . . So now the administration knows that it can make unsubstantiated claims." In fact, the *New York Times*'s reporting on prewar WMD charges by the Bush administration was so sloppy that the paper issued an apology on 26 May 2004, admitting that its coverage was "not as rigorous as it should have been." Thus echoing Arendt and our driving theme of how the pursuit of empire has degraded the norms of public debate, hence dragging America toward the twilight of democracy, Krugman asserts that a lying administration, aided by a largely compliant mass media, can foist on an uninformed public any number of wild assertions, producing consensus not through informed dialogue but orchestrated patriotic ignorance.[75]

Given our critique of President Bush's operation of deception regarding alleged Iraqi WMDs, it comes as no surprise to learn that as of June 2005 the U.S. forces occupying Iraq have found no WMDs. Led by David Kay, the one-time UN weapons inspector, the weapons-hunting Iraq Survey Group spent the summer of 2003 scouring Iraq, finding not one WMD. For Thomas Powers, Kay's findings prove that "the administration's justification for war was not merely flawed or imperfect—it was wrong in almost every detail, and completely wrong at the heart. There was no imminent danger—indeed, there was no *distant* danger." Following Kay's initial reports, the Iraq Survey Group's postwar hunt for WMDs was led by Charles A. Duelfer, a special advisor to the director of the CIA. Duelfer's definitive report of October 2004—running to more than nine hundred pages and drawing on the work of more than twelve hundred agents—revealed that "at the time of the American invasion . . . Iraq did not possess chemical and biological weapons, was not seeking to reconstitute its nuclear program, and was not making any active effort to gain those abilities."[76]

The Duelfer report verifies our claims throughout this chapter: Iraq had no WMDs. In fact, as final evidence of this argument, consider an article printed on 1 May 2005 in London's *Sunday Times* regarding a leaked top secret memo from a meeting on 23 July 2002 between Prime Minister Tony Blair and his inner circle, including Defense Secretary Geoffrey Hoon, Foreign Secretary Jack Straw, Attorney General Lord Goldsmith, JIC head John Scarlett, and Sir Richard Dearlove, head of

MI6 (the British equivalent of the CIA), who is identified throughout the memo as "C." Addressed to David Manning, the British equivalent of the U.S. national security advisor, and written by Matthew Rycroft, the second paragraph of the memo recounts Dearlove's/"C"'s report to the prime minister on his recent meetings with Bush administration officials in Washington. Printed under the heading of "Secret and Strictly Personal—UK Eyes Only," and including the warning that "this record is extremely sensitive," the memo reveals that "'C' reported . . . military action was now seen as inevitable. Bush wanted to remove Saddam, through military action, *justified by the conjunction of terrorism and WMD.* But the *intelligence and facts were being fixed around the policy.*" There you have it: the war was a certainty from as early as July 2002; WMDs and terrorism would be used as justifications for waging war; and intelligence was "being fixed" to meet this agenda. As we have shown here, and as this memo confirms, the president's public address regarding his reasons for waging war on Iraq amounts to a shameful operation of deception.[77]

Epilogue: Speech Kills:
The Productions and Deceptions of Violence

Since 9/11 the Bush administration has been engaged in an operation of deception that has had deadly consequences; indeed, we have illustrated here how by using *argumentum ad ignorantiam,* prolepsis, literalist hyperbole, and position to know, the president has proven once again that speech kills. We are fully aware, however, that reconstructing the president's murderous lies is just one step in the larger project of unraveling the political economy of state-sanctioned violence. We thus close this chapter by expanding our inquiry into the rhetoric surrounding WMDs to consider a series of related examples of mass-produced violence.

For example, consider the fact that over the course of its work in Iraq, from May 1991 through October 1997, the IAEA's "Action Team" of weapons inspectors had a budget of $3 million per year. Projected across this six-and-one-half-year period, this means that the world community spent $19.5 million for weapons inspections. But over the five years including 1998–2002, the U.S. alone spent $78 million in "assistance to the [Iraqi] opposition," meaning that for every $1 spent trying to rid Iraq of WMDs, the U.S. spent $4 trying to topple Hussein by funneling conventional weapons to a wide variety of opposition groups. The figure of $78 million represents only public expenditures, not CIA and other covert Pentagon expenditures, so we have no idea how much money the United States actually spent trying to destabilize Iraq by arming clandestine groups. Moreover, the CIA admitted after the war that it had possessed intelligence on twenty-one suspected WMD sites that it did not share with UN weapons inspectors. The administration was therefore claiming publicly that the inspections were not working, even while privately hamstringing those efforts. Thus, ever since the close of the first Gulf War, the U.S. has spoken publicly about supporting weapons control while both crippling the inspections process and contributing to the mass proliferation of violence in Iraq.[78]

Furthermore, as Chalmers Johnson argues in *Blowback*, any threat Hussein posed to the world was largely the result of reckless U.S. foreign policy, which in the name of combating fundamentalism in Iran armed Hussein throughout the 1980s with a remarkable arsenal of weapons. In this same vein, Peter Dale Scott argues in *Drugs, Oil, and War* that "covert operations, when they generate or reinforce autonomous political power, almost always outlast the specific purpose for which they were designed. Instead they enlarge and become part of the hostile forces the U.S. has to address." Consider, for example, the havoc wreaked in Nicaragua by the Contras, the trail of murder and drugs left by paramilitary death squads in Colombia, the history of violent extremism spawned by anti-Castro fanatics, the prehistoric butchery committed by the Taliban, and of course the military ambitions of Hussein himself—each of these nightmares was fueled at one time, in some cases in explicit violation of U.S. law, by covert U.S. funding, training, and arming. For Johnson and Scott, then, one of the main sources of violence in the world is the United States itself, which by trying to influence political situations via covert operations and alliances with dictators creates networks of heavily armed, highly trained, and utterly lawless mercenaries whose violence inevitably "blows back" as a threat to U.S. security.[79]

Creating mass hysteria regarding WMDs deflects attention from these more pressing causes of violence. For example, Richard Butler opens his venomous memoir, *The Greatest Threat: Iraq, Weapons of Mass Destruction, and the Crisis of Global Security*, with the whopping claim that "the greatest threat to life on earth is weapons of mass destruction." Despite the United States' unquestioned control of Iraqi airspace and the fact that post–Gulf War Iraq never possessed a credible WMD delivery system,

Butler terrifies readers with the hyperbolic threat that Hussein is on the verge of producing chemical rockets so powerful that just one could kill "up to 1 million people." Butler was head of UNSCOM from 1997 to 1999; reading his bitter screed leaves no doubt that UNSCOM was destined to failure, as Butler began his work in Baghdad assuming that Hussein was comparable to Hitler and that he was so dangerous that "a veiled threat of physical violence was always signaled, if only subliminally." Because Butler's cranky book reads like the heralding of a vendetta, a literal call to war in the name of ridding the world of WMDs, it stands along with President Bush's many lies as a strong example of how producing a hysterical discourse of WMDs both diverts attention from more immediate and more deadly forms of violence and short-circuits reasonable deliberation about foreign policy.[80]

Indeed, it is important to acknowledge that the entire debate about WMDs, including both the administration's lies about them and our critique of the "operation of deception," deflects attention from the most pressing causes and weapons of violence. For example, in the first Gulf War coalition forces flew 110,000 air sorties, dropping anywhere from 99,000 to 140,000 tons of explosives, thus unleashing on Iraq an amount of explosives described by Dilip Hiro as "equivalent to five to seven of the nuclear bombs dropped on Hiroshima." Asking at what point the saturation bombing (with conventional weapons) of an impoverished nation crosses over into an act of "mass destruction" demonstrates that overblown fears of WMDs serve to naturalize and justify the United States' use of awesomely devastating conventional weapons.[81]

Some critics have pushed this line of thinking even further by charging that the UN's post–Gulf War sanctions against Iraq—which contributed in some estimates to the death of *half a million* Iraqis—amount to a WMD more deadly than anything Hussein could ever dream of producing. For example, in a blistering article in *Foreign Affairs*, John and Karl Muller argue that "the harm caused by these weapons [chemical, biological, and nuclear WMDs] pales in comparison to the havoc wreaked by a much more popular tool: economic sanctions." The Mullers thus appropriate the notion of WMDs to rename the UN's post–Gulf War restrictions on trade with Iraq as "Sanctions of Mass Destruction." In a similar vein, James Fine refers in the *Middle East Report* to "The Iraq Sanctions Catastrophe." Bush administration spokespersons have repeatedly blamed the sanctions catastrophe on Hussein, charging that he used available funds and resources for his enrichment and armament while his people starved, yet the Mullers, Fine, and a host of other scholars and critics have concluded that the sanctions caused unnecessary hardships and hundreds of thousands of deaths, thus raising the question of what is or is not a WMD.[82]

While some readers may quibble with our thinking critically about what constitutes a weapon of mass destruction, we would like to push this line of argument even further to suggest that the true WMDs are dirty water, hunger, and disease. For example, the World Health Organization reports that in 2002 there were 170 million underweight children globally and that "over three million of them die each year as a result." Another 1.7 million deaths each year "are attributed to unsafe water, sanitation, and hygiene, mainly through infectious diarrhea." Richard Jolly, chairman of the Water Supply and Sanitation Collaborative Council, estimates that "bringing water and sanitation to all would cost $10 billion a year." Along those same lines, the United Nations International Children's Emergency Fund estimates that $2.8 billion per year could provide immunizations for "every child in the developing world," hence dramatically improving the health of millions of children. Compared to the hundreds of billions of dollars the United States has spent leveling Iraq in the name of making the world safe from alleged Iraqi WMDs—with the occupation alone costing $5.46 billion each month—and considering that the U.S. military budget is almost $400 billion per year, it is maddening to wonder how our government can choose to spend billions of dollars on imperial wars rather than on making basic improvements in global access to safe drinking water and disease-blocking immunizations. But no; instead of saving lives from the ravages of real WMDs, the United States wages war against fictional WMDs.[83]

Given the widespread sense that the United States is the world's wealthiest nation, replete with the world's best doctors and scientists and engineers, allowing the destructive forces noted above to continue their death march while waging a costly war in the name of eliminating Iraq's fictional WMDs cannot help but appear to much of the world as unconscionable cruelty. It comes as no surprise, then, to learn that interviews and polls conducted around the world on the two-year anniversary of 9/11 showed increasing hostility toward the United States. As the *New York Times* reported on 11 September 2003, favorable views of the United States had plummeted in Brazil from 56 percent in 2000 to 34 percent now; similar drops were reported in France (from 62 percent to 43 percent), Germany (from 78 percent to 45 percent), Indonesia (from 75 percent to 15 percent), Morocco (from 77 percent to 27 percent), and Turkey (from 52 percent to 15 percent). As the *Times* concluded, "In the two years since Sept. 11, 2001, the view of the United States as a victim of terrorism that deserved the world's sympathy and support has given way to a widespread vision of America as an imperial power that has defied world opinion through unjustified and unilateral use of military force." Two weeks later the president's United States Advisory Group on Public Diplomacy for the Arab and Muslim World reached a similar conclusion, arguing that its assessment of postwar global sentiment suggested that "hostility toward America has reached shocking levels."[84]

President Bush's operation of deception regarding WMDs has thus not only cost innocent lives, subverted the constitutional process of checks and balances, wasted our tax dollars, committed U.S. troops to a bloody quagmire, and left Iraq a devastated and lawless wasteland, but also squandered the world's post-9/11 goodwill, leaving the United States feared now more than ever—and hence more likely than ever to be the target of terrorist vengeance.

War Rhetorics

The *National Security Strategy of
the United States* and President Bush's
Globalization-through-Benevolent-Empire

Condoleezza Rice's comments before the Senate Foreign Relations Committee on 18 January 2005 serve as a grim reminder of the intricate links between an imperial foreign policy and degraded public deliberation. During the first day of the hearings regarding her nomination to be President Bush's post-Powell secretary of state, Rice came under intense questioning from Senator Barbara Boxer (D-CA), whose questions focused on Rice's intimate role in producing what we described in chapter 1 as "the whole operation of deception." Boxer's questions were littered with quotations demonstrating that Rice and her Bush administration allies did everything in their power to portray the invasion of Iraq as a crucial step in the war against terrorism. Like us, Boxer was incredulous about those claims before the war; like us, Boxer approached the hearings wanting Rice to discuss why U.S. foreign policy had become entwined in so many factual distortions, evidential errors, and suggestive innuendos. Demonstrating restraint in her choice of vocabulary, Boxer asked Rice to explain her many pre- and postwar "misstatements." Rice responded, a tone of disdain creeping into her voice, "Senator . . . I would hope that we can have this conversation and discuss what happened before and what went on before and what I said, without impugning my credibility or integrity." Thus, rather than addressing the substance of Boxer's detailed and fact-filled questions, Rice responded as if hard-hitting queries about foreign policy were below-the-belt personal attacks. On this model of nondeliberation, questioning U.S. foreign policy amounts to bad taste, a violation of decorum.[1]

The second day of hearings featured an even more disheartening moment. Boxer again read a long fact-filled statement recounting Rice's pattern of deceptions regarding both the reasons for waging war on Iraq and the status of its reconstruction. To her credit, Boxer marshaled overwhelming evidence illustrating the many ways Rice and her Bush administration allies had systematically misled the American people and the world. Summarizing her thoughts from the first day of hearings, her anger palpable, Boxer expressed the sentiments of millions around the world when she said, "This is why I find it so troubling that the Bush administration used the fear of terror to make the war against Iraq appear to be part of the response to 9/11." In her curt reply, Rice dodged Boxer's questions, evaded their substance, and dismissed their significance; Boxer responded with increasing impatience until finally, after an unproductive round of testy back-and-forth exchanges, Senator Richard Lugar (R-IN, the chair of the committee) intervened, saying, "Now, Senator Boxer obviously had strong points of view and, in fairness, the chair has let the hearing verge out of control." The transcript records laughter at this comment. Lugar continues: "But we're going to come back into control at this stage." Boxer: "I'm finished. You'll be happy." More laughter. The implication of the moment is clear: anything approaching critical questioning of the about-to-be-secretary of state amounts to veering out of control. A hearing ostensibly convened to air legitimate questions about Rice and U.S. foreign policy is thus turned into a prearranged coronation, one where critical questions are dismissively laughed away as off topic and off color. On the first day of hearings, Rice's responses made it clear that the architects of the new U.S. imperial foreign policy would not tolerate criticism; on the second day, Lugar made it clear that the Senate Foreign Relations Committee would support this policy by characterizing the exchange of perspectives—the core activity of democracy—as an unnecessary waste of time, as partisanship verging out of control.[2]

Rice's and Lugar's joint evasion of anything approaching a real debate, their repeated refusal to confront Boxer's and others' dismayed questions about U.S. policy in Iraq—for similarly difficult questions were asked by Senators John Kerry (D-MA) and Christopher Dodd (D-CT) —amounts to a perfect illustration of how the Bush administration's foreign policy works unilaterally, more as the result of imperial dictate than democratic deliberation. To situate Rice's comments and the antideliberative foreign policy they point toward in their post-9/11 context, this chapter addresses the set of assumptions and principles loosely known as the "Bush Doctrine." Articulated initially through the president's post-9/11 speeches and then gathered in a more programmatic sense in the September 2002 *National Security Strategy of the United States,* the Bush

Doctrine amounts not only to a comprehensive statement of post-9/11 U.S. foreign policy but also, as seen in the president's and Rice's and others' handling of tough questions, into an antideliberative discursive strategy.[3]

Analyzing the *NSSUS* is particularly important for our purposes because whereas the WMD lies examined in chapter 1 were time and place conditional, and thus depended on factors pertaining specifically to the war on Iraq, the claims made in the *NSSUS* transcend particular crises, offering instead a broad set of prescriptions arguing for globalization-through-benevolent-empire. Thus, whereas chapter 1 offered a case study of the lies told to drag the nation into war on Iraq, chapter 2 broadens the scope of inquiry by offering an examination of both the principles driving those lies and the rhetorical strategies used to convey these broad policy imperatives. Moreover, because the *NSSUS* speaks on almost every page of the complexities of maintaining U.S. power and privilege in a world ever more united and fractured by technology, capital, and culture, the document offers an unusually comprehensive statement of U.S. anxieties and ambitions regarding globalization and empire. Indeed, because it is so ambitious an attempt to redefine U.S. interests in relationship to globalization and empire, the *NSSUS* is a complicated and at times compelling document. It makes so many claims that touch on so many subjects that we cannot possibly examine them all here. Instead, given our interests in the intersections of globalization, empire, war, and public deliberation, and hoping to provide readers with a sense of analytic clarity, we have distilled what we believe are the *NSSUS*'s five overarching themes:

- First, the *NSSUS* offers *a doctrine of preemption,* by which the United States claims the right to strike against foes wherever and whenever it feels threatened; as a corollary to this first point we examine the impact of this doctrine of preemption on international diplomacy.
- Second, the *NSSUS* proposes *a millennial military state* in which waging war is the chief and perpetual function of the federal government; moreover, President Bush's post-9/11 speeches indicate that this military state strives for a millennial, transhistorical triumph of Good over Evil.

- Third, the *NSSUS* wraps points one and two in *a promise of benign universalism,* in an apparently generous offer to spread U.S. goods, capital, institutions, and values far and wide; as a case study of how this process unfolds, we examine the U.S. response to the postwar looting of Baghdad.
- Fourth, and as a specifically economic version of point three above, the *NSSUS* links U.S. national security, global economic growth, and the fate of foreign governments to their enthusiasm for *evangelical capitalism,* which is portrayed as driving a post-Communist world of globalizing yet gentle free markets.
- And fifth, even while explicitly attempting to avoid this charge, the *NSSUS*'s broad claims about rogue states in a world of Evil, when coupled with President Bush's post-9/11 speeches, hint at a form of conflict some observers have called *a clash of civilizations.*

In addition to pursuing these five themes, we should also note that the *NSSUS* argues time and time again for the rule of law, civil liberties, human rights, gender equality, and a host of other principles generally accepted as some of the best achievements of modernity. For example, the *NSSUS* pledges that "America must stand firmly for the nonnegotiable demands of human dignity: the rule of law; limits on the absolute power of the state; free speech; freedom of worship; equal justice; respect for women; religious and ethnic tolerance; and respect for private property" (3). Likewise, the *NSSUS* promises that the U.S. "will champion the cause of human dignity and oppose those who resist it" (4). In stark contrast to those critics who see the *NSSUS* as a statement of naked U.S. aggression, then, the text actually stands in parts as a testament to progressive humanism, to the Enlightenment promise to spread reason and justice. Indeed, large parts of the *NSSUS* ring with a heroic, almost Wilsonian sense of the need for a cosmopolitan and democratizing politics of justice. Our rhetorical task, then, is to examine the relationship between generous promises to defend "human dignity" and the imperial ways that "those who resist it" are cajoled, threatened, and even attacked. Put differently, our challenge is to figure out the complicated ways the *NSSUS* invokes human rights while in turn proposing a form of U.S.-driven globalization-through-benevolent-empire that many fear amounts to a blueprint for a new Pax Americana.[4]

The *NSSUS* is therefore a curious document, for whereas large parts of it read like a bland policy paper stuffed full of euphemisms, technical jargon, and other forms of bureaucratic prose that seem dedicated to hiding as much as they reveal, other parts of it read like a sermon brimming with uplifting platitudes, nationalist clichés, and bold promises of benevolent leadership. To help us make sense of the *NSSUS* we therefore supplement our analysis of its claims with readings of President Bush's frequently emotional, sometimes theological, and always confident post-9/11 speeches. In comparing these different genres of communication we follow the advice of John Murphy, who has observed that "war rhetoric is a rhetorical hybrid, combining the qualities of what Aristotle termed *deliberative discourse*, arguments to justify the expediency and practicality of an action, and *epideictic rhetoric*, appeals that unify the community and amplify its virtues." This combination of deliberative and epideictic rhetoric is both powerfully persuasive and politically dangerous, for it offers a provocative merging of rhetorical functions. As Murphy describes it, deliberative rhetoric strives to achieve a public display of rationality wherein "the audience makes clear decisions: we should or should not adopt a particular policy." Epideictic rhetoric, on the other hand, both produces and celebrates communal values: "it reflects on the means of honor or dishonor, unity or disunity, community and chaos in public life." That is, epideictic rhetoric fulfills cultural expectations by engaging in value-laden claims that may or may not depend on the norms of evidence and exchange assumed to fuel deliberative rhetoric.[5]

"War rhetoric" therefore amounts to a complicated discursive hybrid where the boundaries between fact and fiction, evidence and ideology, verifiable claim and wish fulfillment bleed promiscuously into the other, leaving readers or listeners in a particularly difficult position. Indeed, following Murphy's suggestive theoretical lead, we proceed with the understanding that by combining deliberative and epideictic rhetoric, the *NSSUS* and the president's speeches work hand in hand, collectively defining post-9/11 U.S. foreign policy. By analyzing the *NSSUS* and President Bush's speeches, then, we hope to offer a comprehensive analysis of the post-9/11 practice of what Murphy calls "war rhetoric."

 ~

Before tackling the five driving themes of post-9/11 war rhetoric it is important to situate the *National Security Strategy of the United States* within some of the larger political concerns dominating Washington at the time of its production. For the same day the president sent the *NSSUS* to Congress, 19 September 2002, he also submitted to that same body his resolution requesting blanket powers to use force against Iraq (House Joint Resolution 114, discussed in chapter 1). The brief remarks made by the president from the Oval Office regarding the transmission of the resolution include the claim that Saddam Hussein is "a true threat to world peace." Within three weeks the president would give his Cincinnati "mushroom cloud" speech, where he employed his most hyperbolic and outlandish claims, charging that those who hesitated to wage total war on terrorists may as well begin planning for the appearance of a mushroom cloud over some unnamed, devastated U.S. city. The *NSSUS* was thus sent to Congress at a pivotal moment, as the Bush White House used the high emotions surrounding the one-year anniversary of 9/11 to shift gears from waging war in Afghanistan to preparing for war on Iraq, all in the name of defending the nation from terrorism.[6]

Two weeks following the *NSSUS*'s submission to Congress, National Security Adviser Condoleezza Rice went on the road to try to explain some of the document's more startling passages. Speaking at the Waldorf Astoria Hotel in New York City, and hence to an audience still reeling from the devastation of 9/11, Rice claimed that "defending our Nation from its enemies is the first and fundamental commitment of the Federal Government." The implication of this claim, delivered in the midst of the early stages of the Bush administration's push for war on Iraq, was that pursuing regime change in Iraq was directly related to "defending the Nation from its enemies." Thus, precisely as Senator Boxer suggested in the confirmation hearing exchanges with which we began this chapter, Rice was implying that the *NSSUS*'s argument for preemptive war in general and the administration's push for regime change in Iraq in particular were both conceived as necessary responses to 9/11.[7]

Taken together, these comments by President Bush and National Security Adviser Rice indicate the deeply troubling purposes the *NSSUS* is meant to fulfill: not only to institutionalize a heightened national security state, one where domestic programs will take a backseat to military considerations, but to demonstrate that the government is so committed to this new national security state that it will fabricate threats to justify its enactment. For as we demonstrated in chapter 1, there were no weapons of mass destruction in Iraq—the "threat to world peace" was manufactured, not real. Nonetheless, the *NSSUS,* the president's resolution and comments, and Rice's speech thus worked hand in hand with the heightened emotions surrounding the one-year anniversary of 9/11 to create a powerful rush of war rhetoric. Indeed, as the administration's official manifesto of post-9/11 U.S. foreign policy, the *NSSUS* argued for a new national security state armed with preemptive strike capacity; as the administration's attempt to persuade Congress to grant war-making powers, the resolution offered the specific (and, as we demonstrated above, false) charges required to invoke the *NSSUS's* policies; and as epideictic support for the deliberative claims of the *NSSUS* and resolution, President Bush and Condoleezza Rice offered fear-mongering speeches implying that war on Iraq was necessary to curtail threats from both al Qaeda and Iraq's alleged WMDs.

Three caveats: first, we are concerned here with the 2002 *NSSUS* as a document that speaks directly to the concerns of post-9/11 America, not as part of a long genre of such texts. We therefore make no attempt to compare this *NSSUS* to the others that have preceded it. Second, like the White House's annual drug war reports, authored collectively by the Office of the National Drug Control Policy, the *NSSUS* was jointly authored by White House officials, thus clouding its authorship (although Rice is believed to have been a key figure in this process). Nonetheless, the text clearly stands as the official version of President Bush's foreign policy. Third, we will not tackle the question of who writes President Bush's speeches, for we assume that as long as he delivers them publicly then he must agree with their content. We therefore proceed with the understanding that a rhetorical analysis of the *NSSUS* and President Bush's post-9/11 speeches offers productive opportunities for studying the White House's efforts to lead the nation to war in Iraq, to justify its ineffectual war on terrorism, and to shift the "first and fundamental commitment of the Federal Government" toward a perpetual war economy fueled by perennial wars waged, if need be, against manufactured enemies.[8]

A Doctrine of Preemption and the End of Diplomacy

On its public release the *NSSUS* garnered immediate attention for its bold forwarding of a doctrine of preemption. Clearly driven by the terror of 9/11, the *NSSUS* claims that "as a matter of common sense and self-defense, America will act against such emerging threats [like Hussein and his supposed WMDs, al Qaeda, and other terrorists] before they are fully formed" (preface, iv). The need to preempt possible alliances between rogue states and terrorists is stated even more clearly in this passage: "We must be prepared to stop rogue states and their terrorist clients before they are able to threaten or use WMD against the United States and our allies and friends" (14). This is a slippery concept, however, for the question of what constitutes a threat is—as demonstrated in chapter 1—open to a wide array of interpretations. For example, when the *NSSUS* claims that "we must adapt the concept of *imminent threat* to the capabilities and objectives of today's adversaries" (15, emphasis added), we are forced to wonder about the criteria that will be used to establish the presence of an imminent threat. Likewise, when the *NSSUS* claims that the presence of WMDs and the possibility of their falling into the hands of terrorists provides a "compelling case for taking *anticipatory action* to defend ourselves" (15, emphasis added), we are obliged to inquire about the amount and quality of evidence required to count as "compelling." For not only was the imminent threat of Hussein's WMDs manufactured, but the alleged links between Hussein and al Qaeda were also shown to be false. So while we heartily support the commonsense argument that the United States has the right to defend itself, and to do so in a manner that precludes catastrophes like 9/11, the war on Iraq demonstrates that slippery notions like *anticipatory action* and *imminent threat* are little more than blanket justifications for U.S. military adventurism. As Carl Kaysen, John Steinbruner, and Martin Malin argue in *War with Iraq*, "The Bush administration's National Security Strategy provides a blueprint for a perpetual series of hot wars and preventive strikes." Using more forceful language, a Foreign Policy in Focus white paper titled "Our Fateful Choice: Global Leader or Global Cop" argues that the *NSSUS*'s doctrine of preemption "establishes the U.S. as an international vigilante—acting at once as cop, judge, and executioner."[9]

The apparent hypocrisy of the *NSSUS*'s principle of vigilante preemption is highlighted by its claim that the United States will "make no distinction between terrorists and those who knowingly harbor or provide aide to them" (5). This claim was first aired on the night of 9/11, when the president spoke to a terrified nation, promising that "we will make no distinction between the terrorists who committed these acts and those who harbor them." In the crucible of national crisis, with many Americans still waiting for word of the fate of their loved ones in New York City, Washington D.C., and the Pennsylvania countryside, this promise to pursue an unwavering, nonnegotiable hunt for the terrorists struck a powerful chord—here was a president who would not waver, who would not bend, who would put the hunt for terrorists ahead of politics as usual. America was both scared and angry that night; the president sought to alleviate the former by stoking the latter, promising not only that the terrorists would be captured but that their financiers, their trainers, their handlers, their many accomplices—all those who harbored and aided them—would also be targeted for U.S. retribution.[10]

A year later, by the time the *NSSUS* was released, this claim of making "no distinction" had been revealed as empty posturing. For by the fall of 2002 even the most casual of news readers had learned that terrorists of various kinds were crawling through Saudi Arabia and Pakistan, that they were powerful in Colombia and Israel, and that they ruled swaths of Russia and Indonesia. In each case, terrorists were working either with explicit or covert support of that nation's intelligence, military, and financial elites—meaning that at least six of our alleged allies in the war on terror could plausibly be charged not only with harboring terrorists but of doing so with the blessings of the United States. Indeed, as Robert Hariman has observed of the Bush administration's use of a notion of Evil (capital E) to try to justify the distinctions it said it would not make, "one problem is that the attribution is so arbitrary. The evil to be found in those regimes [the ones the U.S. has attacked] is much more widely available, not least among American client states who practice state terrorism." Hariman's point is that notions of *anticipatory action* and *imminent threat* have been used selectively, not as all-encompassing policy directives but as rhetorical weapons to be wielded when convenient according to distinctions that appear to have less to do with an across-the-board war against terrorism than supporting those nations, whether democratic or not, that serve the larger macroeconomic and political interests of the United States.[11]

On the other hand, Michael Mann demonstrates in *Incoherent Empire* that one of the chief flaws in the Bush administration's war against terrorism has been its inability to draw useful distinctions between different kinds of terror. For by lumping al Qaeda, a legitimate threat to U.S. interests, together with Chechen rebels, who pose no threat to the United

States, with Hezbollah, who threaten Israel but not the United States, and so on, the United States has inadvertently multiplied the number of groups considered its enemies. Mann thus concludes that making no distinctions among the world's many forms of terrorists "is the perfect way to convert national into international terrorists." Bush's policy of not making distinctions may therefore "end one thousand years of Muslim disunity" and create "exactly what bin Laden is kneeling toward Mecca and praying for."[12]

It would appear, then, that despite the *NSSUS*'s broad claims, the war on terrorism is being fought according to nuanced distinctions that accept some forms of state terrorism and not others (Hariman), even while unproductively lumping together divergent forms of nonstate terrorism (Mann). Moreover, many observers have noted that because of its commitment (albeit confused and confusing) to unilateral and preemptive military strikes, the *NSSUS* sounds the death knell of international diplomacy. Such fears are not unwarranted, as the document claims that "we will not hesitate to act alone" (6) and that "we will be prepared to act apart" (31), meaning that time-tested alliances will be honored only when they fit U.S. interests. London's *Guardian* thus lamented that the *NSSUS* amounts to "a new doctrine of war" that "kills the principle of state sovereignty" by proposing "a new, aggressive Pax Americana." The *Statesman* (India) feared that the *NSSUS* being enacted via a preemptive war on Iraq "will bolster the jehadis' cause." The *Edmonton Journal* lamented that the *NSSUS* marked "the official emergence of the United States as a full-fledged global empire." An editorial in the *Philippine Daily Inquirer* warned that by the United States arguing for the right to attack foes preemptively and unilaterally, "other states such as Pakistan or India may well be encouraged to do the same." These samples of international outrage can by no means claim to be representative of world opinion, yet they indicate a widespread fear that promoting preemptive unilateral military action will make the world a more dangerous place, where multilateral international diplomacy takes a back seat to unilateral firepower launched by any state that claims to feel threatened.[13]

For an example of how applying this doctrine of preemption despite strong international opposition leads to atrophied diplomacy, consider the "Coalition of the Willing" cobbled together by President Bush to wage war on Iraq. During his remarks from the Oval Office to commemorate the submission of his resolution for using force against Iraq, on

19 September 2002—the same day he submitted the *NSSUS* to Congress—President Bush was asked by a reporter, "How many of our friends are willing to join the United States in this effort [to remove Hussein from power]"? Asking simply for the number of coalition partners, the reporter's question was framed as a deliberative moment, a frank request for information. Shifting from this information-based register of deliberative rhetoric to the values-based register of epideictic rhetoric, the president responded in one of his trademark sentence fragments: "I think you're going to see a lot of nations—that a lot of nations love freedom." By shifting from the reporter's deliberative question to his epideictic answer, the president demonstrated how his war rhetoric would be based largely on evasions, on responding to requests for information with clichés and platitudes. Moreover, the president's vague answer created a difficult rhetorical situation for his administration, for whereas the *NSSUS* calls for the right to act preemptively and unilaterally, the president here pointed toward a multilateral attempt to build a coalition. The fact that the proposed war on Iraq was so obviously unnecessary, however, left President Bush scrambling to find willing partners.[14]

Indeed, given the strong-arming that took place in the days leading up to the war on Iraq, what the Bush administration was calling the "Coalition of the Willing" would be described more accurately as a "Coalition of the Coerced." For example, Bulgaria, for its promised support of the United States in its attempt to gain UN approval for the invasion, was guaranteed both U.S. support for its application to enter NATO and continued access to USAID contributions, estimated to be $420 million in 2002. Guinea and Cameroon were promised continued preferential trade status under the Generalized System of Preferences (GSP), a trade agreement that was modified after 9/11 to give the United States the right to revoke preferential trade status from those countries that "have not taken steps to support the efforts of the United States to combat terrorism." Rather than embodying a morally driven policy meant to make the world safer, and rather than rallying a broad coalition of "nations [that] love freedom," then, the *NSSUS*'s controversial doctrine of preemption left the United States scrambling to find allies by pressuring politically insignificant and economically vulnerable states.[15]

Similar economic strong-arming was supposedly applied to Costa Rica, Nicaragua, Guatemala, Honduras, and El Salvador, each of whom was then engaged in negotiations with the United States regarding extending NAFTA-like trading status to a new Central America Free Trade Agreement (The House approved CAFTA by a vote of 217 to 215 on 28 July 2005; President Bush signed it into law on 2 August; we turn to CAFTA in chapter 3). Perhaps out of fear of jeopardizing CAFTA, Honduras committed 370 troops, El Salvador agreed to 360, and Nicaragua offered 115; but holding the world's developing nations hostage to U.S. economic incentives does not amount to a foreign policy—it is simply coercion and is resented as such.[16]

Once the invasion began, President Bush announced that his coalition had grown to forty-five nation-states, but it is clear that this forty-five-nation Coalition of the Willing was but a patchwork of reluctant and sometimes even unaware partners. In fact, apparently assuming that massive drug war assistance to Colombia guaranteed its compliance, President Bush simply listed the nation without consulting any of its leaders—Colombia thus learned of its inclusion in the president's coalition only through the pages of the *Washington Post*. Other states, such as Hungary, allowed themselves to be included in the list while denying any material support; they were members of the Coalition of the Willing only in name, as are the Marshall Islands, Micronesia, and the Solomon Islands. Moreover, by November 2004 the Dominican Republic, Honduras, New Zealand, Nicaragua, the Philippines, Singapore, Spain, and Thailand had withdrawn all their troops from the coalition, whereas Albania was contributing only seventy-two troops, Estonia fifty-five, Kazakhstan twenty-nine, Macedonia thirty-two, Moldova forty-two, and Tonga forty-five. The only nations offering more than one thousand troops were Britain, Italy, the Netherlands, Poland, South Korea, and Ukraine. If we take the sending of one thousand or more troops as a bottom-line figure for indicating a genuine commitment to the war on Iraq, that makes for a coalition, counting the United States, of seven, not forty-five. In fact, by March 2005 the Netherlands had withdrawn its troops, and Italy had announced that it would remove its forces by September, leaving the coalition only five members contributing more than one thousand troops.[17]

But the most damning aspect of President Bush's dwindling coalition—embodying the *by-any-means-necessary* approach championed by Kissinger, Bremer, and Kaplan—is that it amounts to a rogue's gallery of authoritarian regimes. Every year the State Department carries out a human rights survey in which it measures the studied nations' level of respect for the rule of law. That report reveals that the use of "torture and/or extra-judicial killings carried out by security forces" is prevalent in ten of President Bush's coalition members. The killing and torturing states included in the coalition are Albania, Azerbaijan, Colombia, Eritrea, Ethiopia, Georgia, Macedonia, Nicaragua, Turkey, and Uzbekistan. The coalition also includes such notoriously troubled states as Afghanistan, Kuwait, Panama, and Rwanda, thus proving that President Bush's Coalition of the Willing is little more than a gaggle of tawdry authoritarian regimes. The fact that the United States has been reduced to calling these states its allies indicates how the vast majority of the world's major powers, including Germany, France, Russia, India, Canada, and China, but excluding the United Kingdom, found the *NSSUS*'s doctrine of preemption unacceptable. These fears were summarized in a speech by the celebrated historian Paul Schroeder, who argued that the *NSSUS* "would in fact justify almost any attack by any state on any other for almost any reason." Summarizing the international fears that precluded the world's major players from joining the United States in its first war of preemption, Schroeder concluded that "we cannot want a world that operates on this principle."[18]

The irony is thus dark: the *NSSUS* claims to offer a model of uncompromisingly moral behavior meant to protect human rights and extend the rule of law, yet in practice the United States marches off to a war based on false evidence, shoulder to shoulder with a coalition of murderous, undemocratic states. Perhaps the most damning thing to be said about the coalition, however, is that its largest contingent, aside from U.S. forces, is the twenty-thousand-strong army of contractors serving in Iraq as mercenaries. As we argue in chapter 4, this privatizing of the empire by hiring mercenaries demonstrates the utter bankruptcy of any notion of the "Coalition of the Willing" standing as a genuinely international body of allies. Indeed, if the coalition is any indicator, then the *NSSUS*'s promises may prove as hollow as the administration's WMD arguments.[19]

Clearly fearing that the international community would read the *NSSUS* in precisely the manner elucidated here, the Bush administration filled the document with paeans to international cooperation. The preface promises that "in all cases, international obligations are to be taken seriously"; later passages promise "coordination with European allies" (11); one entire section, titled "Develop Agendas for Cooperative Action With the Other Main Centers of Global Power" (pages 25–28), is dedicated to the need for international cooperation and begins with the pledge of future "consultations among partners with a spirit of humility" (25); and the document's closing page acknowledges that "effective international cooperation is needed to accomplish these goals" (31). As our analysis of the "Coalition of the Willing" demonstrates, such promises of humble international cooperation are as flimsy as the president's arguments about Iraqi WMDs. But this comes as no surprise, for as we have shown here, a commitment to lightning-fast unilateral preemptive strikes against perceived foes, justified at least in the case of war on Iraq via WMD lies, cannot coexist with the slow negotiations that mark multilateral diplomacy.

The Millennial Military State

We commented above on National Security Adviser Rice's remarks in New York City in October 2002, where, revising the spirit driving the six enumerated tasks that preface the U.S. Constitution, she argued that the "first and fundamental" task of the federal government was to defend the nation from its enemies. This claim comes directly from the *NSSUS*, which states on the first page of its preface that "defending our Nation against its enemies is the first and fundamental commitment of the Federal Government" (preface, iii). Thus shrinking the many tasks of the federal government to but one, and hence condemning millions of Americans to crumbling schools, spotty health care, dangerous roads, and so on (all results to which we return in detail in chapter 3), the *NSSUS* announces a fundamental shift away from social services in favor of a millennial military state. There is a second, even more dangerous component of this thinking, as the *NSSUS* argues that the U.S. "must build and maintain our defenses beyond challenge," to the point of being so mighty that the United States' strength can "dissuade future military competition" (29). Rather than one power among many, then, and rather than functioning as a state committed to the domestic health and happiness of its citizens, the United States commits itself here to pursuing sole *and perpetual* superpower status.

Supporters of the Bush administration will note that because the United States is the world's only superpower the *NSSUS* is simply stating the obvious. Historically minded critics will respond, however, that international balances of power have always changed over time, rendering any claim to perpetual and unchallenged superpower status a recipe for disaster. For example, the *Boston Globe* editorialized in October 2002 that this refusal to recognize the historically complicated fate of powers, instead proclaiming the unchangeable nature of U.S. supremacy, portrays the United States as "a muscle-bound simpleton afflicted with a fateful case of hubris." Moreover, the *Globe* argues that "Bush's boasting of his determination to keep all possible competitors inferior forever is the surest way to provoke some of them to resist the superpower's designs."[20]

President Bush's unilateral boasting is compromised, however, by the fact that his administration has also called repeatedly for a multilateral balance of powers. To observe this rhetorical tension between claims for unchallenged and perpetual superiority and claims for a balance of powers, we turn back to National Security Adviser Condoleezza Rice's 1 October 2002 speech in New York City, where she tried to explain the *NSSUS*. She claimed on the one hand that "we will seek to dissuade any potential adversary from pursuing a military build-up in the hope of surpassing, or equaling, the power of the United States and our allies." Three sentences later, she referred to "the burden of maintaining a balance of power" ("Rice," 2). The two claims are contradictory: either the United States is preeminent and hence there is no balance of power, just unrivaled U.S. dominance, or the United States works as a partner within a balance of powers, in which case other nations must be military, economic, and political equals (or if not equals, at least respected members of a functional coalition). By thus muddying the notion of balance of powers the Bush administration suggests that it plans to invoke the term only as a placating nod to diplomacy, even while its actions indicate utter disdain for the slow negotiations and multiparty compromises that make diplomacy possible.[21]

Along with the obvious contradiction between arguing for a preeminent state and states in alliance, and hence for a radically unbalanced balance of powers, Rice's (and the *NSSUS*'s) assumptions about state rivalries is historically wrong. She claims that post-9/11 life offers "an historic opportunity to break the destructive pattern of great rivalry that has bedeviled the world since the rise of the nation state in the seventeenth century" ("Rice," 2). Although a strong and united international community is of course preferable to heated rivalries, the fact is that most wars tend to reflect not great rivalries but irresolvable military imbalances between great powers and the minor ones they can swallow. For example, the age leading up to World War I from roughly 1875–1914 was relatively free of major wars because the great powers, Britain, France, Russia, the rising Germany, and the declining Ottoman Empire, were in perpetually shifting alliances—the rivalries of these states kept them for the most part checked, unable to make bold moves against each other (even while viciously colonizing much of the globe). World War I was not launched until these temporary alliances became locked into power blocks and when certain great powers felt strong enough to risk war. In short, Rice's model is exactly backward: nation-state rivalries do not cause war; rather, what causes wars is unchecked powers—like the United States today—who achieve such superiority that they believe they can act without threat of retribution or resistance.[22]

To watch the results of the faulty thinking exposed above in action, we return to President Bush's buildup to war on Iraq, encapsulated for our purposes here in two sentences from a statement delivered from the East Room of the White House on 16 October 2002, at the ceremony marking his signing of the resolution to use force against Iraq. In the first sentence the president said that "the regime [Iraq] is armed with biological and chemical weapons, possesses ballistic missiles, promotes international terror and seeks nuclear weapons." We now know, as demonstrated in chapter 1, that each of those four claims is false. In the second sentence the president claimed that "Iraq's combination of weapons of mass destruction and ties to terrorist groups and ballistic missiles would threaten the peace and security of many nations." Here the president takes false claims about Iraq's military capabilities and inflates them into regional threats to peace, hence making U.S intervention appear necessary. First the *NSSUS* claims that no rivals will be tolerated; then President Bush *invents* a rival on the basis of false evidence; then the logic of the *NSSUS* obliges the United States to invade this trumped-up foe in the name of national security.[23]

Such self-fulfilling and war-producing dynamics obviously could not be possible within the framework of an international balance of powers held together via diplomacy. Indeed, if the process outlined above is indicative of the ways the *NSSUS* will be wielded in the future, then its critics are correct in predicting that the *NSSUS* has ushered in an age of both unilateral and *perpetual* warfare. In fact, the *NSSUS* makes this point clearly when it argues that "the war against terrorists of global reach is a global enterprise of uncertain duration" (preface, iii).

Although the *NSSUS* offers these claims about perpetual war in what we have called above a deliberative register of discourse, the epideictic post-9/11 speeches of President Bush suggest that the *NSSUS*'s unilateral wars of uncertain duration are but one part of a millennial worldview in which historical and political changes give way to a timeless state of evangelical mission. Historians and rhetorical scholars have noted that ever since the founding of the nation presidents have relied on any number of religious phrases, especially the ubiquitous "God Bless America," to signal their assent to general Christian principles. But President Bush offers more than expected ceremonial platitudes, as his speeches since 9/11 demonstrate a deep commitment to an evangelical, missionary, Crusader-like version of Christianity. Indeed, as Lewis Lapham observes in *Theater of War*, President Bush's post-9/11 speeches make it clear that he is "talking about the armies of light come against the legions of darkness on the field of Armageddon."[24]

For example, in the first days following 9/11 the president described the U.S. response to al Qaeda's strikes as part of a "crusade." Speaking from the south lawn of the White House on Sunday afternoon, 16 September 2001, "on the Lord's Day" as he said in his opening remarks, President Bush fielded questions from the press. The repartee between the president and the press was particularly interesting, as the president sought to place 9/11 in some historical framework. He referred to the perpetrators of the terrorist strikes as "a new kind of enemy," but then qualified any sense of newness by saying that "we haven't seen this kind of barbarism in a long period of time." There is a temporal tension here between the claim of an emerging, new enemy and the reprise of an older, familiar form of barbarism. The president then returned to the notion of newness when he said that "this is a new kind of—a new kind of evil." The president thus appeared to invoke the notion of evil as a transhistorical explanation, as a term meant to collapse the old and the new, the familiar and the strange. In the face of his temporal confusions—is it new or old, unique or simply a return of the repressed?—evil pushes the crisis out of any sense of historical explanation and toward a theological sense of timelessness.[25]

Thus, even when a reporter asked the president a deliberative question about the status of civil rights in America, the president continued in his epideictic and theological frame of reference, eventually, as if by chain of association, making the claim that "the American people are beginning to understand. This crusade, this war on terrorism is going to take a while." Given his comments preceding this statement, in which we saw the president lurching out of any sense of historical explanation towards a transhistorical, theological realm of thought, it is fair to assume that he meant the term "crusade" in the general, vague, abstract sense, not in the historical sense of Christian armies invading foreign lands to cleanse Islamic peoples of their sin. Nonetheless, just to make sure the "crusade" slipup was not interpreted as a call for a clash of civilizations, the White House acted quickly to diffuse the scandal; the very next day, the president gave a widely celebrated speech titled "Islam Is Peace" at the Islamic Center of Washington, D.C.[26]

Regardless of the White House's quick-footed reaching out to the Islamic community, the president's "crusade" slipup elicited a firestorm of international criticism. London's *Guardian*, for example, ran a bitter response by Hywel Williams arguing that "crusade" is "an unhappy word. All this started eight centuries ago when Europe unleashed a colonializing campaign to reclaim the holy places. . . . This was when 'Islam' was first invented by the west as a single entity, as the face of the other which could be demonized." In Williams's formulation, then, one cannot say the word "crusade" without invoking the "800-year-old tradition" of bitter religious wars that ravaged Europe, northern Africa, and what we now call the Middle East. Indeed, the term cannot help but invoke the specter of what we will address below as a "clash of civilizations." Writing from Paris, Peter Ford observed in the *Christian Science Monitor* that President Bush's use of the term "crusade" "rang alarm bells in Europe." The French foreign minister, Hubert Vedrine, warned that "we have to avoid a clash of civilizations at all costs," yet given the president's use of the word "crusade" it was clear that many Muslims were worried about exactly this sense of a clash of civilizations. Soheib Bensheikh, the grand mufti of the mosque in Marseille, France, told Ford that the president's use of the term "crusade" "recalled the barbarous and unjust military operations against the Muslim world." President Bush's slipup thus left international observers concerned that the U.S. response to 9/11 would amount to a religious crusade, to yet another colonizing campaign against Islam in the name of Christianity.[27]

We should note here that the U.S. mainstream press completely missed the importance of the moment. Not only did no major U.S. paper criticize the president's infelicitous rhetoric, but William Safire sought in the

New York Times to diffuse anger about the gaffe by linking it to other, less controversial uses of the term "crusade" by Thomas Jefferson, General Eisenhower, and Franklin D. Roosevelt. As we demonstrate below, however, the president's "crusade" slipup is neither simply another example of his troubled relationship with extemporaneous speaking nor an unproblematic invoking of a historically sanctioned term; rather, it indicates precisely his sense that 9/11 launched the United States into a millennial struggle for nothing less than the soul of humanity.[28]

Indeed, we propose that the president's "crusade" slipup amounts to a classic example of what Sigmund Freud called a slip of the tongue. In his *Psychopathology of Everyday Life* Freud notes that "it is a frequent occurrence for the idea one wants to withhold to be precisely the one which forces its way through in the form of a slip of the tongue." For Freud such slips are generated by a double gesture, both "the relaxation of the inhibiting attention" of the speaker and the speaker's immersion in an "uninhibited stream of associations." That is, when a speaker lets his or her guard down, as the president did in his 16 September speech, where he was clearly enjoying his role as sermonist-in-chief, then unfolding strings of associations prod the speaker to reveal thoughts that might otherwise have been self-censored. In this case the dual process enabled the president to work up from thoughts about right and wrong, Good and Evil, to speaking about a crusade. From this perspective, the president's crusader comment was not an error but an expression of his inner thoughts.[29]

Indeed, both before and after his crusade comment, the president relied on a series of terms that suggest Christian and evangelical ambitions. For example, on 14 September 2001—two days prior to the crusade comment—the president spoke at the National Cathedral in Washington, D.C. Although the setting and the moment obviously offered the president an opportunity to invoke the usual religious truisms, he went further, providing a series of radically evangelical pledges. He committed the United States not simply to finding and punishing the perpetrators of 9/11 but to a much more ambitious and divine task: "Our responsibility to history is already clear: to answer these attacks and *rid the world of evil.*" As he would do two days later, the president collapsed history into a timeless religious battle of good versus evil—not some political or economic or cultural systems jockeying against others, but Good battling Evil. History was thus portrayed in millennial terms, as the unfolding of a religious struggle whose preordained conclusion will be the creation of an earthly kingdom of the godly—in short, history is rendered here as a crusade.[30]

Denise Bostdorff has observed that the president has become an astute practitioner of what she calls "covenant renewal discourse." Digging deep into the repertoire of available rhetorical strategies to compare President Bush's post-9/11 speeches to those of late-seventeenth-century Puritans, Bostdorff argues that covenant renewal discourse concentrates on "the threat exposed by an external evil[,] . . . focuses optimistic appeals for the renewal of the church[,] . . . points to crises as tests from God[,] . . . and encourages attempts at faith and good works, implying that they will lead to salvation." By the time the Second Great Awakening swept the United States with a frenzy of religious enthusiasm in the early decades of the nineteenth century, the positions Bostdorff identifies had been transformed into the driving norms of Protestant middle-class culture. For example, the Brick Church of Rochester, New York, rewrote its covenant in 1831; every member subsequently signed this pledge: "We promise to renounce the ways of sin, and to make it the business of our life to do good and promote the declarative glory of our heavenly Father. . . . We promise to make it the great business of our life to glorify God and build up the Redeemer's Kingdom in this fallen world." The repeated references to "business" make it clear that God's work will take the form not only of evangelical zeal but of the making and selling of goods—if nothing else, the Redeemer's Kingdom will be capitalist. As summarized by Paul Johnson, such pledges and the widespread revivalist excitement that drove them suggested that "the millennium would be accomplished when sober, godly men . . . exercised power in this world." Indeed, the coming millennium can only be achieved in God's terms by *the exercise of power:* no call for tolerance and patience, this is an evangelical, capitalist, radically activist call to rid the world of sin.[31]

Given these references to some of the American religious traditions the president can draw on, let us return to his speech in the National Cathedral, where in the fifteen sentences following the quotation from this speech offered above, the president mentioned prayer or asked his listeners to pray eight times. In one of the seven sentences where he did not mention prayer or ask listeners to pray, he offered the theory that "God's signs are not always the ones we look for," thus implying that 9/11 was such a "sign," hence making the U.S. response to 9/11 a God-directed and God-sanctioned action. President Bush then offered the theory that "this world He created is of moral design. Grief and tragedy and hatred are only for a time. Goodness, remembrance, and love have no end," meaning that a U.S. triumph over the forces of Evil is both preordained and ultimately, once accomplished, infinite—the imminent U.S. kingdom of Good will *have no end.* The final two paragraphs of the speech then close with a flourish of requests to "almighty God," "He," or "Him," ending with the supplication "May He bless the souls of the departed. May He comfort our own. And may He always guide our country." Hence merging a seventeenth-century version of Puritan covenant renewal, the nineteenth-century Protestant version of middle-class evangelical activism, and a new, twenty-first-century version of millennial nationalism, President Bush portrayed the U.S. response to 9/11 not as a political or military endeavor but as a religious cause, a crusade, a calling to fulfill God's preordained plan for the eternal triumph of Good over Evil. As Peter Yoonsuk Paik argues, this merging of "millenarian fervor and imperialist domination" amounts to a startling new form of "imperial eschatology."[32]

Critics may respond that such religious rhetoric fulfills long-standing norms of epideictic decorum, which suggest that in times of great crisis and loss the president functions not so much as the nation's political leader as its unofficial priest or minister. Readers who subscribe to this thinking will dismiss our comments above as a stylistic misreading, as bringing to the speech critical criteria that forget or refuse to grant the expected function of the speech. Such a critique suggests that we should forego a rhetorical analysis of the president's comments on the first anniversary of 9/11, delivered from Ellis Island on 11 September 2002, for this speech too, like the one in the National Cathedral a year earlier, was constrained by the norms of such occasions to invoke religious terms to help the nation heal. This perspective asks us to consider these speeches less as moments of political thought than as prayers, less as moments of national policy than as heartfelt meditations and painful reflections. To criticize such speeches therefore, so the argument might go, amounts not only to an analytic misreading but to an act of sacrilege.[33]

Even if we grant this argument, and therefore eschew analysis of President Bush's various speeches commemorating our fallen neighbors on 9/11, his speeches in churches or mosques or synagogues, or his other obviously religious moments, the president's post-9/11 rhetoric still points toward a millennial vision of a perpetual military state. Indeed, even while we will entertain the charge not to introduce politics into the president's more obviously religious performances, it is clear from both our analysis and the observations of other scholars that the president routinely interjects religion into ostensibly political moments. More important, the president's religious beliefs appear to have direct political and military consequences, and vice versa, so it is difficult to distinguish between his deliberative and epideictic moments. By way of comparison, it may be useful to recall President Roosevelt's 8 December 1941 response to Pearl Harbor, or President Eisenhower's 11 May 1960 response to the Francis Gary Powers U2 downing, or President Kennedy's 22 October 1961 speech about the Cuban missile crisis, or President Johnson's 4 August 1964 Tonkin Gulf speech, for each of these responses to grave crises are remarkably full of information—they are measured, deliberative arguments about political matters. President Bush, on the other hand, fills his speeches not with information and specific arguments but with grandiose religious terms that veer dangerously close to his crusade comment.[34]

For example, consider the triumphalist speech following the president's 1 May 2003 "Top Gun" moment on USS *Abraham Lincoln,* where, after climbing out of a Viking S-3B (a four-seat submarine hunting and refueling jet) in a flight suit, he proclaimed the end of the war on Iraq. We examined the many lies and factual errors included in that speech in chapter 1, but want to observe here the speech's closing, which reverts to the religious themes discussed above. After promising the cheering soldiers assembled on the carrier's flight deck that their lost comrades will be reunited with their families "in God's time," the closing paragraph of the speech offers a biblical lesson, complete with a quotation from "the prophet Isaiah," about "the highest calling of history," described by the president as "to fight a great evil." The president therefore invokes a passage from the Bible to bless the efforts of the returning troops, the sacrifices of those lost in battle, and the larger "historical" calling "to fight a great evil." History is thus spun in millennial time, America is portrayed as God's chosen actor, and the troops are blessed as God's warriors for Goodness. It is important to note that our critique of the president's religious rhetoric is not meant as an attack on religion; rather, our analysis of his merging of political and religious claims highlights why his critics have charged him with launching a religious crusade.[35]

For even a cursory review of the book of Isaiah suggests that the president's citing it amounts to a careful rhetorical gesture meant to invoke a series of religious presuppositions. The prefatory comments in the *New Oxford Annotated Bible* situate Isaiah as a response to the Syro-Ephraimite wars, the subsequent Assyrian invasion, the following Babylonian conquest, and the eventual triumph of the Persian Empire. Stretching from roughly 745 BCE, when Tilgath-pileser III became king of the Assyrian Empire, to 539 BCE, when Cyrus, the Persian king, defeated the Babylonians, these wars left the region tattered and ragged, literally stunned by the barbarism of war. Much of Isaiah therefore reads like a grisly string of mass murder and treachery. For example, readers are told early in Isaiah (1.7) that "Your country lies desolate, / your cities are burned with fire; / in your very presence / aliens devour your land; / it is desolate, as overthrown by / foreigners." Anyone who reads the Bible, then, on hearing the president reference Isaiah in his "Top Gun" speech, would immediately understand that the president was suggesting that the war on Iraq was retribution for 9/11, when our cities were indeed "burned with fire" by "aliens" and "foreigners."[36]

But the book of Isaiah offers more than just a model of revenge, as it also calls on God's children to do good works, to "cease to do evil, / learn to do good; / seek justice, / rescue the oppressed, / defend the orphan, / plead for the widow" (1.17, HB 979). Thus offering a rhetorical template for the combination of themes and tones found in the *NSSUS* and President Bush's post-9/11 speeches, Isaiah maps a strange, almost schizophrenic pattern of behavior in which "learning to do good" and "rescue[ing] the oppressed" interweave with righteous acts of terrible violence. Isaiah 2.4 moderates the rush to vengeance with the famous call to "beat their swords into / plowshares, / and their spears into pruning / hooks; / nation shall not lift up sword against / nation, / neither shall they learn war / any more" (HB 980–981). Peace activists have latched onto this phrase for centuries, invoking it as biblical support for their work. But the rest of Isaiah, covering ninety-two pages, is a veritable temper tantrum of rage. Indeed, cycling between brief praise of good followers and lengthy punishment of sinners, Isaiah gains momentum as a chronicle of Heavenly frustration. Retribution therefore explodes forth in regular intervals, such as in 30.27, where readers are told that "the name of the Lord comes / from far away, / burning with his anger, and in thick / rising smoke, / his lips are full of indignation / and his tongue is like a devouring / fire" (HB 1019). By citing Isaiah in his "Top Gun" speech, President Bush invokes this biblical tradition of practicing righteous violence as a form of religious cleansing. Like Isaiah, then, there can be little doubt that the president's war against Iraq is understood as part of a crusade against "those who / despoil us, / and the lot of those who / plunder us" (17.14, HB 1003).[37]

As further evidence of the president's millennial impulses, consider the closing passages from his 28 January 2003 State of the Union address. His many lies in this speech about Iraqi WMDs were exposed in chapter 1, but our comments there did not address his final flourish of millennialism. The president argues that the United States waging its war against terrorism and its war on Iraq prove that "this call of history has come to the right country." But the effect of these wars, which the president claims is to bring liberty to the world, "is not America's gift to the world, it is God's gift to humanity." This remarkable claim is followed by a nod to "the ways of Providence," which although unknowable are not cause for hesitation, for "we can trust in them, placing our confidence in the loving God behind all life, and all of history." So here again "history" is collapsed into a millennial unfolding of "the ways of Providence," and the United States is portrayed as the chosen agent of that Providence, literally as the carrier of "God's gift to humanity." As Martin Marty wrote in *Newsweek,* "The problem isn't with Bush's sincerity, but with his evident conviction that he is doing God's will." Indeed, President Bush proposes that both the United States in general and he in particular have been chosen to do God's work in the millennial war against Evil—whereas other nations pursue national interests, the United States defends "the ways of Providence."[38]

The president's allies at "Bush Country," a group dedicated to "Promoting the Ideals of Conservatism," support our analysis above, as they claim that their group's chief goal is to help the president "bring our nation back to its Judeo Christian roots." However, those "roots" are grounded in the born-again theology that foresees the return of Christ to rule the earth for a thousand years. Millennialists thus await the end of historical and political time in the form of Christian time; hence the popular phrase "end times," meant to indicate the history-ending cataclysm—"Wail, for the day of the Lord is near; / it will come like destruction from / the Almighty!" (Isaiah 13.6, HB 997)—that will mark the arrival of Christ, born again, to rule an earthly and eternal Kingdom of Goodness. For forecasts of when such events may unfold, readers may go to the Rapture Index Web site, where forty-five factors of evil (including the rise of "false Christs," "Satanism," "Globalism," "Liberalism," and "plagues") are rated, hence constituting a predictive index foretelling the coming Rapture. As of June 2005 the Index stood at 144 (the high for the year was 155); any score over 145 suggests readers should "fasten your seat belt," for the Rapture is imminent. Perhaps not surprisingly, the Index's record high was 182 in the weeks following 9/11, indicating that at least for the architects of the Index, al Qaeda's strikes were not political events but religious signs, not human catastrophes but Heavenly indicators.[39]

This cosmological vision has become remarkably popular in the past decade, in turn spawning a flood of critical commentary. For example, according to Melani McAlister, as many as a third of those Americans polled describe themselves as evangelical or born again. Jim Aune claims that "the nineteen million Christian Right voters . . . are now the single most influential voting bloc in the United States." Likewise, Howard Fineman argues that "Bible-believing Christians are Bush's strongest backers." The president's millennial and perpetual war rhetoric thus speaks directly to this section of the population, offering them daily doses of theological support, daily Isaiah-derived indications that the Rapture is coming and that they are fighting the Good fight against Evil. Given the fact that, according to Fineman, "evangelical missionaries don't hide their desire to convert Muslims to Christianity," and given the clear and deep links to the religious far right described above, there can be little wonder that "to many Muslims, especially Arabs, he [Bush] looks sinister: a new Crusader, bent on retaking the East for Christendom." Whereas John Sutherland has argued that "eschatology has filled the vacuum where Cold War ideology used to be," our comments here suggest that eschatology has not so much replaced cold war ideology as given it expanded meanings. That is, President Bush has deftly combined religion, history, and politics, producing an evangelical, war-making version of globalization-through-benevolent-empire.[40]

By combining our rhetorical analyses of the *NSSUS*'s deliberative arguments for the United States as an unchallenged and perpetual superpower with the president's epideictic invocations of the righteousness of Heavenly directed violence, we have demonstrated that post-9/11 U.S. foreign policy amounts to a form of *millennial militarism*. As the embodiment of this policy, consider Lieutenant General William Boykin. The deputy secretary of defense for intelligence, and hence one of the top figures directing the war on terrorism, Boykin barnstormed the nation in 2003 and 2004, speaking at twenty-three Christian churches, where, appearing in uniform, he told listeners that the United States should "come at them [the terrorists] in the name of Jesus." The *New York Times* excoriated the Bush White House for not rebuking Boykin for his uniformed "brimstone bigotry," but the administration's nonresponse should come as no surprise, for as we have shown here, merging the military and the millennial is one of the defining characteristics of this administration. Given this troubling fact, the *NSSUS*'s and President Bush's broad claims that the United States has embarked on a mission to bring U.S.-style democracy and free markets to the rest of the world amounts to a chilling prospect. Indeed, as we demonstrate below, the version of benign universalism trumpeted in the *NSSUS* and President Bush's post-9/11 speeches may in fact amount to a prescription for cultural homogenization, theft and destruction carried out in the name of Goodness.[41]

Benign Universalism and the Dynamics of Cultural Homogenization

Our comments above focus on the combination of militarism, nationalism, and millennialism, with all three driven by an evangelical worldview that sees life in terms of a struggle between Good and Evil, the God-chosen United States and those miscreants who oppose it. Critics of both the *NSSUS* and President Bush have tended to see these ideas as justifying the spread of globalization-through-benevolent-empire. Although such fears obviously beg for evidence, and can often lean perilously close to crackpot conspiracy theories, they nonetheless raise the important question of whether the spread of U.S. cultural norms and economic practices is little more than a covert means of recolonizing developing nations. This question has been taken up in an economic sense by Joseph Stiglitz in *Globalization and Its Discontents*, where he argues that the International Monetary Fund's "approach to developing countries has had the feel of a colonial ruler." We want to supplement Stiglitz's economic analysis by considering the broad question of whether the *NSSUS* and President Bush have portrayed U.S. (and IMF) relations with the developing world in a manner that invites comparisons to the assimilating, homogenizing goals of colonialism. Put simply, is the *NSSUS*'s and President Bush's benign universalism rhetorical cover for globalization-through-benevolent-empire?[42]

The *NSSUS*, President Bush's post-9/11 speeches, and the comments of the president's supporters have done little to temper such questions about neocolonialism and cultural homogenization. For example, the opening sentence of the *NSSUS* proclaims triumphantly that the twentieth century concluded with a "decisive victory for the forces of freedom— and *a single model of national success:* freedom, democracy, and free enterprise. . . . These values of freedom are right and true *for every person, in every society*" (preface, iii, emphasis added). Whether President Bush and the authors of the *NSSUS* intend such phrases to be read in this manner, it is hard not to interpret the italicized phrases above—*a single model of national success . . . for every person, in every society*—as anything other than a call for the homogenization of the world's riotous political, economic, and cultural differences under the banner of U.S. military, political, economic, and cultural leadership. Such fears cannot help but be reinforced by the *NSSUS*'s claim that the United States "will actively work to bring the hope of democracy, development, free markets, and free trade *to every corner of the world*" (preface, iv, emphasis added). In a similar vein, in a speech before an appreciative U.S. Congress on 17 July 2003, when he confronted the rising tide of British anger toward him by celebrating British involvement in the wars on Iraq and terrorism, Prime Minister Tony Blair argued that "ours are not Western values, they are the *universal values* of the human spirit."[43]

We will turn our attention to globalizing free markets and their supposed "universal values" in chapters 3 and 4 and so will retain the bulk of our comments on those topics for that later work. But we will offer here the simple reminder that *every corner of the world* might not want grease-spewing fast-food restaurants cluttering its landscapes, that bombastic pop culture might not be welcome in some communities, that strip malls, drug wars, a flood of alcohol, gleaming prisons, and any number of the other prominent and unfortunate features of contemporary U.S. culture might strike many people in developing nations as things to be feared. Eric Hobsbawm's *The Age of Empire* is useful here, as it reminds us that in the wave of modern colonialism covering roughly 1875 to 1914, the military and economic imbalance between world-encircling European states and their targets of aggression was so great that the less-developed nations "were all equally at the mercy of the ships that came from abroad bringing cargoes of goods, armed men, and ideas against which they were powerless." Thus, "progress outside the advanced countries was neither an obvious fact nor a plausible assumption, but *mainly a foreign danger.*" Hobsbawm's argument is cause for alarm, for it suggests that President Bush's, the *NSSUS*'s, and Prime Minister Blair's benign universalism may likely appear to much of the world as "a foreign danger," as imperialist self-interest hiding behind the justifying rhetoric of benevolence.[44]

Indeed, although the *NSSUS* boldly proclaims that U.S. values "are right and true for all people everywhere" (3), this surely cannot be true, let alone desirable, for two reasons. First, the norms of democratic deliberation suggest that "right and true" can only be determined by local cultures enacting locally determined political and cultural practices in dialogue with the forces of globalization. Although the United States cannot shrug its shoulders and walk away when confronted with slavery and terror, neither can it swagger into foreign lands and declare by fiat what shall be true and right. To assume that it can do so flies in the face of all notions of diplomacy and influence, turning the slow process of cultural transformation into what feels to many critics like another cultural invasion of the kind Hobsbawm described above. Second, those of us who live in the United States know that our "values" are constant sites of contestation: there is not one set of U.S. values but many, in endless dialogue and messy debate. The *NSSUS*'s claims regarding the inherent rightness of U.S. values thus collapses the wonderful complexity of American life into a monolithic caricature while in turn assuming the power to foist these values on others. Surely even the staunchest allies of President Bush can see that this reduction of U.S. society to one set of values that are then magically extended as "right and true" for everyone everywhere cannot help but smack of the arrogance that drove late-nineteenth- and then twentieth-century colonialism.

To pursue this argument we ask what recent U.S. actions indicate about the *NSSUS* and President Bush's claims regarding global culture in the face of post-9/11 U.S. imperatives. Indeed, rather than speculating on what the *NSSUS* might mean when it talks about spreading U.S. values far and wide, let us instead look at the available evidence of what happens to local cultures when the U.S. flexes its military, political, and economic power. Let us turn, then, to the question of what happened to Iraq in the days following the U.S. invasion. For if readers accept our premise that the war on Iraq is but the first and most direct embodiment of the broad principles outlined in the *NSSUS*, then we may safely postulate that the treatment of postwar Iraq's cultural landmarks reveals much about what

every person, in every society may expect at the hands of the U.S.'s benevolent empire.

We begin our observations on the looting of Iraq as a test case of benign universalism by noting that although wars destroy things—that is
their function—they are always fought in the name of preserving higher
values, many of which are embodied in a given culture's art, antiquities,
and architecture. War thus carries the paradoxical function of trying to
destroy parts of a culture while simultaneously trying to preserve other
parts. And while the United States is unchallenged in its capacity for the
former, its abysmal record of the latter in postwar Iraq is widely considered damning evidence not only of its cultural insensitivity, even imperial
arrogance, but of the fact that while claiming to fight for democracy and
justice, the arrival of U.S. forces signals the beginning of a dual process of
cultural expropriation and imposition.

As for the latter, MedAct reports in *Continuing Collateral Damage: The
Health and Environmental Costs of War on Iraq* that the U.S. Department
of Defense, when asked about an influx of applications from entrepreneurs wanting to open McDonald's franchises in Baghdad, said, "The
Iraqi people would love a Big Mac and fries as much as the rest of the
world." Such cavalier claims follow the logic of the *NSSUS*, which argues
that "if others make something that you value, you should be able to buy
it. This is real freedom" (18). In fact, the Coalition Provisional Authority's
advertising pamphlet for the reconstruction of Iraq, titled *Trade and Foreign Investment Opportunities in Iraq,* argues that "the economic development underway in Iraq will favor certain industries," including, as the
second entry on its list, "branded foods and beverages, fast food." So
bringing Coca-Cola, McDonald's, and other branded and fast foods to
Iraq is not the stuff of conspiratorial cynics but actual U.S. policy, the
institutionalized state version of Friedman's "Golden Arches Theory of
Conflict Resolution."[45]

In contrast to such cheerfully crass thinking, it is clear that some if not
many aspects of U.S.-style consumer culture strike many Iraqis as nothing less than imperial offenses, as crude impositions that besmirch indigenous cultural practices. In fact, Ann Simons has reported that the
Iraqi Shiites she interviewed were deeply worried that "pornography and
other vices typically associated with Western societies are beginning to
seep into their culture." The fact that these Iraqis make the leap from
McDonald's and other corporations that sell a variety of goods to con-

cerns about "pornography and other vices"—and this interview was conducted before the atrocities at Abu Ghraib were revealed—indicates how broadly U.S. cultural practices appear tarnished, as if even hamburgers carry the taint of imperial aggression and cultural debasement.[46]

Given the chaos of postwar Iraq, in which many of its museums and libraries were looted, some of its archaeological treasures were stolen, and many of its architectural achievements were damaged, such fears make sense. Indeed, while the *New York Times* reported in its understated manner that "postwar lawlessness in Iraq is far more pervasive and intractable than they [the United States and Britain] had originally expected," European journalists portrayed a culture under siege, where arts and antiquities were stolen in plain view of U.S. troops who did nothing to stop such crimes. In fact, in the face of U.S. inaction, literally working in the shadow of the occupying forces, thieves began selling real and fake artifacts on street corners, causing one curator to call the looting of the Baghdad Museum "the most catastrophic theft of antiquities since the second world war." (Note that sources variously refer to this museum as The National Museum in Baghdad, the Iraq National Museum, or Baghdad Museum; we use the last term.) As Eleanor Robson lamented in the *Observer*, "The collection lies in ruins, objects from a long, rich past [lie] in smithereens." Robert Fisk dramatically portrayed these acts of cultural theft and destruction as part of "the sacking of Baghdad."[47]

Although it was initially reported that more than 170,000 precious items had been stolen from around Baghdad during the April 2003 postwar looting, it was soon discovered that many of the treasures thought to have been lost were not stolen but kept safe by Shiite elders. Initial statements lamenting the loss of world history had thus been blown out of proportion; in the words of one reporter they were "bollocks." In fact, by early May 2003 it was conceded that some of what had originally been reported as missing was safely stored in underground vaults in the National Bank. It will therefore take years to fathom how many of Iraq's cultural treasures were stolen or destroyed as compared to how many of them were shepherded to safety by Baghdad's religious elite. Jennie Matthew has reported in *Middle East Online* that the situation is made more difficult by the fact that Iran, Kuwait, Saudi Arabia, and Turkey are "continuing to drag their feet in retrieving goods secreted across their borders."[48]

Although it is too early to evaluate the long-term damage done to ancient items held in Iraq, the immediate rhetorical dilemma is clear: the combination of secretive (but necessary) Shiite protective actions, global black-market opportunists, and U.S. ineptitude has left many Iraqis convinced that the U.S. occupying forces lack any sense of cultural sensitivity. Indeed, Iraqis believe that the U.S. forces did nothing to protect their culture, literally standing idly by as it was smashed and stolen before their very eyes. As Mark Danner reported from Baghdad, "This was an enormously important political blow against the occupation, undermining any trust or faith Iraqis might have had in their new rulers." Expecting Iraqis to welcome the U.S.-led administration of post-Hussein Iraq is thus compromised if not made impossible by this simple fact: the postwar looting of Iraq's art, libraries, and antiquities, done with what appeared to be U.S. assent, has sent the clear message that the occupying forces cannot protect let alone honor or respect the cultural achievements of the people they now rule.[49]

Moreover, whereas early reports of U.S. complicity with this cultural destruction and thievery focused on art and antiquities in Baghdad, later reports broadened the scope of the crisis to consider the irreversible damage done to Iraq's outlying archeological and architectural sites. For example, Ed Vuillamy reported in the *Observer* that a pyramid built by the Sumerians in 4000 BC, near the historically rich town of Ur, now stands awkwardly next to a U.S. military base. Imagine the outcry if such a humiliation were imposed on the Smithsonian or the Library of Congress or the National Gallery of Art, with a U.S. cultural treasure debased by concertina wire, the roar of base construction and traffic, and the presence of an occupying foreign force that showed such landmarks no respect. Worse yet, Vuillamy observes that the walls of this ancient cultural treasure are now covered with graffiti, including the words *semper fi*, the motto of the U.S. Marines. Ur is the birthplace of the biblical patriarch Abraham, it is where the wheel was invented some 5,000–6,000 years ago and where the *Epic of Gilgamesh* was written on twelve clay tablets, circa 2500 BC. Occupying U.S. forces know little of this history and so accord the culture they have invaded little respect. We attribute no malevolence to the troops who debased the pyramid with *semper fi* graffiti— they were simply expressing typical nationalist and militarist glee in a form of communication largely sanctioned by U.S. cultural norms. Nonetheless, the boyish ineptitude of the gesture is deeply troubling, for it demonstrates profound cultural insensitivity—*why ruin a six-thousand-*

year-old pyramid?—precisely the kind of cultural chauvinism that enabled troops to stand idly by as Baghdad was looted. The stories recounted above demonstrate why, when the *NSSUS* and President Bush proclaim the spread of U.S. values to "every person, in every society," much of the world trembles.[50]

The cultural destruction in Iraq has roots in Gulf War I and the brutal UN-sponsored postwar sanctions. During the 1991 Gulf War, museums in outlying Iraqi cities (but not Baghdad) lost as many as four thousand objects. In 2001, on the ten-year anniversary of that first round of war-enabled cultural destruction, the Baghdad Museum was reopened with the support of international scholars, volunteers, and private donors. By 2003 the museum contained twenty galleries housing 100,000-year-old stone tools, Babylonian tablets, medieval manuscripts, gold, ivory, Sumerian jewels, and other ancient treasures. The collection has rightly been hailed as containing crucial evidence of "the cradle of civilization." While these cultural treasures have come under intense pressure from the two Gulf wars, the archaeological sites from which many of them emerged were hard hit by the postwar sanctions. Indeed, many of Iraq's ten thousand registered archeological sites are located in the southern regions that were devastated by economic sanctions during the 1990s. In the face of starvation and other sanction-fueled hardships, impoverished and desperate villagers began selling relics and artifacts to black market dealers. In fact, Edmund Andrews reported in the *New York Times* that after the first Gulf War the market for ancient material "grew so prevalent that cuneiform tablets are even now regularly advertised on e-Bay, and can sell for less than $100."[51]

Thus spurred by the sanctions of the 1990s and continuing through the latest war on Iraq, the black market has continued to grow, and archeological sites have continued to be stripped of their resources, not by powerful Western experts but by desperate civilian diggers. According to one British scholar, no British archeologists have touched Iraq since 1990; whereas prior to the first Gulf War there were approximately one hundred registered projects in the countryside, that number had dropped by 2002 to twenty. Instead of international archaeological experts working according to established norms of scholarship and preservation, then, southern Iraq's key sites were being looted by armed groups of mercenaries and desperate locals, with both parties serving what the *Times* calls a "global network of plundering that is rapidly depleting the immense reserves of ancient art and historical data that lie buried in cities that once made up the Babylonian and Sumerian empires." Despite the debate regarding the extent of cultural destruction in Baghdad, then, it is clear that a decade of brutal UN sanctions and the inaction of U.S. occupying forces produced a situation in which Iraq's archaeological treasures were stripped by thieves and thugs.[52]

Lest readers assume that we are asking too much of the occupying U.S. forces, who from one perspective cannot be asked to play the role of cultural protectors while still fighting a guerrilla war and trying to secure a war-torn nation, it is important to recall Joanne Mariner's point that "under the laws of war, the United States is obligated to ensure public order in territories that it occupies, and to prevent looting and other forms of lawlessness." Indeed, the UN Convention for the Protection of Cultural Property in the Event of Armed Conflict, introduced to the Hague on 14 May 1954 and ratified on 7 August 1956, mandates that occupying powers must "undertake to prohibit, prevent and, if necessary, put a stop to any form of theft, pillage or misappropriation of, and any acts of vandalism directed against, cultural property." Acknowledging the widespread sense that the United States was violating this law, the UN Educational, Scientific, and Cultural Organization (UNESCO) issued a September 2003 declaration stressing the responsibility of occupiers to prevent the intentional destruction of culture.[53]

These concepts regarding the legal obligation of military forces to protect the cultures of the states they occupy were introduced to the 108th U.S. Congress on 7 May 2003, when the Iraq Cultural Heritage Act (H. R. 2009) was referred to the Committee on Ways and Means (where it still languishes as of June 2005). The bill intends "to provide for the recovery, restitution, and protection of the cultural heritage of Iraq." H. R. 2009 is similar in this regard to the UNESCO report, "Iraq—Heritage in Danger," which maps the "precious legacy for all humanity" contained throughout Iraq and in the Baghdad Museum. Likewise, the International Criminal Police Organization (Interpol) features on its Web site pictures of pieces stolen from the Iraq Museum, thus aiding the international search for stolen art and artifacts. While the U.S. and UNESCO acts call for the protection of art and artifacts from the ravages of black-market dealers, they also offer working definitions of culture, hence raising interesting questions regarding the power of culture in an age of globalization and empire. For example, H. R. 2009 distinguishes between two material conceptions of "cultural heritage." The first covers archeological material "discovered as a result of scientific excavation, illegal or clandestine digging, accidental discovery, or exploration" that is more than a century old and was produced by humans (including human skeletal remains). The second covers cultural material that might not fulfill the above criteria for age but is "of historic, artistic, religious, scientific, or cultural interest." If passed, the bill would restrict importation of both categories of materials and would require their return to Iraq.[54]

Although we applaud these efforts, it is important to notice how the definitions employed here limit the notion of culture to ancient artifacts, high art, and other saleable materials that circulate in the world of museums. Such definitions are helpful for thinking about ways to prevent the theft of specific cultural objects, yet they limit the notion of culture to commodities. We should remember, however, that the fears with which we began this section on cultural destruction were of "pornography and other vices" that might be imposed on Iraqis by corporate U.S. consumer culture. Although pornography and vice are certainly commodities, their cultural power, their ability to incite fear in Iraqis, transcends their status as saleable goods. The question of cultural destruction thus has two aspects: first, the material theft of cultural artifacts—that is, *the expropriation of culture* for the purposes of capitalist profit; second, the introduction of cultural forms (like McDonald's, *semper fi* graffiti, and pornography)— that is, *the imposition of culture* for the purposes of imperialist control.

The bodies of governance noted above have responded admirably to the first and not at all to the second of these concerns. For example, UN Resolution 1483, passed 22 May 2003, "stress[es] the need for respect for the archeological, historical, cultural, and religious heritage of Iraq, and for the continued protection of archeological, historical, cultural, and religious sites, museums, libraries and monuments." The resolution accordingly encourages member states to facilitate "the safe return to Iraqi institutions of Iraqi cultural property and other items of archeological, historical, cultural, rare scientific, and religious importance." Invoking what might be called an international cultural policy, the UN recognizes "Iraqi cultural property" as belonging to the nation and argues that the task of "continued protection" requires international cooperation. This is a good start, one that problematizes the relationship between international norms of culture and those of the indigenous people such laws are meant to protect. But how can such laws account for the more immediate question of what will happen to Iraqi daily culture in the face of globalizing U.S. corporate interests? The question then is not only about what happens in response to the theft of ancient Iraqi artifacts, but what happens to daily life, the myriad forms of culture that escape the U.S. and UN definitions discussed above, when McDonald's, militarist graffiti, and pornography come to town?[55]

To try to answer that question we turn to reports of life in postwar Baghdad. For example, Max Rodenbeck observed in 2003 that "with its anxious daytime throngs and eerie nighttime emptiness, Baghdad remains a dazed city. The armed American presence adds a particular note of unreality. The giant hulking vehicles, coils of concertina wire, and sweating, gear-laden troops patrolling in combat formation all have an embarrassed air." The combined brutality of the occupation and the insurgency has turned embarrassment into fear, however, as Iraq has slid ever closer toward chaos. After witnessing one of the daily car bombings that rocked Baghdad in 2004, Christian Parenti described a scene "illuminated by orange flame, the surrounding streets are strewn with debris: twisted metal, broken glass, part of a tweed jacket, a steering rod, half of a severed human foot." For Parenti, the repetition of such violence has turned Baghdad into "Armageddon in miniature." While Rodenbeck and Parenti emphasize the violence and absurdity of the U.S. occupation of Iraq, Rory McCarthy, writing for the *Guardian* from Baghdad, describes occupied Iraq as such a desperate place that Iraqis gather around the garbage dumps of U.S. bases, scrounging through the trash for food or saleable items to help them survive.[56]

It comes as no surprise, then, to find Neil MacFarquar reporting in the *New York Times* that "humiliation and rage stalk the Arab world." In fact, Iranian media reported early in the war that America's invasion of Iraq exemplified attempts by the West to wipe out Eastern culture altogether. Although such claims strike us as both theoretically sloppy, for we refuse any homogenized notion of West and East, and practically untenable—indeed, as further evidence of how cultural claims may function as propaganda for different regimes—our point in these past few pages has been to demonstrate how plausible they might appear to Iraqis, who find themselves in a strange new world where their streets rock from the weight of passing U.S. tanks, where their museums appear to have been stripped of ancient treasures, where their archaeological wonders are slipped over porous borders to enrich European dealers, where their architectural wonders are debased and even shelled, where all that is local and familiar feels threatened by what is assumed will be an onslaught of capitalist, secular, U.S. "culture."[57]

Indeed, it is increasingly clear that spreading U.S. "values" "to every corner of the world" may well be a recipe for the two forms of cultural destruction described here: *the expropriation of indigenous cultural goods* and *the imposition of foreign cultural practices.* In closing this section on cultural destruction we turn to *Globalization and Culture,* where John Tomlinson argues that "cultural signification and interpretation constantly orientates people, individually and collectively, towards particular actions." Moreover, the intense connectivity of globalization "matters for culture in the sense that it brings the negotiation of cultural experience into the centre of strategies for intervention in the other realms of connectivity: the political, the environmental, [and] the economic." For Tomlinson, then, the ways specific forms of political action and allegiance are negotiated hinge in no small part on the more slippery question of how "cultural signification" orients individuals to certain norms and expectations.[58]

The communicative facts of globalization multiply the power of this equation, for as time and space appear to shrink, so "the negotiation of cultural experience" becomes increasingly international. If Tomlinson's analysis is correct, then the cultural destruction of Iraq—like the horrible photographs of abuses at Abu Ghraib—is not a local but a global phenomenon, one that will hereafter compromise all U.S. attempts to speak as if its actions are intended to promote anything other than expanded U.S. power and privilege. Indeed, if we accept Tomlinson's thesis that cultural experiences inevitably fuel political allegiances, then the cultural destruction and homogenization of Iraq cannot help but cast U.S. political goals in a dubious light.

We have argued here that the looting of Iraq is a local yet globally important example of benign universalism in action; we now expand the scope of that argument from analyzing the cultural destruction of one nation to observing how the *NSSUS* and President Bush have argued for the global spread of what we call evangelical capitalism. Offered as the only path toward peace and prosperity, evangelical capitalism calls for the spread of U.S.-driven post-Communist capitalism, albeit with a familiar missionary twist. Like benign universalism, then, evangelical capitalism suggests a form of cultural arrogance, a willingness to override local norms and values on behalf of what the U.S. deems "right and true for every person, in every society."

Evangelical Capitalism

Linking our comments in the preceding section about cultural destruction with our analysis of how the *NSSUS* trumpets the spread of democracy, decency, and dignity, we demonstrate here how recent U.S. economic policies pursue and how their rhetorics propose a version of "human dignity" that we call *evangelical capitalism*. Indeed, using its supposed triumph in the cold war as its driving explanation of the unquestioned efficacy and even ethical importance of free-market capitalism, the *NSSUS* and President Bush strive to collapse both specific democratic and broad human rights into a call for benevolent free markets. For example, the first sentence of the *NSSUS*'s preface proclaims that "the great struggles of the twentieth century between liberty [U.S. democracy] and totalitarianism [Soviet Communism] ended with a decisive victory for the forces of freedom—and a single sustainable model for national success: freedom, democracy, and free enterprise" (iii). Likewise, the document's closing sentence argues that the future security and happiness of the United States—and hence of the world—"comes from" the nation's "entrepreneurial energy" (31). Thus offering a blueprint for precisely the kinds of cultural homogenization and destruction addressed above, the Bush Doctrine begins and ends with the understanding that democracy *is* capitalism, that capitalism *is* democracy, and that both terms are universally applicable around the globe.

The president's speeches on the topic reproduce this theory, albeit with the added evangelical dimension of claiming that enabling capitalist success is a form of godly righteousness. In this sense, then, the *NSSUS* and President Bush offer a blueprint for what Ellen Meiksins Wood calls "commercial imperialism," a scenario in which local cultures, economic practices, and political norms are homogenized under the banner of U.S.-led evangelical capitalism. Examining the president's and the *NSSUS*'s versions of globalization-through-benevolent-empire thus offers a remarkable rhetorical opportunity to watch the world's superpower think aloud about its ambitions for controlling globalization by establishing a Christian empire of gentle, post-Communist free markets.[59]

We should note that we have found the claims stated above some-
what startling, for whereas we opened the *NSSUS* assuming it would
speak to questions of international politics, military force, national security, and so on, the curious fact is that it reads in large chunks more like
a manifesto—like the Brick Church covenant of 1831—for a renewed version of evangelical capitalism. As we read the *NSSUS*, there are three
chief benefits of the gentle power of post-Communist free markets. First,
"free trade and free markets have proven their ability to lift whole societies out of poverty" (preface, v). This is an especially important task, for
the *NSSUS* acknowledges that "a world where some live in comfort and
plenty, while half of the human race lives on less than \$2 a day, is neither
just nor stable" (21). In a similar vein, the *NSSUS* argues that U.S.-driven
free markets will enable people in developing countries to "fight against
corruption" (17). Evangelical capitalism is therefore a movement for social
justice, a systemic attempt to use U.S. economic might to alleviate global
poverty and to remove criminals from positions of economic and political
power.

Second, whereas any number of historians, philosophers, economists,
and cultural critics have written about capitalism as a system of profit
making based on the exploitation of workers' labor, the carnivalesque
creation of new "needs," the rapid expansion of markets, and the constant
search for cheaper raw materials, the *NSSUS* proclaims that the markets
of exchange that fuel capitalism in fact offer "real freedom" (18). So rather
than oppressing workers, stripping away nature's bounty, and devouring
local cultures, evangelical capitalism offers its participants free choice—
"this is real freedom" (18). There is of course much truth to that claim, as
some forms of capitalism in some countries under certain conditions have
indeed improved peoples' living standards. But as with the Bush administration's rhetoric of certainty regarding WMDs, the cheerful claim that
capitalism is always and only a provider of "real freedom" amounts to a
half-truth and hence to a tool of propaganda.

Third, whereas numerous critics have observed that unrestricted capital markets (where speculators pursue profit via exchange rates, futures,
stock markets, and other forms of paper profit divorced from material
production) have destabilized developing nations, the *NSSUS* argues that
"international flows of investment capital are needed to expand the productive potential of these [developing] economies" (18). To demonstrate

the deep commitment driving this claim, the *NSSUS* argues for "an increase of development assistance that is provided in the form of grants instead of loans" (22).

The *NSSUS* offers many more pronouncements regarding the benefits of evangelical capitalism, but we will stop here, summarizing what we read as the document's three main claims. First, evangelical capitalism is a system of social justice that strives to eradicate poverty and eliminate corruption. Second, evangelical capitalism proposes a version of free markets without economics, where what matters are not laborers and resources, the old competitive strife that marked prior forms of capitalism, but the joy of consumers offered a new world of unlimited choice—this capitalist joy is real freedom. Third, evangelical capitalism eschews predatory investment strategies, instead offering developing nations hope and opportunity in the form of grants, not interest-compounding loans. These are remarkable, even utopian claims that point to a world of justice, equality, and opportunity, all fueled by the remarkable energy and dynamism of U.S.-driven evangelical capitalism.

Moreover, the president has repeated the *NSSUS*'s visionary arguments again and again, adding to them a tone of sermonic fervor. For example, speaking at the Inter-American Development Bank in Washington, D.C., on 14 March 2002, President Bush repeated the three main claims summarized above and added detail to his vision by promising that he would establish a "New Millennium Challenge Account" in to which he would put $5 billion over three years to help developing nations. The speech reaches its evangelical crescendo when the president moves from discussing economic details to broad moral commitments. "People across the world are working to relieve poverty and suffering, and I'm proud of their efforts. . . . Some were motivated by simple decency, some serve a God who is impatient with injustice. And all have made this commitment. We cannot leave behind half of humanity as we seek a better future for ourselves. We cannot accept permanent poverty in a world of progress. There are no second-class citizens in the human race." This is a stunning and seductive passage, for the president here turns evangelical capitalism into a missionary service charged with doing God's work, one job at a time, redeeming the brilliant promises of progress by linking them to simple decency, turning each act of production and exchange into a quest for social justice.[60]

A fourth key aspect of evangelical capitalism regards national security, as the *NSSUS* pledges to "diminish the underlying conditions that spawn terrorism" (6) by using benevolent free markets to help failing states reassert local political and economic authority. President Bush was clear in his Inter-American Development Bank speech that "poverty doesn't cause terrorism. Being poor doesn't make you a murderer. . . . Yet persistent poverty and oppression can lead to hopelessness and despair. And when governments fail to meet the most basic needs of their people, these failed states can become havens for terror" (2). Hence, in addition to fulfilling the righteous task of advancing the wishes of "a God who is impatient with injustice," evangelical capitalism produces the added bonus of strengthening weak states, thus short-circuiting the spiral into depression and alienation that leads to what the *NSSUS* calls the "the embittered few" (1) to commit acts of terror.

Having thus established the four primary claims of the *NSSUS* and President Bush regarding evangelical capitalism (it is a form of social justice, it offers real freedom, it undoes predatory capitalism, and it supports national security), we now briefly examine the plausibility of the first two parts of this theory (with parts three and four addressed in chapters 3 and 4). First, consider the claim that evangelical capitalism strives for social justice by diminishing poverty and corruption. Although we applaud the *NSSUS* and President Bush for foregrounding the horror of global poverty we would remind readers that poverty, especially for the young, is at near epidemic proportions in the United States and caution them that poverty is a deeply embedded structural phenomenon that cannot be erased with giant loans and grants. For as Stiglitz argues in *Globalization and Its Discontents,* "Lack of food leads to ill health, which limits their [the developing world's poor] earning ability, leading to still poorer health. Barely surviving, they cannot send their children to school, and without an education, their children are condemned to a life of poverty. Poverty is passed along from one generation to another," thus fueling an inherited sense of powerlessness and insecurity. Flooding failed economies with U.S. dollars may well support local capitalist elites, yet without addressing the deep structural causes of developing nation poverty such actions may actually exacerbate the problem.[61]

Indeed, according to Amy Chua's *World on Fire,* globalization in the form of spreading capitalism intensifies disempowerment, for by generating "not only new opportunities and hopes, but also new social desires, stresses, insecurities, and frustrations," it produces violence rather than

new and empowered middle classes. The theory that evangelical capitalism is a form of social justice is therefore both materially wrong and yet
another example of what we have been calling rhetrickery, for it ignores
the deep structural causes of global poverty, it proceeds as if poverty were
not a pressing problem in the United States, and it promises global uplift
when in fact, in many cases, offering humiliation.[62]

As an example of this combination of material error and rhetorical
trickery, consider the Millennium Challenge Account. For whereas we
noted above that the president promised in 2002 to create a $5 billion
Millennium Challenge Account to help developing nations fight their
way out of poverty, the *New York Times* reported on 29 January 2004 that
even while the president continued to trumpet the claim in his speeches
around the nation, the fact is that he had released but $2.5 billion to the
fund. This is a massive amount of money, but as only 50 percent of
the promised amount, it cannot help but leave the president looking like
a liar, an exaggerator, or a particularly bad mathematician. Worse yet,
David Harvey reports in *The New Imperialism* that "the U.S. now plans
to attach a condition of open market access on the U.S. model to the
Millennium Challenge Grants," thus suggesting that the president's proposed move against poverty is in fact an attempt to "create opportunities
for monopoly powers to proliferate." The White House's materials on the
subject reflect this ambivalence, for they claim that the Millennium
Challenge Account is part of the "moral imperative" to "combat poverty,"
yet they clearly impose the same U.S. standards of neoliberalism that
Stiglitz, Chua, Harvey, and others have argued fuel economic injustice. In
fact, the conditions the White House imposes on its Millennium Challenge Account are so stringent that as of June 2005, only four nations
have qualified for assistance packages totaling $610 million. Of this sum,
only $400,000 has been spent. The president therefore drapes grandiose
economic policies that few experts believe work in the moralizing language of an evangelical mission, all the while deflecting attention from
the failure of the Millennium Challenge Account.[63]

The claim that evangelical capitalism will diminish poverty and corruption is therefore both hopelessly naïve regarding the causes of developing nation poverty and deeply suspect regarding the rhetorical work
fulfilled by celebrating the "moral imperative" of the Millennium Challenge Account. In fact, the United Nations' *HDR* notes that of the
twenty-two countries that constitute the Development Assistance Com-

mittee (DAC) of the Organization for Economic Cooperation and Development (OECD), "the U.S. gives the second highest amount *but the lowest proportion*" of gross national product (GNP). Indeed, even if factoring the full $5 billion Millennium Challenge Account into the calculation, the United States gives but 0.15 percent of GNP in the form of grants to developing nations, whereas tiny Ireland and Luxembourg offer 0.30 percent and 0.71 percent of GNP respectively. Despite President Bush's boasting, then, the *HDR* demonstrates that the United States gives proportionally less of its GNP to developing nations than any other member of the OECD, including half of what Ireland offers and less than one-quarter of what Luxembourg gives.[64]

Regarding the claim that evangelical capitalism spreads the "real freedom" of consumer choice, it is important to examine some of the implications of spreading U.S.-style consumerism to the developing world. For example, consider Wal-Mart, one of the largest corporate contributors in the 2003 election cycle, when its political action committee gave $1 million, 85 percent of which went to Republicans. In return for its campaign generosity, Wal-Mart's lobbyists were successful in including in CAFTA provisions further enabling it to lower costs by relying on goods made abroad with cheaper materials and cheaper labor than possible in the United States. So while consumers may find lower prices on the shelf, U.S. workers are undercut by Wal-Mart's relying on foreign parts and labor. Moreover, Wal-Mart's founders, the Walton family, who are worth over $100 billion, have committed themselves not only to selling cheap goods but also, as is consistent with the economic dogma known as the Washington Consensus (which we address in chapter 3), to privatizing America's schools, hence, according to Glen Ford and Peter Gamble, striving to "destroy public education in the United States." Further embodying Washington Consensus principles declaring that all public services should be privatized, with governments and corporations cutting their obligations to citizens and workers alike, Wal-Mart has also sought to curtail employee health benefits; as a result, as many as one-third of all Wal-Mart employees do not have health insurance. This combination of leveraging political clout via massive campaign contributions, cutting product cost by relying on outsourcing, and minimizing employee benefits drives Wal-Mart's profitability, making it an engine of global consumerism but also a harbinger of neoliberalism's many fault lines. For while Wal-Mart operates production facilities in twelve nations, sold goods in 2002 valued at $245 billion, and runs three thousand stores in the United States alone, which are visited by shoppers representing a stunning 80 percent of all U.S. households, the company also champions antilabor practices, low wages, environmental destruction, and the spread of a culture of homogenized banality. The supposed moral imperatives driving neoliberal development are therefore compromised by the real world practices of that vision's chief practitioners.[65]

Indeed, while Wal-Mart and massive stores like it offer the promise of almost infinite consumer choice, their overall impact on the United States demonstrates that expanded consumerism is not necessarily a route to long-term development. In fact, Aaron Bernstein reports that for the nearly 25 percent of those Americans trapped in low-paying, dead-end jobs—precisely the kind offered by Wal-Mart—the market offers not so much real freedom as the humiliation of living in the shadow of unfulfilled promise. Paul Krugman echoes these claims, observing that so many Americans are stuck in unfulfilling and unpromising jobs, leaving them both poor and angry, that "the distribution of income in the U.S. has gone right back to Gilded Age levels of inequality." Moreover, Bernstein has reported in *Business Week* that the premise that low-paying jobs of the kind offered by Wal-Mart create upward mobility, in turn opening up consumer choices, is largely fictional. He reports that "though the boom lifted pay rates for janitors and clerks by as much as 5% to 10% in the late 1990s, more of them remained janitors or clerks; fewer worked their way into better-paying positions." In short, Bernstein argues that even during the huge market advances of the 1990s, when newly minted dot.com millionaires were supposedly the norm, upward mobility was a dream, not a reality. Globally, the problem only worsens because when new markets are opened up at the behest of American-style free trade, workers in developing nations are not generally capable of participating in the consumer societies their labor helps produce. The *New York Times* thus editorialized in December 2003 that "the rigged trade game is not only harvesting poverty around the world, but plenty of resentment as well."[66]

What the *NSSUS* and President Bush portray as evangelical capitalism is therefore understood in many parts of the world as little more than market-imposed humiliation. For the "freedom" of consumerism is experienced by the world's poor, including those in the United States, not as an actual possibility for a better life but as the intense lure of something unattainable. For example, Chua describes "the uneducated, disease-ridden, desperately poor but numerically vast Indian- or African-blooded majorities of Latin America," who "experience little or no economic benefit from privatization and global markets while finding themselves suddenly filled with contradictory new materialistic and consumerist desires." As suggested in our comments in the introduction on Waldman and Roy's writings on India, Chua argues that the promises of evangelical capitalism are not only unstable and perhaps even surreal, but also capable of fueling the conditions of violence.[67]

Along with these international dangers it is equally important to notice how the promises of evangelical capitalism serve the domestic function of enriching a small group of weapons manufacturers. Indeed, cynical readers may be tempted to argue that the president's grandiose version of evangelical capitalism is just rhetorical window dressing, a moralizing distraction meant to obscure the devastating domestic effects of his perpetual military state. For regardless of one's position regarding the coming Rapture, the assumed wishes of God, or the morality of tackling developing nation poverty via massive U.S. loans and grants, the economic and political needs of the perpetual military state demand dramatic transformations in the ways Americans live. Even a cursory glance at the status of the military-industrial complex demonstrates a thriving, ever-expanding, globe-encircling behemoth that devours resources, produces massive pollution, turns the areas surrounding its bases into alcohol- and pornography-flooded ghettoes, and leaves democracy in America in an increasingly tenuous position. We are pointing, then, to yet another dark irony within the Bush administration's post-9/11 rhetoric, for while it has championed a justice-building and hope-spreading form of international evangelical capitalism, its reliance on the military-industrial complex has continued a process of slashing social services while practicing domestic cronyism.[68]

For example, most Americans do not know that many of the contractors who provide the weapons to the U.S. military are tax cheats. But the *Wall Street Journal* reported in February 2004 that "more than 27,000 defense contractors" owe the IRS a total of $3 billion in unpaid taxes. Despite the fact that these contractors have not paid their taxes, the U.S. military continues to purchase arms and services from them. So U.S. taxpayers pay the government, which buys weapons from companies who do not pay taxes yet reap massive profits, and the government punishes these tax cheats by granting them more contracts! In essence, our tax dollars are being given to military contractors. Imagine the benefits the nation would enjoy if that $3 billion was recycled into our roads and schools and health care. But instead of improving the daily lives of Americans, the government enriches its tax-cheating military contractors. Moreover, the amount of money circulated through these contractors is staggering. Lockheed Martin, the biggest U.S. defense contractor (which was not named in the report on tax cheats) made $344 million in the fourth quarter of 2004 alone; this was based on sales of $8.98 billion—that's $8,980,000,000 worth of weapons sales for just three months. The president's sermonic claims about the "moral imperative" of evangelical capitalism thus strike us as deeply compromised by the facts offered above, which demonstrate a nation sinking under the excesses of the military-industrial complex.[69]

We offer lengthier economic analyses of globalization and empire in chapters 3 and 4, and more detailed examinations of crony capitalism and the military-industrial complex in chapter 4, and so will cut short our comments here regarding these aspects of evangelical capitalism. Our arguments here have demonstrated, however, that the promises of the gentle power of post-Communist free markets, offered as what we have called *evangelical capitalism*, are economically dubious at best, rhetorical justifications for accelerated U.S. profits and power at worst. Moreover, given the *NSSUS* and President Bush's related comments regarding the cultures likely to become the recipients of evangelical capitalism, it is hard to imagine the missionary imperative behind this project as anything other than a call for cultural homogenization, if not outright colonization. Our comments on the military-industrial complex add another layer of concern regarding the promises of evangelical capitalism, for they demonstrate that even while speaking of a "moral imperative" to render contemporary economics more just—hence pursuing globalization-through-benevolent-empire—such claims amount to rhetorical justifications for imperial cronyism.

The Ontologically Damaged
and the Clash of Civilizations

One of the most curious aspects of the *NSSUS* and President Bush's post-9/11 speeches is that even while they stand among the major political documents of our age, their terms of description often sound less like government pronouncements than ventures into that branch of philosophy known as ontology. Traditionally understood as the philosophy of being (as compared to *epistemology*, the philosophy of knowledge; or *axiology*, the philosophy of values; or *phenomenology*, the philosophy of perception; and so on), ontological questions address the nature of being, with the implied sense that large parts of what constitutes being are inherent, literally organic, never-changing components of life itself. A. R. Lacey argues in *A Dictionary of Philosophy* that "ontology borders on philosophy of religion." A modified, postmodern version of such thinking, known as "weak ontology," steers away from these religious overtones to ask a frank question: "What does it mean to be? . . . How do we as human beings meaningfully go about our everyday lives?" But if we recall the deeply religious character of both the *NSSUS* and many of President Bush's post-9/11 speeches—which taken together amount to a proposed philosophy of being, a new dogma of post-9/11 righteousness—then we may argue that these texts offer a worldview that is fundamentally ontological. Moreover, throughout these documents terrorists and rogue states are portrayed as *ontologically damaged:* their actions are not political choices (weak ontology) but inherent flaws (strong ontology), their beliefs are not simply different from ours but unrecognizable on any moral compass—*their condition is not chosen or situational but organic, an ontological matter of being itself.* The rhetorical function of arguing from this ontological position is to turn political and therefore negotiable differences into essential and therefore nonnegotiable differences. The relevant question, then, becomes not what do you believe or what do you do, but *what are you?*[70]

For example, notice the *NSSUS*'s claim that our nation's enemies "reject basic human values and hate the U.S. and everything for which it stands" (14). Whereas the political left has tended since 9/11 to see our nation's enemies' anger as the result of specific foreign policies with which they take offense, the political right has tended to think of our enemies in the way described above, as ontologically damaged maniacs driven by their "reject[ing] basic human values." From this latter perspective, the anger of those who attack us is not situational but foundational: *they hate us.* The dilemma is therefore not caused by clashing beliefs, incommensurable cultural fictions, or irresolvable political differences (weak ontology), but by a more foundational problem with being itself. The

NSSUS cautions against drawing too stark a conclusion from such thinking, warning that "the war on terrorism is not a clash of civilizations" (31), yet as we demonstrate below, the president's speeches have called that cautionary passage into question.

Indeed, on 11 October 2001, just one month following 9/11, the president claimed in a press conference that al Qaeda's strikes were "an attack on the heart and soul of the civilized world." This was the same speech in which he referred to terrorists as "the parasites." One month later the president again relied on these terms in a speech on homeland security in Atlanta, where he said that "we wage a war to save civilization itself." Two months later, in his January 2002 State of the Union address, the president pledged to "eliminate the terrorist parasites." Four months later, speaking in the German Bundestag on 23 May 2002, President Bush again claimed that "we are defending civilization itself." Another six months later, when he signed the Homeland Security Act into legislation on 25 November 2002, the president noted that the war to save civilization was being fought against foes who "hate us because of what we love." The war to save civilization is therefore between the moral and God-loving United States and foes who are so ontologically damaged that they are devoid of basic human values: they are parasites, inhuman foes of civilization itself. In this regard, "clash of civilizations" may be too soft a term for describing what the president proposes here, for his terms make it sound more like a clash of species: humans against parasites, those capable of love and intelligence against senseless killing machines. Thus illustrating a pattern that Robert Ivie argues is central to America's "republic of fear," President Bush used clash-of-civilizations rhetoric to fuel the "chronic paranoia" underlying our nation's long history of "extreme Othering."[71]

As we have suggested above, the rhetorical problem with this strategy is that it implies, or some would even say explicitly calls for, a form of universalizing colonialism in which world cultures are homogenized under the banner of U.S. values and norms. The president appears internally conflicted on this issue, for even while his speeches lean perilously close to calling for a clash of civilizations, or even a clash of species, he seems to understand that such a position is potentially inflammatory. For example, in a June 2002 speech before the graduating class of the U.S. Military Academy at West Point, New York, the president cautions that "there is no clash of civilizations," yet he also claims that "moral truth is *the same in every culture, in every time, in every place.*" Thus, even while saying there is no clash of civilizations, and hence while trying to avoid what he rightly perceives as an unproductive rhetorical strategy, the president makes it clear that "moral truth," which he clearly understands to mean U.S. truth, will be spread across the globe, thus amounting to a universalizing discourse. This of course means that anyone or anything that opposes this universalizing discourse is essentially, ontologically damaged, and therefore needs to be either absorbed or destroyed.[72]

Given the recurring presence of such thinking in the *NSSUS* and the president's speeches, it is plausible to conclude that U.S. national security hinges less on historically specific sets of political challenges than on a religious crusade against those who are ontologically damaged. The logical consequence of this strategy is that the ontologically damaged cannot be persuaded to change their ways, for change is impossible; instead, they can only be quarantined or eliminated. The *NSSUS* and some of President Bush's post-9/11 speeches thus verge precipitously close to declaring what can only be described, to borrow a phrase from Samuel Huntington's celebrated and controversial 1993 essay in *Foreign Affairs,* as a "Clash of Civilizations."[73]

As the Eaton Professor of the Science of Government at Harvard University and one of the nation's premier scholars of political science, Huntington's arguments in the essay were received almost as if they were fixed government doctrine, as if they had somehow both revealed the essence of recent U.S. foreign policy and pinpointed the future obstacles threatening its success. Thirteen years now since its publication, the article has entered the realm of myth, circulating in academic and political circles alike as a talisman, meaning for many users whatever they want or need it to mean. In fact, the public response to the article was so heated that Huntington expanded his ideas in a 1996 book of the same title. Since then, the notion of a clash of civilizations has become a rhetorical triggering mechanism fulfilling multiple, and contradictory, functions. For those on the left it serves as a warning of the worst-case consequences of the neocolonial ambitions of the Bush administration. For those on the right it points toward the utter depravity of U.S. enemies, whose terrorism poses a threat not to specific U.S. foreign policies but to civilization itself. For those in the shrinking middle it stands as an alarming term of debate and contention regarding the sweeping claims of those on the left and the right. Huntington's notion of a coming "clash of civilizations" is thus used to predict an imminent global conflagration prodded toward fruition by U.S. bullying and arrogance, to diagnose an already engaged war between those who defend civilization—the United States and its ever-dwindling allies—and those who threaten it—al Qaeda, Saddam Hussein, Colombian drug lords, the Russian Mafia, and an apparently ever-expanding list of bad guys—and to call for a moment of reflection, a pause to consider the dire ramifications of such increasingly extreme responses to the dilemmas of globalization and empire.[74]

Rather than descending into these debates, let us instead turn to the article to see if and how Huntington's essay applies to our question regarding the ways the *NSSUS* and President Bush have portrayed U.S. relations with the ontologically damaged. We should note first that although Huntington opens his article with the claim that "the clash of civilizations will dominate global politics" (1), he does not "advocate the desirability" of such conflicts; rather, he hopes "to set forth descriptive hypotheses as to what the future may be like" (14). For Huntington, this future will not be driven by ideological commitments, as was the cold war, nor will it be driven by nation-state competition, as were the two world wars; instead, future conflicts will be driven by fundamental clashes between irreconcilable ways of being in the world—in short, by the hatreds spurred by the ontological differences between civilizations. Indeed, Huntington notes that whereas "which side are you on?" was the pertinent question in earlier forms of conflict, the new phase of civilizational conflict will leave combatants asking "what are you?" (4). When Huntington talks about the clash of civilizations, then, he may as well say the clash of ontologies, for the definition of civilizations employed here is not so much political as organic, not changing but static, not complex and fluid but monolithic and frozen—in a word, ontological.

For Huntington there are eight such ontologically distinct civilizations: "Western, Confucian, Japanese, Islamic, Hindu, Slavic-Orthodox, Latin American, and possibly African" (2). Michael Ignatieff, whom we discussed briefly in our introduction, questioned the accuracy of this partitioning, noting that Huntington's civilizations "are unified, self-contained compartments, not the promiscuously interacting, heterogeneous and constantly changing amoebas we know them to be." Although we share Ignatieff's doubts about the accuracy of Huntington's list of civilizations, we will bypass this question to proceed to the heart of

Huntington's thesis: that the shrinking of time and space that marks globalization brings these civilizations into increasing contact and that this contact does not elevate the intermingling entities into a higher realm of tolerance and even neighborliness—as multiculturalists would have it—but rather "invigorates differences and animosities stretching or thought to stretch back deep into history" (3). Whether we accept Huntington's notion of what is or is not a civilization, his argument succinctly summarizes one of the startling contradictions of globalization: that increasing global consciousness appears in many cases to lead to rededicated commitments to local prejudices. For Huntington, the more our worldly consciousness expands, the more provincial we become.[75]

This thesis has been pursued in Amy Chua's 2004 *World on Fire*, where she studies recent explosions of ethnonationalist violence in Africa, Latin America, the Middle East, and Asia. She concludes that in each case the aggressive pursuit of U.S.-driven free markets and democracy fueled long-simmering local hatreds. Chua argues that "in societies with a market-dominant ethnic minority, markets and democracy favor not just different people, or different classes, but different ethnic groups. Markets concentrate wealth . . . in the hands of the market-dominant minority, while democracy increases the political power of the impoverished majority. Under these circumstances the pursuit of free market democracy becomes an engine of potentially catastrophic ethno-nationalism." One of Chua's prime examples is the riots that rocked Indonesia in May 1998, when rampaging *pribumi*, the overwhelmingly poor ethnic majority of the nation, attacked Chinese merchants, who constituted a wealthy market-dominant ethnic minority. Chua notes that while they constitute "just 3 percent of the population, the Chinese controlled approximately 70 percent of the private economy"; moreover, she claims they did so as the appointed "handful of cronies" working as the economic elites propping up Suharto's rotten regime. The explosion of violence in Indonesia was therefore, for Chua, the inevitable outcome of ethnonationalist tension over control of markets. Although Chua does not invoke the notion of a clash of civilizations to explain these riots, her point squares with Huntington's thesis that deep notions of ethnic nationalism cannot be overcome, for they are ontologically rooted, meaning globalization under the guise of democracy and free markets can only produce ethnonationalist—what Huntington would call civilizational—bloodshed.[76]

We should note here that Chua's analysis of the Indonesia riots is deeply flawed, for Chalmers Johnson has shown in *Blowback* that the riots were not spontaneous eruptions of ethnonationalist hatreds but the carefully orchestrated results of the Indonesian military. With the Suharto regime wobbling under mounting domestic and international pressure in the spring of 1998, and with Suharto out of the country on a trip to Egypt, the Indonesian military sought to trigger a coup by instigating what would appear to be populist ethnonationalist violence. But the riots that ensued were conducted in a clockwork-like, even military manner; erupting at forty different locations *at the same time*, 2,470 shops were burned, 1,119 cars were destroyed, and 1,188 people—mostly Chinese—were murdered. The violence contributed powerfully to the sense that the nation was disintegrating and that Suharto should resign, which he did on 21 May. Although the corporate media reported these events—in a line Chua swallows whole—as a regime change spurred largely by the instability caused by rampaging ethnonationalist hatreds, Ariel Heryanto argues that the riots "were not racially motivated mass riots but racialized state terrorism." Chua's example thus amounts not to an indictment of globalization so much as a demonstration of her taking misleading media reports at face value. In fact, we suspect that such arguments about clashes of civilizations and ethnonationalist hatreds generally fall into this same analytic error: *they skim the surface effects of events and call them causal, they mistake complex political crises for ontological damage.*[77]

Nonetheless, the Chua/Huntington thesis that globalization recharges the flagging batteries of ethnonationalism has become popular, in turn justifying slackening commitments to notions of universalism, let alone any sense of multilateral internationalism. As Huntington observes, in a passage that describes recent U.S. actions perfectly, "A world of clashing civilizations . . . is inevitably a world of double standards: people apply one standard to their kin-countries and a different standard to others" (8). Given this reduction of international diplomacy to self-civilization-serving double standards, it is logical to charge that "the very phrase 'world community' has become the euphemistic collective noun . . . to give global legitimacy to actions reflecting the interests of the U.S. and other Western powers" (10). Moreover, Huntington notes that the central values the United States offers under the guise of improving the "world community," including democracy and free markets, which as we have already demonstrated above form the entwined heart of the *NSSUS,* cannot possibly feel to members of other civilizations like anything other than an imposition of foreign, imperial power. "Western efforts to propagate such ideas" as "individualism, liberalism, constitutionalism, human rights, equality, liberty, rule of law, democracy, free markets, [and] the separation of church and state," Huntington warns, "produce instead a reaction against 'human rights imperialism' and a reaffirmation of indigenous values" (11). Huntington thus argues that the ontological differences between civilizations are so broad, and that each civilization's commitment to its own ontologies is so unwavering, that attempts to pass one civilization's ideals off onto another cannot result in anything but war.

Huntington's "Clash of Civilizations" and Chua's *World on Fire* thus warn against precisely the kind of universalizing rhetoric that drives the *NSSUS.* Indeed, their shared central thesis, that globalization increases ethnonationalist tension, leads them both to call for a patient and prudent foreign policy of tactful engagement. Avoiding a clash of civilizations will therefore require, for Huntington, that the "West develop a more profound understanding of the basic religious and philosophical assumptions underlying other civilizations" (15). Chua's answer, defined in her closing chapter, "The Future of Free Markets," is to pursue benign capitalism rather than shock therapy (see pages 259–288). Although their conclusions thus stand as ringing indictments of the Bush administration's post-9/11 rhetoric and policies, the foundational ideas of both authors—that there are such things as civilizations (Huntington) and/or distinct ethnonationalist affiliations (Chua), that they are ontologically distinct, and that they inevitably clash when they contact each other— actually serve the Bush administration nicely.

Indeed, if one accepts the premise that 9/11 stands as the opening shot in a civilizational clash, with al Qaeda striking not at U.S. foreign policy but at Western civilization itself, then it follows that the United States must defend both itself and the larger civilization it supposedly leads. This clearly explains the attraction for the Bush administration of rhetoric that evades time- and space-specific politics in favor of a sweeping and benign universalism, for such grandiose benevolence enables the United States to avoid discussion of its actual political actions, instead behaving as if it were the defender of the timeless values of Western civilization. Moreover, if Western values cannot appear to other civilizations as anything other than imperialism, and given the fact that the West must deal

with these other civilizations because it needs their markets and resources, then both Huntington's and Chua's positions explain the need
for imperialism. For while the stealth imperialism of markets and multilateral agreements works slowly and still elicits fears of civilizational
clashes and ethnonationalist violence, then why not move more quickly,
using the military, while facing similar charges yet reaping more immediate, more complete, and more controllable benefits? That is, if diplomacy is likely to fail due to the constraints of ontologically distinct civilizational norms and ethnonationalist commitments, then realists must
face the fact that imperialism is not only the best but the only option for
protecting U.S. interests abroad.

As Edward Said lamented in his review of Huntington's book, "Un-
countable are the editorials in every American and European newspaper
and magazine of note adding to this vocabulary of gigantism and apoca-
lypse, each use of which is plainly designed not to edify but to inflame
the reader's indignant passion as a member of the 'West.'" Ironically, then,
while Huntington's and Chua's conclusions explicitly caution against the
reckless maneuvers that characterize post-9/11 U.S. foreign policy, their
underlying assumptions about the ontological status of civilizations and
ethnonationalisms lend the Bush administration's recent claims and actions not only an air of intellectual legitimacy but a whiff of inevitability.
Indeed, by creating a rhetorical strategy that relies on the notion of unchangeable truths and errors, on a sense of being that is ontological rather
than political—*they hate us for what we are, not what we do*—the president
ends up proposing a familiar version of the necessary burden of pursuing
an evangelical colonialism, one that strives to homogenize the world in
the name of defending civilization.[78]

Epilogue: "This Should Give Us Pause"

Our rhetorical analysis of the *NSSUS* and President Bush's post-9/11
speeches reveals that their war rhetoric is based on five central ideas regarding the future of globalization and empire: (1) *a doctrine of preemption,* which we have shown to compromise any sense of international diplomacy; (2) *a millennial military state,* which we have described as an
evangelical and perpetual post-9/11 version of the cold war's military-
industrial complex; (3) *a promise of benign universalism,* which we have
demonstrated amounts to a blueprint for cultural theft and homogeniza-

tion; (4) *a post-Communist world of evangelical capitalism,* which we have analyzed as a rhetorically astute way of justifying continued U.S. economic domination of world markets; and (5) *a clash of civilizations,* where our enemies are portrayed not as political actors but as ontologically damaged subhumans. These five central ideas constitute a bold vision of a new U.S. empire, a new Pax Americana where U.S. military might, economic power, and cultural norms spread across the globe in the name of defending both U.S. national security and civilization at large. Thus linking McDonald's and McDonnell Douglas, the *NSSUS* and President Bush's post-9/11 war rhetorics announce a new U.S. foreign policy of pursuing globalization-through-benevolent-empire.

To demonstrate how this new posture is based largely on a profound misunderstanding of the bases of our enemies' anger, we will close this chapter on war rhetorics by turning again to the findings of the *Report of the Defense Science Board Task Force on Strategic Communication.* Based on a Zogby international poll conducted in July 2004, the report measures public opinion about the United States in Morocco, Saudi Arabia, Jordan, Lebanon, and the United Arab Emirates. The poll is broken down into ten categories: four aspects of U.S. foreign policy and six aspects of U.S. culture. To take Morocco as an example, its favorable ratings for the cultural categories are 90 percent for science/technology, 53 percent for freedom/democracy, 59 percent for people, 60 percent for movies/TV, 73 percent for products, and 61 percent for education. However, its unfavorable ratings for foreign policy aspects are 90 percent for policy toward Arabs, 93 percent for policy toward Palestinians, 82 percent for policy on terrorism, and 98 percent for policy on Iraq. Moroccans therefore have strongly favorable views of U.S. values and cultural practices and intensely unfavorable views of U.S. foreign policy. In short, they do not hate us because of what we are and how we live—the essentialist, ontological argument discussed above—but because of what we do as an international colossus. Moreover, the report notes that the unfavorable numbers have been rising since the U.S. invasion of Iraq and that throughout the Islamic world "Americans have become the enemy." The report concludes that "opinion is hardest against America in precisely those places ruled by what Muslims call 'apostates' and tyrants," including "the tyrannies of Egypt, Saudi Arabia, Pakistan, Jordan, and the Gulf states"—all U.S. allies. "This," the report suggests, "should give us pause."[79]

The report's findings should give us pause indeed, for they suggest,

counter to everything the president and the *NSSUS* postulate, that international anger is not directed at our values but at our policies. If these
findings are accurate, then they suggest that the war rhetorics examined
here will inflame already rising anger toward the United States. Indeed,
as we have argued here, the report demonstrates that the Bush administration's policy of globalization-through-benevolent-empire may well
prove to be a recipe for catastrophe.

3
"It Is Accelerating"

The Rhetorics of Globalization and
the Dilemmas of U.S. Power

Anticipating the arrival of upward of one hundred thousand protesters in mid-November 2003, Miami placed itself in a state of military lockdown while leaders from thirty-four countries met for weeklong negotiations—formally called a "ministerial"—regarding the Free Trade Area of the Americas (FTAA). Hoping to become the permanent headquarters of the FTAA, and thus needing to prove to the assembled international capitalist elites that it could thwart the supposed anarchy of antiglobalization activists, Miami appropriated $12 million for security, deployed twenty-five hundred police officers, and called on the support of the U.S. Marshals Service, the Federal Protective Service, and the Coast Guard. Demonstrating that the Bush administration perceives activists fighting for global economic justice as terrorists, $8.5 million of Miami's FTAA security budget came from President Bush's emergency $87 billion spending package for waging war on Iraq. Thus, at the week's largest march, on 20 November, self-proclaimed "RoboCops" armed in full riot gear, backed up by tanks, snipers, and helicopters, and largely paid for with war monies, launched tear gas into the assembled crowds and harassed protesters in the name of defending both national security and regional economic development.[1]

The overwhelming police and military presence suggested to many observers that the architects of economic globalization envisioned their work unfolding in a war zone, as if protesters exercising their right to free speech and assembly were not part of the democratic process but threats to be feared, silenced, and arrested. Indeed, groups of heavily armed police patrolled downtown Miami on horseback, apparently ready at a moment's notice to ride down marchers. And so RoboCop met the cavalry, the technological met the premodern, protesters met the full force of the powers that would be used to protect FTAA ministers from the people they were supposedly meeting to help. By late afternoon the police had arrested nearly one hundred of the ten thousand mostly peaceful protesters, dumped the personal belongings of arrestees into the street, shot at them with rubber bullets and pepper spray, and used shock-inducing tasers to control marchers.[2]

Two months prior to the Miami ministerial, in the troubled tourist paradise of Cancún, Mexico, about ten thousand people gathered outside the gates of a meeting of the World Trade Organization. As Mexican peasants and village children dressed in bright colors scurried about, singing songs of hope and solidarity, and as activists from around the world chanted slogans against corporate globalization, a Korean farmer, newspaper publisher, father, widower, and former provincial congressman, Lee Kyung Hae, climbed to the top of a chain-link fence and stabbed himself in the heart with a Swiss army knife. Facing the trade ministers and bearing a sign that read "WTO Kills Farmers," Lee fell into the arms of shocked protesters and died shortly thereafter. Before committing his act of ritual suicide, Lee wrote a scathing letter to the WTO arguing that "soon after the Uruguay Round Agreement was sealed, we Korean farmers realized that our destinies are no longer in our own hands. We cannot seem to do anything to stop the waves that have destroyed our communities where we have been settled for hundreds of years." Emphasizing his experience of globalization as a form of foreign-imposed cultural destruction, Lee concluded that "uncontrolled multinational corporations and a small number of big WTO members are leading an undesirable globalization that is inhumane, environmentally degrading, farmer-killing, and undemocratic."[3]

Much like the Vietnamese Buddhist monk Thich Quang Duc, who committed self-immolation in Saigon on 11 June 1963 to protest the murderous policies of the U.S.-backed Diem regime, and much like the 1965 ritual suicides of Alice Herz, Norman Morrison, and Roger LaPorte, Americans dismayed at the atrocities of the U.S. war in Vietnam, Lee sacrificed himself to help incite concern for a cause. As described by Michael Biggs, such acts of politically motivated self-sacrifice attempt to "appeal to others by means of a costly signal, and [to] incite potential sympathizers." Lee thus sought to express his despair at the consequences of globalization and to electrify the movement against it by repeating Quang Duc's gesture of offering himself as "a donation to the struggle."[4]

These instances of state-sanctioned police violence against protesters in Miami and self-imposed violence-as-protest in Cancún illustrate the complicated relationships among world economic systems and the individuals who experience them. In both Miami and Cancún consumer decadence parades next to crushing poverty; in both cities the utopian promises of globalization-as-salvation crash into harsh realities that speak less to the hopes of a better twenty-first century than to the horrors of Dickens's bleak nineteenth century; in both cities observers are forced to ponder the complicated relationships among state sovereignty, local cultures, corporate powers, and international institutions; in both cities the presence of FTAA and WTO elites highlights contradictions between the hopes of agency and the sorrows of disempowerment, between the many ways violence both sustains and critiques the economic and political powers driving globalization.

One popular response to globalization is to suggest that it amounts to the homogenization of daily life under the banner of U.S. corporate capital. But the stories above also indicate a process of imposed alienation and fragmentation, where a Korean farmer feels overwhelmed by waves of economic and cultural destruction launched by nameless forces assembled in Mexico, where American protesters practice their democratic rights only to be intimidated and even beaten by mounted police, all the while wondering, *On whose behalf do the police ride those horses? What forces lie behind the FTAA and WTO?* Thus reprising our comments in the introduction on Fredric Jameson's and Arundhati Roy's notions of cultural schizophrenia, the glimpses of globalization offered above point to a world where power and responsibility feel increasingly dispersed, where the causes of events seem evermore uncertain. Indeed, while our opening stories may illustrate a world that is jelling into a homogenous capitalist whole ruled by what Lee characterizes as "uncontrolled multinational corporations and a small number of big WTO members," they simultaneously point to a world that is fragmenting into a terrifying cacophony of confusion, where cultures bleed into each other or slowly collapse in the face of new technologies, where national boundaries shift or simply do not matter, where agency and causality are increasingly difficult if not impossible to pinpoint, and where expressions of dissent are met with violence, as in Miami, or produce violence, as in Cancún.

In both of these cases we want to highlight the relationship between violence and discourse, with state-imposed violence attempting to silence debate in Miami and self-imposed violence attempting to trigger debate in the face of institutionally sanctioned silence in Cancún. And of course there is the violence of those who refuse these models of discourse altogether, of those whose only response to globalization is to resort to murderous fanaticism, hence turning violence into an especially bloody form of outraged expression. We therefore want to consider globalization as driving a dialectic of universalizing *and* particularizing energies, of homogenization *and* fragmentation, with both impulses often expressing themselves through violence. Studying public arguments regarding these topics is especially important, for as Stephen Lucas argues, "actual economic conditions are less important than how people perceive or react to those conditions. . . . What people believe to be true is more important than what actually is true." If Lucas is correct, then understanding the relationships among globalization and violence entails both traditional economic analysis of "actual economic conditions" and rhetorical analysis of "what people believe to be true."[5]

For example, for many on the left, the U.S. invasion of Iraq was, as Kurt Campbell warned in a 2001 *Washington Post* editorial, "the first major conflict to occur in the age of globalization." Although the causal chain linking globalization and war was not specified in Campbell's editorial, Steven Staples of the Polaris Institute produced a poster that was widely distributed in the days leading up to the U.S. invasion of Iraq claiming that "Globalization Promotes War." Staples argued that "globalization promotes the conditions of war," that it "promotes military spending over social spending," that it "requires police and military protection of corporate interests," that it "undermines grassroots peace work," and that it "promotes corporate security over human security." These five charges appeared beneath an image of two octopi, one wearing a military cap with a dollar sign and holding a missile, the other with a tentacle full of dollars—the joined octopi of militarism and greed thus encircle the globe. Embodying popular responses to globalization, Campbell's editorial and Staples's poster argued that globalization amounts to the mutually reciprocal advancement of the interests of economic elites, the military-industrial complex, and U.S. empire, with democracy and justice the first casualties of these entwined powers.[6]

An opposite argument may be found in Thomas Barnett's *The Pentagon's New Map*. Whereas Campbell implies and Staples charges that globalization causes war, Barnett argues that globalization creates stability and that a *lack of globalization* causes war. "Show me where globalization is thick with network connectivity, financial transactions, liberal media flows, and collective security, and I will show you regions featuring stable governments, rising standards of living, and more deaths by suicide than by murder," Barnett promises. Hence echoing the globalization-as-freedom-and-progress mantra examined via Thomas Friedman's McDonald's thesis in our introduction and President Bush's speeches in chapter 2, Barnett concludes that "a country's potential to warrant a U.S. military response is inversely related to its globalization connectivity." For Barnett, globalization is the surest way to heal failed or failing states, hence preventing terrorists from arising from the ashes of shattered hopes. Thus echoing the *NSSUS*'s strategy of globalization-as-national-security, Barnett explicitly collapses the spread of U.S. economic interests and cultural norms with global peace.[7]

Given the disparity of these positions, our task in this chapter is to examine how violence in general and war in particular filter through recent discourses about globalization and empire. Our survey of the available literature suggests three main arguments regarding the relationships among globalization, empire, and violence: one argues that state violence is used to impose a form of U.S.-driven empire and corporate globalization; another claims that political violence erupts as a response to empire's and globalization's injustices; and the third claims that the violence spawned by failed states spreads because of a lack of U.S.-led globalization. Despite their differences, all three arguments assume various links between globalization, empire, and violence.

Benjamin Barber has sought to analyze these links by foregrounding an anarchy-producing and democracy-destroying clash between the homogenizing corporate powers of what he calls "McWorld" and the tribalizing resistances that have recently taken the form of fanatical jihads. Like Barber, M. Lane Bruner focuses on the tension between "the impulse toward a universal market and the contrary impulse toward local tribalization." The problem with such formulations is that neither globalizing capitalism nor the supposedly tribal resistances that erupt against it are homogeneous: for as we demonstrate here, McWorld and jihad are both riven with contradictions. Moreover, the history of post–World War II U.S. relations with Middle East dictators and tyrants, many of whom have relied on strains of Islam to enforce political rule, suggests that the problem is not McWorld versus jihad, but what Timothy Mitchell calls "McJihad." This jarring term suggests that local religious fundamentalisms, political regimes, and globalizing market forces have found common cause. If we throw into these comments what feels like the rising tendency to resort to violence—as an attempt to impose U.S. state and economic power, as a desperate response to such attempts, or as the implosions of failed states that suffer from a lack of globalization—then it makes sense that many observers are stunned, literally bewildered in the face of life's apparently accelerating complexities and dangers. In this regard we agree with the diagnosis of the *NSSUS*, which declares that globalization has reached the dizzying point where, whether we call it McWorld or jihad or McJihad or some baffling combination of the three, we all face "*a new condition of life.*"[8]

As argued throughout this book, we assume that making sense of this new condition of life requires understanding the intricacies of globalization and its many forms of violence, how globalization both influences and is influenced by U.S. foreign policy in general and the U.S. war on Iraq in particular, and how various publics argue about these topics. Whereas chapter 1 analyzed the Bush administration's lies regarding Iraq's supposed WMDs, thus exposing the rhetoric used to drag the United States into an unnecessary war, and whereas chapter 2 analyzed the *NSSUS* and President Bush's post-9/11 rhetoric, thus addressing the broad principles of what we called the United States' new "war rhetoric," this chapter asks broad economic questions about globalization, thus examining the rhetorical strategies used both to champion and criticize the spread of a U.S.-driven model of economic development. Thinking in terms of concentric circles, then, each chapter has expanded our scope of inquiry, moving from specific WMD lies in chapter 1 to the broad principles of U.S. empire in chapter 2 and now to the question of how our first two issues exemplify and confound various aspects of economic globalization. To answer that question, the chapter unfolds in three stages:

- First, to forestall any sense of theoretical simplicity or historical naiveté, we open with a review of some of the prior modes of globalization, thus placing our current moment within a long trajectory of different forms of market expansion and nation-state adventurism.
- Second, to explicate the institutional architecture of economic globalization, and to explain how it simultaneously supports and hampers the political ambitions of the United States, we offer analyses of the rise of multinational corporations (MNCs); the

agencies charged with overseeing the economic aspects of globalization, including the International Monetary Fund, World Bank,
and World Trade Organization; and the U.S.-led regional and bilateral agreements meant to sidestep and sometimes to supplement these international bodies, including the North America
Free Trade Agreement (NAFTA), the Central America Free
Trade Agreement, the proposed Free Trade Area of the Americas,
and other pending free trade agreements (FTAs) with Middle
Eastern states.

- Third, having established the broad historical contours and specific institutional parameters of globalization, we examine four of
its difficulties, focusing on:

  (1) Tensions between the border-crossing freedoms of transnational capital and geographically rooted consumers, workers, and states. We characterize this as the dilemma of spa-
  tially fixed human needs and national boundaries clashing
  with mobile economic opportunities.

  (2) Tensions between the needs of developing nations for economic growth and the damage this wreaks on U.S.-based
  workers and the U.S. trade deficit, which, as it escalates,
  hampers developing world growth. This is the dilemma of
  the United States becoming a postindustrial nation that exports jobs and imports products, thus both driving and, para-
  doxically, hindering global development.

  (3) Tensions between the enabling rhetoric of liberalizing free
  markets and the fact that what economists call "hot money"
  or "vulture funds" actually destroy developing nations. This
  is the dilemma of unregulated financial practices, which produce profit without making goods, thus exacerbating developing world debt while enriching first-world elites.

  (4) Tensions between promises of liberatory technological revolu-
  tions and the persistence of stifling industrial barbarism. This
  is the dilemma of horrible nineteenth-century labor practices
  thriving in the shadow of twenty-first-century innovations.

Our task is to address the broad contours of globalization and to suggest how the tensions outlined above produce political and economic
problems, leading not to healthy democracies but violent responses, not
to economic opportunities but a new age of exploitation, not to re-

newed internationalism but invigorated empire. Indeed, Walden Bello and Aileen Kwa have argued that "the Bush administration has supplanted the globalist political-economy of the Clinton period with a unilateralist, nationalist political-economy that intends to shore up the global dominance of the U.S. corporate elite" and an "aggressive military policy that is meant to ensure the military supremacy of the U.S." Our comments in chapter 2 confirmed the latter claim via rhetorical analyses of the *NSSUS* and President Bush's related speeches. Our task in this chapter, beginning with Bello and Kwa's assertion yet hoping to add historical depth and theoretical flexibility to it, is to make sense of the economic intricacies of globalization, to examine the claims of those who support and critique it, to observe the many ways violence circulates throughout these questions, and to locate each of these questions as part of the broad historical and cultural milieu fueling the United States' pursuit of empire.[9]

Globalization's Histories

We begin our discussion of the competing histories and theories of globalization by turning to William Greider's *One World, Ready or Not*, where he describes a wonderful yet vicious machine running out of control, smashing across the land in a frenzied whirl: "Think of this awesome machine running over open terrain and ignoring familiar boundaries. It plows across fields and fencerows with a fierce momentum that is exhilarating to behold and also frightening. As it goes, the machine throws off enormous mows of wealth and bounty while it leaves behind great furrows of wreckage. Now imagine that there are skillful hands on board, but no one is at the wheel. . . . And it is accelerating." This passage is representative of much of the literature on globalization because it foregrounds three tensions: first, between the familiar spatial enclosures of borders and territoriality ("fields and fencerows") and the transspatial flights of capital and culture that mark globalization; second, between the fact that globalization is the product of human actions ("skillful hands") yet is widely experienced as if it were a machine with a will of its own; and third, between the fact that globalization creates astronomic wealth for the lucky few while leaving "great furrows of wreckage" for the many.[10]

Two key questions lurk behind these metaphorically expressed tensions. First, given the sense of velocity and destruction implied in the passage, what is the role of violence in generating and/or resisting this scenario? Second, given the ways the passage problematizes any sense of control or agency, who or what is at the wheel of this machine? Our comments in this first section strive to situate these three tensions and their overarching concerns about violence and agency within a historical framework, hence offering readers a sense of the complicated historical developments that have led to our current moment of globalization.

Globalization and the Tension between States and Capital, with the Invasion of Iraq as a Case Study

The first broad historical point suggested by Greider's metaphor regards the tension between the spatial enclosures of states and the transnational flights of capital and culture. Although this tension has certainly accelerated in recent years with new developments in the technologies of communication and distribution, and although the collapse of Communism has opened vast new territories to the spread of capitalism, the historical fact is that capitalists have always struggled to realize profitability regardless of national allegiances or territorial boundaries. In this sense, globalization may amount to little more than a buzzword for the inherently expansive energies of capitalism. Nonetheless, the different stages of these expansive powers need to be studied if we want to ground our current moment within its proper historical context.

For example, Malcolm Waters maps out five stages of globalization, each of which corresponds roughly to a new stage in capitalism, including "the germinal phase (Europe, 1400–1759)," "the incipient phase (Europe, 1750–1875)," "the take-off phase (1875–1925)," "the struggle-for-hegemony phase (1925–1969)," and "the uncertainty phase (1969–1992)." This last-mentioned stage has been called "late capitalism" by Ernest Mandel, "the society of the spectacle" by Guy Debord, and "postmodernity" by Fredric Jameson and his legion of followers. Waters (uncertainty phase), Mandel (late capitalism), Debord (spectacle), and Jameson (postmodernity) each strive to offer sophisticated portrayals of the situations they address, yet their arguments are each rooted to the same assumption driving Greider's metaphor: that capital always strives to break free from the landed boundaries of national allegiance, hence functioning as the wedge cracking open new lands, markets, and aspects of daily life to economic exploitation and eventual political domination.[11]

Indeed, Waters, Mandel, Debord, Jameson, and Greider all build their arguments on a tradition of thought addressing the relationships among capitalism and empire. For example, in the opening pages of *The Communist Manifesto* (1848), Karl Marx diagnosed the ever-expanding needs of capitalism in terms that haunt our present moment. "The need of a constantly expanding market for its products chases the bourgeoisie over the whole surface of the globe," Marx argued, professing that the global search for profit would force capitalists to "nestle everywhere, settle everywhere, establish connections everywhere." Globalizing capitalists would achieve this goal, Marx feared, by pursuing "the conquest of new markets" via the "enforced destruction" of folk customs, religious traditions, national boundaries, and other impediments to profit. One can hardly imagine a better description of the war on Iraq. As we discussed briefly in chapter 2 in our section on cultural destruction, and as we detail in chapter 4 in our materials regarding crony capitalism and the "reconstruction" of Iraq, the theft and/or destruction of literally every facet of Iraq's civil infrastructure means that U.S. corporations will reap hundreds of millions of dollars of profits from rebuilding Iraq for decades to come.[12]

We have examined the causes of the war in chapters 1 and 2, yet it is clear that regardless of why the war was fought, breaking Hussein's stranglehold on Iraq means the United States has conquered a nation and opened a new market of twenty-five million consumers, most of whom will depend on U.S.-made or U.S.-traded goods of an infinite variety in the near future. On the one hand, then, and just as Marx predicted, the military destruction of the existing regime and the subsequent conquest of new markets in Iraq have worked hand in hand in a wondrous manner: where once there were crippling sanctions, mass poverty, and thuggish authoritarianism, there is now—so the Bush administration would have us believe—a land of unfettered capitalist opportunity, beckoning adventurous empire builders to remake the blood-stained desert into a free market.

On the other hand, we know that the war on Iraq and its occupation have proven staggeringly expensive. So even while a handful of elite U.S. megaconstruction and military contractors have been enriched by both wartime and postwar reconstruction contracts, the U.S. Treasury has been devastated. Indeed, the war on Iraq illustrates how state-sanctioned political goals may be pursued even at the cost of broad capitalist interests and the health of the nation's economy. For example, the government's postwar estimate is that occupying Iraq will cost $3.9 billion per month; if projected over the anticipated five years of the occupation, that would leave the United States with a bill for roughly $234 billion. That's $234,000,000,000 of U.S. taxpayer money spent to supposedly stabilize a nation that posed no direct threat to U.S. national security and therefore did not need to be invaded. That five-year estimate is too low, however, for Andrew Natsios, the administrator of the United States Agency for International Development (USAID, the U.S. government agency responsible for overseeing many of the contracts for reconstructing Iraq), indicated in a 17 March 2004 speech before the Washington Foreign Press Center that rebuilding Iraq will more likely take until "the end of this decade." But even by then, Natsios admits, he expects not to see an established free nation and a functioning free market, but rather an Iraq "begin[ning] to show signs of being a functioning, parliamentary market economy and democratic political system." The fact that Natsios calls it a "parliamentary market economy" indicates yet again how Bush administration officials link the language of political systems (parliamentary) with economic systems (market economy), in this case conflating the two as if they were automatically the same thing, as if capitalism *is* democracy and democracy *is* capitalism.[13]

Whereas Natsios's comments illustrate both the slippage from economic to political terms and the uncertain duration yet astronomically costly nature of the U.S. presence in Iraq, other sources indicate that U.S. troops in Iraq are encountering a humanitarian disaster, amounting on some estimates to as many as sixteen million starving Iraqis who need food, water, shelter, and medical attention. Recognizing a prewar malnutrition rate for children of 23 percent, the United Nations asked member nations to donate $124 million for emergency humanitarian relief, yet responding to this crisis in even a minimal manner has been estimated to cost at least $10 billion. Along with humanitarian aid, the cost of reparations is stunning, for the United States, as the occupier of the nation, is legally obliged to address reparations claims from a wide array of parties. For a useful guideline on how much reparations will cost, consider the facts from the first Gulf War. For studying the environmental damage caused by that war, Iraq's neighbors (not including Turkey) were given $243 million. In other war-related payments, Israel was given $20 million; British companies received $23 million; Kuwait was paid $780 million— all told, over $43 billion has thus far been awarded as war reparations for the first Gulf War. It is still too early to know the full extent of war reparations costs for the most recent war on Iraq, but one estimate has put the figure at as much as $361 billion.[14]

It will take years, perhaps even decades, to document the total costs of the invasion of Iraq; nonetheless, the figures offered above suggest that a comprehensive, long-term rendering of the costs would point toward expenditures of as much as $675 billion. There has been some loose talk of covering these costs with money made from selling Iraqi oil, yet many observers believe that the only way the U.S. government can possibly pay such exorbitant bills is by siphoning funds from domestic programs and by mortgaging our collective future economic security by assuming giant loans. Writing in a blistering tone, the editors of the *Nation* warned that by embarking on this expensive venture, "Bush has signed a death warrant for many social welfare programs and damaged our society for years to come."[15]

This claim rings true, for notice that while the Bush administration is spending hundreds of billions of dollars first on destroying Iraq and now on rebuilding it, U.S. national parks receive an annual budget of $2 billion, the National Cancer Institute receives $5 billion, NASA receives $15 billion, and grade schools and high schools receive $34 billion—meaning that preserving our wildlife, advancing our medical and scientific research, and educating our young are all relegated to budgetary afterthoughts in comparison to the hundreds of billions of our tax dollars the Bush administration is pouring into Iraq. Indeed, the Coalition on Human Needs reports that President Bush's fiscal year 2005 budget will worsen already crushing social problems, including the fact that "more than 43 million [Americans] lack health insurance, 8.4 million are unemployed, 35 million are poor, and 3.5 million people, 1.35 million of whom are children, will likely experience homelessness this year." Hence illustrating the social costs of waging imperial wars, these figures demonstrate how invading Iraq has compromised what the U.S. Constitution refers to as the "general Welfare."[16]

We suspect that President Bush knows that most Americans would be appalled to learn that their neighbors were suffering because tax dollars were being diverted to Iraq, which explains why he has refused to address the real costs of the war and the occupation. A report released in March 2003 by the Council on Foreign Relations (CFR), written by such Republican luminaries as James Schlesinger, Thomas Pickering, and Jeanne Kirkpatrick, argued in a masterstroke of understatement that President

Bush has "failed to fully describe to Congress and the American people the magnitude of the resources required to meet the post-conflict needs" of Iraq. In its story on the CFR report, the *New York Times* noted that "the Bush administration was planning to put Iraqi soldiers to work and to pay the salaries of more than two million Iraqi civil servants to enable them to rebuild the country. . . . But officials declined to estimate how much such support would cost." Furthermore, the Congressional Budget Office (CBO) reported in March 2003 that the budget deficit of $300 billion (which had rocketed up to $427 billion by January 2005) *did not include any projected war costs,* meaning that the real cost of the war and the real extent of the deficit were both being hidden from the public. Republican Senator Chuck Hagel protested the administration's refusal to address these issues, complaining that the administration was providing the Senate Foreign Relations Committee with "No answers. . . . No answers. . . . No answers."[17]

A telling exchange regarding the cost of the war took place on 16 September 2002—three days before President Bush would submit to Congress the *NSSUS.* In that morning's *Wall Street Journal,* Lawrence Lindsey, head of the White House's National Economic Council, was quoted as projecting that a war in Iraq would cost between 1 percent and 2 percent of U.S. gross domestic product (GDP), thus amounting to anywhere between $100–200 billion. This was a safe estimate, for according to William Nordhaus, the Sterling Professor of Economics at Yale, the first Gulf War also cost roughly 1 percent of U.S. GDP, which in 2002 dollars would amount to $76.1 billion. Nordhaus's projections for the second war on Iraq indicated that it would cost, if fought under "favorable" conditions, $99 billion; if fought under "protracted and unfavorable" conditions, Nordhaus's estimate jumps to $1.9 trillion. Lindsey's estimate was therefore cautious and well within the bounds of past experience—he was simply reporting the facts.[18]

Nonetheless, despite their prudent nature, by 9:30 that very morning, while on Air Force One en route to a day of presidential events in Iowa, Deputy Press Secretary Scott McClellan sought to cast Lindsey's estimate as foolish. When asked to comment on the figure, McClellan said, "I think it's premature to speculate about any particular course of action," hence making an estimate about the cost of the war impossible. When pressed for a comment on the probable cost by a reporter, McClellan dodged the question again, saying, "Well, this is a national security issue.

Let's keep that in mind." An outraged reporter then asked, "Is the idea that you're just going to tell the American people what it's going to cost after the decision has been made? Do they not have a right to know as the debate is going on?" McClellan's stonewalling response to that question spoke volumes about the administration's policy regarding the likely cost of war in Iraq. Indeed, McClellan's attempt to squash Lindsey's estimate, in conjunction with the administration's ongoing silence on the topic, demonstrated that President Bush was committed to hiding the facts from both congressional oversight and the American people—in both cases subverting the public scrutiny that guarantees the legitimacy of the democratic process. The fact that this exchange took place three days before the *NSSUS* was sent to Congress makes the matter even more complicated, for it suggests that the Bush administration feared the *NSSUS*'s rhetorical thunder might be lost amid any debate about the astronomical cost of realizing its call for wars of preemption.[19]

This brief digression through the costs and cover-ups of the war on Iraq offers a crucial counterpoint to Marx's argument about the relationship between states and capital, territory and mobility. For whereas Marx predicted that capitalists would roam across the globe in the search for profit, acting even to the detriment of their home countries' economic and political goals, President Bush's handling of the war on Iraq offers a complicated twist to this theory. For on the one hand the war has enriched a handful of elite U.S. contractors, hence fueling a new round of globalizing capitalism, yet on the other hand the war has clearly created a budgetary crisis in the United States that will hamper future economic development and force subsequent administrations to cut social spending. So in the case of the war on Iraq, the nation's perceived political interests have trumped its economic interests.

Recalling Marx's dire—and 158-year-old—prediction in this regard helps demonstrate that much of what passes for new forms of globalization in fact amounts to little more than the latest stage in the history of the tension between the landed interests of states and capitalism's pursuit of profitability across space. In this sense, the histories of capitalism and empire are forever entwined. Ellen Meiksins Wood's *Empire of Capital* traces this relationship through global history, marking the subtle differences in economic policies within the Roman, Spanish, Arab Muslim, Venetian, Dutch, and British empires. For Wood, what makes the new U.S.-dominated stage of globalization unique is not only the United

States' unchallenged military supremacy but its reliance on the justifying rhetorics of free trade and democracy. For whereas previous empires explained their actions according to doctrines of self-defense or racial supremacy or state supremacy or progress itself, the new phase of U.S.-led globalization is based largely on the promise of spreading democracy and free markets. But as Wood observes, globalization in fact means "the opening of subordinate economies and their vulnerability to imperial capital, while the imperial economy remains sheltered as much as possible from the obverse effects. Globalization has nothing to do with free trade. On the contrary, it is about the careful control of trading conditions, in the interests of imperial capital."[20]

From Wood's historical perspective, then, the start of the twenty-first century feels strangely like the seventeenth, with capitalist elites and rival nation-states jockeying for control of resources, markets, and political authority, only now doing so in the name of free markets and democracy. Indeed, Wood seems to imply that our current stage of globalization is not so much a new form of balance between the space-hopping needs of capitalists and the territorial ambitions of states as simply *a new discursive arrangement,* a new means of justifying processes of dominating "subordinate economies" while protecting home markets. In short, contemporary globalization is as much a rhetorical as an economic phenomenon.

Although Wood's argument rebukes those who perceive globalization as a new phenomenon, we want to push forward from her historical claims to try to determine what makes the contemporary notion of globalization so compelling, so rhetorically powerful. We therefore turn to David Harvey's *The New Imperialism,* which analyzes the ways globalization stands as both a deeply historical and contemporary question. Like Wood, Harvey argues that whereas the power of states is always based in large part on their control of "territorialized space" and geographically rooted electors, "the capitalist operates in continuous space and time." For Harvey, then, "the fundamental point is to see the territorial and the capitalist logics of power as distinct from each other. Yet it is also undeniable that the two logics intertwine in complex and sometimes contradictory ways." For example, since the end of World War II the United States has imbricated its state needs and the needs of its capitalist elites via "means of imperial domination that nominally respected the independence of [some] countries yet dominated them through some mix of privileged trade relations, patronage, clientelism, and covert coercion."

Rather than engaging in outright colonialism, then, in actually setting up U.S. troops and administrators as occupying forces in foreign lands, Harvey suggests that post–World War II U.S. foreign policy has sought to balance the appearance of respecting indigenous sovereignty with unfettered access to local markets and goods.[21]

Chalmers Johnson reminds us, however, that in many cases, including most notably Japan and South Korea, the "most effective nonmilitary policies" of post–World War II U.S. international relations hinged on "trading access to our markets for East Asian toleration of the indefinite billeting of our soldiers, aircraft, and ships in their countries." In Harvey's model, states and capitalist elites strive to balance their mutual needs; in Johnson's model there are certain national security imperatives (or obsessions), in this case maintaining military bases with which to contain Communism (and in our case waging war on Iraq), that override the long-term economic interests of capitalists. For Wood, Harvey, and Johnson, the tension between state-protected territoriality and the space-transcending needs of capitalists therefore exist in historically inflected tension, hence demonstrating that the new dynamics of globalization are, at least in this regard, simply the latest round of developments in a very old dynamic.[22]

The *New* in Harvey's *New Imperialism* suggests, however, that our current stage of globalization has produced some unprecedented conditions. For Harvey, the *New* may be summarized simply as the reflection of the United States' post–cold war international supremacy, where any semblance of delicate international politicking has given way to unchallenged U.S. dominance in two key categories. First, whereas the cold war forced the United States to at least appear to honor the wishes of its NATO partners and to seek mutual alliances with states committed to containing the Soviet Union, the collapse of Communism has enabled the United States to pursue its political goals free from any threat of rival superpower retaliation or any constraints imposed by allies. Second, whereas globalizing capital might once have clashed with perceived U.S. security interests—say in seeking profits in the Soviet Union, or China, or Egypt, or India, or any number of states that at some point during the cold war were ostensibly off limits to U.S firms—the collapse of Communism has opened the entire globe to new rounds of capitalist activity.

The combination of these two factors, leaving the U.S. free to pursue its political goals without rivals and its economic goals without opposition, means that prior tensions between state security and capitalist profits, between entrenched territoriality and fluid capital, have been reduced dramatically. This is significant for Harvey because it means that the territorial ambitions of the state and the profit ambitions of capital now appear almost synonymous. Harvey thus calls our moment one of "globalization through Americanization," meaning that each new foreign market that is opened up to U.S. interests amounts at the same time to a new beachhead of U.S. political, economic, and cultural power.[23]

Wood takes this point further, arguing that our new stage of globalization is based largely on the increased significance of state support for capitalist investment. For example, late-fifteenth-century Spanish conquistadores engaged in capitalist endeavors that eventually led to the imposition of formal colonization; early seventeenth-century Dutch merchants roamed widely, exceeding the formal reach of the Dutch state; in both cases profit-seeking capitalists were the initial wedge of empire, opening markets first before the state sought to formalize market dominance as political and military dominance. In contrast, the Roman Empire waged war first, only engaging in long-term economic development after a territory had been conquered. The situations in Afghanistan and Iraq appear close to this latter model, for in both nations U.S. military forces preceded economic forces, thus suggesting that the new U.S. empire resonates more closely with the Roman than the Dutch or Spanish empires. Indeed, focusing on the "indispensable" power of the state to create new opportunities for capitalist profit, Wood argues that "no other institution, no transnational agency, has even begun to replace the nation state as an administrative, and coercive guarantor of social order, property relations, stability or contractual predictability." This confusion—or perhaps conflation—of the state's military power and capitalist elites' economic power perhaps explains why Iraqi and Afghani insurgents make little distinction between civilian and military personnel, for the difference is irrelevant to them because both modes of power are U.S. power, both styles of intervention support "globalization through Americanization."[24]

Although the tension between territory-transcending capital and border-defending states is therefore ancient, we will conclude this section of our analysis by suggesting that our current stage of globalization amounts to a dangerous fusing of these interests, with U.S. state adventurism and U.S.-led or U.S.-friendly corporations working more than ever in conjunction, amounting in a worst-case scenario to an imperial juggernaut. We should remember, however, that previous eras have felt similar fears. For example, Hobsbawm notes in *The Age of Empire* that the late nineteenth century witnessed "a growing convergence between politics and economics," meaning that "the economic motive for acquiring some colonial territory becomes difficult to disentangle from the political action required for the purpose." Indeed, the sheer historical familiarity of this fusion underlies Greider's offering the specter of fascism as one possible result of our current moment. The fact that our current moment speaks to Hobsbawm's nineteenth century and Greider's twentieth century may well indicate that twenty-first-century globalization is based on amplifications of prior crises, where economic instabilities led capitalist elites to forego free markets in favor of heavy—and heavily armed—state intervention.[25]

Indeed, we argue that increasing market and political instabilities since the mid-1960s have taught the United States to rely increasingly on its military supremacy to intervene in situations that once might have been viewed as opportunities to exercise legitimacy-enhancing political diplomacy or market-building economic negotiations. Harvey observes, however, that "whenever there was a conflict between democracy, on the one hand, and order and stability built upon propertied interests, on the other, the U.S. opted for the latter." Citing the cases of U.S. military operations in the Dominican Republic, Brazil, and Chile, and citing U.S. military support for dictatorial regimes that did business with U.S.-based MNCs, including Argentina, Saudi Arabia, Iran, and Indonesia, Harvey argues that the United States has become increasingly willing to see its state interests and the interests of its capitalist elites as coterminous, thus devaluing a sense of international cooperation and truly free markets in favor of an activist state that does not shy away from using its military to support the interests of its capitalist elites.[26]

The problem is that this transformation demonstrates to the world that the United States is not interested in leading by positive example, instead resorting to actions that look increasingly like empire building. But as the United States acts more and more like an empire, then the rest of the world loses incentive to engage it as anything other than a threat, hence producing a sense of both political and economic wariness that damages international relations and leaves the United States more likely to act unilaterally. As Harvey concludes, "If [U.S.] hegemony weakens, then the danger exists for a turn to far more coercive tactics." Our fear, then, is that our current moment of globalization may signal a new stage in the long process of balancing state interests and capitalist interests, one where the United States, faced with increasing economic competition and political complications, fuses its responses to the two in a capitalist empire that wages preemptive wars.[27]

Globalization-as-Machine:
The Spectacular World of Commodity Fetishism

The second broad historical point suggested by Greider's metaphor of a monstrous and miraculous machine running out of control is that each new stage of economic development produces its own forms of oppression and mystification. The agrarian production of feudalism, for example, was based on tightly controlled local markets, the forced impoverishment of peasants, and the supposedly God-granted privileges of landed aristocrats. Seventeenth-century mercantilism controlled burgeoning international markets of exchange under the rubric of the emerging discourses of human and property rights. For while Fernand Braudel has argued in *The Wheels of Commerce* that "mercantilism was none other than the insistent, egoistic and vehement forward thrust of the modern state," Wood has demonstrated that this thrust was couched in terms, coined originally by Hugo Grotius in the early seventeenth century, justifying the individual's and state's rights to "appropriate territory" from those who were not cultivating it to its full market potential. Eighteenth-century economic development was fueled largely in the then globe-straddling British colonies by slavery and indentured servitude, with imperial actions justified in the name of science, reason, modernity, and racial supremacy. Nineteenth-century industrialism created new ways to harness technology, to exploit human labor, to produce weapons, and to justify an age of colonialism under the banner of modernization and ongoing racial supremacy. These are of course suggestive rather than comprehensive categories, each of which carries its own complexities and contradictions, yet they demonstrate that as the economic means of production change and as the political needs of states evolve, so the claims used to legitimize these transformations are adjusted. Given this premise, it will be instructive to try to unravel what is actually new about our current age of globalization at the level of economic or political fact and what is new at the level of rhetorical justification.[28]

Let us return, then, to Greider's claim that the "awesome machine" of globalization has "skillful hands on board, but no one is at the wheel." This image raises the question of control: who or what drives this machine? For that matter, who built it, who fuels it, and who maintains it? To address these questions about the waning sense of agency under rapidly changing systems of capitalist production, we turn to a suggestive passage from Karl Marx's 1867 *Capital,* where he offered this definition of the "fetishism of commodities": "It is nothing but the definite social relation between men themselves which assumes here, for them, the fantastic form of a relation between things. In order, therefore, to find an analogy we must take flight into the misty realm of religion. There the products of the human brain appear as autonomous figures with a life of their own. . . . So it is in the world of commodities with the products of men's hands." Marx thus argues that commodities, the physical embodiment of human labor, tend to be perceived as things with a life of their own, as if they dropped from the sky. By obscuring the labor relations that constitute the commodity—just like hiding the human hands behind the supposedly godly wisdom of the Bible, just like the *NSSUS's* version of evangelical capitalism as free markets without economics—this process of fetishism masks the violence inherent in capitalism. For Marx, then, the task of critical thinking was to restore to every object or relationship its hidden labor and violence, thus demystifying the fetishism of commodities by analyzing them as repositories of political, economic, and cultural power.[29]

Greider's metaphor points directly to Marx's critique of the fetishism of commodities, for it clearly implies that the machine—a product of human choices, of human labor, of human intentions—has assumed a life of its own, roaring across fields like a tornado, like a force of nature beyond control. It is therefore useful to think of our current moment of globalization as representing a new stage of commodity fetishism, where the global market has become so complicated that it appears to be a self-motivated machine, even while we know that it is the product of human choices. In this sense, Greider's metaphor demonstrates a new stage of global activity in which any sense of control is impossible. Put differently, Greider's metaphor suggests a stage of history where commodity fetishism has reached unprecedented levels, where the ability to locate human actions and their attendant violence has disappeared into a massive, incomprehensible swirl of commodities and confusion.

We saw above how Waters calls this historical stage the "uncertainty phase" of capitalism, with Mandel calling it "late capitalism" and Jameson calling it "postmodernity." Guy Debord called this precarious situation the "society of the spectacle," arguing in 1967 that "it is doubtless impossible to contrast the pseudo-need imposed by the reign of modern consumerism with any authentic need or desire that is not itself equally determined by society and its history. . . . The commodity's mechanical accumulation unleashes a *limitless artificiality*. . . . The cumulative power of this autonomous realm of artifice necessarily everywhere entails a *falsification of life*."[30]

Thereby anticipating Greider's metaphor, Debord places the mechanical at the heart of his argument, suggesting that the technologies of both production and consumerism have reached a stage where organic, authentic needs cannot be distinguished from needs taught by markets. Even if we question the efficacy of this nostalgic notion of the unsullied authentic, and even if we foreground the fact that DeBord's claim is now almost forty years old, his characterization of our world as awash in limitless artificiality and falsification strikes a resonant chord. Indeed, as numerous observers have noted, one of the functions of modern capitalism is to produce needs, to inculcate endless desires for endless goods. When spread across the globe, "everywhere" as Debord calls it, globalizing capitalism amounts to an increasingly all-encompassing society of the spectacle, where commodity fetishism becomes not only an economic phenomenon but a way of life, "a world view transformed into an objective force." Because this objective force is committed not to satisfying basic human needs but to creating consumerist fantasies, and because the economic relations needed to make this scenario possible produce resentment among those whose labor is exploited and resistance by those who cling to a sense of cultural autonomy, Debord warns that the society of the spectacle must be based on "permanent violence."[31]

The U.S.-run Coalition Provisional Authority in Iraq made many of these theoretical claims concrete in its remarkable pamphlet, *Trade and Foreign Investment Opportunities in Iraq*. For although the CPA's rule in Iraq was based on the firepower of the U.S. military, the CPA was also deeply concerned with seducing Iraq into the society of the spectacle. That is, if the rule of the United States and its chosen Iraqi allies is to ever appear legitimate, as anything other than an occupation, then the hard power of the military must be replaced by the soft power of the society of the spectacle. In fact, like many scholars and critics of the society of the spectacle, the CPA understood that its necessary production of what Debord called "limitless artificiality" depended largely on television.

It is therefore revelatory to find that the CPA's advertising pamphlet, intended to lure MNCs to the reconstruction effort in Iraq, places on its second page a graph demonstrating the lack of televisions in Iraq and the Middle East. According to a 2000 study by the Annenberg Public Policy Center, 57 percent of U.S. children between the ages of eight and sixteen had televisions in their bedrooms. The study found that children from low-income households are more likely to have televisions in their bedrooms than children from wealthy homes; that on average children spend 6.5 hours *a day* interacting with some form of screen media; and that the average American family owns 2.5 television sets. Seduction into the commodity fetishism driving the society of the spectacle is thus largely accomplished by television. Bringing more TVs to the Middle East appears in this context as nothing short of a national security imperative, for in the CPA's graph Oman is shown to possess roughly six hundred TVs for every one thousand people; Bahrain and Kuwait are near four hundred; Turkey is around three hundred, and Saudi Arabia is around two hundred; but Jordan, Iraq, and Iran all lag beneath one hundred. The graph demonstrates that those states that are either oil rich (Oman, Bahrain, Kuwait, Saudi Arabia), and/or U.S. allies (Bahrain, Kuwait, Saudi Arabia), and/or NATO partners (Turkey) have more TVs than the region's two chief troublemakers (Iraq and Iran) and one of its badly lagging monarchies (Jordan). Without making this argument explicitly, the graph assumes that states on the road either to development or democracy possess TVs and that possession of them—like McDonald's for Friedman—is a marker of civilizing modernity, of a state's entrance to the global economy of images, of its integration into the society of the spectacle.[32]

Next to the graph is a photograph of a store in downtown Baghdad, complete with a large Siemens sign; beneath this image the CPA announces that Iraqis possess "strong pent-up demand for products forbidden or unattainable under the former regime," including "satellite dishes, electronic equipment, phones, internet services." The implication is clear: like Siemens, U.S.-based MNCs should do the patriotic work of enabling previously shackled Iraqi consumer desires to erupt into the society of the spectacle by raising Iraq's TVs-per-person ratio. The brochure says nothing of establishing democracy; rather, it entices corporations to come to the desert to participate in the twenty-first century's first great business bonanza: turning Iraq into the newest outpost of the society of the spectacle.[33]

We should be careful, however, not to jump too quickly to the conclusion that our current moment of globalization, which relies so heavily on the fetishism of commodities and the society of the spectacle, is that dramatically different from or more violent than prior historical moments. For the sheer fact that Marx flagged this problem in 1867 indicates that the dilemma of disentangling individual needs from the market's mass-produced needs is as old as industrial capitalism. In fact, the larger cultural questions raised by this notion of the fetishism of commodities were addressed in eloquent detail by Ralph Waldo Emerson in his 31 August 1837 lecture before Harvard's Phi Beta Kappa Society. Titled "The American Scholar," Emerson lamented the fact that the "One Man" of old, the individual organically linked to a larger, holistic community, "has been so distributed to multitudes, has been so minutely subdivided and peddled óut, that it is spilled into drops, and cannot be gathered. The state of society is one in which the members have suffered amputation from the trunk, and strut about so many walking monsters,—a good finger, a neck, a stomach, an elbow, but never a man." Hence, "man is metamorphosed into a thing" by modernity's alienating divisions of labor, its nascent Industrial Revolution, and its merciless attack on existing social orders.[34]

It would still be another eleven years before Marx would argue in *The Communist Manifesto* that "owing to the extensive use of machinery and to division of labor, the work of the proletarians has lost all individual character. . . . He becomes an appendage of the machine." In a passage that sounds like he was cribbing from Emerson's "American Scholar," Marx then warns that modernity's transformations in labor practices, notions of the self, and community culture amount for the disempowered laborer to "a mere training to act as a machine." These are terrifying images in which the rapidly modernizing countrysides of both Emerson's America and Marx's Europe are littered with "so many walking monsters" violently ripped from their once-bucolic worlds and thrust into the mechanized alienation of modern capitalism. Emerson and Marx thus diagnosed in 1837 and 1848 respectively a scenario that haunts Lee's 2004 letter to the WTO.[35]

Indeed, for our purposes it is historically important to note that many of the fears raised today about twenty-first-century globalization are central to Emerson's and Marx's nineteenth-century concerns. Both periods feature grave debates about the compromising of human choice and dignity in a world increasingly besieged by mass-produced products, the cultural confusions that arise in cities that are expanding at exponential rates due to emigrating strangers from faraway places, and the unsettling intrusions of factory life that slowly but surely erode centuries-old work habits and life patterns. Both Emerson and Marx recognized that modernity was realigning political orders, changing work habits, transforming notions of space and time, and therefore shattering old notions of community and self. Both men saw these transformations as opportunities, as occasions for leaping boldly into the future, but also as catastrophes, as the enforced destruction of established ways of being in the world. And both men, Emerson watching the nascent U.S. empire stretch westward, Marx watching nationalism rip Europe into war after war, understood that the confusions and complications caused by new stages of capitalism both surfaced in and sometimes caused shockwaves in nation-states.

What makes the CPA's advertising brochure so chilling, then, is not its promotion of empire via the society of the spectacle—for this has been at the heart of capitalism since the days of Emerson and Marx, simply taking new forms with each new wave of technological progress and cultural fashion—but its inability to see the current moment as anything other than an "investment opportunity in Iraq," as anything other than an opportunity to push TVs and related electronic goods on starving Iraqis. As Debord warned, "The [society of the] spectacle manifests itself as an enormous positivity, out of reach and beyond dispute." The CPA's brochure confirms this thesis, demonstrating that the reconstruction of Iraq will not be a nuanced process of thinking about the needs and values of that shattered nation but a crass rush toward enforced yet cheerful participation in the society of the spectacle. Indeed, the "enormous positivity" expressed in the CPA's banal brochure indicates that the goal of postwar reconstruction in Iraq has less to do with empowering citizens to engage in democracy than numbing them—like so many good Americans—into televisual oblivion.[36]

Globalization as Mass-Produced Poverty:
The History of Accelerating Wealth Gaps

The third broad historical point suggested by Greider's metaphor regards the ways globalization produces astronomical wealth for the few and crippling poverty for the many, thus creating an unprecedented wealth gap. Waters argues in *Globalization* that the rich-to-poor ratio for "income per head" achieved historically unmatched levels over the past decades, for whereas "the rich-to-poor income ratio was about 2:1 in 1800, by 1945 it was 20:1, by 1975 it was 40:1, and by 1990 it was 64:1." These startling figures, which we have found difficult to corroborate, demonstrate that the growth of income inequality follows the slow march of modernity. Indeed, beginning roughly with the early stages of the Industrial Revolution, these figures indicate the structural ways that modern capitalism has learned to produce wealth for the few by exploiting the labor of the many. We should remember, then, that vast wealth gaps are not new. For example, Hobsbawm reminds us in *The Age of Revolution* that the laboring poor of mid-nineteenth-century England experienced industrial capitalism as "a social catastrophe they did not understand," as a "social and economic cataclysm." And the cataclysm was spreading, as Hobsbawm notes in *The Age of Empire* that "between 1750 and 1800 the *per capita* gross national product in what are today known as the 'developed countries' was substantially the same as in what is now known as the 'Third World.' . . . But in the nineteenth century the gap between the western countries . . . and the rest widened. . . . By 1880 the per capita income in the 'developed' world was about double that in the 'Third World,' [and] by 1913 it was to be over three times as high, and widening."[37]

These preliminary comments suggest two findings. First, over the past two centuries the world's already wealthy have multiplied the income differences between themselves and the world's poor—*meaning there has been an accelerating domestic wealth gap between elites and masses within all states.* Second, modernization in Europe and the United States has progressively widened the wealth gap between "developed" and "developing" states—*meaning there has been an accelerating international wealth gap be-*

tween northern and southern states. Our current moment of globalization is therefore but the extension of these two foundational economic processes, and hence the logical outcome of modernity's production of *an increased domestic wealth gap* and *an increased international wealth gap.*

Moreover, some observers—including Harvey and Wood, who were discussed above, and Joseph Stiglitz and Mike Davis, to whom we turn below—have argued that globalization at the opening of the twenty-first century is marked by an especially aggressive state that struggles, in the face of unstable global markets, to insure profitability to capitalist elites by orchestrating policies that lead to increased global poverty. Yet Braudel reminds us that from as early as the sixteenth century, "the state was there to preserve inequality, the cornerstone of the social order. Culture and its spokesmen were generally on hand to preach resignation to one's lot, obedience and good behavior, and the obligation to render unto Caesar that which was Caesar's." Put simply, Braudel argues that the chief function of states since the sixteenth century has been to appropriate wealth for ruling classes. Joseph Stiglitz's *Globalization and Its Discontents* makes it clear, however, that although neither poverty nor states enforcing it are new phenomena, the sheer scale of global poverty has reached unprecedented levels. In fact, Stiglitz argues that "despite repeated promises of poverty reduction made over the last decade of the twentieth century, the actual number of people living in poverty has actually increased by almost 100 million." Thus linking Stiglitz's arguments with Greider's, we argue that the production of poverty, one of the chief effects of U.S.-led neoliberal globalization, "is accelerating."[38]

In fact, Benjamin Friedman notes in the *New York Review of Books* that "of the fifty countries where per capita incomes were lowest in 1990 . . . twenty-three had lower average incomes in 1999 than they did in 1990." Friedman thus proposes that the so-called developing nations would more accurately be called "the non-developing economies." He notes, for example, that "in Uganda, or Ethiopia, or Malawi, neither men nor women can expect to live even to the age of forty-five. . . . In Sierra Leone 28 percent of all children die before reaching their fifth birthday. . . . In India more than half of all children are malnourished. . . . In Bangladesh just half of the adult men, and fewer than one fourth of adult women, can read and write." The crucial question is whether the past decades of globalizing neoliberalism have inflated these problems or reduced them. For B. Friedman, Stiglitz, Harvey, Greider, Davis, and many of the other scholars, journalists, historians, and activists cited herein the answer is a qualified yes: globalization has, in tandem with complicated local factors, fueled increases in poverty.[39]

But as each of these commentators agrees, figuring out the relationships between globalization and poverty is complicated. For example, in *One World: The Ethics of Globalization,* Peter Singer addresses the question of whether income inequality is increasing and whether, if so, it is related directly to globalization. He concludes that the charge that inequality has deepened because of globalization not only lacks factual concreteness but serves as a red herring, deflecting debate from the local causes of poverty toward abstract questions about global ethics and fairness. For Singer, then, the question is not about globalization but about the ways local elites, local economies, and local cultures experience both wealth and poverty. Singer therefore argues that "the more important issue about the opening up of world trade may be whether it has made the world's poor worse off than they would have otherwise been, not relative to the rich, but in absolute terms."[40]

A group of economists from Columbia University have devoted themselves to this question of measuring poverty in "absolute" versus "relative" terms. In a working paper for the National Bureau of Economic Research, Xavier Sala-i-Martin argues that under his model "global inequality . . . has fallen substantially over the last twenty years." He argues that the number of poor people has decreased by three hundred million to five hundred million since the 1970s, for although economists have calculated increasing disparities between rich and poor on a global average, he explains that "most of the global inequality in the world comes from the fact that the average American income is . . . much larger than the average Senegalese." So although the poor in developing nations may be *relatively poorer* compared to citizens of G-8 states, they are *not absolutely poorer,* for their living standards have been rising in terms of local norms. Economic growth in China and India alone means that hundreds of millions of people who are relatively poor compared to global elites are less poor in absolute terms within their home states. Sala-i-Martin acknowledges, however, that continued economic stagnation and even decline in Africa, especially because of AIDS, threatens this trend.[41]

Understanding the links between poverty and globalization is therefore remarkably complicated. Branko Milanovic, a World Bank associate committed to finding ways to measure local and even household poverty against macroeconomic factors, admits that "our measurement tools are rather blunt." Milanovic's confession is confusing, however, for the World Bank relies on hundreds of "Development Indicators," separated by region and category, including such groupings as: people (life expectancy, mortality rates, literacy, malnutrition, AIDS/HIV prevalence); environment (water access, deforestation, energy use, CO_2 emissions, sanitation); economics (income, GDP per capita, purchasing power parity—which is adjusted for local economies, exports in goods and services); states and markets (military expenditures, research and development, telephones, personal computers, paved roads, high-tech exports); and global links (trade, private capital, debt, foreign direct investment, aid, and tourism). Adding another layer of complexity to this picture, the bank's 2004 *World Development Report* (*WDR*) focuses on services and demonstrates that although the number of people living in abject poverty—which it measures as living on less than $1 a day, adjusted for local economies—has decreased, local social services, including education, health care, and public access to clean water, are increasingly failing. So whereas incomes may be rising in absolute terms, the *WDR* suggests that *quality of life* may be falling.[42]

For confirmation of that thesis we turn to Mike Davis's stunning 2004 essay, "Planet of Slums," where he examines the global production of massive slum populations. Davis addresses the rise of megacities such as Tokyo, Moscow, and Mexico City, noting that by 2025 sprawling giants like Jakarta, Dhaka, Karachi, and Bombay are estimated to house between twenty-five million to thirty-three million people. Because of the ways "silicon capitalism delinks the growth of production from employment"—hence the revealing *New York Times* headline for 6 May 2004: "Low-Tech or High, Jobs Are Scarce in India's Boom"—and because of the ravaging of developing nation agricultural communities at the hands of subsidy-aided U.S. and EU products, these megacities are now and will increasingly be home to megaslums, teeming with recently unemployed workers victimized by downsizing, with farmers and peasants chased from their land, with the hungry and the resentful, the dirty and the starving.[43]

Thus offering strong humanistic counterevidence to Sala-i-Martin's statistical attempt to claim that increased wages have pulled millions out of poverty globally, Davis argues that slums already house "78.2% of the urban population of the least developed countries and fully a third of the global urban population." Like Harvey, Davis sees this production of slums as one result of a decade's worth of IMF-imposed neoliberalism, leading to what he calls "the equivalent of a great natural disaster." Regardless of whether one uses relative or absolute terms of economic measurement, then, these slums stand as a sickening testament to the production of global poverty. In Latin America, for example, Davis observes that "in Buenos Aires, the richest decile's share of income increased from 10 times that of the poorest in 1984 to 23 times in 1989. In Lima, where the value of the minimum wage fell by 83 percent during the IMF recession, the percentage of households living below the poverty threshold increased from 17 percent in 1985 to 44 percent in 1990. In Rio de Janeiro, inequality as measured in the classical Gini coefficients soared. . . . Throughout Latin America, the 1980s deepened the canyons and elevated the peaks of the world's most extreme social topography." Although growth in China and India may partially skew the statistical picture of global economic trends, Davis concludes that over the past two decades globalizing neoliberalism has in fact created "a mass pauperization almost without precedent in history."[44]

Davis's scathing arguments are supported by the UN's *HDR*, which moves beyond simply measuring income to inquire about "building human capabilities" and "the range of things that people can do or be." For example, whereas Sala-i-Martin and his Columbia colleagues argue that absolute poverty levels are dropping, the *HDR* also factors in these chilling figures: "Since 1990 an estimated 220,000 people have died in wars between states—compared with nearly 3.6 million in wars within states"; "civilians have accounted for more than 90% of the casualties—either killed or injured—in post–Cold War conflicts"; and "at the end of 2000 more than 12 million people were refugees, 6 million were internally displaced and nearly 4 million were returning refugees"—leaving roughly 25.8 million people either dead or displaced by war since 1990. Even while granting the mathematical accuracy of Sala-i-Martin's claim that absolute poverty within states is decreasing slightly, the more broadly construed factors offered above by Davis and the UN make it clear that the recent history of globalization has produced declining "human capabilities."[45]

In fact, given the ubiquity of globe-straddling communications technologies, which make the wealth of Hollywood superstars feel as real to street sweepers in Hyderabad as if it was next door, relative wealth differences increasingly affect what the UN calls human development. And the *HDR* is clear that relative wealth differences across nations are expanding, claiming unequivocally that "the world has become more unequal. Between 1970 and 1990 the world was more unequal than at any time before 1950." No knee-jerk liberal conclusion based on soft observational evidence, the claim rests on the UN's calculating life expectancy, educational opportunities, and standard of living, and then factoring these against its Human Poverty Index (HPI), Gender-Related Development Index (GDI), Gender Empowerment Measure (GEM), Human Freedom Index (HFI), and Political Freedom Index (PFI).[46]

Despite the dizzying complexity of these questions, and bracketing for the moment the question of how they relate to globalization, it is clear that global poverty persists at shocking levels. Moreover, as our closing comments in our "Speech Kills" epilogue to chapter 1 indicate, the prevalence of global poverty is enabled if not fueled by the military choices of the United States. Indeed, we observed above how health experts estimate that $10 billion per year would enable developing nations to provide clean drinking water to their populations, thus decreasing sickness and in turn increasing productivity and happiness, yet the United States is instead spending billions of dollars per month waging war in Iraq. In short, the United States has chosen to invest in war rather than water.

Thus, although trying to pinpoint the causal relationships between globalization, accelerating wealth gaps, and declining living standards is difficult, there can be little doubt that the military and economic strategies of the U.S. empire exacerbate the problem. Nonetheless, collapsing globalization into the United States is a mistake, for we demonstrate below that the most important institutions supporting economic globalization do not simply do the United States' bidding; rather, they constitute a complicated web of competing hopes and practices, some of which support U.S. interests but many of which leave the United States in an increasingly tenuous position regarding both economic growth and political power.

Institutions of Globalization

Thus far we have demonstrated how our current moment of globalization stands as the culmination of economic, political, and cultural processes that are as old as modernity itself. Given this historical grounding, it is nonetheless important to analyze *if* and *how* our contemporary stage of globalization demonstrates new factors, new forms of power and privilege, commerce and communication, development and destruction, that distinguish it from prior modes of international capitalism. Whereas we have shown above that capitalists have always sought profit in faraway places, that states have always sought to balance their landed security needs with their economic interests in supporting globe-trotting elites, that commodity fetishism has been producing alienation, confusion, and violence since at least the late 1830s, and that modernity has exacerbated both domestic and international wealth gaps, it seems to us that the global economy has indeed entered *a new phase of both integration and competition,* where political, cultural, and economic powers are increasingly managed not by warring capitalists or rival states but by colossal new institutions that sometimes transcend states, that sometimes support the interests of states, and that frequently compete against each other.

The integration thesis has become very popular in recent years; as Prime Minister Tony Blair put it in a triumphant, postwar speech before the U.S. Congress in July 2003, "we are bound together as never before." To explicate the institutional architecture of this new phase of global integration, we offer analyses of the rise of MNCs and the agencies charged with overseeing globalization, including the IMF, World Bank, and WTO. However, because this institutional architecture of economic globalization and integration appears to be slowly but surely diffusing U.S. power, both the Clinton and Bush administrations have pursued a series of geographically specific and politically laden trade agreements, including NAFTA, CAFTA, and FTAA. We argue that these regional and bilateral FTAs amount to attempts to counter the effects of globalization by bolstering localized versions of U.S. power and privilege, even while trumpeting the rhetoric of free trade.[47]

Analyzing these institutions of globalization and regional FTAs will enable us to demonstrate how our current moment of globalization depends on increasingly powerful networks of institutions that manage— and sometimes compete over—the flows of international capital and political power, often exercising authority against the wishes of local governments and citizens alike. Indeed, the combination of this institutional architecture of globalization and regional FTAs poses serious threats to state sovereignty, worker rights, local cultures, and any sense of representative government.

Multinational and Transnational Corporations and the Extension of Traditional Powers

In the prior stages of globalization considered above, state political power and capitalist economic powers existed in constant tension, sometimes working together, sometimes butting heads, but generally working along independent, albeit related, paths of interest. Contemporary MNCs further complicate this relationship, for although they straddle many nations and many markets, their chief concern is always defending their own profit; MNCs therefore sometimes work hand in hand with developing nations against the best interests of the United States, they sometimes support U.S. interests against developing nations, they almost always exploit workers mercilessly, and they sometimes combine these actions in confusing ways. Whereas multinational corporations are understood as companies that engage in international business while still maintaining clear bonds to a home state, some observers have argued that transnational corporations (TNCs) are so global in their reach of operations and organizational structure that they are no longer rooted in any clear home. As Waters argues in *Globalization*, "One would be hard pressed to decide whether Unilever or Shell were Dutch or British, whether News Corporation was Australian, British, or American, whether ABB was Swedish or Swiss, whether Airbus was British, French, German, or Spanish," and so on in a dizzying list of TNCs that defy any clear linking to a home state. The rise of such TNCs, according to Waters, complicates the already tense relationship between the landed interests of states and the roaming interests of capital. Nonetheless, even while the relationships between globe-straddling corporations and their home states have become clouded, the overwhelming majority of these companies are still rooted in G-8 and other traditionally elite states. Indeed, despite confusions regarding their nationality, the giant corporations considered herein tend to enrich the already rich. To avoid confusion, then, and to move against the notion that such companies somehow float above national interests, we use the phrase multinational rather than transnational corporation.[48]

Regardless of whether we call them MNCs or TNCs, the corporations addressed here roam widely across the globe in a mercenary manner, seeking profit rather than anything resembling long-term commitments to their host communities; they accordingly function with a dramatically diminished sense of responsibility to any specific state, locale, or community. Developing nations, markets, and labor pools are thus perceived by MNCs as raw material to be manipulated, wrung dry of profitability before moving on to another fresh zone of activity. On the one hand, then, MNCs contribute mightily to the fragmentation of lived experience, turning once-organic communities into atomistic production sites, destroying unions and crushing local producers, and leaving communities to pick up the pieces when they move on in search of cheaper goods, materials, or labor. On the other hand, the international actions of MNCs mean that they inevitably tie the world together, hence creating an ever-stronger sense of global integration, of a shrinking planet, of being linked to a world community of fellow producers and consumers.[49]

At first glance, the rise of MNCs may be linked to a post–World War II boom in international commerce. Forced by World War II to confront the global war triggered by Germany and Japan, who sought to create immense empires by absorbing nation after nation, the United States was wrenched out of its isolationist slumber. Although its new sense of internationalism began as a military response, it was not long before the United States and U.S. corporations were embarking on a new generation of international activity, slowly but surely encircling the world with both military bases and capitalist outposts. Such activity had actually begun much earlier, however, as the Spanish-American War closed the nineteenth century by serving notice that the United States was entering the world stage as an empire builder. In fact, even before the 1898 invasion of Cuba, Puerto Rico, and the Philippines—ostensibly launched in response to crises created by the collapse of the Spanish empire—U.S. troops had landed in Mexico in 1846, in Argentina in 1852, in Nicaragua in 1853 and 1854, in Uruguay in 1855, in China in 1859, in Angola in 1860, in Hawaii in 1893, and in Nicaragua again in 1894. Although each of these military actions inevitably led to new market opportunities for U.S. elites, Howard Zinn reports that as late as 1898 "90% of American products were sold at home." So although the United States was regularly flexing its muscle as a state, mid- to late-nineteenth- and early twentieth-century U.S. capitalists were still, even while drawing material from abroad, overwhelmingly engaged in domestic markets. That fact would change dramatically, first with the push toward internationalism triggered by the Spanish-American War, then again by World War I, and then again by World War II, which closed with the United States' troops and capitalists dispersed across the globe, eager to cement U.S. global supremacy.[50]

Like their U.S. counterparts, European capitalists spent the closing decades of the nineteenth century exploring new ventures in the lands conquered during what Hobsbawm calls *The Age of Empire;* interrupted only by the cataclysms of the two world wars, European capitalists had a long history of international activity in both formal and informal colonies. The close of World War II therefore found both U.S. and European elites eager to spread their activities on a global scale. In fact, Sidney Rolfe and Walter Danim argue in *The Multi-National Corporation in the World Economy* that by 1970, a mere twenty-five years after the close of World War II, between "75 to 85 of the largest American corporations and 200 of the biggest European companies" had investments or employment commitments of "at least 25% of total turnover" in countries other than their home. Likewise, Kenneth Simmonds and Courtney Brown observe in *World Business* that by 1969 "71 of the 176 largest U.S. concerns" worked with as many as 33 percent of their employees overseas. Thus beginning after the close of World War II and heightening by the midperiod of the Vietnam War, covering roughly a generation, U.S. and European companies were slowly but surely encircling the globe.[51]

It would take roughly another generation for these early forays into globalization to culminate in the situation faced today, where many observers perceive a world economy driven almost entirely by MNCs. Consider these facts: In 1998 the largest 20,000 MNCs accounted for "75% of international commodity trade" and "80% of international exchanges of technology and managerial skills"; the largest 300 MNCs accounted in 1988 for "25% of the world's capital"; in 1987 MNCs employed roughly 33% "of the 90 million manufacturing workers in the world"; and of the 100 largest economies in the world, *including states,* 51 are MNCs. The world's economy is therefore increasingly run by MNCs, many of them with budgets larger than a majority of nation-states. It is important to note, however, that by 1990 "over 90% of foreign direct investment (FDI) was sourced in ten developed countries, and two thirds originated in only four (US, UK, Japan, and Germany)." This means that MNCs, despite their global activities, are rooted in traditionally wealthy nation-states. Waters notes in *Globalization* that "the Asian share of FDI rose from 3.6% in 1973 to 9.3% in 1988," yet even while new players entered the world market, the United States maintained "45% of FDI" as late as 1978.

Taking the long view, then, we may situate the current world domination of MNCs based in the United States, United Kingdom, Japan, and Germany as the culmination of roughly a century of capitalist development that has been both triggered by and sometimes interrupted by colonial and global wars.[52]

Moreover, although the MNCs driving globalization build factories in developing nations, purchase materials and labor in developing nations, and invest in technologies in developing nations, much of their business actually flows between their foreign subsidiaries, consumers in traditionally wealthy states, or other MNCs. For example, Greider notes that whereas MNCs sold goods worth $721 billion in 1971, they sold $5.2 trillion in 1991. Although such inflated numbers might appear to indicate the rise of stable middle and working classes in the developing world, where MNCs bring jobs, investment opportunities, affordable goods, training and skills, and financial stability, many of these skyrocketing sales were not to developing nation consumers, companies, or state agencies, but to other MNCs. Greider reports that "more than 40 percent of U.S. exports and nearly 50 percent of its imports are actually goods that travel not in the open marketplace, but through these intra-firm channels." Likewise, Joseph Nye reports in *The Paradox of American Power* that "nearly a third of [global] trade occurs within transnational corporations." In fact, even as international trade within MNCs has skyrocketed, global development has crashed, for as Jan Nederveen Pieterse observes, "In 1980 the share of world trade of manufactured goods of the 102 poorest countries of the world was 7.9 percent of world exports and 9 percent of imports; ten years later these shares fell to 1.4 percent and 4.9 percent respectively." Rather than expanding opportunities for developing nations to participate in globalizing networks of production and consumption, then, neoliberal globalization amounts to a shrinking of such opportunities for the poor and an expansion of them for the rich.[53]

Indeed, rather than creating consumer choice and economic uplift for new parts of the world, MNCs maximize profits by seeking out the most favorable rates of production, even if that means goods must travel through a remarkably complex circuit of international subsidiaries. Thus, rather than building stable middle and working classes in developing nations, MNCs use whatever aspects of a given situation suit their business interests of gathering together a global network of suppliers. Subcontractors and workers in developing nations therefore amount to little more than fractured and alienated subsets of a global economic system that leaves them marginalized at best, impoverished at worst.

This means that while the web of MNCs increasingly stretches across the globe, enabling local entrepreneurs to enjoy new possibilities, bringing much-needed jobs to the unemployed, and offering host nations some tangible benefits, globalization nonetheless amounts to the spread not so much of "Americanization" (as we saw Harvey call it above) as capitalization at the hands of a small number of MNCs linked to each other, based in traditionally wealthy states, and supported by U.S.-led regional trade pacts. For example, according to the U.S. Census Bureau's February 2004 figures, the United States' top four trade partners are Canada (20 percent), Mexico (12 percent), China (9 percent), and Japan (8 percent)—that is 49 percent of U.S. trade with our two partners in NAFTA and the two economic giants of Asia, hence rendering globalization less a global than a regional phenomenon, less a broadly spreading system of free trade than a series of tightly monitored trading blocs based on selective protectionism and inter-MNC trade.[54]

The key task then, as we have addressed above in a preliminary manner, is to fathom the relationships among capitalist elites, the MNCs they manage, the states who host them, and the workers and consumers who fuel their profits. To reduce these complicated relationships to two questions, we might ask, *What are the valences of power driving the globalizing web of MNCs?* and *Who oversees globalization?* As we will demonstrate below, the answers to these questions increasingly point not to sovereign nation-states or empowered workers and enlightened consumers but to international governmental organizations (IGOs) such as the IMF, World Bank, and WTO.

The IMF, World Bank, and WTO: The Institutional Architecture of Globalizing Capitalism

The World Bank (formally called the International Bank for Reconstruction and Development) and IMF were formed at the Bretton Woods Conference in New Hampshire in the summer of 1944; the WTO was created in 1995 to supersede the 1947 General Agreement on Tariffs and Trade (GATT); the World Bank, IMF, and WTO thus share roots in attempts to rebuild the world economy following World War II. Helping with the reconstruction of shattered European countries and striving to bring order to the devastated world economy, these institutions framed a structure of global economic oversight based largely on the success of the managed economies instituted by the New Deal in the United States and by Keynesian-led policies in Britain. Their intention, then, as described by Walden Bello in *The Future in the Balance: Essays on Globalization and Resistance,* was to create a system that would be "the guardian of global liquidity." These guardians of a now-rationalized post–World War II capitalism, these institutional architects of globalization, would fulfill their functions by "monitoring member countries' maintenance of stable exchange rates and providing facilities on which they could periodically draw to overcome cyclical balance of payment difficulties." Thus, whereas the preceding century of international capitalism had led to constant wars, brutal colonization, stability-destroying boom and bust cycles, and a general pattern of competition-driven waste and ruin, the IMF, World Bank, and GATT were instituted following World War II to manage a new age of globalizing free markets.[55]

The Bretton Woods system therefore institutionalized a global structure of checks and balances: thinking globally but acting locally, the World Bank would rebuild Europe and eradicate global poverty by working within (and ideally with) host nations; thinking in sweeping macroeconomic terms, the IMF would monitor the world economy by supplying funds or applying financial pressure as needed to maintain stability; enabling the individual ambitions of capitalists, GATT (and now the WTO) would encourage the reduction of tariffs and other blockages to increased international commerce. Hence aiding individual capitalists (GATT/WTO), helping nations (World Bank), and managing global financial affairs (IMF), the troika of post–World War II economic institutions was poised to usher in a new age of rationalized international capitalism. For proponents of this system, the new institutional architecture of globalization insured that the best aspects of capitalism—its infinite dynamism, technological creativity, motivational power, and uplifting promise—would not be overrun by its worst aspects—its cyclical meltdowns, mechanical drudgery, deadening labors, and hope-destroying reality. As explained by Michael Moore (not the populist filmmaker but the former head of the WTO) in his *World without Walls,* the institutional checks and balances of the IMF, World Bank, and WTO were meant "to ensure access to globalization's advantages, and to maintain rules and regulations for safety and fair play." Indeed, while the contemporary manifestations of these institutions are hardly recognizable in such terms, it is important to remember that their original function was to monitor markets, to control capitalism, to make development decent and free markets more fair.[56]

It would not be long, however, before these new institutions of global capitalism served, as Fred Block argues, "to legitimize the exercise of U.S. power on a global scale." Indeed, as we have demonstrated above via a host of examples, the utopian promises of this new institutional architecture of globalization foundered on a number of complicated contradictions. For example, Block shows how the United States initially relied on the Bretton Woods institutions to "persuade non-communist trade unionists to cooperate with economic policies that were disastrous for the working class." Along with thwarting worker organizations, institutional tensions flared as well, for whereas the stated purpose of the IMF is to oversee macrodevelopment, often by working hand in hand with the World Bank, the IMF's macroeconomic policies tend not to attend to the intricacies and nuances of the countries it deals with. The site-specific strategies of the World Bank and the macrostrategies of the IMF often clash, leaving host nations caught between their immediate needs and the wishes of warring foreign institutions, both of which have the power to offer great help or devastating punishments. Given this complicated institutional arrangement, it comes as no surprise to learn that many people in developing nations fear both the IMF and World Bank as little more than covert weapons of colonization.[57]

The World Bank has attempted to counter such fears by trying to build what Leo Panitch calls "a post-Washington Consensus" of "globalization with a social-democratic face." For example, while the bank admits in its *World Development Report 2004* that "there have been spectacular successes and miserable failures in the efforts by developing countries to make services work," it attributes these successes and failures largely to "the degree to which poor people themselves are involved in determining the quality and quantity of the services which they receive." That is, the bank understands that globalizing neoliberalism can only succeed with more input from the world's poor, from those whose lives are directly affected by the bank's development efforts. Given the remarkably closed nature of bank deliberations and decision-making processes, however, it is difficult to take such claims seriously. Indeed, the bank granted $28.9 billion to more than eighty countries in 2003, making any attempt to involve "poor people themselves" more directly and more powerfully in the bank's business, at least as it is currently structured, an unfathomable proposition.[58]

For even while the bank tries to render global macroeconomics in the familiar language of individual choice and democratic representation—suggesting that it would like to work hand in hand with empowered agents in developing nations—the fact is that its and the IMF's policies are inevitably informed by the larger political, social, and military interests of G-8 nations. For example, widespread starvation and general economic decay in Kenya were not as compelling to the IMF as local political corruption, which prompted the IMF to withdraw its support from programs in Kenya. Yet the IMF offered Russia an $11.2 billion loan in the summer of 1997, despite widespread acknowledgment that the Russian economic elites who would be handling the loan were little more than a gang of thieves. In comparing the two scenarios Stiglitz observes that "no one really expected the IMF to treat a nuclear power the same way that it treated a poor African country of little strategic importance." This is where the reality of power politics shines through, proving that the IMF is not so much dedicated to global macroeconomic stability as to propping up regimes useful to the larger geopolitical needs of the United States. Indeed, Stiglitz reports that "to some, it seemed that while the Fund was overlooking grand larceny, it was taking a strong stand on petty theft." Such duplicitous behavior can only tarnish the legitimacy of the IMF and World Bank, making them seem less like independent institutions for promoting economic growth than reliable tools of U.S. empire.[59]

Indeed, the key fact about IMF, World Bank, and other elite development institutions is that the billions of dollars of loans and other forms of assistance they grant to developing nations generally return to developed-world elites via criteria-laden contracts. That is, the leading institutions of globalization credit money to developing nations with the understanding that such money will be spent on projects run by developed-nation MNCs. Hence, Global Exchange reports that "for every $1 the U.S. contributes to international development banks, U.S. exporters win more than $2 in bank-financed procurement contracts." Seen in this light, the institutions of globalization amount to little more than conduits of international corporate welfare (what we describe in chapter 4 as crony capitalism), to means of globalizing the reach of MNCs in the name of development.[60]

Along with the IMF and World Bank, the third key IGO for our purposes is the WTO. Although it was officially launched in 1995, discussions about it began in the early 1980s as part of the so-called Uruguay round of trade negotiations, when economic elites explored the possibility of expanding both the scope and membership of GATT. Launched a half-century after the 1944 Bretton Woods conference, and institutionalizing business practices that had begun accelerating toward the end of the cold war, as national and regional economies became more entwined and technology enabled goods to be produced and transported at unprecedented speed, the WTO emerged as the official body governing international trade. Speaking both as the retired head of the WTO and as a representative of the emerging "Washington Consensus" driving its policies (to which we turn below), Moore expresses great faith in expansive trade in an age of globalization. His thesis is that cooperation without coercion and overall "good governance—the establishment of honest transparent public services and responsible, accountable, replaceable politicians—is not some warm, fuzzy, liberal do-gooder theory, it is sound economics, and it works best." Thus inhabiting the language of pragmatism, Moore and other WTO supporters have argued that installing a process of governing global trade is the only practical way to manage globalization; from this perspective the WTO is not so much a political institution meant to shape the world as simply a fair, functional, and necessary response to the complexities of globalization.[61]

Whereas global justice advocates argue that the WTO's procedures are undemocratic and coercive and that they force nations into a system of global corruption and subservience, Moore holds that "negotiating a WTO investment agreement is not synonymous with surrendering national economic sovereignty to global capitalism." However, Moore acknowledges that many decisions are made not as part of transparent democratic meetings but as part of "green room" negotiations—private, behind-closed-door meetings—among elite states. Indeed, Peter Singer explains in One World that what is called "consensus" is actually an agenda "set by informal meetings of the major trading powers." In short, "consensus" is but a euphemism for continued elite leadership.[62]

This perhaps explains why, if members reject the proposals as they did in Cancún, then the meeting results not in negotiation but in a breakdown, for the meeting was never meant to be a negotiating session; rather, it was a façade, a gathering of nations meant to mimic democracy when in fact elite "green room" members had a preset agenda. Bello pushes this argument even further, arguing that the WTO's "main purpose is to reduce the tremendous policing costs to the stronger powers that would be involved in disciplining many small countries in a more fluid, less structured international system." In other words, although the WTO purports to trigger developing-nation growth by lowering international tariffs, hence facilitating more and more profitable global trade, and although it claims to do so via transparent methods of negotiation, Bello charges that the WTO's policies serve as an appendage to U.S. foreign and economic policy.[63]

Although the IMF, World Bank, and WTO each carry different tasks, many of which conflict at times, they nonetheless combine to support what has come to be known as the "Washington Consensus." The three key strategies of the Washington Consensus, each contributing to the rise of what has come to be called neoliberalism, are fiscal austerity, privatization, and market liberalization. *Fiscal austerity* means developing nations are forced to cut social spending, hence reducing state expenditures and ideally state dependence on loans from the World Bank and other developed-nation lenders. *Privatization* means that those social services cut by the state are supposed to be absorbed and made more productive by private capitalists, hence creating an environment ripe for an entrepreneurial takeoff into accelerated development and profitability. *Market liberalization* means that trade tariffs, banking regulations, and other state-imposed market controls must be lifted to enable international entrepreneurs to move more quickly and effectively into the developing nation opportunities created by the first two parts of the Washington Consensus, hence fueling globalization and local development.[64]

As expressed by President Bush in his 22 March 2002 speech before the United Nations Financing for Development Conference, "The lesson of our time is clear: when nations close their markets and opportunity is hoarded by a privileged few, no amount—no amount—of development aid is ever enough." But when those markets are opened up, liberalized, they become hotbeds of trade, which the president characterized a week earlier at the Inter-American Development Bank (IADB) as "the engine of development." Summarizing the utopian hopes driving the Washington Consensus, the president concluded that "the advances of free markets and trade and democracy and rule of law have brought prosperity to an ever-widening circle of people in this world."[65]

We will turn to some of the complications and contradictions of this vision below, where we address five of the pressing dilemmas of globalization, but for now we will focus on the president's linking the economic aspects of the Washington Consensus with democracy. For as noted above, one of the most stringent critiques of the IMF, World Bank, and WTO is that their deliberative procedures are remarkably, even shockingly secret. Put simply, no one is elected to be a representative to these bodies, and no one outside of them is allowed to monitor their internal functioning; so although they are charged with governing the global economy, they are not democratic or even vaguely representational in terms of their makeup. In fact, according to Global Exchange, "voting power at the World Bank and IMF is determined by the level of a nation's financial contribution. Therefore, the U.S. has roughly 17% of the vote, with the G7 holding a total of 45%." Even while arguing for their roles in supporting the economies and governments of developing nations, then, the bank and IMF function under the leadership of United States and G-8 elites, hence treating the developed nations they "serve" as little more than semicolonies. Indeed, despite the president's describing the IMF, World Bank, and WTO as spreading democracy, they are closed institutions, modeling not democracy but oligopoly, not broad inclusion but elite privilege. The institutions charged with driving the Washington Consensus therefore amount, as argued by Stiglitz, to "*global governance without global government.*"[66]

In fact, the supersecretive nature of the WTO's ministerial meeting in Cancún in September 2003 prompted representatives from the global south to mobilize a walkout to protest what they believed were the obvious links between the old political elitism of colonialism and the new political elitism of the WTO. The curious rhetorical inflections of the WTO's description of the collapsed talks, posted on its Web site, illustrate the simmering tensions between secrecy and disclosure, Old World elitism and supposed New World democracy. For although the WTO's version of events is full of what appear to be meticulously detailed entries, such as telling readers the exact times at which meetings or debates occurred, the actual content of the descriptions of each moment is remarkably vague. For example, the chairperson of the sessions, Luis Ernesto Derbez, acknowledged that when the negotiations began to break down, on 13 September, he initiated all-night consultations "in a variety of formats . . . with a smallish group of participants." The entry appears to convey important information, yet the key phrases here, "a variety of formats" and "a smallish group of participants," are so elastic as to mean nothing. Clearly, such rhetorical evasions hide the fact that the "smallish group of participants" consisted largely of representatives from G-8 states trying to bully their counterparts from developing nations. These vaguely described "green room" meetings were not successful, however, so Derbez adjourned the meeting the next day, 14 September 2003.[67]

The collapse of the Cancún talks was caused, according to the *New York Times,* by a "coalition of the unwilling," who, mocking the elitism of the G-8, referred to themselves as the G-20 (or sometimes G-22 or G-23 depending on sources). Members of the G-20 disagreed over agricultural subsidies, intellectual property laws, and the "green room" nature of the meetings, which left many WTO ministers feeling less like participants in a round of international negotiations than colonial supplicants. The *New York Times* editorialized that "the world's poorest and most vulnerable nations will suffer most. It is a bitter irony that the chief architects of this failure were nations like Japan, Korea and European Union members, themselves ads for the prosperity afforded by increased global trade." This is a curious charge, for most observers agree that the talks failed not because of recalcitrant Japanese, Korean, or EU representatives but because the United States refused to negotiate its astronomical agricultural subsidies, which give large U.S. farmers unfair advantage over farmers from developing nations. Furthermore, most observers, including the *Times*'s Elizabeth Becker and the editors of *Business Week,* agreed both that the walkout was led by Brazil's president, Luiz Ignacio Lula de Silva, and that the walkout was a principled response to the United States' refusal to negotiate. Moreover, by focusing on what we believe is a misreading of both the economic causes and political leaders of the breakdown, the *Times*'s editorial missed the important point that the walkout was also about the mechanics of decision making at the WTO.[68]

No rash act by a "coalition of the unwilling," the walkout was a clear statement that globalization could not proceed under the rubric of unchallenged U.S. and other elite state leadership. Indeed, the walkout indicates that some members of the global south—and their developed nation allies—have begun to realize that you cannot spread democracy and free trade at the hands of oligopolistic institutions whose actions tend to enrich elites from the developed world. As economists Dean Baker and Mark Weisbrot argue, "The whole notion of the WTO as an organization designed to promulgate and enforce rules for 'free trade' is a misrepresentation," for the WTO has used "green room" tactics to push the Washington Consensus on developing nations even while leaving massive U.S. tariffs and domestic subsidies in place.[69]

Nonetheless, although the IMF, World Bank, and WTO appear at first glance to support the economic and political interests of the United States and G-8, thus enabling what we saw Harvey call "globalization as Americanization," the fact is that U.S.-based MNCs require both geographic and legal flexibility to achieve maximum profits. So although the IMF, World Bank, and WTO may be useful to MNCs in many instances by forcing developing nations to open their markets under the guise of the Washington Consensus's neoliberalism, they also hinder MNCs in other instances, for global agreements by definition open markets to foreign competition and produce new and expansive legal parameters, both of which threaten existing trade arrangements and practices. This inherent tension between the ways the institutions of globalization both aid and hinder the interests of U.S.-based MNCs may help explain the rise in recent years of regional trade agreements. We therefore argue below that NAFTA, CAFTA, and the FTAA amount to attempts by the United States to combine the global coverage and support of the IMF, World Bank, and WTO with the regional backing of localized FTAs. We thus examine the ways these FTAs amount to subglobal trade agreements meant to lock in geographically specific trade advantages and regional political alliances. Moreover, as we demonstrate in our comments on the United States' new bilateral trade agreements with Singapore and Chile and the president's proposed FTAs with Middle Eastern states, the United States is increasingly turning to subglobal arrangements as a way of avoiding global political accountability and maximizing U.S. influence.[70]

NAFTA, FTAA, and Regional and Bilateral Responses to Globalization

The 2004 *Economic Report of the President* forwards the premise that "free markets allocate resources to their highest-valued uses, avoid waste, prevent shortages, and foster innovation." But as noted above, the flexibility implied in this claim clashes with the fact that the IMF, World Bank, and WTO exist to regulate global markets, hence producing a tension between global economic needs, regional needs, and local state needs.

Ideally these different geographical and political levels of economic development would work together, but of course they do not, at least not much of the time. For example, the president's *Economic Report* subtly flags the tension between global and subglobal trade practices. It declares that "the Administration has pursued, and will continue to pursue, an ambitious agenda of trade liberalization through negotiations at the global" level, yet it concludes that sentence by also promising to pursue trade agreements at "regional and bilateral levels." As suggested by the report, NAFTA, CAFTA, and the proposed FTAA exist as local forms of access and leverage meant both to supplement but also at times to counter the globalizing dictates of the IMF, World Bank, and WTO. The president's pursuit of globalization-through-benevolent-empire thus proceeds not only at the global level enabled by the IMF, World Bank, and WTO, but also through the regional levels delineated in the bilateral FTAs addressed below.[71]

The subject of fierce debate within the United States for many years, NAFTA was approved by Congress on 20 November and signed into law by President Clinton on 8 December 1993. Prior to its passage, the general argument for NAFTA, as encapsulated in the title of an article in the *Economist* from 1991, was that "Mexico Beckons, Protectionists Quaver." Neoliberals thus hoped that NAFTA would pull Mexico into modernity, break down protectionist barriers to trade, and hence improve production and profitability in both Mexico and the United States. Summarizing these promises nine years later, in an article analyzing how they have proven illusory, Celia Dugger recalled in the *New York Times* that according to President Clinton and his NAFTA allies, "foreign investors would make Mexico an economic tiger, turning its poor workers into middle-class consumers who would then buy U.S. and Canadian goods, creating more jobs in the high-wage countries."[72]

Despite their illusory nature, these claims have been repeated in the office of the United States Trade Representative's 2004 *NAFTA: A Decade of Strengthening Dynamic Relationships,* which boasts that if the NAFTA nations are considered one entity, then their GDP would be $11.4 trillion, making NAFTA the world's largest trading bloc and its member nations responsible for as much as one-third of global GDP. The report gushes that NAFTA encompasses continentwide trading that reaches $1.2 million *every minute.* Like the *NSSUS* and President Bush's post-9/11 speeches, such claims point to the underlying assumption that increasing trade in both volume and speed—*it is accelerating*—inevitably improves democracy, that integration into globalizing neoliberalism inevitably raises the quality of life of all participants.[73]

Or consider the claims of Robert Zoellick, the U.S. trade representative, who, speaking before the National Foreign Trade Council in Washington, D.C., on 26 July 2001, celebrated not only NAFTA's economic dynamism but the fact that it was pulling Mexico into the world of globalizing neoliberalism, thus enabling the United States "to plant the standards of free trade, democracy, and support for developing nations." In short, NAFTA was reforming Mexico, turning the straggling and impoverished oligopoly into a thriving and wealthy democracy. Like the *NSSUS* and the U.S. trade representative's report cited above, Zoellick's speech amounts not only to a blueprint for the Washington Consensus but also to a dramatic illustration of the utopian impulses driving neoliberalism.[74]

To situate these claims regarding neoliberalism in general and NAFTA in particular in some helpful historical perspective, it is important to review Mexico's economic plight dating back to the early days of the Reagan presidency, which urged Mexico to gouge public spending, hoping that doing so would help create a budget surplus that could be used to repay outstanding loans to developed nation banks. Mexico was also pressured to privatize its state industries—it has sold one thousand since 1983—and to join GATT, thus beginning the process of both privatization and market liberalization. But opening its borders to cheap imports devastated local manufacturing, in turn triggering unemployment and cutting tax revenues, transforming an anticipated budget surplus into an escalating deficit. As a result, during the 1980s, "real wages (adjusted for inflation) fell in Mexico by 75%," leading many to lament the 1980s as "the lost decade." By the early 1990s the trade deficit began to soar. When the peso eventually collapsed in 1995, triggering interest rates too high for local business owners to handle, wealthy foreign investors moved in to take advantage of the mess, thus effectively turning much of Mexico's once locally owned private and state property into foreign-owned investments. Thus, by March 2004, 85 percent of Mexico's banking assets were held by foreign firms; according to the *Wall Street Journal*, this means that Mexico's banks suffer "the highest ratio of foreign ownership in Latin America."[75]

Whereas Zoellick celebrated recent Mexican economic history as evidence of how the United States is using neoliberalism "to plant the standards of free trade, democracy, and support for developing nations," our overview demonstrates that in fact Mexico has been colonized by investors from developed nations, hence illustrating what John Gray calls "the absurdity of neo-liberal reforms in Mexico." Indeed, given our summary, there can be little wonder why some Mexicans view the recent economic history of neoliberalism as an act of neocolonialism.[76]

Despite the obvious fact that these early attempts to wrench Mexico into the system of globalizing neoliberalism were dismal failures, and despite the fact that NAFTA was designed to accelerate the Washington Consensus model that had already damaged Mexico so badly, NAFTA was touted (and is touted still) as a means of recharging Mexico's economy. Yet since NAFTA was passed, eight million Mexicans have fallen into poverty; Mexican real wages in manufacturing have dropped 13.5 percent; income for salaried workers has fallen 25 percent while income for self-employed workers has fallen 40 percent; and heavily subsidized U.S. agricultural products have decimated Mexico's small farmers, driving as many as one million of them into poverty. Moreover, whereas Mexico's total foreign debt was $57 billion in 1982, it rose to $99 billion by 1997—so since NAFTA was passed the nation has not become enriched but more indebted. In fact, based on his fact-finding travels through Mexico in November 2003, Congressman Bernie Sanders (I-VT) reported that he "encountered horrendous poverty, environmental degradation, and a lawless and corrupt environment."[77]

While the economic effects of NAFTA on Mexico have therefore been devastating, we are equally concerned about how NAFTA established a precedent for using internationally sanctioned laws written by unelected corporate elites to subvert democratically sanctioned local laws. Take for example Chapter 11 of NAFTA, which enables MNCs to sue governments and localities for lost profits and to overturn local environmental and public health laws. According to John Echeverria, a law professor at Georgetown University, such NAFTA-based reviews of U.S. laws amount to "the biggest threat to U.S. judicial independence that no one has heard of and even fewer people understand." One case among the slew of companies bringing these suits is the U.S.-based Metaclad Corporation, which claimed that a 1997 environmental decree issued in the Mexican state of San Luis Postosi was unfairly restrictive. Marshalling NAFTA's environmental laws against the local Mexican laws, Metaclad forced the government to pay $16 million in damages. But NAFTA's Chapter 11 does more than enable U.S. companies to flout local Mexican laws, as illustrated by the case of the Loewen Group, a Canadian funeral home chain, which won $750 million from the U.S. government after a Mississippi court held the chain responsible for malicious and fraudulent business practices. The Metaclad case illustrates how NAFTA enables MNCs to trample local laws, and the Loewen Group case demonstrates that what Mississippi law calls fraud, NAFTA calls good business.[78]

Moreover, NAFTA has dramatically harmed both the U.S. trade deficit and U.S. workers. For example, the Economic Policy Institute (EPI) reports that since the passage of NAFTA the United States has witnessed a "growth in imports of 195.3% from Mexico and 61.1% from Canada," thus "overwhelmingly surpass[ing U.S.] export growth." In 2003 alone, the U.S. trade deficit with Mexico was $40.6 billion; with Canada it was $54.4 billion—that means the U.S. trade deficit with its NAFTA partners was $95 billion. Put simply, we are buying more from our NAFTA partners than we are selling to them, leaving the United States with an escalating NAFTA-fueled trade deficit and NAFTA-fueled unemployment. Indeed, ten years after NAFTA's implementation more than one million U.S. workers had lost their jobs, mainly in manufacturing industries that produce textiles and apparel, vehicles, computers, and electrical appliances. According to the Center for American Progress, "In January 2004, manufacturing lost another 11,000 [jobs] in its 42nd monthly decline in a row." As higher-paid, skilled workers move from declining industries to the service sector, which pays on average only 81 percent of manufacturing jobs, wages are driven down across the board. Evaluating the national economy is of course a perilously complicated issue, one that we cannot hope to accomplish here in anything but the most cursory manner. Indeed, it is difficult to disentangle the numbers offered above from NAFTA-driven effects and the more broadly construed consequences of outsourcing; nonetheless, we have shown here that NAFTA has hurt both the U.S. trade deficit and U.S. workers.[79]

The complicated twist to this story, however, as noted above in our comments on MNCs, is that the increasing U.S. trade deficit with Mexico is not enriching that nation because the vast bulk of the profits made from this NAFTA-fueled trade resides not with Mexican workers, the Mexican nation-state, or Mexican-owned corporations, but with the U.S.-based MNCs straddling the Mexican/U.S. border in "development

zones" populated with what have come to be known as *maquiladora* factories. The *maquiladoras* make up more than one-fourth of direct foreign
investment and almost half of all export production in Mexico. But because they export most of their output, they leave little in the way of more
affordable goods for Mexican consumers, and because of the lowered tariffs and taxes established under NAFTA, such exports bring little money
to the Mexican government. Moreover, despite widespread pre-NAFTA
concerns over brutal labor standards, the *maquiladoras* remain sites of
unsafe working conditions. In fact, the turnover rate in *maquiladoras* is
between 15 and 25 percent per month, and "the average work-life of a
maquila worker is only ten years because of injuries, health problems, and
the firing of women workers who become pregnant." The *maquiladora*
factories triggering much of the U.S. trade deficit therefore rely on a combination of exploited cheap Mexican labor, credit-driven U.S. consumers, and NAFTA's lowered tax laws, labor standards, and environmental
guidelines to reap astronomical profits. NAFTA therefore amounts not
to an attempt to accelerate development and protect jobs but to stream-
line the profit opportunities of MNCs.[80]

As a corollary to this frightening charge, consider how the financial
practices of regional trade pacts and their partner institutions influence
the pace and kinds of economic development possible in the twenty-first
century. As an example, we turn to the financial practices of the Inter-
American Development Bank, which plays a major role in lending and
granting money to Latin America. Founded in 1959 and based in Washington D.C., the IADB was the world's first regional lending institution.
Like the governance structure of the IMF and World Bank, each of the
IADB's forty-six member countries—several European countries and Japan are also members—enjoys voting rights based on how much capital
it has invested in the bank. The United States holds 30 percent of total
voting power; half of the voting power resides in Latin American and
Caribbean countries combined; and the remaining 20 percent is held by
Canada and the other nonregional member countries.[81]

One of the chief tasks of the IADB is to provide the financial support
needed to enable MNCs to siphon oil and other resources out of the
global south. For example, between 1992 and 2004, the IADB lent $6.2
billion for fossil-fuel projects, in some cases using such money as political
leverage (working closely with U.S.-based fossil-fuel interests) to squash
alternative energy research. The Sustainable Energy and Economy Net-

work (SEEN) argues that "in 2000 the IADB forced the Nicaraguan government to cancel a wind-energy project as a condition for receiving a power sector reform loan." In addition to the information offered above demonstrating how NAFTA's Chapter 11 enables MNCs to subvert local trade and environmental regulations, this example from Nicaragua illustrates how the IADB uses its massive financial clout to support existing fossil-fuel corporations by determining that alternative energy resources will not be developed in Nicaragua.[82]

In fact, many of the top recipients of IADB financing are fossil-fuel MNCs, including Spain's Endesa corporation, which used $1.28 billion of IADB money to pursue energy projects in Argentina, Brazil, El Salvador, Guatemala, Honduras, Panama, and Uruguay. Second on the list is the AES corporation, based in the United States, which received $1.07 billion for energy-related projects in Argentina, Columbia, and El Salvador. Overall, more than half of the top fifteen corporate beneficiaries of IADB fossil-fuel financing projects in Latin America from 1992 to 2004 were U.S.-based MNCs, including Enron, Shell, General Electric, and Bechtel. These U.S.-based and fossil-fuel-driven MNCs used their IADB loans to build pipelines and power plants and to continue privatizing once-public resources while marginalizing local projects that pursued more ecologically sustainable models of development and energy production. Likewise, only 3 percent of the World Bank's energy lending is granted to renewable and energy efficient projects.[83]

In many areas these actions have been so unpopular that MNCs have been forced to rely on repressive regimes and human-rights-violating paramilitary squads to keep the local population in order. For example, Chevron-Texaco, which controls more than half of an Amazonian region of Ecuador, has been accused of working closely with that nation's repressive military in order to continue its appropriation of natural resources. In a similar vein, Shell's environmental rampage in Nigeria, where it has spilled more than 1.6 million gallons of oil since 1982, has so outraged locals that it has been forced to protect its operations with human-rights-violating paramilitaries. Likewise, Exxon-Mobil relies on three thousand Indonesian troops to protect its gas fields in Lhokseumawe, in northern Indonesia, from an unstable mix of outraged locals and separatist rebels, both of whom resent the MNCs' exploitative presence. In other words, the same MNCs that purport to bring jobs and security to developing nations, aided by trade pacts like NAFTA and regional superbanks like the IADB, sometimes stand shoulder to shoulder with the corrupt governments and paramilitary death squads that repress the local populations.[84]

Expanding and cementing the globalizing neoliberal practices discussed above, the proposed FTAA planned to encircle the entire Western hemisphere, from the Arctic Circle to the southernmost tip of South America; it will encompass eight hundred million people in thirty-four nations in North, Central, and South America and the Caribbean, covering everybody but the still-impoverished Cubans. We wish the life-improving promises of its supporters were true, for as of 2002, 220 million people in Latin America and the Caribbean lived in poverty, while there were 35 million people subsisting below the poverty line in the United States, including its 8.5 million unemployed. Considering that it is modeled on NAFTA, however, we suspect that FTAA will not solve these problems so much as exacerbate them.[85]

The FTAA was first formally discussed at the Summit of the Americas in Miami in 1994, but its first ministerial declaration was issued at a 1995 meeting in Denver. Following the general principles of the Washington Consensus, the declaration claimed that "in view of the wide differences in levels of development and size of economies, we will actively look for ways to provide opportunities to facilitate the integration of the smaller economies and increase their level of development." Thus focusing on integration and development, the FTAA sought to break down trade and investment barriers, assuming that doing so would promote democracy and development, thereby stabilizing a region that has been rocked by decades of cyclical depressions and political upheavals. While ignoring the deeper cultural, political, and structural causes of these depressions and upheavals, the ministerial declaration claimed that applying the principles of neoliberalism would enable it to "build one existing subregional and bilateral arrangement in order to broaden and deepen hemispheric economic integration." The repeated emphasis on integration, both here and in related NAFTA and FTAA documents, has led critics to fear that this version of globalization amounts to a blueprint for cultural homogenization rather than locally sensitive development.[86]

Moreover, like NAFTA, the proposed FTAA will be armed with expansive powers that may compromise and even challenge local laws. Neither NAFTA nor FTAA can actually overturn or rewrite established laws, but they can award large damages to corporations like Metaclad and the Loewen Group, hence providing financial incentive to break the law. The Methanex case is especially interesting because it demonstrates how the institutions governing trade are not beholden to local laws or political norms. Methanex, a Canadian-based manufacturer of the gasoline-additive MTBE, was banned from the United States after thirty California public water systems, thirty-five hundred groundwater sites, Lake Tahoe, and Lake Shasta were found to be contaminated with MTBE. Leaky storage tanks and pipelines throughout California were allowing MTBE to seep into the water table, hence putting millions of Californians at risk for MTBE-triggered cases of asthma, nausea, respiratory failure, and eye irritation. Arguing in 1999 that U.S. environmental standards were unfair, however, Methanex used NAFTA's Chapter 11 to take the United States to court, claiming that it had lost $970 million in profits. Methanex's suit raised two startling countercharges against California's initial decision. First, the company claimed that the contaminations were California's fault for allowing tanks, pipelines, and other facilities to decay beyond any reasonable standard of safety. Rather than an example of corporate malfeasance, then, the trouble in California reflected that state's budgetary crisis and its inevitable environmental fallout. Second, Methanex argued that the charges against it were motivated by the protectionist desire to squeeze out a Canadian product to make market space for the chief competitor to MTBE, ethanol made by Archer Daniels Midland (ADM), a U.S.-based MNC. What at first looks like NAFTA being used to subvert environmental laws thus turns out to be a representative case of the complexities of contemporary capitalism. Methanex eventually sued the United States for $1 billion for lost profits; the U.S. State Department, which oversees NAFTA-based investor-to-state claims, has released preliminary findings; as of June 2005 the case continues to weave its way through the courts, embodying the complications of agency and responsibility in an age of globalization.[87]

Given the NAFTA track record, it comes as no surprise to learn that the proposed FTAA triggered massive protests, including the Miami march with which we opened this chapter. In fact, it appears that resistance to the proposed FTAA has crystallized the movement against many of the global institutions examined here. For example, protesting the many ways globalizing free trade is not so much free as rigged for the benefit of MNCs, a group of twenty-three developing countries—the so-called G-23—banded together to walk out of the WTO meeting in

Cancún in September 2003. Carrying over from that protest, members of the G-23 convinced their fellow ministerial negotiators in Miami, in November 2003, not to adopt the FTAA as planned. Instead, negotiators agreed on an à la carte version, what critics are calling "FTAA-lite," which enables countries to adopt only the specific policies they see as valuable yet "fudges how broad and deep the FTAA will be." Widespread anger at the proposed FTAA therefore appears to have alerted many observers to the problems we have discussed above, perhaps signaling a turning point in the development of NAFTA-like attempts to blanket entire regions with globalizing neoliberalism.[88]

Indeed, Sarah Anderson and John Cavanagh argued in the *Nation* in December 2003, following the WTO walkout and the FTAA's collapse, that "doctrinaire pro-free-trade leaders were voted or driven out of office in Ecuador, Brazil, Argentina, and . . . Bolivia" in recent years. Brazil in particular, with its President Lula, has been remarkably successful in reforming the policies of its previous president, Cardoso. Because he was beholden to the landowners, banks, and media moguls who brought him to power, Cardoso felt obligated to stick to what historian Perry Anderson has characterized as "a plainly calamitous path" during his eight years in office. But whereas Cardoso was a throwback to old elitism, and was reviled as such, Lula is a populist with broad support; he was elected in a landslide and is widely revered as the peoples' president, at least in part because of his successful advocacy for *fair trade* instead of Washington Consensus–style free trade. Even in the United States, more than two-thirds of the respondents in a recent poll agreed that "if another country is willing to lower its barriers to products from the U.S. if we lower our barriers to their products," then the United States should agree to do so. In other words, G-23 ministers, widespread protesters, Brazil's President Lula, and two out of three Americans want free trade to be fair, not rigged to benefit MNCs.[89]

In closing this section on the institutional architecture of globalization we should note, however, that the fair-trade wishes expressed in the paragraph above collide with the imperial ambitions of the United States. For example, consider the bilateral free trade agreement signed by the United States and Singapore on 6 May 2003 (hereafter US-SFTA). A similar bilateral FTA with Chile (US-CFTA), one that had been under consideration for much longer than the Singapore pact, was temporarily put on hold, presumably to punish Chile for opposing the U.S invasion of Iraq.

But Singapore, a strong supporter of the war, despite the protests of most of its citizens, was rewarded for supporting the war with an agreement that immediately erased all tariffs on U.S. goods imported by Singapore and that phased out all tariffs on Singaporean goods imported into the United States. In announcing the pact President Bush praised Singapore for being "a strong partner in the war on terrorism and a member of the coalition on Iraq." Although the United States and Singapore trade as much as $33.4 billion worth of goods each year, the president's comments make it clear that the US-SFTA's chief function is to reward Singapore for supporting the United States' recent military actions. Indeed, far from the glowing claims that globalizing free trade will create opportunity and democracy wherever it spreads, the US-SFTA illustrates how the United States is happy to make agreements with authoritarian regimes as long as they support the United States' imperial actions. As Thomas Carothers lamented in the *Washington Post*, "The administration is rewarding a dictatorship . . . for overriding the views of its people, a majority of whom . . . opposed the war."[90]

We should note that President Bush signed both the US-SFTA and the US-CFTA on 3 September 2003. In his comments during the signing ceremony, echoing the *NSSUS's*, Friedman's, Zoellick's, and Barnett's theory that globalization promotes peace, the president argued that "economic integration through trade can also foster political cooperation by promoting peace between nations." Both FTAs were authorized under "fast track" agreements, meaning Congress could vote on them but not negotiate their provisions; the US-SFTA and US-CFTA therefore amount not to broad-reaching attempts to foster development in struggling nations but to institutionalized examples of executive privileges, for they are bilateral economic treaties formed at the president's discretion to serve his foreign policy objectives.[91]

This use of FTAs as weapons of empire, as economic means of rewarding or punishing states for their support or resistance to U.S. military aggression, has historical roots in the cold war. For example, when Salvador Allende was elected president of Chile in 1970, President Nixon pressured the World Bank to suspend its lending—amounting to as much as $234 million a year before the election—to Allende's allegedly Communist government. In fact, Nixon's National Security Decision Memorandum No. 93 outlined a series of steps amounting to economic warfare, including not only halting World Bank loans but similar support from the U.S. Export-Import Bank, the United States Agency for International Development, and the IADB. When Augusto Pinochet took the reins of power in a 1973 coup aided with U.S. money, weapons, and other logistical support, installing a military dictatorship that would last for seventeen brutal years, Nixon encouraged the bank and other key lenders to resume relationships with Chile. The institutions of globalization examined herein were thus used as economic tools for fighting the war against Communism, even if that meant supporting a human-rights-abusing tyrant who assumed power after the assassination of a democratically elected president.[92]

Whereas our comments above on the IMF, World Bank, and WTO have argued that globalizing capitalism is an inherently unstable phenomenon, one that may well be slipping away from U.S. or G-8 control, the US-SFTA, US-CFTA, CAFTA, NAFTA, and FTAA point to a new phase of globalization, where bilateral trade pacts fulfill explicitly military functions, serving as little more than imperial alliances between the United States and its client states. In fact, FTAs are currently being negotiated with Bahrain and Morocco, with the Bush administration beginning work on a broadly construed Middle East FTA as well, in each case forging economic, political, and assumedly military alliances with nondemocratic states that will be useful in cementing U.S. power in the region. This is hardly a recipe for spreading democracy. But as we demonstrate below, the dilemmas of globalization may well escape even these attempts at imperial control.[93]

Four Tensions of Globalization and Possible Fractures in International Capitalism

Having established the historical background to our current moment of globalization in the first section of this chapter, and having examined both the institutional architecture of globalization and politically motivated regional and bilateral FTAs in the second section, we now address four of the most pressing dilemmas of globalization. These are by no means the only dilemmas we could address, but they are the ones that speak most directly to our interests in locating the relationships among globalization, empire, and the causes of violence. These four dilemmas are as follows: first, the spatial dilemma of fixed human needs clashing with mobile economic opportunities; second, the economic dilemma of the United States becoming a postindustrial nation that exports jobs and imports products, thus both driving global development and hindering it; third, the dilemma of unregulated financial practices, which produce profit without making goods, thus exacerbating developing world debt while enriching first-world elites; and fourth, the dilemma of horrible nineteenth-century labor practices persisting in the shadow of twenty-first-century innovations. Focusing on these four dilemmas will enable us to locate the instabilities within the new institutional architecture of globalization, recognizing its fault lines and weak spots by analyzing its perhaps crippling internal contradictions. Ultimately, we suspect that as the United States loses any sense of control over these dilemmas, and as globalization therefore teeters closer to market-induced anarchy than U.S.-controlled neoliberalism, so the United States becomes increasingly likely to rely on military force to achieve its economic and political goals.

Tension One: Transnational Capitalism Enriches Elite Nations and Hinders Global Development

In our comments above regarding the historical roots of MNCs and globalization we noted that U.S. capitalists began roaming the globe as early as the mid-nineteenth century, reaching truly global proportions following the 1898 Spanish-American War, and that Europeans followed a similar course, one that reached its apex in the closing decades of the nineteenth century, when Britain, France, Germany, Belgium, Portugal, the Netherlands, and to a lesser degree Spain colonized much of the globe. For both U.S. and European capitalists the point of international trade was clear: to make profits not possible in domestic markets and to aid the political ambitions of their home states. Limited local economic development may have been one result of such actions, but it was not the goal; in fact, most historians agree that globalizing U.S. and European capitalists sought to "develop" their colonial or semicolonial host countries only so far as was necessary to aid their own profit interests. As Michael Hardt and Antonio Negri argue in *Empire,* summarizing what has become known as the underdevelopment and/or dependency thesis, "to say that the subordinate economies do not develop does not mean that they do not change or grow; it means, rather, that *they remain subordinate in the global system.*"[94]

What distinguishes contemporary MNCs from these early practitioners of globalization is not that they produce underdevelopment or selective development in their host countries, for that has always been the role of international capitalism, but that their relationships with home states are now tenuous at best. That is, whereas the actions of late-nineteenth-century globalizing capitalists clearly supported both their domestic home economies and the political ambitions of their home states, today's MNCs increasingly pursue interests that transcend localizable states or markets. We have demonstrated this point above in our comments on *maquiladora* plants in Mexico, where MNCs use border-straddling "development zones" to achieve astronomical corporate profits while costing U.S. workers their jobs, leaving Mexico little gain, and exploiting local Mexican workers. To supplement that example, consider the complicated global production process leading to a Gap sweatshirt.

The story begins in Uzbekistan, where Gap Inc. pays two cents for a pound of cotton; the cotton is then ground-shipped through Iran to the Arabian Sea, where it is floated to Korea, where it is woven by workers who make $4 an hour; the material is then shipped by boat and rail to Russia, where it is sewn together by women who make between $39 and $69 per month; from Russia the sweatshirts are floated to California; from there they are trucked to Fishkill, New York, where they are sorted, packaged, and shipped to stores where U.S. consumers purchase them for roughly $48. The Gap's cheerful sweatshirts thus embody a new stage of global capitalism, where the production process spans multiple continents. The Gap presumably maximizes its profit by engaging in this circuitous production process, but does this process help the United States? No, for the completed sweatshirt consists entirely of foreign materials and mostly foreign labor—so a U.S.-based corporation makes a profit, and U.S. consumers get their sweatshirts, but the U.S. economy as a whole receives little jolt of employment and material sales; instead U.S. citizens play the limited roles of shippers, sorters, and sales clerks. Expanding from the question of how the Gap's global production process affects the United States to how it impacts its many global partners leads us to the heart of one of the key debates about globalizing capitalism: *does the Gap provide necessary and much-appreciated jobs or does it engage in reprehensible exploitation?*[95]

To answer that question we turn to the Gap's 2003 *Social Responsibility Report* (*SRR*). An extensive attempt to chronicle Gap's international labor practices, the *SRR* illustrates some of the core issues surrounding MNCs and the new global economy. For example, the *SRR* observes that in fiscal year 2003 Gap sold $15.9 billion worth of goods while employing 150,000 workers in three thousand garment factories in fifty countries. Hence illustrating what is meant by the term "post-Fordism," where modernity's giant centralized factories have given way to postmodernity's interlinked networks of small contractors and subcontractors—thus making the Gap's use of the word "factory" highly misleading—Gap stretches across the globe, managing a dense chain of independent producers, hence providing it remarkable flexibility in terms of where it chooses to do business and under what conditions. In fact, the *SRR* reports that Gap's social responsibility code obligated it to "revoke the approval of 136 factories" in 2003 alone. This practice of refusing to do business with "factories" that break key aspects of the Gap's social responsibility code indicates a MNC trying to maximize the benefits of globalization while minimizing its abuses.[96]

However, the *SRR* also acknowledges that "no garment manufacturer or factory is in full compliance with all the requirements all of the time." For example, consider the testimony of Carmencita Abad, who worked for a Gap-contracted manufacturer in Saipan (one of the Mariana Islands, south of Japan). Abad was appalled at the working conditions in her facility and tried to organize a union; she was intimidated by factory owners who were committed not to upholding social responsibility codes but to the bottom line. She then approached Global Exchange, the San Francisco–based workers' rights organization, which produced "Gap's Code of Conduct vs. Carmencita Abad's Reality." A stunning point-by-point refutation of the Gap's *SRR*, Abad's report portrays an independent contractor struggling to succeed by ruthlessly oppressing workers and cutting business expenses. Indeed, in *No Logo*, her popular exposé of globalization's production of the spectacles and miseries of consumerism, Naomi Klein reports that "seamstresses at a factory sewing garments for the Gap, Guess and Old Navy" in the Philippines were under such intense quota-driven pressure that "they sometimes have to resort to urinating in plastic bags under their machines." While MNCs like the Gap thus author social responsibility codes like the *SRR*, the reality of transnational production processes means that the application of such standards amounts to what Abad portrays as and what Klein calls "a haphazard and piecemeal mess of crisis management."[97]

Thus, even while U.S. workers are hurt by the Gap and Gap-like MNCs "outsourcing" their labor, so workers in developing nations—like Abad in Saipan, Klein's interviewees in the Philippines, and the Uzbeki,

Korean, and Russian workers mentioned above—find themselves laboring under hellish conditions that make a mockery of the glowing promises of the proponents of globalizing free markets. In the long run, even though the Gap's practices do not benefit the United States as a whole, the widespread sense that such companies are American, that they somehow support an American agenda and benefit the U.S. economy as a whole, can only produce animosity toward the United States, hence undercutting U.S. attempts to manage the consequences of globalization. If the global war on terrorism is largely a war of ideas, a cultural battle fought for the hearts and minds of the world, then this first tension of globalization points to a damning conclusion: that U.S. legitimacy around the world suffers because of the perceptions of injustice that circulate around the Gap and its fellow MNCs.

Tension Two: How the United States Both Drives and Hinders Development

Our second dilemma follows logically from the first: whereas the practices of underdevelopment create long-term structural advantages for U.S. and European-based MNCs, the ability of MNCs to locate the cheapest labor possible means that even while MNCs may make great profits, workers in developed nations suffer from their outsourcing of production. Indeed, as demonstrated above in our examples from *maquiladora* plants and the Gap, American workers will almost always be undercut by workers in developing nations, where wages, taxes, environmental standards, and other production costs are lower and more pliable. The Gap's economic advantage thus hurts the U.S. national interest, for the Gap's purchasing Uzbeki cotton means U.S. cotton is not being bought; its contracting Korean weavers means Americans are not doing that work; its hiring Russian seamstresses means U.S. laborers who once did that work are out of a job. The MNC roams the globe, seeking profits by maximizing economic advantages, but the nation-state (and its workers) is geographically fixed, leaving the United States with the dilemma of unemployed or underemployed workers whose jobs have gone overseas. The larger problem here—illustrating what Giovanni Arrighi calls the "Catch 22 that always confronts incumbent leading centers of capitalist development"—is that as these processes slowly but surely sap the United States of economic vitality, so a slowed-down U.S. economy in turn places a heavy burden on global development.[98]

For an example of these claims, let us return once again to NAFTA.

Vigorously promoted by the Clinton administration both as a vehicle for creating jobs for American citizens and as a harbinger of the heady possibilities of globalizing free markets, it is now clear that even while NAFTA has enabled large corporate profits, it has proven disastrous for American workers. Indeed, Public Citizen's Global Trade Watch released a report in 2001 chronicling the effects of NAFTA on Alabama's family farmers. Titled *Down on the Farm: NAFTA's Seven-Years War on Farmers and Ranchers in Alabama,* the study concludes that "non-corporate Alabama farm operations fell 74% between 1993 and 1999." As a result, "2,000 farms have disappeared during the seven years of NAFTA." The culprit here is peanuts. Since NAFTA was passed, the United States has increased its consumption of imported Mexican peanuts by 1400 percent. Peanuts accounted for as much as 70 percent of Alabama's crop income as late as 1998, meaning that whereas the state's noncorporate peanut farmers were once the backbone of the state's farming community, now they are being driven out of business by MNCs importing peanuts farmed under cheaper conditions in developing nations. Although these imported peanuts are cheaper to produce than their Alabama-farmed counterparts, the puzzling fact is that since the implementation of NAFTA "prices for food eaten at home in cities with fewer than 50,000 residents in the South increased by 23%." So as the wholesale commodities purchased on the globalizing free market cost capitalists less, the retail commodities purchased in small-town domestic markets cost Americans more—this is a recipe for profit at the top of the social ladder and mass-produced poverty at its bottom.[99]

Furthermore, the corporations importing these Mexican peanuts are ostensibly American, which explains the massive tariffs still imposed on foreign-made peanut butter. So while American-based MNCs show increased profits, Alabama peanut farmers lose their jobs while simultaneously being forced to pay more for their daily sustenance; and while MNCs obtain cheaper raw materials, U.S. companies are protected by exorbitant tariffs that in turn hurt development elsewhere. Hence, in the name of free markets and their globalization, NAFTA enables U.S. corporations to roam far and wide, regardless of national interests or boundaries, all the while eroding farming life in Alabama and quashing development in other nations.[100]

Expanding from the plight of out-of-work farmers and overcharged consumers in Alabama to a macrological perspective that considers the nation as a whole, it is clear that as MNCs use NAFTA and NAFTA-like arrangements to increase profits by importing goods from their developing-nation subsidiaries or from foreign firms that rely on cheap labor, so the nation as a whole suffers. In fact, Greider reports that since 1980 "Americans have bought $1.5 trillion more than they sold in their merchandise traded with foreign nations." The catch is that many of these trade-deficit-ballooning imports come from U.S-based MNCs that have shifted their production to foreign locations. Thus, whereas the United States was once the world's preeminent manufacturer of goods, it has become the world's most overgorged consumer. This shift from being an exporting to an importing nation explains in part how the United States "went from holding a net surplus of foreign assets equal to 30 percent of its own annual economic output in 1970 to a debtor position by 1994 of −8.5 percent." In Greider's estimation this change from being an exporting nation to an importing nation has led to "an epochal shift of wealth, probably unmatched in human history."[101]

Thus, whereas many observers portray globalization as but a euphemism for expanding U.S. economic privilege and cultural dominance, the fact is that America as a whole is increasingly a loser in the game of globalization. This in turn means that the engine of globalization—the United States—is dragging, likely leading to economic difficulties elsewhere. Whereas a United States that is too successful breeds animosity and poverty globally, leading to political instability and economic uncertainty (tension one above), a United States that is not successful enough drags down the economic possibilities of developing nations, also leading to political instability and economic uncertainty (tension two). Finding a productive balance point in this complicated equation is made more difficult by the ways MNCs transcend national interests and local markets. A further complication, addressed below, is that profits increasingly have little to do with goods, instead circling the globe in an instantaneous market of financial speculation.

Tension Three: The Financial Piracy of Hot Money and Vulture Funds

Although the United States' position as leader of global production has steadily declined since the early 1970s, it has cemented its role as the world's banker. David Harvey's 1990 *The Condition of Postmodernity* offers a lucid analysis of this shift from the U.S.-based Fordist factories of modernity to the international flexible accumulation practices of postmodernity, arguing that one of the many ways the United States has sought to counter the challenges of globalization is by resorting to "paper entrepreneurialism." Locating the 17 October 1973 OPEC oil embargo as a key moment in the history of global capitalism, in part because it offered President Nixon the occasion to decouple the U.S. dollar from gold, Harvey argues that "since 1973, money has been de-materialized in the sense that it no longer has a formal or tangible link to precious metals. . . . Nor does it rely exclusively upon productivity within a particular space," meaning that "speculative shifts bypass actual economic power and performance." We do not mean to romanticize the gold standard, yet we agree with Harvey that the new post-Fordist world of flexible accumulation and loose money amounts to what he calls a "casino economy."[102]

Harvey's 2003 *The New Imperialism* updates this thesis, demonstrating how a post-1973 "explosion in the quantity of 'fictitious' capital in circulation lacking any prospect of redemption" has resulted in "a wave of bankruptcies . . . uncontainable inflationary pressures, and the collapse of fixed international arrangements that had founded U.S. super-imperialism after WWII." Perhaps the most startling aspect of our current moment of globalization, then, is how it has produced an international free market not so much for goods as for speculation on goods, leading to a new phase of capitalism in which power resides less with captains of industry than with bank managers—hence Harvey's characterization of globalization as an age of "financialization." One of the problems with this new age of casinolike financialization is that it breeds economic and political instability, adding yet another level of uncertainty to globalization. Indeed, market-playing investors and globe-straddling MNCs alike have come increasingly to rely for short-term profits on the vicissitudes of stocks, bonds, currencies, and the many forms of paper money that circulate the world regardless of national borders or the actual sales of goods. The great American novelist Don DeLillo characterizes such profits-without-products as "instantaneous capital that shoots across horizons at the speed of light." Although there are astronomical profits to be made from manipulating this instantaneous capital, the results of doing so, as we illustrate below, can be devastating for entire nations.[103]

Thinking historically, developing nations have been handcuffed, and in some cases devastated, by their post–World War II indebtedness to developed nations, banks from Europe and the United States, and the quasigovernmental institutions examined above, including the World Bank, IMF, and IADB. For example, Mandel notes in *Late Capitalism* that by the end of 1972 "the accumulated outstanding debts of the semi-colonies had grown to $100 billion. Debt service by now absorbed 31.5% of the export revenues of The United Arab Republic, 37.5% of those of Uruguay, 25% of those of Pakistan, 24% of those of India, 22% of those of Argentina, 20% of those of Afghanistan, and 19% of those of Turkey." Thus ranging from a low of 19% in Turkey to a high of 37.5% in Uruguay, these developing nations were forced to commit vast amounts of revenue from their exports to covering both the principal and the ever-piling interest on loans originally intended to help these nations catch up to the United States and Europe.[104]

In fact, Catherine Caufield notes in *Masters of Illusion* that beginning in the mid-1970s most of the loans going to Latin American states were not intended to aid economic development but to enable them to cover existing debt payments. So immediate loan defaults were prevented with more loans that in the long run only made the debt trap deeper. The accumulating mountain of interest on loans (and then additional loans to cover the interest on these loans) meant that these nations found themselves getting poorer, not wealthier, thus turning what were originally hope-laden loans into the shackles of long-term indebtedness. For critics of the World Bank and its fellow developed-nation institutions, these lending practices amount to financial colonization. Kristen Forbes, a member of President Bush's Council of Economic Advisers, argues that 2004 will mark the first year since the 1970s that Latin American states will pay back more to the IMF than they will borrow, hence indicating that the burden of the debt trap may, finally, be lessening. Yet the United Nations' *HDR* demonstrates that the combination of foreign direct investment (2.5 percent of GDP), foreign aid (.5 percent of GDP), and NGO grants (.1 percent of GDP) amounts to less than half of the 6.3 percent of GDP developing nations spend on average for debt servicing—which means that for every $1 coming in to a developing nation, roughly $2 leaves to service debts. Hence Joyce Kolko's bitter charge that "the IMF has effectively decapitalized the recipient countries."[105]

This systematic process of extracting capital from the developing world even while purportedly engaging in development is what economists call "unequal exchange." When calculated as a gross economic effect, as what happens when developing nations enter into loan-driven relationships with already developed nations, the results of unequal exchange can be shocking. For example, Samir Amin has estimated that from as early as the mid-1960s the United States and elite European states gathered as much as $22 billion per year from developing nations via the benefits of unequal exchange. This "outflow of value toward the metropolitan countries at the expense of the countries economically dependent on them," as Mandel describes it, means that the casinolike post-Fordist economy of financialization accelerates existing inequalities between developed and less-developed states.[106]

Our current moment of globalization has added a new twist to this phenomenon, for the early 1990s saw the bosses of the casino economy turning such loans and debts into the raw material for market speculation, literally transforming developing nation debt into an investment option for developed nation elites. Known as "the Brady Plan," the idea was to repackage developing nation debt as collateralized bonds that could be traded by investors, with the bonds guaranteed by the U.S. Treasury. Speculators could then buy debt low and, assuming developing nations managed to pull themselves out of depression, sell their bonds high, hence making a profit while encouraging development. Thus forming a mutually reinforcing triangulation of responsibilities between lending institutions, individual (or group) bondholders, and developing nations, with arrangements and payment schedules overseen by the IMF, the Brady Plan sought to turn disadvantage to advantage, to make developing-nation growth not only a political and moral imperative but an occasion for enlightened investment. The problem, of course, as any critic of capitalism could have predicted, is that the arrangement enabled rogue investors to sidestep the triangulation process by bypassing the IMF-imposed payment schedule to sue for full repayment of debt. The Brady Plan thus quickly devolved into what are known as "vulture funds."[107]

As reported by the European Network on Debt and Development, a particularly egregious example of a vulture fund involves the American financial firm of Elliott Associates (EA), which in 1996 used the Brady Plan model of packaged-debt-as-bond to pay $11 million to purchase $20 million of Peru's national debt. Although Peru originally owed the $20 million (and skyrocketing interest on it) to the World Bank, IMF, IADB, and other elite lender institutions, it was widely known that its debts could never be repaid at face value. Simply put, Peru could not afford to repay its $20 million debt, the banks knew this, the value of the loan was therefore diminished, and so the banks sold the rights to the loan to EA for $11 million, hence cutting their losses and disentangling themselves from a sticky situation that would likely have drawn on for years in tedious negotiations. Under the Brady Plan the repackaged loan would have been paid off slowly at discounted value, thus enabling EA to make a profit while helping Peru climb out of the debt trap.[108]

But EA, not bound by any of the quasigovernmental developmental agreements that underwrote the original loan, instead bundled Peru's debts into a package and began legal proceedings, suing for complete and immediate repayment of the loan. By arguing that it had preferred creditor status, EA was able to leap ahead of other nation-state creditors—including Canada, Belgium, Luxembourg, the Netherlands, Germany, and the United Kingdom—in the queue to receive payments. Thus, instead of gradually paying back long-standing loans to the World Bank, the IMF, and the European nations noted above, Peru was legally forced to repay Elliott Associates *first and in full.* Including owed back interest, Peru eventually paid EA $58 million, producing a $47 million profit for clever American bankers while leaving Peru evermore incapable of making the infrastructural investments required to pull its economy out of its decades-old doldrums.[109]

Elliott Associates first practiced such a plan in Panama in 1995, when it took advantage of the Brady Plan to pay $17.5 million for $28.75 million of Panama's debt. EA then sued for full and immediate payment of the original loan, all accrued interest, and legal costs, eventually receiving payment of $57 million, leaving them with almost $40 million of profit. In both the Peru and Panama cases, the market liberalization dictated by globalizing neoliberalism enabled EA to make money by manipulating developing-nation debt, thus further enriching the already wealthy while further impoverishing the poor. EA has reportedly wangled millions of dollars in similar maneuvers against Ecuador, Poland, the Ivory Coast, Turkmenistan, and the Democratic Republic of Congo. Appropriately named because they are acts of predatory capitalism in which the mighty prey on the weak, figuratively sweeping like carnivores down on the carcasses of the damned, vulture funds illustrate how globalizing financial markets can be manipulated to produce profits for a few first-world elites by exploiting the most vulnerable players in the globalizing free market.[110]

Moving from the specific example of how Elliott Associates used vulture funds to devastate Peru, Panama, and others, to the macroeconomic results of such actions, Harvey reports in *The New Imperialism* that since 2000 "some 37 countries" have been forced into "debt rescheduling." Although tweaking the particulars of these nations' permanent indebtedness by rescheduling their payments may postpone short-term economic crises, Harvey argues that the overall picture is one of "capital bondage," with developing nations literally held hostage by developed-nation financial institutions. In fact, Harvey claims that the "volatility" of global markets since the 1980s "was clearly manipulated, if not directed, by the Wall Street–IMF complex to the advantage of finance capital, Wall Street, and the U.S. economy." Thus, whereas many observers see the results of globalizing hot money as part of the unintended consequences of a new phase of international capitalism, Harvey attributes causality and intentionality to the institutions of globalization discussed above. He thus views the Asian crisis of 1997 as an intentional "attack" on rival economic models and as "the disciplining, even destruction, of the developmental states centered in East and South-East Asia." More generally, he sees the repeated financial crises that have erupted in recent years as part of "the visitation of crises" on the developing world, as "crises [that] may be imposed" by the World Bank, IMF, and other institutions of globalization. For Harvey, then, financialization amounts to a new weapon in the already large arsenal of tools used by developed states to enforce poverty and dependence on developing states.[111]

Harvey's concerns in *The New Imperialism* are shared, albeit rendered in a more cautious tone, by Stiglitz's *Globalization and Its Discontents*, which argues that IMF policies not only exacerbated the financial crises in Africa, East Asia, and Russia, but were largely responsible for them. Indeed, when considering the 1997 financial crash that began in Thailand but that rapidly spread to Malaysia, Korea, the Philippines, and Indonesia, Stiglitz argues that "I believe that capital account liberalization was *the single most important factor leading to the crisis.*" Likewise, Stiglitz argues that the torturous decline of post-Communist Russia was largely caused by the fluctuations and predatory actions of hot money. For while the IMF, World Bank, and other major developed nations offered Russia an emergency package of $22.6 billion in the summer of 1997, the Russians responded by suspending all debt payments and devaluing the ruble (which fell in value by 75 percent by January 1999). The Russian economy collapsed soon thereafter, leaving as many as 40 percent of all Russians to live on less than \$4 a day. Stiglitz notes with dismay that within days of the 1997 bailout, billions of dollars began "showing up in Cypriot and Swiss bank accounts," meaning that Russian elites swindled the bailout for their personal advantage, hence turning their nation toward poverty-stricken depression. Stiglitz thus reports that "there are many in Russia (and elsewhere) who believe the failed policies were not just accidental; the failures were deliberate, intended to eviscerate Russia." Stiglitz later discounts this argument, however, arguing that the horror story told above was not the result of intentional actions so much as poor planning and the organizational insensitivity that follows from developed-nation institutions meddling in the affairs of nations they know little about.[112]

Using Harvey and Stiglitz as our representative critics, then, the question boils down, again, to causality: *are the ravages of financialization the result of intentional actions or the inherent irrationality of globalizing capitalism?* Our examples from Elliott Associates and Harvey's *New Imperialism* point to the former; Stiglitz wants to cling to the latter. But even if we accept Stiglitz's answer, we are obliged to recognize that the architects of the financial catastrophes he analyzes appear to have learned little from recent history. In fact, at the G-8 Summit of 2001 in Genoa (but four years after financial crashes rocked Asia), the IMF, World Bank, and other regional development banks released a joint report on globalization and poverty in which they emphatically suggested that the neoliberalization of finances would benefit struggling economies. Addressing Asia in particular, where but four years earlier the predatory actions of unregulated hot money had led to economic devastation, the report claimed that "access to long-term international capital, including private direct investment, will also help expand economic opportunities and mitigate the impact of external shocks." Thus the same logic of championing liberalization, free markets, and venture investments that backfired only years before repeated like a broken record.[113]

Moreover, U.S. investors, having witnessed EA's use of vulture funds to score astronomical profits, are trumpeting the practice as the new wave of high-risk investment; hence the happy "how to" articles in *Forbes* and *Business Week* teaching speculators how to profit from vulture funds, hence the spring 2003 efforts by U.S. investors to repeat EA's tactics against Argentina. Given what we know about the roles of financialization in fueling the crashes of the late 1990s, however, and given the excitement among U.S. investors over vulture funds, the G-8's dogmatic repetition of neoliberal mantras cannot help but sound like an excuse for precisely what Harvey calls "the visitation of crises."[114]

As the vulture fund examples from above suggest, globalizing free markets tend to heighten the opportunities for manipulating what DeLillo calls "instantaneous capital." Greider reports that by the early 1990s, "foreign-exchange trading totaled more than $1.2 trillion *a day*." This means that profit is being made on trading not goods but paper—speculating on profits has become as lucrative as actually making a product. Contrary to the dream of such speculation opening doors to previously impoverished nations and entrepreneurs, the trading of this instantaneous capital was "mostly transacted by a very small community: the world's largest thirty to fifty banks and a handful of major brokerages." Despite the prevalent rhetoric claiming that the spread of free markets will inevitably produce economic opportunity and political democracy far and wide, Greider thus demonstrates that the "enormous mows of wealth and bounty" produced by globalization tend to accumulate in the hands of a relatively small clique of banks and MNCs, with the largest twenty of them based in the United States, the United Kingdom, Switzerland, the Netherlands, Italy, France, Germany, and Japan, essentially the G-8. In short, the old powers still dominate the new world of globalization.[115]

Because of these exploitative practices, especially in the form of hot money and vulture funds, many citizens in developing countries have come to view globalization as a form of neocolonialism disguised in the rhetoric of free markets and expanding democracy. In fact, the United Nations Development Programme conducted a survey of 18,643 Latin Americans in the spring of 2004, finding that "a majority say they would support the replacement of a democratic government with an 'authoritarian' one if it could produce economic benefits." As noted throughout this chapter, globalizing neoliberalism has proven disastrous to many developing nations, yet the survey found that many of the victims of this economic process "are faulting democracy itself." Rather than making international capitalism seem more fair, then, linking it with democracy has actually left democracy's reputation in tatters, as a political order besmirched with globalization's failures.[116]

Tension Four: New World Technology and Old World Barbarism

We noted above that many victims of international capitalism's injustice mistakenly blame democracy as the cause of their troubles. We add to our analysis of the production of resentment by noting the strange clash between the utopian promises of New World technology and the reality of Old World barbarism. We have been influenced here by Kevin Bales's *Disposable People*, which offers a grueling account of how globalizing neoliberalism's search for cheap labor leads to working conditions that recall the horrors of slavery. Bales argues that "as international business now seeks to buy labor at the lowest cost, often through subcontractors, some of these contractors achieve the lowest cost by using slave labor." In short, New World technology and Old World barbarism go hand in hand. As Bales notes, and as we examine below, this relationship is also fueled by the use of subcontractors.[117]

Following Bales and others' leads, our comments fall into two categories, regarding domestic and international effects. Domestically, the role of technology is complicated, for while its advances are making life more convenient for the lucky in an apparently infinite number of ways, that same technology makes more and more workers redundant, thus eroding the economic stability of one of the classes on whom our national economic health depends. Recognizing both its genius and barbarism, this is how DeLillo describes a new, super high-tech auto plant: "The system flows forever onward, automated to priestly nuance, every gliding movement back-referenced for prime performance. Hollow bodies coming in endless sequence. There's nobody on the line with caffeine nerves or a history of clinical depression. Just the eerie weave of chromium alloys carried in interlocking arcs, block iron and asphalt sheeting, soaring ornaments of coachwork fitted and merged. Robots tightening bolts, programmed drudges that do not dream of family dead."[118]

This posthuman landscape of brilliantly efficient robotic drudges increasingly spans the globe. In fact, although the popular press portrays America as the world's forerunner in all things technological, the country's economic stability suffers because of its inferior technological sophistication. For example, at Toyota's Tahara plant, where they build the luxury Lexus LS 400, cars were assembled in the late 1990s with only 18.4 hours of human labor; similar high-end vehicles were built by General Motors and Ford in factories in Michigan where the labor hours required to finish a vehicle were 39 and 34 hours respectively. Adding the saved labor time and the saved warranty charges enabled by its robotic efficiency, Toyota thus made luxury cars for as much as $1,000 less per vehicle than GM or Ford. The logic of capitalism dictates that GM and Ford must play technological catch-up; to a large extent they have, but in the process of advancing their technology they have left thousands of workers unemployed. For example, whereas it took 4,720 workers to build 960 Ford Granadas a day in 1979, it took 1,880 workers to build 1,200 Escorts a day in 1990. In the case of the auto industry, then, globalizing technological innovation means more unemployed Americans and more cars flooding an already saturated market.[119]

Recent information confirms these theses while adding an ominous touch: while U.S. auto manufacturers still take longer to make cars than their Japanese competitors, and while U.S. companies continue to play catch-up by adding new technologies at the cost of jobs (Chrysler, for example, cut 800,000 hours of human labor-time in 2002), some U.S. firms are now actually losing money on each car they make. For example, Ford lost $114 for each vehicle it made in 2002. And although General Motors made $701 on each car it made, this pales in comparison to the $1,214 made by Toyota, the $1,581 made by Honda, and the $2,069 made by Nissan. These examples from the auto industry by no means represent the fate of all U.S. manufacturers, but they indicate the ways *technology has no flag*—innovations transcend borders, in many cases leaving U.S. workers and U.S. firms at a disadvantage. (As a side note, we should re member that U.S. auto manufacturers pay as much as $5 billion per year in health care benefits for their workers, whereas Japanese and German companies have no such expenditures due to nationalized health care. So here is an example of how U.S. state policies—refusing to do what every other major Western state does: offer universal health care—hurts the competitiveness of U.S. capitalists.)[120]

The new technologies that leave increasing numbers of U.S. workers unemployed also sit side by side with ongoing barbarism, especially in developing nations. As Greider puts it, "The great paradox of this economic revolution is that its new technologies enable people and nations to take sudden leaps into modernity, while at the same time they promote the renewal of once-forbidden barbarisms. Amid the newness of things, exploitation of the weak by the strong also flourishes again." In short, the flip side of globalizing New World technology is increased Old World barbarism. Indeed, whereas Toyota and other cutting-edge com panies seek economic advantages in global free markets via the use of remarkable, truly fantastic automation, many companies pursue the old-fashioned route of exploiting workers too poor or too powerless to fight for basic human rights.[121]

Perhaps the most famous example of this thesis is the Kader Industrial Toy Company, where, in a fire in its factory outside Bangkok on 10 May 1993, 188 workers were killed and 469 were injured. The death and injury toll was so high not only because of a lack of safety precautions and dubious building practices—including the fact that the four buildings that burned to the ground had no fire escapes and no fire alarms—but because workers were locked inside the factory, trapped like slaves. In fact, the *New York Times* reported that even after the fire erupted, security guards blocked exit points, acting on management's fears "that workers would steal toys as they fled." The *Multinational Monitor* reports that workers at the plant were being paid $5 for working fourteen-hour shifts. Following an investigation, Kader was fined $12,380 for building code violations; considering that Kader's annual business runs in the billions of dollars, that fine amounts to an endorsement of its labor practices. Indeed, the Kader fire and its aftermath indicate that for globalizing capitalists, Old World barbarism is an accepted part of doing business.[122]

The toys those trapped Thai workers were producing were purchased by such familiar U.S. corporations as Toys "R" Us, Fisher-Price, Hasbro, Tyco, Arco, Kenner, Gund, and J.C. Penney. In this case, globalization means that first-world consumers purchase toys produced by subcontracted workers who labor in Bangkok under slavish and even deadly conditions. In an article championing free markets, the *Economist* repeats one of the key premises of the Washington Consensus when it argues that globalizing MNCs "transfer technology and know-how to their host economies," yet the Kader story illustrates the opposite: that while ramped-up technology makes production cheaper for some MNCs and their subcontractors, those who cannot afford the technological edge are forced to resort to even more egregious worker exploitation to keep up with their more technological competitors. Not so much contradictions as complicated partners, New World technology and Old World barbarism therefore interweave in a dangerous dance of mutual dependence and influence.[123]

Epilogue: "Blame for What Happened . . ."

From the perspective of neoliberalism's proponents, the future of globalization depends on denying the links articulated above between consumerism, New World technology, and Old World barbarism. For example, responding to blistering coverage of the Kader fire, David Miller, president of the Toy Manufacturers of America, argued in a letter to the *New York Times* that "blame for what happened rests with Thai managers . . . not with the American companies that contracted with Kader." Hence illustrating what we discussed earlier as the fetishism of commodities, Miller, like the *NSSUS* and President Bush, recognizes responsibility only for the finished products his group sells, not for the trail of death and exploitation that follows his toys to the market. In contrast to the capitalist truth-tellings of Bremer and Friedman, Miller's denial offers a model of the ways globalizing neoliberalism is based on refusing to see the inherent connections among profit and pain, desire and death, toys and terror.[124]

Attempting to dig beneath such self-serving denials, we have argued here that globalization is both hellish and utopian, that it is a truly paradoxical phenomenon marked by the four tensions discussed above: the tension of fixed human needs clashing with mobile economic opportunities; the tension of the United States both driving global development and hindering it; the tension of unregulated financial practices exacerbating developing-world debt while enriching first-world elites; and the tension of New World technology flourishing side by side with Old World barbarism. As argued here, technological advances shrink time and space yet make workers redundant; financial advances give capitalists more accounting flexibility yet lead to predatory dealings with developing nations; opening labor markets enables companies to reduce their production costs while pitting worker against worker, forcing wages downward; and so on in a dizzying spiral of contradictions, where all that matters is efficiency and profit. Calling for old-fashioned nation-defending regulations will likely trigger regional and even global tariff wars; calling off all trading regulations will only accelerate the damage to workers; and building NAFTA-like FTAs will continue to drag down wages, leaving the U.S. middle class with fancy goods purchased at the cost of working-class jobs in the United States and wasted lives elsewhere. Like capitalism in general, then, globalization is an inherently unstable, always changing, ethically dubious, mysteriously fluid process.

Nonetheless, we have argued here that globalization is enmeshed in a slow but sure transfer of power: global U.S. market dominance is shrinking, U.S. standards of living are declining, and anyone with access to easy capital and proliferating technology can now enter the game, likely with workers willing to labor for wages less than those required to survive in the United States. It is hard not to suspect, then, that the war in Iraq, the war on terror, the principles articulated in the *NSSUS*, and the bilateral FTAs discussed above are at least indirect responses to the dilemmas of globalization. As Mitchell Koss asked in a scathing editorial in the *Los Angeles Times* in the early weeks of the war on Iraq, "How do you re-impose force in a world that has been slipping beyond control?" Koss answered that question by charging that the United States chose to wage war on Iraq in order "to show its prowess in a globalized world." The direct intentionality of that statement is hard to support, for as we have shown here, globalization is not monolithic, it serves no one master, its effects are diffuse and complex; nonetheless, our analyses in this chapter (and of the Bush Doctrine in chapter 2) suggest that the rise of a U.S. empire—fueled both by military adventurism and bilateral FTAs—is closely related to the desperate attempt to control the inherently uncontrollable process of globalization. To watch how such attempts to control globalization leave the United States in increasingly compromised positions, both economically and politically, we turn now to the reconstruction of Iraq.[125]

4

Privatizing the Empire

Globalizing Crony Capitalism and the Rhetoric of "Renewal in Iraq"

Speaking before the House Appropriations Foreign Operations Subcommittee on 30 September 2003, Andrew Natsios, the administrator of the USAID, argued that the United States has done a herculean job of rebuilding roads, schools, water treatment plants, and other crucial components of Iraq's devastated infrastructure. Regarding health care, for example, Natsios reported that the United States has

> rehabilitated 20 delivery rooms in care centers serving 300,000 residents in Basra. An additional 29 hospital rehabilitations have been completed in other areas and 131 more are planned or underway; 600 primary health centers have been re-equipped. . . . [The United States has] distributed most of three million packets of Oral Re-hydration Salts to children with diarrhea, and provided 2.5 kilograms of supplementary food rations to more than 100,000 pregnant, nursing mothers and malnourished children under 5 years. We have procured 4.2 million vaccinations, with approximately 1.4 million children vaccinated through July [2003].[1]

And on and on it goes, a dazzling list of humanitarian achievements that have improved the lives of once-desperate Iraqis. Similarly remarkable reports of postwar achievements were available via the Coalition Provisional Authority's "Administrator's Weekly Report" and are still available via USAID's "Weekly Update" of "Iraq Reconstruction and Humanitarian Relief" and the materials posted by the U.S. Embassy in Baghdad. The question, then, given what appears to be an unprecedented offering of health care and other social services to Iraqis—ironically surpassing what is available in many U.S. inner cities—is Why has the reconstruction of Iraq taken on such an ominous tone? Why do U.S. actions in Iraq appear so calculated, so instrumental, so hypocritical? If CPA, USAID, and U.S. Embassy claims are true, then how can an internal U.S. military report lament "the disaster that is the reconstruction of Iraq"?[2]

One answer may be that many observers intuitively understand the argument we offered in chapter 1: that the United States' claims about Iraqi WMDs were sheer fabrications and that the war was fought by choice, presumably to advance U.S. economic and political interests. From this perspective, no amount of reconstruction can make up for fighting an unnecessary and unethical war. A second answer may be that many observers grasp the argument we offered in chapter 2: that the *National Security Strategy of the United States* claims the right of the United States to wage war when and where it pleases, hence making Iraq but the first step in an anticipated string of wars of empire. From this perspective, no amount of reconstruction can hide the fact that the United States' actions in Iraq amount to a new stage of U.S. colonialism. Indeed, Tariq Ali, noted scholar of and frequent traveler through the Middle East, reports that "the peoples of the Arab world view Operation Iraqi Freedom as a grisly charade, a cover for an old-fashioned European-style colonial occupation." A third answer may be that many observers, following the arguments we presented in chapter 3, see the reconstruction of Iraq as a case study in what we saw David Harvey call "globalization through Americanization." From this perspective, no amount of reconstruction can hide the fact that it has been undertaken almost exclusively by U.S.-based firms (and their international subcontractors, most with deep ties to the military-industrial complex), hence rendering reconstruction as little more than state-to-corporation welfare, as an attempt to wrench—"integrate" was the word we saw the proponents of NAFTA and the FTAA use in chapter 3—Iraq into the globalizing network of neoliberal free markets under the blanket of U.S. consumer goods and cultural norms. These three arguments render the United States' reconstruction efforts in postwar Iraq as little more than the veneer of altruism covering self-interest, as a hypocritical and largely botched show of nation building meant to try to persuade a skeptical world that the United States is actually concerned with the well-being of both individual Iraqis and the nation as a whole, even while turning it into a fully franchised outpost of U.S. military, corporate, and political power.[3]

Yet a fourth answer, hearkening back to our introduction, is that the horrible images of torture at Abu Ghraib prison made explicit what many Iraqis have feared ever since 9/11 gave the Bush administration an excuse to pursue regime change in Baghdad: that imperial U.S. culture is irrevocably laced with pornography and brutality. From this perspective, no amount of reconstruction can hide the fact that the occupation of Iraq has become a shame-producing nightmare haunted by U.S. soldiers and contractors. For example, in a conversation with Mark Danner in Baghdad, a young Iraqi disgustedly spit out the word *shame* five times in five sentences to describe how Iraqis feel about the U.S. occupation. The young man concluded his discourse on shame by saying "The Americans *provoke* the people. They don't *respect* the people." Working in tandem with the military, political, and economic arguments noted above, this position sees the reconstruction of Iraq as a form of cultural imperialism, as imposed debasement.[4]

A fifth reason the reconstruction of Iraq has become so controversial is that it has been driven thus far by what we call in this chapter "crony capitalism." Indeed, the materials presented in chapters 2 and 3 point to the conclusion that when President Bush and his supporters say *free market*, they mean *crony capitalism*. Whereas the World Bank, IMF, WTO, IADB, CAFTA, NAFTA, and the many pending FTAs discussed previously are all couched in the language of free markets meant to extend political democracy, consumer choice, technical innovation, and the rule of law, we showed in chapter 3 that the driving force of globalizing capitalism remains a relatively small clique of G-8-based multinational corporations that share members of their boards of directors, lobbying influence, trading relationships, and the coterie of "experts" who glide through the revolving doors linking corporate power, government power, and military power. We argued in our introduction that free trade is a lie, and we showed in chapters 2 and 3 how globalizing neoliberalism is a rigged game; in each instance we pointed to the crucial fact that the ever-widening gap between the lived realities of globalization and the Bush administration's vacuous rhetoric about free markets has left U.S. claims to be spreading democracy and opportunity looking compromised at best, malevolent at worst. When coupled with the WMD lies examined in chapter 1 and the *NSSUS*'s provocative blueprint for empire studied in chapter 2, the reality of crony capitalism underlying the rhetoric of free markets has thus left the United States facing a global legitimacy crisis.

We also argued in chapter 3, however, that the success of G-8-based multinational corporations does not directly translate into U.S. economic or political power. In fact, we argued that neoliberal globalization is slowly but surely stripping the United States of its once-unchallenged status as both the engine and chief beneficiary of global capitalism. Following Harvey, Johnson, Wood, and others, then, we argued that this process has led to an increasingly desperate United States using its military power to try to defend and extend its waning economic power. The remarkably limited parameters of participation in the reconstruction of Iraq support this thesis, as only the United States and handpicked U.S. allies have been allowed to enter the new, post-Hussein market. In contrast to the promises of open free markets, what we see unfolding in Iraq is closed crony capitalism, a system where contracts are awarded without public bidding and without international competition, where links to the military-industrial complex function as a form of state-to-corporation welfare, where democratic checks and balances are thwarted by laws protecting corporate secrecy, and where national security is used as a justification for corporate malfeasance. The reconstruction of Iraq therefore looks startlingly similar to the imperial scenario we discussed in our introduction, where we saw J. A. Hobson argue that "the only possible answer" to the question of how such economic excess and waste could be pursued in the name of the nation "is that the business interests of the nation as a whole are subordinated to those of certain sectional interests that usurp control of the national resources and use them for their private gain." Updating Hobson's thesis about imperial usurpers, Antonia Juhasz has characterized the reconstruction of Iraq as "capitalism gone wild." Gordon Adams echoes this charge in a slightly different tone, calling postwar Iraq "a Wild West atmosphere." But Christian Parenti has put it most succinctly, arguing that "one dynamic above all others has destroyed the American project in Iraq: fraud."[5]

Thus, while USAID's Natsios proudly boasts of U.S. accomplishments in bringing social services to needy Iraqis, the means of providing these services are attracting scrutiny because they appear to suggest that Iraq is systematically being carved up into corporate fiefdoms. The triumphs Natsios trumpets to Congress therefore simultaneously terrify much of the world, for they indicate how the United States is selling off Iraq's economy, bit by bit, turning it into a colonial outpost of U.S-based corporate interests. Moreover, many observers worry that Iraq's nascent democracy cannot survive alongside globalizing crony capitalism. Such fears follow clearly from the fact that some Washington insiders appear more interested in establishing neoliberal markets than building democratic polities. For example, Robert Kaplan, noted neoconservative journalist, argues that "our goal in Iraq should be a transitional secular dictatorship that unites the merchant classes across sectarian lines and may in time, after the rebuilding of institutions and the economy, lead to a democratic alternative." Kaplan's capitalist truth-telling makes this chilling point: the reconstruction of Iraq should be focused first and foremost on cementing a "transitional secular dictatorship" of crony capitalists, hence leaving Iraq less as a fledgling democracy than as a privatized fiefdom.[6]

The postwar reconstruction of Iraq therefore serves as a laboratory for witnessing how the United States is trying to circumvent the dilemmas of globalization by imposing a state-run yet thoroughly privatized economy—that is, by merging the rhetoric of multinational neoliberal capitalism with the realities of U.S.-driven military Keynesianism. To support this thesis our argument here unfolds in four sections. First, to debunk Bush administration claims regarding the heroic march of democracy and self-rule in Iraq, we recount what critics are referring to as "the handover that wasn't." Second, we engage in a sweeping examination of how crony capitalism compromises U.S. efforts to bring economic rejuvenation and political democracy to Iraq. Third, merging stories from Iraq and the United States, we offer a series of example-driven definitions of crony capitalism. And fourth, to demonstrate the depth of illusion driving U.S. polices in Iraq, we analyze the Bush administration's claims regarding the politics and economics of reconstruction. The chapter then closes with an epilogue arguing that privatizing the empire via crony capitalism amounts to nothing less than an assault on democracy itself.

The Handover That Wasn't

In an editorial published in the *Washington Post* on 27 June 2004, the about-to-be-installed-as-prime-minister Ayad Allawi prophesied that with the handover of authority from the United States to Iraq, scheduled for the thirtieth, "the Iraqi people will take their first step toward a free and prosperous future." Apparently hoping to preempt expected terrorist strikes on the thirtieth, the United States disbanded the CPA and

handed power over to a supposedly rebuilt and sovereign Iraqi government on the twenty-eighth, thus formally ending the U.S. occupation.
President Bush and Prime Minister Tony Blair held a joint press conference during a NATO summit to mark the transfer of authority. Speaking
from Istanbul, the president announced that the handover marked "a
proud moral achievement for members of our coalition. We pledged to
end a dangerous regime, to free the oppressed, and to restore sovereignty.
We have kept our word." Blair corroborated Bush's claims and called the
day "an important staging post on the journey of the people of Iraq towards a new future, one in which democracy replaces dictatorship; in
which freedom replaces repression; and of which all the people of Iraq
can look forward to the possibility and the hope of an Iraq that genuinely
guarantees a future for people from whatever part of Iraq they come."[7]

Despite such grand claims regarding Iraqi independence, the fact is
that at the time there were still 138,000 U.S. soldiers, 20,000 coalition
troops, and more than 20,000 U.S. contractors on the ground, all faced
with a rising insurgency (to which we return below) that in the following
months would become a full-scale war. On the day of the transfer, fewer
than 140 of the slated 2,300 reconstruction projects had been started,
largely because many contractors were forced to devote as much as 20
percent of their money to hiring security contingents rather than workers.
Moreover, although there were supposed to have been at least fifty thousand Iraqis employed in local reconstruction efforts by then, only twenty
thousand Iraqis were working on such projects at the time of the handover of authority. While President Bush and Prime Minister Blair thus
boasted of their efforts to "restore sovereignty" to Iraq, and while Allawi
envisioned "a free and prosperous future," it was clear to many observers
that Iraq was in a shambles: economically devastated, politically crippled,
culturally fractured, and suffering from an increasingly deadly anti-U.S.
insurgency, the nation was hanging by a thread.[8]

Moreover, the CPA became defunct on June 28 in name only, for before departing Baghdad CPA Administrator Paul Bremer bequeathed
economic and political control of Iraq to the thirty-year exile and ex-CIA
informant, Prime Minister Ayad Allawi, and stacked every ministry with
U.S.-appointed officials serving five-year terms. Bremer also assigned a
list of one hundred orders that would direct Iraq's transition "from a cen-
trally planned economy to a market economy." The CPA's Program Management Office, which was responsible for overseeing the reconstruction

effort, was not dissolved; it simply underwent a change in name, becoming the Project and Contracting Office (PCO). According to its own press release, the PCO "will now report to the U.S. Department of State, which is responsible for setting priorities and requirements, and to the U.S. Department of the Army, which is responsible for program management and contracts." Ellen McCarthy reported in the *Washington Post* that despite the fanfare about Iraqi independence and full sovereignty, "U.S. contractors working in Iraq will be exempted from the legal processes of the country's new interim government when they are performing official duties." This means that as long as contractors' actions fall within their officially sanctioned PCO duties, they are not beholden to Iraqi laws. With Iraq run by a U.S.-picked prime minister, U.S.-stacked ministries, U.S.-authored orders, and U.S.-directed PCO development agreements, the notion that Iraq was now a free and independent republic was farcical. The *New York Times* accordingly referred to the administration's claims regarding Iraqi independence as "ludicrous." Indeed, the so-called transition at the end of June 2004 from an occupied to an independent Iraq can more accurately be described as, in Juhasz's terms, "the handover that wasn't."[9]

Although the transfer of authority was therefore largely symbolic, it nonetheless meant that the operational center of U.S. efforts was shifted from the CPA to the new (and then still under construction) embassy of the United States in Iraq. In Colin Powell's words, the new embassy was "bound to be one of the largest, most complex, and most important in the world." During the ceremonial swearing-in of Ambassador John Negroponte as the head of the embassy on 13 June 2004, Powell's comments drew laughter from an all-star crowd of Washington insiders when he remarked, "John, we save the most challenging jobs for you." Indeed, Negroponte's history of "challenging jobs" is extensive, for he has served in some capacity in every presidential administration since Dwight Eisenhower. His foreign service began in 1960; he was then transferred in 1964 to the U.S. Embassy in Saigon, hence placing him at the center of the diplomatic office that would lead the failed U.S. war on Vietnam. From 1971 through 1973 Negroponte advised Henry Kissinger, objecting during the Paris peace talks that Kissinger was "making too many concessions to the North Vietnamese." Negroponte was subsequently posted, some say exiled, to appointments in Ecuador and then Greece. From 1981 to 1985, during the Contra wars, he was the ambassador to Honduras, heading an embassy that was charged with collaborating with both the Contras and human-rights abusers in Honduras. From 1987 to 1989 he served as deputy assistant to the president for national security affairs; then, from 1989 to 1993, during the Zapatista uprising in Chiapas, he was the ambassador to Mexico, thus again overseeing an embassy caught in the middle of a violent civil war. From 1993 to 1996 he served as ambassador to the Philippines; he was posted to Panama in 1996; in 1997 he became executive vice president for global markets at McGraw-Hill, where he worked until President Bush nominated him to be the ambassador to the UN in September 2001. Given the long-standing arguments of his critics that Negroponte has spent much of his career supervising U.S. allies engaging in lawbreaking, human-rights-destroying, democracy-crushing, empire-defending violence, it comes as no surprise that Stephen Kinzer argued that "sending him to the UN serves notice that the Bush administration will not be bound by diplomatic niceties as it conducts its foreign policy." Three days after the attacks of 9/11, Congress confirmed Negroponte's appointment to the UN, "with unexpected ease" as the *New York Times* put it; less than three years later he was sworn in by Powell for the "challenging job" of ambassador to Iraq, again gaining congressional approval with little controversy.[10]

In chapter 1, we noticed how a compliant Congress abdicated its duty of raising questions about the rush to war on Iraq; Negroponte's breezy confirmation hearings illustrate again how that body has lost any sense of critical engagement with evidence countering the president's wishes, for it is widely known that Negroponte's record is dubious, if not criminal, especially because of his involvement in the Contra affair during the time of his post in Honduras. For example, the *Baltimore Sun* ran a four-part series in the summer of 1995 detailing how in the early 1980s the Honduran death squad known as Battalion 316 systematically kidnapped, tortured, and murdered civilians. Part of President Reagan's effort to eliminate the scourge of Communism supposedly stalking Central America, Battalion 316, like many of the death squads in El Salvador, Guatemala, and Nicaragua, allegedly depended on the United States for military training, arms, finance, and other covert logistical support. While Negroponte was ambassador to Honduras, from 1981 to 1985, he was repeatedly presented with evidence chronicling Battalion 316's butchery, yet he consistently proclaimed, both in public forums and before the Senate Foreign Relations Committee, that Honduras was free of death squads and human-rights abusers. But as one of the key staging grounds for the Contra wars that killed as many as fifty thousand men, women, and children in Nicaragua alone, and hence as a nation torn both by its own internal strife and by violence spilling over from Nicaragua, there can be little doubt that Negroponte's frequent denials were little more than empire-protecting deceptions.[11]

So although the *Baltimore Sun* has chronicled his connections to the Iran-Contra scandal, and regardless of the fact that Negroponte has been publicly accused of deceiving Congress—"Congress was deliberately misled," says the *Sun*—Negroponte slipped with almost no opposition into the Bush administration by becoming the ambassador to the UN in 2000 and then head of the U.S. Embassy of Iraq in 2004. Negroponte will be dogged in his new position, however, by critics who remember that the accounts of those tortured by Battalion 316 in Honduras echo with the same sense of horror that marks the abuses at Baghdad's Abu Ghraib prison. For example, here is one passage describing Battalion 316's torturing of Ines Consuelo Murillo: "Her captors tied the 24-year-old woman's hands and feet, hung her naked from the ceiling and beat her with their fists. They fondled her. They nearly drowned her. They clipped wires to her breasts and sent electricity surging through her body." Along with engaging in such dreadful, Abu Ghraib–like torture, Battalion 316 "disappeared" as many as two hundred Hondurans who are now presumed dead. From 1981 to 1985, then, Negroponte ran a U.S. embassy in a country where CIA-trained military units supposedly gathering intelligence from subversives were charged with "stalking, kidnapping, torturing and killing," yet he repeated over and over again, and did so in the hearings during which he was appointed ambassador to Iraq, that all was well in Honduras. Given this record of presiding blithely over U.S.-orchestrated mayhem, we can only imagine what awaits Iraq after the handover that wasn't.[12]

(Negroponte switched jobs again when he was appointed President Bush's new director of national intelligence in the spring of 2005; the *Washington Post* reported that April that Negroponte had "worked hard to maintain the fiction that Honduras was not serving as the logistical base for as many as 15,000 anti-Sandinista rebels." This ability to maintain the imperial fictions orchestrated by the White House will serve Negroponte well in his new position.[13])

But we need not speculate on that scenario, for despite the president's and his supporters' buoyant claims regarding Iraq's brave march toward freedom and development, the *New York Times* reported in July 2004 that government officials had received a dour report portraying postwar Iraq as a looming catastrophe. The classified *NIE* in question was reportedly pessimistic about Iraq's future, indicating that the worst-case scenario would be Iraq falling into civil war. The *Washington Post*'s Dana Priest and Thomas Ricks spoke with "career professionals within the national security agencies" who corroborated the *NIE*'s assessment, portraying postwar Iraq as "a disaster." Indeed, since the summer of 2004 Iraq has slipped ever closer to chaos. The number of examples we could marshal as evidence for that claim is stunning; here are but a few of the hundreds of telling events[14]:

- On 28 July 2004, one month after the transfer of sovereignty, seventy people were killed and fifty-six wounded when a suicide car bomber pulled up alongside a group of police recruits seeking jobs in Baquba. Then, on 14 September 2004, a car bomb exploded outside police headquarters in Baghdad, killing 47 and wounding 114 young men who were waiting to join the police force. In October 2004, fifty newly trained Iraqi soldiers were found executed on a deserted road near the Iranian border; members of the "al Qaeda in Mesopotamia" group had lured three busloads of soldiers into a fake checkpoint and then murdered all of them. These and other strikes like them demonstrate how the attempt to build indigenous security forces, whether police or army, is failing.[15]
- Whereas at the beginning of the U.S. occupation it was estimated that the insurgency comprised approximately twenty-five hundred Iraqis and fifty or so foreign jihadis, those numbers were revised upward by July 2004 to twenty thousand and five hundred, respectively. Fifty cells of insurgents supposedly draw on unlimited funding from "an underground financial network run by former Baath Party leaders and Saddam Hussein's relatives." Thus, while building Iraqi security forces is failing, the insurgency is growing.[16]
- Newspapers have reported that most of western Iraq, including the entire Anbar Province, is considered a no-go zone for U.S. military and contractors, with former Baath Party and Hussein loyalists joining fundamentalists to fight against occupiers and

Iraqis collaborating with the United States. While the so-called
Sunni triangle is increasingly considered off-limits to U.S. forces,
the violence has become so widespread in a region south of Baghdad that U.S. troops now refer to it as "the triangle of death." U.S.
forces are thus increasingly limited to heavily fortified enclaves,
thereby ceding much of Iraq's countryside and outlying towns to
insurgents. (U.S. forces did, however, attack supposed insurgent
strongholds in Karabila, Qaim, and Haditha, towns along Iraq's
western border, in May and June 2005.)[17]

- The Center for Strategic and International Studies released a report in September 2004 finding that security in Iraq was in the
  "danger zone" (as were the areas of governance and participation,
  economic opportunity, health care, and education). Basic policing
  functions have been so eroded by the occupation that whereas
  Baghdad experienced 14 violent deaths each month in 2002, by
  early 2004 it suffered 357 each month, therefore averaging more
  than 10 murders each day; by the summer of 2004 that monthly
  murder number had almost doubled, reaching "at least 600." The
  U.S. occupation has thus released a tidal wave of violence, leaving
  much of Iraq a crime-infested nightmare. As characterized by
  David Remnick, "A tyrant is gone, but much of Iraqi society
  has been reduced, at least sporadically, to a Hobbesian state of
  chaos."[18]

- And most dismaying of all, we learned in fall 2004 that as many
  as one hundred thousand civilians were killed in Iraq due to the
  war and fighting during the U.S. occupation. The president's war
  to preempt possible mass deaths possibly caused by WMDs has
  thus proven shamefully deadly.[19]

Alongside these terrible facts, consider the status of some of Iraq's
most important cities. For example, in Baghdad, although the amount of
electricity was finally restored to prewar levels around the date of the
"handover," the modernization of the power grid was still far behind
schedule, and most Baghdadis were still experiencing regular blackouts.
On 12 September 2004, mortar attacks in several Baghdad neighborhoods, four suicide car bombings, and innumerable gunshots into the
fortified "Green Zone" rocked the city before sunrise, killing approximately sixty Iraqis. The United States responded with air strikes, killing

an undetermined number of suspected guerillas and innocent civilians. In Baghdad alone in the month of September, there were nearly one thousand attacks on military and civilian targets (almost half of the national total of twenty-three hundred incidents of insurgent violence that month). On September 30, two car bombs struck a street celebration in Baghdad, killing 41 Iraqis, most of them children, and wounding 139 more. The violence continued into October, when early in the month two car bombs exploded, one near a police recruiting center and another near the interim Iraqi government headquarters and American embassy, killing fifteen and wounding eighty-two. The same day, another seven people were killed and twenty wounded by another car bomb near the Baghdad Hotel, where many journalists and foreign contractors stay. In one of his many brave reports from the streets of Baghdad, Christian Parenti described Baghdad as "this politically diseased metropolis . . . tormented by a fever of violence, social breakdown, administrative anarchy, and economic decline." Hardly an emblem of flowering democracy, postwar Baghdad amounts in these reports to a city under siege, a deadly war zone teetering on the brink of anarchy.[20]

The situation in Falluja has been equally bleak. After at least six hundred Iraqis, an estimated half of whom were women and children, were killed in clashes between insurgents and U.S. forces in early April 2004, the United States declared a brief cease-fire in the city. Although residents were spared from heavy artillery and major bombings, neither U.S. nor Iraqi forces could guarantee the safety of citizens. In fact, Rahul Mahajan reports seeing ambulances with "neat, precise bullet-holes in the windshield on the driver's side, pointing down at an angle that indicated [snipers, allegedly United States] would have most likely hit the driver's chest." Dahr Jamail, another reporter who braved Falluja around the same time, saw similar U.S. sniper attacks on ambulances and civilians, even during the cease-fire. (U.S. troops apparently feared insurgents were using ambulances as cover for ferrying weapons and fighters.) And in villages surrounding Falluja, hundreds more civilians were killed in "a kind of urban warfare that most marines know only from the movies." In the fall of 2004, attention was drawn again to Anbar Province when nearby Ramadi began to slip beyond control. Similar struggles were reported in Najaf, Karbala, Kufa, Mosul, and then Falluja again in November 2004. By June 2005 James Glanz was thus characterizing Iraq as suffering the dual fate of "insurgent mayhem and political stalemate."[21]

Rather than proudly speaking of the transition to democracy and free-dom, then, the situations in Baghdad, Falluja, Ramadi, Najaf, Karbala, Kufa, and Mosul—to say nothing of the "triangle of death"—would appear to oblige the president to discuss the status of an ongoing guerilla war, one the United States is by no means assured of winning. Indeed, in stark contrast to the Bush administration's cheerful claims regarding its benevolent role in bringing democracy and free markets to a sovereign Iraq, the U.S. reconstruction—*the handover that wasn't*—has thus far been a disaster of incomprehensible proportions. In fact, as a final insult to anyone who wanted to believe that Iraq was on the road to independence, consider the fact that when Prime Minister Allawi ventured to the U.S. Congress in September 2004, ostensibly to thank the United States and report the good news from Baghdad, he functioned as little more than a hired mouthpiece for the Bush administration. The *Washington Post* reported that Dan Senor, former spokesman for the CPA (who left the CPA to join the Bush presidential campaign team), was "heavily involved in drafting" Allawi's speech and that "the U.S. Embassy in Baghdad and British Foreign Service officials" also "helped Allawi with the text and delivery of his remarks." In short, the prime minister of Iraq came before the U.S. government to speak words written for him by U.S and U.K. officials. These facts perhaps explain Susan Watkins's jarring argument comparing Allawi's administration to the loathed Vichy regime in occupied France.[22]

The "handover that wasn't" was followed in January 2005 by Iraqis voting for a new parliament. As the *New York Times* described one polling area, "The mood turned joyous, with Iraqis celebrating their new-found democratic freedoms in street parties that, until the election, were virtually unknown in this war-ravaged land." Ignoring a wave of violence meant to intimidate would-be voters, millions of Iraqis marched to polls, voting for the first time in a free election. Like most observers, we found such scenes heartwarming, for here was democracy flourishing in a formerly authoritarian state, here was hope rising from the ashes of war. Our comments on the handover that wasn't indicate, however, that appearances may be deceiving. In fact, although the corporate mass media celebrated election day as a U.S.-led triumph, Iraq was hit with as many as 260 guerrilla strikes that day, making it among the most violent of the occupation. And while Kurds and Shiites voted in large numbers, Sunnis shunned the polls. In another of his insightful reports from Baghdad,

Mark Danner argued that "the political burden of the elections was to bring those who felt frightened or alienated by the new dispensation into the political process, so they could express their opposition through politics and not through violence," thereby enabling the new government "to isolate the extremists. And in this . . . the election failed." Indeed, as of 13 June 2005 the Transitional National Assembly, led by President Jalal Talabani and Prime Minister Ibrahim al-Jaafari, but crippled by the lack of Sunni representation, had yet to agree on the composition of the committee charged with drafting a new constitution. Although it is too early to know whether the new assembly will eventually succeed in that important task, our analysis of the "handover that wasn't" and Danner's observations on the election suggest that democracy in Iraq is more a dream than a reality. Moreover, we demonstrate below that the hope of bringing democracy to Iraq is compromised by crony capitalism, which is turning Iraq into a franchised outpost of U.S. economic interests.[23]

Privatizing the Empire via Crony Capitalism

Among the many reasons why the U.S. reconstruction of Iraq has gone so badly, we focus here on how crony capitalism has rendered U.S. efforts dubious at best, criminal at worst. For while the dealings among numerous U.S. firms and the Pentagon have fallen under increasing legal scrutiny, the larger political problem is that the reconstruction has proven to many observers that the United States is attempting to privatize the empire via crony capitalism, hence turning Iraq into the land of opportunity for scandal-ridden U.S. corporations linked to the military-industrial complex. International outrage over the handling of the reconstruction began almost as soon as the war on Iraq supposedly concluded in the spring of 2003, for the billions of dollars President Bush earmarked for reconstruction were at first limited only to U.S.-based firms and then to companies based in countries who participated in the "Coalition of the Willing." By December 2003, when the Pentagon released a directive limiting bidding on newly announced contracts to firms from those countries that fought in the war or provided military aid, the White House found itself immersed in international diplomatic tension. Canada, which although opposed to the war on Iraq has been committed to the war against terrorism, providing two thousand troops to Afghanistan and pledging more than $225 million in aid to Iraq, criticized the Bush administration for excluding it from bidding on reconstruction contracts. Heading off a diplomatic disaster with Canada, and facing increasing pressure from Britain, President Bush thus agreed to open the bidding process on $18.6 billion in reconstruction projects, yet as of April 2004 the companies receiving awards continued—despite minor contracts awarded to Canadian, British, Egyptian, Australian, and Chinese firms—to be overwhelmingly U.S based.[24]

Moreover, the Government Accountability Office (GAO) released a report in June 2004 finding that all of the fourteen new contracts it investigated for fiscal year 2003 were no-bid contracts, that contractors were not in compliance with task orders on a widespread scale, and that "the Army and its contractors have yet to agree on key terms and conditions, including the projected cost, on nearly $1.8 billion worth of reconstruction work." Before the House Committee on Government Reform on 15 June 2004, the GAO explained that task orders were being made beyond the scope of existing contracts in some instances and not being carried out at all in other instances. Task orders were frequently revised as well; for example, a $426 million contract with an unnamed company that provides support to U.S. troops in Kuwait was changed 18 times in four months, sometimes on consecutive days, amounting in total to 176 modifications. Likewise, a CPA audit released in July 2004 revealed that it was pursuing sixty-nine criminal investigations surrounding fraud, abuse, and other contract improprieties. Privatizing the empire via crony capitalism has thus created a cascading series of contract disputes, leading many observers to suspect that reconstructing Iraq will initiate corruption.[25]

Along with doubts about the bidding process, many observers have expressed concern about the ways the reconstruction of Iraq has appeared to be an open bazaar of opportunities for White House friends. The story of New Bridge Strategies (NBS) illustrates how such fears are well founded, as the firm's leadership amounts to a choice list of Washington and London power brokers, including Joe Allbaugh, appointed by President Bush to head the U.S. Federal Disaster Agency; Edward Rogers, deputy assistant to the White House chief of staff under President George H. W. Bush; Richard Burt, ambassador to Germany under President Reagan; and Lord Powell, a former military advisor to Prime Minister Margaret Thatcher. Much like Paul Bremer's firm from our introduction, NBS thus relies on political access to translate into corporate riches. In fact, NBS's Web site announces itself as a consulting firm "with the aim of assisting clients to evaluate and take advantage of business opportunities in the Middle East following the conclusion of the U.S.-led war in Iraq." NBS thus makes the fears illustrated above about crony capitalism concrete, for by merging corporate and political elites, and by using the reconstruction of Iraq as an opportunity to pursue riches, it hopes *to take advantage* of the destruction of Iraq.[26]

As case after case demonstrates, uniting crony capitalism and empire enables elites to take advantage of war by circumventing democratic checks and balances. For example, in September 2004 the Center for Public Integrity (CPI), a nonprofit watchdog group, reported that its study of Pentagon contracts worth more than $900 billion had found a startling pattern: 60 percent of Boeing's $81 billion in Pentagon contracts over the past five years had been awarded without competitive bidding; 74 percent of Lockheed Martin's $94 billion in contracts over that same period were awarded in the same no-bid process, as were 67 percent of Raytheon's $40 billion in contracts. The implication of the CPI's study was clear: even while working under the guise of expanding and protecting "free markets," the military-industrial complex was functioning as a favor-extending, riches-sharing, checks-and-balances-destroying form of state-to-corporation welfare. Despite the Bush administration's initial posturing and then begrudging willingness to bend on contracts in the early months of 2004, reconstructing Iraq appears to be less about rebuilding that shattered nation than about providing lucrative contracts to well-connected U.S. firms, hence making the reconstruction seem more like state-to-corporation welfare than international relief.[27]

Kellogg Brown & Root, Bechtel, and Reconstruction Crony Capitalism

Critics have been especially angered by the prominent role played in Iraq by Kellogg Brown & Root (KBR), a subsidiary of Halliburton, the company previously led by Vice President Cheney. We will turn to KBR's post–Iraq war activities below but want to mention first that even before the war, Halliburton had received $37 million to build prisons in Guantánamo Bay and $100 million to build an embassy in Kabul, Afghanistan; that despite the broad and crippling UN sanctions following the first Gulf War, it sold $73 million in "oil field supplies" to Saddam Hussein between 1997 and 2000; and that "it paid $1.2 million in criminal fines to the Justice Department and $2.6 million in civil penalties to the Commerce Department for violating the 1986 presidential embargo restricting trade with Libya." We mention these facts to reveal how even prior to the current Iraq war, KBR/Halliburton has been one of the military-industrial complex's contractors of choice, both helping the United States punish suspected terrorists and doing business with states supposedly supporting them. As Dan Baum observes, "KBR/Halliburton got rich doing business with Iraq, it got rich preparing to destroy Iraq, and now it's getting rich rebuilding Iraq."[28]

Before turning to KBR/Halliburton contracts in postwar Iraq, it is important to recall that before the war Halliburton held contracts for general wartime tasks totaling $830 million. Granted under the 2001 Logistics Civil Augmentation Program (LogCAP), Halliburton was contracted to function as a logistical branch of the U.S. armed services, building housing, supplying food, and supporting other empire-building operations in, among others, Afghanistan, Djibouti, Georgia, Jordan, and Uzbekistan. This lucrative 2001 LogCAP was awarded to Halliburton despite the fact that it was denied the 1997 LogCAP after the GAO found that Halliburton had overrun its estimated costs on a prior LogCAP job in the Balkans by 32 percent. Under this same LogCAP from the early 1990s, Halliburton fulfilled military-related tasks in Haiti and Somalia, generating more than $100 million in revenue in each case. Prior to the U.S. invasion of Iraq, then, Halliburton had a long history of making money by the United States waging war.[29]

Moreover, the contractor's responsibilities lie not solely in cleaning up war-torn countries after the fact but in overseeing the war process from start to finish. For example, Halliburton has conducted studies for the Pentagon on how military operations can best be supported by civilian employees who wash laundry, cook and serve meals, and do janitorial work. While Cheney was at the helm, Halliburton was paid $3.9 million for conducting such a study; an additional $5 million was later granted for a follow-up analysis. Halliburton was thus in the enviable position of diagnosing the conditions under which it could recommend additional contracts for its own services. Accordingly suspicious of the vice president's involvement in the war on Iraq from the earliest preplanning stages through the awarding of contracts, Congressman Henry Waxman (D-CA) sent a letter in mid-June 2004 to Cheney urging that he "disclose all contacts between your office and the Defense Department relating to the

Halliburton contracts." Citing new information that the office of the vice president had talked with the Pentagon in the fall of 2002 about hiring Halliburton to restore Iraq's oil infrastructure, Waxman's eight-page request casts deep doubts about Cheney's many public proclamations that he had no involvement in the Pentagon's dealings with Halliburton.[30]

The link between crony capitalists such as Halliburton and U.S. empire is so strong that it has inspired countless newspaper articles, editorials, opinion pieces, and political cartoons. In Jeff Danziger's cartoon of 13 April 2003, for example, coming during roughly the fourth week of the war on Iraq, two U.S. Air Force pilots sit in the cockpit of a fighter plane, reviewing their instructions. One pilot turns to the other, a piece of paper in his hand, and says, "Here's the target list, including all the places Halliburton and others have contracts to re-build." The implication is that U.S. war strategies are determined by crony capitalism, that the bombings are not used to strike at the supposed threats posed by Hussein's feeble armed forces but to ensure fat postwar contracts for Vice President Cheney's corporate colleagues.[31]

Although such charges may be discounted as the stuff of conspiratorial cynics, the fact is that KBR's contracts with the military-industrial complex are astronomical (totaling $3.9 billion in fiscal year 2003 alone), largely secret, and laced with improprieties. One contract to reconstruct postwar Iraqi oil fields has been estimated to be worth as much as $1.2 billion, but because the contract is open-ended and includes no set time line or dollar amount, KBR's services (and hence profits) will stretch into the indefinite future at indefinite costs. The open-ended contract is an example of both "indefinite delivery" (no time frame) and "indefinite quantity" (no set limits on tasks), or what are known as ID/IQ contracts. While KBR's ID/IQ contract was awarded without public bidding, the firm has announced that it will subcontract much of its work to Boots & Coots International Well Control (BCI) and Wild Well Control Inc. (WWC), two Houston-based firms. It is difficult to learn that KBR will subcontract its work to BCI and WWC without wondering why the U.S. government did not contract with these companies directly, hence saving the costs of paying KBR to oversee its subcontractors. Indeed, the fact that KBR was awarded this contract without any public bidding—the very process that may have led to better bids from BCI or WWC—indicates that it is likely the product of crony capitalism.[32]

Moreover, because the contract is ID/IQ, it includes a "cost plus" agreement, meaning that the U.S. government is bound to cover all of KBR's costs and an agreed-on percentage of profit, with a guaranteed profit ratio of 1 percent supplemented by an additional 2 percent if certain criteria are met. Although the overall 3 percent profit ratio is low compared to other KBR projects, the "cost plus" and ID/IQ nature of the contract means that KBR is under no pressure to minimize its costs or the length of its job. This means that the normal rules of capitalism do not apply—performance-enhancing competition, market-heightened efficiency, and profit-protecting cost reductions are explicitly not parts of this arrangement. Halliburton's CEO, David Lesar, has thus cooed that with such contracts "you have no risk of losing money." In fact, George Anders and Susan Warren argue in the *Wall Street Journal* that Halliburton/KBR uses such "no risk" military contracts to help it "weather the intense boom-and-bust cycles of the energy business." The KBR contract for postwar Iraq therefore exemplifies many aspects of crony capitalism: it was awarded with no public bidding, the cost-plus nature of the deal encourages profligate spending, and, even though signed by archproponents of neoliberalism, the contract amounts to a form of guaranteed, "no risk" capitalism in which the military-industrial complex functions as the provider of state-to-corporation welfare.[33]

Along with Halliburton/KBR, many of the largest Iraq reconstruction contracts have gone to Bechtel. One contract is ostensibly for $34.6 million, yet the ID/IQ nature of the deal has led one commentator to estimate that the work contracted to Bechtel may eventually cost as much as $680 million. It would be hard not to reach this figure, for according to the *New York Times* the contract "covers virtually all the major projects in Iraq, including two international and three domestic airports, ensuring potable water is available, reconstructing electric power plants and rebuilding roads, railroads, schools, hospitals and irrigation systems." If Bechtel's previous giant operations are any indication, then these tasks will take a very long time, will be done poorly, and will cost the earth. Take Boston's infamous "Big Dig" project, which Bechtel has managed to stretch into eighteen years of work, running the original cost projection of $3.5 billion up to a stunning $15 billion (and note that USAID Administrator Natsios was once director of the Big Dig). Or consider the San Onofre (CA) nuclear reactor, built by Bechtel but quickly mothballed because it was built so poorly that it needed $125 million worth of repairs. Although it has not signed a contract to clean up the San Onofre mess—

described by the Sierra Club as "an unequivocal environmental and economic disaster"—Bechtel has won a $3 billion contract to clean up nuclear messes in Idaho and Colorado, where as many as fifty-two aging nuclear reactors and their respective work sites need attention. Or consider Bechtel's trail of misery in Cochabamba, Bolivia, where it won a contract to privatize the town's water. Bechtel then doubled the price of water, leaving thousands of peasants and urban poor with no access to water. Protests ensued at which Bolivian police injured locals. Bechtel was eventually thrown out of Bolivia, but it has responded by filing a suit with the World Bank asking for $25 million in damages because of lost profits. These examples demonstrate that Bechtel is not a company one can trust; its record of cost overruns and shoddy work is apparent.[34]

In fact, on 5 April 2004 the consumer watchdog group Public Citizen sent a letter to the inspector general of the U.S. Department of Defense charging that Bechtel "has failed its contractual mandate to develop essential water delivery and sewage disposal" services in Iraq. Bechtel was awarded a $1.03 billion contract for such services in April 2003; according to Public Citizen the contract specified dates at which services were supposed to be running in "Hilla, Najaf, Diwaniyah, Sadr City, and smaller villages where families face crisis conditions." But one year later such services were not being provided. Bechtel's failure in this regard leads us to wonder about the accuracy of USAID Administrator Natsios's glowing review of other U.S. accomplishments in Iraq. For although Natsios proclaimed that "we have renovated 1,500 schools," Pratap Chatterjee and Herbert Docena were doubtful—so they visited schools renovated by Bechtel's subcontractors in Baghdad. What they found at the Al-Harthia, Al-Wathba, Al Raja, and Hawa schools was shoddy work, numbing cost overruns, and playgrounds littered with the waste left by rushed and/or careless workers. Batool Mahdi Hussain, the headmistress at the Hawa school, fumed that "the condition of our school was better before the contractors came." Bechtel apparently agrees, for it is reportedly withholding 10 percent of the payment due to subcontractors until they fix the jobs.[35]

These stories of Bechtel's failures in renovating both water services and schools cast Natsios's testimony about heroic U.S. reconstruction efforts in a dubious light, suggesting that the shabby work encouraged by "cost plus" and no-bid crony capitalist contracts may well undermine U.S. claims to be rebuilding Iraq. Along these same lines, USAID's "Weekly

Update" of "Iraq Reconstruction and Humanitarian Relief" includes claims that stretch the imagination. For example, in Update #30, dated 4 May 2004, USAID claims to have "trained 860 secondary Master Trainers during September 2003 to January 2004 nationwide" and to have "trained 31,722 secondary school teachers and administration staff." We have not spoken to any of these teachers, but as teachers ourselves, and hence as authors with an acute sense of the complications of teaching, let alone teaching in a war zone, we find USAID's claims incredulous. For it is simply impossible to retrain 32,582 teachers and master trainers in five months—unless of course the training is the most rudimentary, amounting to little more than a crash course, and hence to precisely the kind of rushed and shallow training that leads to jobs done poorly.[36]

In another example of a failed reconstruction project, the *New York Times* reported that Creative Associates, the firm charged with overseeing a pilot program for schools in six Iraqi cities, had reached only 650 children among the nation's millions of dropouts. By merging Public Citizen's information on sewage and waste, Chatterjee and Docena's reporting about shoddy school construction, the *Times*'s reporting on Creative Associates, and our own concerns about USAID's dubious claims regarding teacher training, it is hard not to suspect that USAID's "Updates" amount largely to wish fulfillment.[37]

Our comments thus far indicate a yawning abyss between Bush administration claims and on-the-ground facts regarding reconstruction in Iraq, with each failure undercut by the practice of crony capitalism. Given the stunning number and size of reconstruction contracts, and considering the stories of flourishing crony capitalism discussed above, it is difficult not to imagine Iraq sliding into a morass of corporate corruption. For in addition to the contracts discussed above for KBR/Halliburton (totaling as much as $11.4 billion for Iraq and Afghanistan) and Bechtel ($2.8 billion), here are some of the other key reconstruction contracts awarded thus far:

- The Parsons Corporation, which among other technological and engineering tasks oversees the disposal of captured enemy weapons, has Department of Defense contracts in Iraq valuing $5.3 billion.
- The U.S. Department of Defense has contracted Perini Corporation, Fluor Corporation, and Washington Group International

for "field support" in Iraq via contracts that may cost as much as $500 million each. Total contracts in Iraq and Afghanistan for Fluor Corporation, Washington Group International, and Perini Corporation are valued at $3.8 billion, $3.1 billion, and $2.5 billion, respectively.

- The Department of Defense hired the Shaw Group to renovate military bases and work on environmental and infrastructural projects in Iraq for $3.1 billion.
- Rebuilding Iraq's local governance and improving its public services has been awarded by USAID to the Research Triangle Institute (RTI), with projected costs of as much as $466 million.
- General Iraq reconstruction tasks have been contracted by USAID to Bearing Point Inc., with projected costs of $240 million.
- Rebuilding Iraq's primary and secondary education system has been awarded by USAID to Creative Associates International, at a cost as high as $157 million.
- The U.S. State Department has contracted DynCorp (purchased in March 2003 by Computer Sciences Corporation) to rebuild Iraq's law enforcement capabilities; the contract is worth as much as $50 million.
- CACI International Inc., a private contractor implicated in the Abu Ghraib prison torture scandal, was hired by the Department of the Interior to conduct $66 million worth of interrogation and intelligence analysis.[38]

The process by which many of these massive contracts were awarded was so secretive that the GAO, suspecting the foul play of crony capitalism, initiated an investigation, finding in June 2004 that numerous contracts had been unfairly awarded, that taxpayers were being overcharged, and that the terms of most of the contracts were not being carried out.[39]

Indeed, by autumn 2004, the State Department recognized that not only was Iraq in shambles, but the plan to rebuild it was insufficient. Dreams of megasized water and power projects, those "prime contracts" of more than a billion dollars awarded to select firms, were becoming more and more unrealistic as Iraq slipped further into violence. Moreover, sewage was flowing in the streets of Sadr City, children were splashing in a river of antifreeze in the slums of Baghdad, 20 to 40 percent of Iraqis were still without potable water, and major projects in Erbil, Jalabja, Baquba, and Nasiriya had been delayed. On the day of the so-called handover of authority, the *New York Times* reported that communications, power, sewer, and water systems were "agonizingly slow" and that contractors were spending 20 percent or more of their budgets on security measures following beheadings, kidnappings, and other attacks on Westerners (that figure would rise to 30 percent by the fall of 2004). Thus, realizing that the lack of security in Iraq was preventing the fulfillment of reconstruction projects, the Bush administration proposed in September 2004 to shift money designated for water, power, and sewer projects in Iraq to improve security, increase oil output, and help establish a sovereign government. The announcement confirmed the fact that Iraq was in a state of utter disrepair and incipient civil war.[40]

The fallout from diverting money from rebuilding infrastructure to security for Western contractors, however, is a looming health and humanitarian disaster. For example, Christian Parenti reported in the *Nation* that because Bechtel failed to repair the two sewage plants that handle all of Baghdad's waste, "their daily flow of 780,000 cubic yards of human and industrial waste—a nasty cocktail of organic solids, heavy metals, and poisonous chemicals from a battery factory, a soap factory, an electronics plant and other light industry—goes directly into the Diyala River, which joins the Tigris seven miles southwest of the plants." The Tigris River winds through Iraq, flowing all the way down to the Persian Gulf, hence providing water to dozens of villages and even some larger towns like Basra and Amarah; millions of people who draw water from, fish in, and depend on the Tigris for sustenance are therefore now at risk of disease from the contaminated sewage gurgling its way downstream from Baghdad. As a result, Iraq is suffering from outbreaks of waterborne hepatitis E and diarrhea, both of which are especially deadly when contracted by pregnant women and small children.[41]

While the GAO, State Department, Public Citizen, CorpWatch, and others investigate the inner workings of crony capitalism in the reconstruction of Iraq, its implications reverberate not only in Iraq but also around the world, in many cases proving the worst fears of America's critics true. For example, Frances D. Cook, former ambassador to Oman and a consultant to Middle Eastern business concerns, worried that "they are already screaming in the Middle East—you call us corrupt, look at you giving contracts to American companies and no one else." Or consider the complaint of Fareed Yaseen, an Iraqi ambassador, who lamented the fact that "there was practically no Iraqi voice in the disbursement of these [reconstruction] funds." Cook's and Yaseen's complaints demonstrate how relying on crony capitalism damages the credibility of U.S. efforts, suggesting that it is less interested in spreading "free markets" than in guaranteeing giant contracts to corporate insiders for rebuilding the countries it has destroyed. Indeed, to many observers this appears to be nothing less than a program of state-to-corporation welfare following this crude plan: invoke national security to justify destroying developing-world infrastructure, then use U.S. tax dollars to pay your friends to rebuild the nation you have just leveled.[42]

Naomi Klein forwarded a scathing version of this thesis when she argued in the *Guardian* that the war in Iraq was but a shortcut to market dominance. Impatient with the slowness of "Free Trade Lite, which wrestles market access through backroom bullying" and "negotiations with sovereign countries [that] can be hard," Klein argues that the United States has waged war in order to create "Free Trade Supercharged, which seizes new markets on the battlefields of pre-emptive wars." Echoing the themes raised in the Danziger cartoon discussed above, Klein argues that whereas the dialectics of free-market transformation are slow and difficult, for crony capitalists it is "far easier to just tear up the country, occupy it, then rebuild it the way you want." From this perspective, which again returns us to our question regarding the relationships among globalization, empire, capitalism, and the production of violence, the soldiers of empire are but the advance wave of free marketers, conquering the world in the name of democracy while in fact spreading crony capitalism.[43]

The Scandal Sheet

To return now to our initial question about how crony capitalism is destabilizing U.S. efforts to restore Iraq, let us consider some of the corporate scandals and apparent improprieties that have rocked the main contractors in Iraq. Some of these cases may involve criminal activity; others hint at favoritism in ways that, whether true or not, give the impression of crony capitalism. For an example of the latter, consider the case of Nour USA, which in January 2004 was awarded a Pentagon contract worth anywhere from $327 million to $500 million to help outfit the Iraqi army. The losing firms in the bidding process were so convinced that it was rigged that they protested, leading the Pentagon to suspend and then cancel the contract in March 2004. Although the Pentagon has subsequently denied that favoritism played any role in awarding the original contract, the *Wall Street Journal* has noted that "Nour is headed by A. Huda Farouki, a longtime Washington insider who also has a business connection to Ahmed Chalabi," the exile figure we examined in chapter 1, where we concluded that he played a significant role in shaping White House WMD lies and postwar hopes. What matters here is not whether the Pentagon picked Nour to favor Chalabi, a White House confidant and longtime CIA informant, but the fact that his relationship with Nour looks dubious; it appears to be another example of reconstruction business being handed out to friends and insiders. Rather than illustrating the free flow of ideas and opportunities supposedly driving free markets, the Nour contract illustrates the ways crony capitalism depends on favoritism.[44]

Whereas the Nour case hinges on the appearance of impropriety in the bidding process, the examples provided below demonstrate how crony capitalism in the cause of empire produces waves of corporate malfeasance. For example, consider KBR/Halliburton's performance in Iraq thus far. KBR's LogCAP commitments are so vast that, like its using BCI and WWC to rebuild the oil fields, KBR has had to subcontract much of its other LogCAP work in Iraq as well. The subcontracts are so valuable that competition for them is intense, leading some firms to resort to bribery. In fact, the *Wall Street Journal* reported in January 2004 that two KBR employees in Iraq had taken kickbacks "valued at up to $6 million" from a Kuwaiti firm hoping to secure a subcontract. Halliburton said a "routine internal audit" discovered $6.3 million in employee kickbacks; the company terminated all those involved in the scandal and repaid the government in full. Nonetheless, whereas the Bush administration is trumpeting neoliberalism in general and the reconstruction of Iraq in particular as examples of the moral power of capitalism to spur creativity and hard work, here we have a bribery scandal regarding a contract awarded with no public bidding, thus amounting to corruption on top of corruption. In fact, Halliburton's handling of such contracts and the dubious nature of their procurement in the first place is so controversial that Bunnatine Greenhouse, "the top civilian contracting official for the Army Corps of Engineers," has called for a federal investigation to study the scandal.[45]

In addition, the *Wall Street Journal* reported in February 2004 that another KBR subcontractor, Tamimi Global Co., from Saudi Arabia, had been billing the Pentagon for 42,042 meals a day while serving only 14,053 meals per day, resulting in an overcharge of $3.5 million in July 2003 alone. Over a seven-month period, Halliburton/KBR overcharged the U.S. government by $16 million "for meals at a single U.S. military base in Kuwait." Moreover, the *New York Times* reported in February 2004 that KBR's billing improprieties to date had totaled as much as $27.4 million, prompting the Pentagon to investigate fifty-three other food operations at military bases in Iraq and Kuwait. If such problems occurred at one or two bases we might be able to discount them as random examples of incompetence, but the fact that they spread so widely indicates that the problem is likely systematic fraud. In fact, Halliburton's contracts for supplying food to U.S. troops include such astronomically inflated figures that, when facing questions regarding a "discrepancy" in one contract with the Defense Department, Halliburton lopped $700 million from its bid without explanation or protest. In short, the original bid contained $700 million worth of pork. Nonetheless, rather than repaying the moneys earned in the contract scandals described herein, or suffering a fine, or losing its contracts, KBR will temporarily keep its misbegotten $16 million, slowly deducting it from future bills tendered to the U.S. government. While these scandals were unfolding, pressure on Washington to make the reconstruction process more transparent led to the rebidding of the oil field contract discussed above. Despite the examples of crony capitalism noted in this paragraph, KBR was again awarded the contract, estimated in January 2004 to be worth $1.2 billion. Congressman Waxman protested the deal, saying that "serious questions have been raised about millions in dollars in overcharges.... It's special treatment to reward the company with yet another contract in the face of these unresolved questions." But as we have argued here, special treatment for insiders who inflate contract costs and then dissemble about their fulfillment is the essence of crony capitalism.[46]

Yet another example of crony capitalism in the reconstruction of Iraq involves Altanmia, a Kuwaiti company hired by KBR to orchestrate shipments of gasoline from Kuwait into Iraq, provide tanker trucks, house KBR employees in upscale apartments near Kuwait City, and even set up fast-food stands like Nathan's Famous hot dogs and Arthur Treacher's Fish and Chips—both part of another Altanmia affiliate—near U.S. military camps in the region. When the Pentagon audited KBR, it found that the gasoline Altanmia was supplying at $2.27 per gallon could have been bought from a Turkish subcontractor for $1.18 and that Altanmia was taking an average cut of 10.5 cents per gallon sold to KBR. Moreover, why

KBR could not have dealt directly with Kuwait's national petroleum company rather than hiring Altanmia has become cause for a criminal investigation by the Justice Department. In the meantime, Altanmia has broadened its scope into supplying telecommunication services, fast food, real estate, jewelry, firearms, and military goods such as gas masks, night-vision goggles, and chemical-neutralization agents for other U.S. military contractors. Although the Pentagon has estimated that KBR's work with Altanmia resulted in overcharges of $20 million between May and September of 2004 alone, the puzzling fact is that Washington's champions of lean-and-mean free markets have continued to do business with such inefficient firms, hence proving that the rhetoric of globalizing neoliberalism is little more than a chant used to justify continued crony capitalism.[47]

The thesis that crony capitalism is driving U.S. empire via its forays in Iraq is further confirmed by considering the practices of DynCorp's employees. DynCorp, which has handled civilian policing overseas since 1994 and receives most of its $2.3 billion yearly revenue from the U.S. government, was accused of widespread sexual improprieties during the Balkan wars. A Nebraska police officer working for the DynCorp-administered International Police Task Force in Bosnia, working in conjunction with a British subsidiary of the company, was awarded the equivalent of $200,000 by the U.K. court that heard her case charging "sexual misbehavior by colleagues." A Texas mechanic working on helicopter repairs in Bosnia for DynCorp charged that coworkers were procuring underage prostitutes. According to the *Wall Street Journal,* "An internal U.S. Army investigation cleared DynCorp of involvement in 'white slavery' but found that two employees 'could have been charged . . . with procuring and pandering.'" But its employees engaging in such acts—sexual harassment in the first case, prostitution in the second—has apparently not deterred the U.S. State Department from sending DynCorp to Iraq. Given their track records, there can be little wonder that Iraqis have learned to fear contractors such as DynCorp and KBR and to suspect that the kinds of prison abuse discussed in our introduction were not isolated incidents but the consequences of a system that rewards scandal-ridden firms.[48]

Privatizing the Empire

Stepping back from the immediate question of how scandal-ridden crony capitalism is compromising U.S. efforts in postwar Iraq, we want to conclude this section of our chapter by considering some of the implications of the ways the Bush administration is *privatizing the empire* by contracting more and more subsets of the nation's war machine to private corporations that are not accountable in the same ways as official government agencies. For example, Executive Order 12600, signed into law by President Reagan on 23 June 1987, exempts companies that do contract work for the U.S. government from Freedom of Information Act (FOIA) filings. The order enables companies to reject FOIA requests on the grounds that their "trade secrets and commercial or financial information" are "privileged and confidential" information that, if released, could aid competitors. The contractors working in Iraq are therefore protected from careful scrutiny by this executive order, in essence putting their corporate profits above the nation's democratic system of checks and balances.[49]

In a similar vein, privatizing the empire provides the U.S. government and its contractors greater flexibility in skirting and even destroying labor laws. For example, the CPA's 5 June 2003 Public Notice Number One has been interpreted as banning unions in postwar Iraq. Stevedoring Services of America (recently renamed SSA Marine) has been contracted by the USAID to rebuild the port of Umm Qasr, reportedly for as much as $14 million. When that company's long-standing antilabor practices are paired with the CPA's law, critics predict that Iraq's dock workers will face severe cuts in wages and services, if not outright dismissal. Oil industry workers face a similar prospect, as Dathar Al-Kashab, manager of an oil refinery in Baghdad, told David Bacon of CorpWatch that "if I put on the hat of privatization, I'll have to fire 1,500 [of the refinery's 3,000] workers."[50]

While privatizing the empire thus costs Iraqis precious jobs and circumvents U.S. norms of checks and balances, it also fuels the collaboration of crony capitalism with the military-industrial complex. Critics of the military-industrial complex have been arguing for years that it is a sprawling machine organized to produce excess, for its chief goal is not simply to build the weapons needed to defend the United States but to build the overcapacity of weapons needed to keep its manufacturers among the world's largest, most wealthy, and most powerful corporations. Chalmers Johnson's *The Sorrows of Empire* provides a grueling critique of the military-industrial complex, arguing that the combination of weapons-driven pork barrel politics at home and imperial aggrandizement abroad, with both cloaked in the secrecy supposedly needed to protect national security, has left the U.S. Congress with little to no control over spending, programs, or implementation. The military-industrial complex has thus produced a situation where there is "an almost total loss of accountability for public money spent on military projects of any sort." Indeed, "Special Access Programs," those super secret operations over which Congress has no supervision, now total as many as 185, costing on Johnson's estimate as much as $35 billion per year. For Johnson, this sprawling empire of secret appropriations, secret weapons systems, and secret operations points to a republic rapidly sliding toward a military-industrial complex–driven empire run by crony capitalists and what he calls "a Pentagonized presidency."[51]

Given the depth and breadth of Johnson's study, we will keep our comments on the military-industrial complex and its reliance on crony capitalism brief. First, we want to highlight the ways the military-industrial complex produces massive excess military capacity, hence draining the U.S. treasury of billions of dollars that could be spent elsewhere. For example, William Greider reports in *Fortress America* that by the end of the cold war the United States had purchased so many extra tanks that it began dumping them in the ocean and giving them away to friends. In fact, the army "dumped 100 old Sherman M-60s into Mobile Bay off the Alabama coast to form artificial reefs for fish in the Gulf of Mexico. . . . One year it gave 45 tanks free to Bosnia and another 50 to Jordan. It shipped 91 tanks to Brazil under a no-cost, five year lease, and 30 to Bahrain on the same terms. . . . Egypt got 700 free by picking up transportation costs." Greider's point is that the U.S. taxpayer has been duped—essentially defrauded—by lobbyists of the military-industrial complex and their compliant congressional allies into funding colossal weapons systems at astronomical costs, hence turning taxpayers into indirect donors of free weapons to such troubled nations as Bosnia, Jordan, Brazil, Bahrain, and Egypt. In essence, U.S. taxpayers are funding state-to-corporation welfare for weapons manufacturers while arming developing nations.[52]

Or consider the strange history of Lockheed Martin's F/A-22 fighter jet, also called "the raptor," a weapon that has taken twenty-three years to develop, with the cost of each plane rising to a stunning $258 million—that's $258,000,000 for one plane. Considering that the Soviet Union collapsed over a decade ago, it is boggling to fathom how this incomprehensibly expensive fighter, originally designed for air battles against jets that were never built by a now-defunct enemy, could still be constructed. Indeed, building the raptor and other such weapons would appear to be driven not so much by legitimate military threats as by military Keynesianism that uses the production of weapons as a form of state-to-corporation welfare, thereby keeping favored parts of the troubled U.S. economy floating in hard times. The *9/11 Commission Report* renders the political implications of this claim in stark terms when it observes that "with an annual budget larger than the GDP of Russia," the Department of Defense "is an empire."[53]

While the cronyism driving the military-industrial complex's empire thus wreaks havoc on the U.S. Treasury and the U.S. political process itself, some observers have noted that the long-term international political implications of this process are terrifying. As John Tirman argues in *Spoils of War*, the U.S. military-industrial complex arming foreign nations slowly but surely "militarizes a society, in effect, encouraging military and police domination" of the political process. Worse yet, Tirman observes that the United States then tends to "turn a blind eye to the internal consequences of the political hegemony that accrues to the military" in such states—he cites Afghanistan, Iran, Iraq, and Turkey as examples— hence sowing the seeds for both domestic and regional conflicts that in many cases have dramatically harmed U.S. national interests. In fact, the Center for Defense Information (CDI) reports that U.S. arms sales have expanded dramatically since 9/11 because the United States has "waived restrictions on arms or military assistance to Armenia, Azerbaijan, India, Pakistan, Tajikistan, and Yugoslavia." These are but a few of the nations to whom the United States sells billions of dollars of weapons (the CDI's list of weapons buyers comes to thirty-eight pages!), yet they indicate what the CDI calls a "dangerous trend" in weapons proliferation. Rather than helping to defend the United States, then, the military-industrial complex may be charged with creating militarized hot spots around the globe, with fueling regional rivalries and arms races, and, as demonstrated below, in supporting authoritarian regimes.[54]

Indeed, P. W. Singer's *Corporate Warriors* offers staggering insights into how "private military firms," what he calls PMFs, are becoming global mercenaries hired out to the highest bidder. Echoing our concerns from chapter 3 about the ways multinational corporations pursue profits across the globe regardless of national affiliations, Singer fears that PMFs, pursuing profits above patriotic duty, will sell their services to nations regard-less of their political goals, hence fueling regional conflicts and support-ing dubious regimes. Singer notes, for example, that PMFs "practically run the national armed forces" of Saudi Arabia, an autocratic regime that might well, without PMF support, face intense internal political pressure. The rise of PMFs means, then, that corrupt regimes can hire military support that would otherwise be lacking and that regional rivals can hire armies without seeking domestic support (as the British did in trying to suppress the American Revolution, an act so unpopular in England that King George was forced to hire more than thirty thousand Hessian mer-cenaries, a force described by Lord Camden in Parliament as "devoted wretches purchased for slaughter"). In fact, Tom Barry argues in a report for Foreign Policy in Focus that the proliferation of PMFs has led to "the rise of a new warlordism" both in the United States and abroad. "The new warlordism," Barry claims, "keeps counsel not with diplomats but with arms merchants." As a blossoming subset of corporate interests within the larger military-industrial complex, PMFs thus enable states to bypass any sense of political accountability while waging covert and overt wars both at home and abroad.[55]

This charge is particularly true regarding U.S. actions in Iraq, where by using as many as twenty thousand private contractors, many of them PMFs, President Bush has tried to shield aspects of the botched occupa-tion from public scrutiny. Knowing that reinstituting a military draft to supplement beleaguered and stretched-thin troops would be wildly un-popular, the president has instead overseen the hiring of PMFs, thus pri-vatizing the empire, quietly contracting occupation work to mercenaries. We want to be clear that this strategy crosses party lines, as President Clinton relied heavily on PMFs in the Kosovo war, where Singer reports that "KBR built 192 barracks housing over 7,000 troops, thirteen heli-pads, two aviation-maintenance facilities, and 37 temporary bathing fa-cilities . . . [and] delivered 1,134,182 high-quality meals, 55,544,000 gallons of water, and 383,071 gallons of diesel fuel." Singer thus concludes that KBR "was the U.S. force's supply and engineering corps wrapped into one corporate element." Given our comments above regarding the nu-merous scandals involving KBR's actions in Iraq, all of them serving as case studies of crony capitalism, this example of President Clinton relying on KBR in Kosovo demonstrates how privatizing the empire transcends party affiliation, amounting instead to a bipartisan strategy for avoiding public scrutiny of war-making functions.[56]

Finally, it is important to consider how since 9/11 the practices of the military-industrial complex have transformed into what some observers are referring to as a "Homeland Security-Industrial-Complex" (HSIC). For with federal spending of antiterrorist security measures approaching $50 billion per year, and with private expenditures ranging from $40 billion to $50 billion per year, suppliers of weaponry, intelligence, surveillance, security, and other services of the military-industrial complex are rapidly entering the blossoming domestic market. Given our many examples above detailing how crony capitalism is fueling the reconstruction of Iraq in particular and the military-industrial complex in general, it is logical to assume that the new HSIC will also be riven with procurement illegalities, budgeting improprieties, subcontractors bungling tasks, and oceans of wasted U.S. tax dollars. In fact, Northrop Grumman, one of the "Big Three" military contractors of the military-industrial complex, has won a $175 million contract from the Department of Homeland Security to "develop, manage, and run the new agency's personnel system." Grumman already holds government contracts for running personnel systems from the Department of Defense for $281 million and from the Treasury Department for $114 million. One of the leading members of the military-industrial complex's gravy train is therefore contracted to complete $575 million worth of domestic work, hence demonstrating how privatizing the empire abroad in turn leads to a militarized United States—what Barry calls the new warlordism—where weapons manufacturers with intimate contacts with the military-industrial complex blur into domestic service providers for the HSIC.[57]

Privatizing the empire via crony capitalism thus contributes to the production of massive corporations profiting from the military-industrial complex, the HSIC, and Iraq reconstruction all at the same time, hence creating conflicts of interest and opportunities for corporate corruption. This does not bode well for Iraq, for we have shown here how the excesses of the military-industrial complex, fueled now by the rich combination of a rising HSIC and the reconstruction of Iraq, are proceeding under the banner of the Washington Consensus's dogmas: reduce costs by slashing payroll, even if that creates massive unemployment; attack or even outlaw unions, regardless of what this means for working conditions; and turn once-government-controlled industries over to private capitalists, even if that means fueling shady accounting practices, sloppy work, and massive cost overruns. Although these shock therapies may produce more profitable industries in Iraq in the long run, their immediate consequences cannot help but convince Iraqis that the reconstruction is less about their national and personal well-being than about the U.S. corporate bottom line. Indeed, we have shown here how the reconstruction of Iraq amounts to a crass privatizing of the empire, where the military-industrial complex and the HSIC bury public checks and balances and any notion of the common good beneath a sea of favoritism, corruption, and shoddy work.

Crony Capitalism Defined

On the basis of the findings offered above, we define crony capitalism as a version of neoliberalism where corporate and political corruption is the norm rather than the exception, as a "Wild West" version of capitalism where fraud and cheating are rampant. By merging our critique of the reconstruction of Iraq with additional examples from recent U.S. scandals, we have uncovered what we believe are the three major subcategories of crony capitalism: first, *institutionalized profiteering;* second, *corporate secrecy and the assault on democracy;* and third, *fossil-fuel cannibalism.* Each subcategory is intimately linked to the excesses and abuses of the military-industrial complex and is deeply implicated in the Bush administration's empire building.

Institutionalized Profiteering

Consider the case of Enron, which reported profits to shareholders from 1996 through 2000 of $3.3 billion while reporting profits to the Internal Revenue Service (IRS) of only $76 million. Thus, instead of paying $1.1 billion in taxes during this period, Enron paid $63 million, cheating taxpayers out of roughly $1,079,000,000. According to the Senate Finance Committee's Joint Committee on Taxation (JCT), Enron accomplished this accounting trickery by sheltering money in "Cayman Islands entities." Furthermore, Enron was aided in this institutionalized theft by a series of prominent Wall Street accounting firms and banks, including Bankers Trust, which earned $40.2 million for helping Enron prepare its taxes. Enron's early corporate successes were therefore based on a coterie of cheating executives, lying accountants, and pliable banks, many of them conspiring to defraud U.S. consumers and taxpayers of billions of dollars. Indeed, Enron's criminality was based not only on individual acts of cheating but on a network of conspiring crony capitalists—the problem is therefore systemic.[58]

Although appalling, Enron's circumventing tax payments to the IRS is not anomalous, for many companies shift income out of the United States in order to avoid paying taxes. In fact, the JCT estimates that tax shelters enable U.S.-based firms to deny the IRS as much as $50 billion *every year*. For example, while serving as CEO of Halliburton from 1995 to 2000, Vice President Dick Cheney oversaw that company's dealings with as many as twenty subsidiaries claiming the Cayman Islands, not the United States, as their home base of operations, hence cheating the United States out of billions of tax dollars. Furthermore, the *Wall Street Journal* reported on 4 August 2004 that a Securities and Exchange Commission (SEC) audit had found that Halliburton's reported pretax income for the second quarter of 1998 was wrong by as much as $87.9 million, or roughly 46 percent of their announced profit. The *New York Times* then reported on 12 August 2004 that a Pentagon audit had found that Halliburton's "accounting system was inadequate in nearly every way." The *Times, Post*, and SEC all agree, then, that Halliburton misled investors, the DOD, and the IRS alike. One of the key aspects of crony capitalism, therefore, is the drive to minimize taxes via creative accounting practices, hence destroying social services in the United States and fueling neoliberal arguments for the ongoing privatization of as many aspects of our lives as possible. Thus linking our comments from chapter 3 on "hot money" to our concerns here with the reconstruction of Iraq, Enron's and Halliburton's crony capitalist practices illustrate why free trade is an increasingly discredited doctrine, a "rigged game" indeed.[59]

Interested readers will find an avalanche of material regarding what one critic has called "the Enron stage of capitalism" in the hundreds of newspaper stories written about recent scandals involving Xerox, Adelphia, Tyco, ImClone, Qwest, Global Crossing, HealthSouth, Ahold, and twelve additional Wall Street firms tied up in conflicts of interest with investment banks. We are concerned here, however, with locating crony capitalists involved specifically with the U.S. government and its spreading empire. For example, consider the case of MCI, formerly WorldCom; although the *Wall Street Journal* reported that MCI "committed one of the largest corporate frauds ever," the company received a ten-year, $360 million contract for State Department communication services. The fact that the U.S. government would reward MCI with such a lucrative contract, despite the relative glut of other firms fully capable of handling the job, indicates how the federal government encourages crony capitalists engaged in institutionalized profiteering.[60]

Consider the case of the sneaky Boeing/Pentagon deal regarding new aerial refueling tankers. The Pentagon wanted one hundred of these planes; Boeing wanted to sell them, each one at a cost of $138 million; but the government could not afford them—so the Pentagon agreed to create a company that would lease the planes to the Pentagon, thus giving Boeing its profits, the Pentagon its planes, and taxpayers an estimated $8 billion of additional costs above and beyond the price of the planes just to cover the interest on the long-term leases. Public outrage over the audacity of this deal forced the Pentagon to postpone it, yet the World Policy Institute reports that Boeing nonetheless enjoyed $17.3 billion worth of Pentagon contracts in fiscal year 2003 alone. And these contracts were awarded despite the fact that Boeing had been caught in a scandal regarding the theft of documents related to a proposed satellite-launching program. Then, in October 2004, another Boeing-Pentagon scandal broke when Darlene A. Druyun, a former high-ranking air force official, was sentenced to prison after pleading guilty to conspiracy. During her tenure as a procurement officer for the air force, Druyun favored Boeing as the recipient of billions of dollars worth of contracts for U.S. aircraft and a $100 million NATO early warning system. According to a report in the *New York Times,* she selected Boeing for a $4 billion contract, despite there being four other lower bidders, "out of gratitude to Boeing for having hired her daughter and son-in-law." In 2002, Druyun ended her thirty-year air force career to become a Boeing executive. All three cases, the Druyun conspiracy scandal, the document theft scandal, and the aerial refueling tanker scandal, provide examples of Boeing breaking or bending the law in the search for profits while exploiting contacts with the military-industrial complex. We should note that Boeing's actions were aided by the Pentagon. In fact, one e-mail exchange within the Pentagon revealed an official saying "we all know this [the tanker deal discussed above] is a bailout for Boeing." Thus defining crony capitalism, the e-mail suggests that the Pentagon was more concerned with bailing out its friends at Boeing than with spending taxpayers' money wisely.[61]

Moreover, the chief practitioners of crony capitalism are so assured of long-term profit-making relationships with the U.S. military-industrial complex that they view laws constraining their environmental, labor, health, and financial practices as little more than nuisances. Because the penalties to be paid for breaking these laws are so insignificant, crony capitalists can break the law at will, seemingly considering criminal fines as little more than short-term taxes on the assured long-term march to profits. For example, note that ten U.S. companies with contracts for work in Iraq totaling in the billions of dollars have, according to Matt Kelley of the Associated Press, "paid more than $300 million in penalties since 2000 to resolve allegations of bid rigging, fraud, delivery of faulty parts, and environmental damage." Historically, such infractions would have barred a company from receiving additional contract work with the U.S. government, but President Bush rescinded this long-standing policy in December 2001. It may come as no surprise, then, to learn that these lawbreaking yet contract-winning companies amount to a laundry list of companies with close ties to the Bush administration, including, among others, Halliburton, Bechtel, Fluor, and Northrop Grumman.[62]

In fact, William Hartung notes that the "Big Three," Lockheed Martin, Boeing, and Northrop Grumman, "get one of every four dollars the Pentagon doles out for everything from rifles to rockets." Given the fact that each of these companies can count on crony connections to ensure massive government contracts, paying fines for breaking the laws regulating capitalism amounts to a minor inconvenience. Halliburton, for example, holds contracts worth more than $11.4 billion for reconstructing Iraq and Afghanistan, making its 2002 fine of $2 million for price rigging on a prior contract—coming to less than 2¢ out of every $100—a trifling slap on the wrist. Indeed, crony capitalists are so confident of their long-term associations with the U.S. military-industrial complex that they appear to view fines and other penalties for breaking laws as little more than an inconvenience, a troublesome morality tax. This means that crony capitalism breeds lawbreaking, creating a culture where labor, health, environmental, financial, accounting, and other business practices are denigrated—*capitalism gone wild* indeed.[63]

As a closing flourish to this section on institutionalized profiteering, consider the stunning practices of Custer Battles (CB), one of the many PMFs helping to privatize the empire via the reconstruction of Iraq. CB has contracts worth more than $100 million in Iraq, yet a suit filed by Pete Baldwin, a former employee disgusted by CB's practices, alleges that CB padded its profits from work in Iraq by engaging in "a pattern of fraudulent billing practices." For example, while CB subcontracted the construction of a helicopter landing pad for $95,000, it billed the CPA $157,000, hence making a $62,000 profit on one bill alone. In another case of alleged fraud, CB employees repainted old Baghdad Airways forklifts but then billed the CPA "thousands of dollars a month" as if they were leasing new forklifts. Among its many reconstruction tasks, CB is contracted to provide security for Baghdad's airport and "to safeguard Iraq's new currency as it was being distributed." Much like the cases recounted above regarding Enron, Halliburton, KBR, MCI, and Boeing, CB's practices demonstrate how crony capitalism has become a government-subsidized policy of institutionalized profiteering.[64]

Corporate Secrecy and the Assault on Democracy

As the examples offered above demonstrate, privatizing the empire via crony capitalism depends for its success on collusion between corporate and government players—secrecy is therefore a crucial element of crony capitalism, meaning that successful crony capitalists must do everything in their power to shield their institutionalized profiteering from the public scrutiny enabled by a process of checks and balances. Put simply, privatizing the empire via crony capitalism subverts democracy. One obvious background example of this thesis is the link between the war on Iraq, rising U.S. empire, and the politics of oil. For although President Bush and his allies have repeatedly said that the war was not about oil—"It has nothing to do with oil, literally nothing to do with oil," claimed Secretary of Defense Rumsfeld in a November 2002 news conference—vast majorities believe that the war was indeed about oil, hence the ubiquitous "No Blood For Oil" signs at virtually every antiwar protest around the world in the spring of 2003, in the days leading up to the U.S. invasion of Iraq. The problem for the Bush administration is that talking about the political economy of oil would force it to explain its too-cozy (and some suspect criminal) relationship with a handful of fossil-fuel-driven corporations, thus revealing its dependence on crony capitalism.[65]

For example, it is widely known that Vice President Cheney's Energy

Task Force (ETF) was a friendly colloquium with Cheney's old business partners from the oil business. Given the Bush administration's radical plans for drilling in the Arctic wilderness, invading Iraq, and rejecting all calls for energy conservation, many observers suspected that the vice president's ETF was little more than a front for his friends in the energy business and hence a government-sponsored gathering of crony capitalists. Suspecting foul play and facing relentless White House stalling, the GAO took the unprecedented step of suing a vice president for access to his files from those meetings. The Natural Resource Defense Council (NRDC) and the Sierra Club also sued the National Energy Policy Development Group for access to the files from the meetings in question. In all three cases (the GAO, NRDC, and Sierra Club cases), Cheney's stonewalling indicated that his first allegiance was to his old business friends, not to the transparent give-and-take of information that renders democracy legitimate. Indeed, by hiding the information regarding how his oil-baron friends have shaped U.S. energy and foreign policy, Cheney has not only proven himself a strong supporter of crony capitalism and a foe of democracy, but has fueled suspicions regarding the dubious fossil-fuel imperatives driving the U.S. invasion of Iraq.[66]

In a bizarre twist that appears to point toward their assumed guilt, the Bush administration asked the U.S. Court of Appeals for the District of Columbia to intervene in the lower court's hearing of these cases. The court of appeals refused to act, but at Cheney's urging the Sierra Club case was forwarded to the Supreme Court, which agreed to hear it on 15 December 2003. Less than one month later, Supreme Court Justice Antonin Scalia boarded Air Force Two for a vacation in Louisiana, where he, Cheney, and a small group of fellow power brokers enjoyed several days of duck hunting with their gracious host, Wallace Carline, the president of a Louisiana oil services company. When the hunting story broke, critics suggested that Scalia, due to an obvious conflict of interest, should recuse himself from the ETF case, but he wrote a twenty-one-page public response rejecting such calls, finding the idea "that a Supreme Court justice can be bought so cheap" appalling. No one can force a Supreme Court justice off a case, meaning that Scalia alone has the power to set standards of appropriateness among cronies. Scalia is known for his gregariousness, his lively writing that, especially on dissenting opinions, sometimes verges toward imprudence, and his affinity for what the *New York Times* calls "verbal jousting." Scalia maintains a high profile in

Washington and associates regularly with his old friends from the Nixon and Ford administrations, on which he served before being appointed to the Supreme Court by President Reagan in 1986. His friendship with Vice President Cheney, however, and his refusal to abstain from the ETF case, reveal how crony capitalism subverts checks and balances in general and the impartiality of the Supreme Court in particular, by shrouding joint government/corporate decisions in secrecy.[67]

In fact, in a remarkable editorial titled "Behind Closed Doors," noted conservative journalist William Safire argued that Cheney's keeping his task force's files secret amounted to an attempt to "place the vice president above the law" and "to erect a high barrier to finding out who is advising whom about the public's business behind closed doors." Reminding Republicans of the ferocity of their pursuit of White House documents in their endless search for wrongdoings during the Clinton years, Safire wagged a scolding finger, warning that "what is sauce for the Clintons is sauce for the Bushies."[68]

As Cheney's handling of the ETF illustrates, even to the dismay of some of his fellow conservatives, such as Safire, crony capitalism's penchant for secrecy, avoidance of public scrutiny, and aversion to checks and balances amount to nothing less than an assault on democracy. This is particularly important regarding the reconstruction of Iraq, for as noted above, President Reagan's Executive Order 12600 exempts companies that do contract work for the U.S. government from FOIA filings, meaning contractors working in Iraq are largely protected from careful scrutiny, in essence putting their corporate profits above the nation's democratic system of checks and balances. According to Paul Light of the Brookings Institution, "the shadow government" of contractors fulfilling U.S. government tasks has blossomed to include as many as 5.6 million workers, hence amounting to a giant parallel economy driven by U.S. tax dollars yet exempt from public scrutiny. The military contracts privatizing the empire in Iraq, then, illustrate how crony capitalism institutionalizes fraud and theft and assaults democracy at the same time.[69]

Indeed, the Center for Public Integrity released a report in September 2004 examining Defense Department spending and the Pentagon's dealings with private contractors for a period of six years, from fiscal year 1998 through fiscal year 2003. In that period alone, Lockheed Martin, the Pentagon's biggest contractor, received $94 billion in contracts. Next on the list was Boeing, with $82 billion; Halliburton came in fourteenth with a total of roughly $6.8 billion. More troubling than the sheer number of dollars spent by the Pentagon on private contracts—amounting to almost half of the Defense Department's total budget!—are the ways in which such contracts are allocated, spent, and recorded. First, fewer than half of the Pentagon contracts were awarded under "full and open competition," meaning that contractors did not go through the process of competitive bidding. Second, nearly one-third of the contracts awarded were "cost-plus," which, as detailed earlier, means that contractors have little incentive to keep their costs down and can charge the Pentagon for extra, often frivolous expenditures. Third, although the awarding of contracts is supposed to be public knowledge, and although the Pentagon keeps a Web-accessible database containing information on spending, the Center for Public Integrity found deep inaccuracies in how Pentagon information was recorded. For although the Pentagon even hires contractors to advise it on procuring contractors, the publicly posted contract data often failed to match companies to their corporate parents, contained multiple identification numbers for a single company, and mistook some companies for those with similar-sounding names. The effort to reconstruct Iraq using corporate cronyism, then, follows a pattern of dubious defense budget allocations, profligate contract spending, and fraudulent record keeping, with each part of the process protected as much as possible from public scrutiny, hence amounting to nothing less than an assault on the checks and balances that render democracy legitimate.[70]

Fossil-Fuel Cannibalism

As demonstrated above, crony capitalism in general and the "shadow government" of contractors in particular pursue wealth and power even to the detriment of the nation as a whole. This amounts to a form of cannibalistic capitalism, where cronies devour the state's long-term health and prosperity in their pursuit of immediate profits. This cannibalistic crony capitalism is particularly evident in the deep links among fossil-fuel-based firms, the military, and Washington insiders. Our third subcategory of crony capitalism therefore addresses what we call *fossil-fuel cannibalism.*

For example, consider the findings in *Crude Vision: How Oil Interests Obscured U.S. Government Focus on Chemical Weapons Use by Saddam Hussein.* In this astounding report based on analysis of recently released materials from the National Security Archive (NSA), Jim Vallette, Steve

Kretzmann, and Daphne Wysham demonstrate that the same Rumsfeld who claimed in 2003 that the war "has nothing to do with oil, literally nothing to do with oil," repeatedly ventured to Baghdad in the mid-1980s to try to negotiate with Saddam Hussein for the construction of a Persian Gulf–avoiding pipeline that would have shipped Iraqi oil westward, through Jordan to the Red Sea port of Aqaba. The proposed pipeline was to have been built by Bechtel, the same company now reaping giant contracts for rebuilding Iraq, with the funds for construction forwarded (and guaranteed) by the U.S. Export-Import Bank. In a fine example of how the language of news reporting depends on understatement and prudence, Richard Oppel referred in an article about the failed Aqaba project to Bechtel as a company with "longstanding ties to the national security establishment." The real scandal here, however, regards how the drive for oil blinded Bechtel and U.S. government officials to the use of chemical weapons for it was well known in October 1983, before Rumsfeld's first visit with Hussein on 20 December, that Iraq was using chemical weapons against Iran. Yet the NSA documents show that Rumsfeld only considered Hussein's use of chemical weapons in terms of their likely "embarrassment" to ongoing pipeline negotiations. That is, as long as Hussein appeared likely to do business with U.S. oil interests, his using chemical weapons was merely a possible embarrassment, not the cause for war that it would become twenty years later.[71]

Because of fears for the proposed pipeline's security from Israeli air strikes, Hussein rejected the Aqaba project in December 1985. Now, supposedly driven by a fear that Hussein *might* use the chemical weapons that Rumsfeld knew he had used repeatedly from 1983 to 1985, the United States finally controls that oil. The lesson is clear: chemical-weapons-using oil-rich dictators who play along with U.S.-based fossil-fuel capitalists are acceptable partners in crony capitalism. Furthermore, the list of insider players associated with the first attempt to gain access to Iraqi oil, including Rumsfeld, George Shultz, Lawrence Eagleburger, Caspar Weinberger, and Dick Cheney, reads like a casting call of the current team leading the reconstruction of Iraq's oil fields. It is difficult to learn of such dealings without suspecting that crony capitalism and the pursuit of oil have driven our nation to make war on another hapless foe, making empire look like the stepchild of greed and corruption. The Aqaba project debacle thus demonstrates our third definitional claim regarding crony capitalism: that the search for fossil-fuel profit drives foreign policy, even prompting an administration to overlook the use of chemical weapons. In short, fossil-fuel cannibalism corrupts the foreign policy process, not enhancing the U.S. national interest but devouring it.[72]

Another of the damning aspects of fossil-fuel cannibalism is that it drives the United States to form alliances with dictators. We have already established how the United States sought to work with Saddam Hussein in the 1980s, and the United States' long relationship with the oppressive government of Saudi Arabia is well known; post-9/11, however, the United States appears to be using the war against terrorism as rhetorical cover for expanding relationships with oil-rich tyrants. As reported by Lutz Kleveman, "The most tyrannical of Washington's new allies is Islom Karimov, the ex-Communist dictator of Uzbekistan, who allowed U.S. troops to set up a large and permanent military base on Uzbek soil during the Afghan campaign in late 2001." Kleveman argues that the push to control Caspian oil by establishing U.S. bases throughout the region, justified in the name of supporting local regimes who are supposedly our allies in the fight against terrorism, is leading the United States, yet again, to form alliances with regimes that do not support democracy or human rights.[73]

In fact, Greg Palast has argued on AlterNet that "the Bush administration made plans for war and for Iraq's oil before the 9/11 attacks." No war to establish democracy in Iraq, or to rid the region of alleged WMDs, Palast suggests that the United States invaded Iraq because the Bush administration was "intent on using Iraq's oil to destroy the OPEC cartel." Although such a charge might be dismissed as a typical conspiratorial delusion, Aijaz Ahmad supports it, noting that "when the Taliban refused to cooperate fully with the United States in its designs on Central Asian oil, the U.S. decided to invade. Niaz Naik, the dean of Pakistan's diplomatic corps, said on the BBC that he had been told by the Americans during the summer of 2001 that the invasion [of Afghanistan] would begin in October [2001]." Michael Klare's analysis of the 17 May 2001 *National Energy Policy* (*NEP*) supports Palast's and Ahmad's arguments. The cause of intense political controversy, the *NEP*—also known as the Cheney Report—outlined the Bush administration's long-term energy strategy, including what Klare characterizes as "an explicit emphasis on securing more oil from foreign sources." Released roughly four months before 9/11, and targeting the Caspian Sea Basin, home to Azerbaijan, Georgia, Kazakhstan, Kyrgyzstan, Turkmenistan, Tajikistan, and Uzbekistan, the *NEP* gave "every indication that the United States plans to maintain a permanent military presence and to strengthen its ties with friendly regimes in the area." Hence, even before the wars in Afghanistan and Iraq brought U.S. troops to the region, Klare concludes that the Bush White House was intent on forming relationships with Caspian Sea Basin states regardless of their dubious human rights records.[74]

Moreover, on 13 May 2005, Uzbekistan forces opened fire on protesters in Andijon, killing anywhere from 173 (the government's figure) to 745 (the protesters' figure), prompting Human Rights Watch to call the event a "massacre." Following the massacre, HRW chronicled a systematic crackdown in which Uzbekistan was "targeting human rights defenders and opposition activists for arrest, beatings, and intimidation." Although claiming to support the spread of democracy, the Bush administration has formed an alliance with an oil-rich regime in which, according to HRW, the human rights record is "abysmal. . . . Elections are an empty exercise. There is no independent media or genuine opposition parties," and there is "extensive use of torture." Thus supporting the claims made by Kleveman, Palast, Ahmad, and Klare, HRW's reports offer damning evidence of how fossil-fuel cannibalism devours the national interest, driving the United States to form political partnerships, military alliances, and economic deals with oil-rich authoritarian regimes, hence compromising U.S. claims to be spreading democracy while fighting its war against terrorism.[75]

We have thus far offered three claims regarding crony capitalism. First, it amounts to *institutionalized profiteering* meant to cheat consumers, taxpayers, and states out of billions of dollars. Such institutionalized profiteering results in a devastated tax base, thus enabling neoliberals to argue for the further privatization of social services. Second, the depth of corruption and deception forces crony capitalists and their government allies to try to subvert both specific laws and the larger cultural expectations that major development projects will fall under the public scrutiny of checks and balances. In short, crony capitalism breeds subversion and secrecy, amounting to an *assault on democracy.* Third, these first two points culminate in the *fossil-fuel cannibalism* that compromises long-term U.S. national interests in the cause of pursuing short-term, oil-based profits. Crony capitalism thus amounts to the highest stage of economic and political corruption, where "free markets" means corruption and where political power is bought and sold.

More important for this chapter, however, the proliferation of crony capitalism compromises all U.S. claims to global legitimacy as a purveyor of democracy and opportunity. Indeed, one of our key points in this chapter (and in chapters 2 and 3) has been to notice how by President Bush and his supporters so stridently linking democracy to morality to globalizing neoliberalism, hence producing what we have called *evangelical capitalism*, democracy as a political system has increasingly come to be seen as the tarnished and ineffectual handmaiden of crony capitalism. And given that many observers conflate globalization with Americanization, as if globalization were a euphemism for U.S. empire, then it should come as no surprise to learn that the global onslaught of crony capitalism has led cynics to believe that democracy is little more than empire's rhetorical justification. When that rhetorical slippage happens, with democracy taking the fall for the injustices produced by crony capitalism and U.S. empire, then claims to spread democracy appear hypocritical at best, malicious at worst. In short, the malfeasance of crony capitalism—especially when paired with a drive to privatize the empire—discredits the hopes of democracy. To watch this process unfolding before our very eyes, we turn now to a rhetorical analysis of the Bush administration's claims regarding the reconstruction of Iraq.

A Rhetorical Analysis of the Bush Administration's Claims for "Renewal in Iraq"

We begin our rhetorical analysis of the Bush administration's claims for "Renewal in Iraq" by turning to a 28 April 2003 speech by President Bush in Dearborn, Michigan. A suburb of Detroit, Dearborn is situated in a part of southeast Michigan that houses the nation's largest Arab American community, totaling in some estimates to as many as three hundred thousand people. As Gary Younge writes, Dearborn is "the hub of Arab America"; according to Steven Gold, the "first Islamic mosque in America" was built in the region in 1919, meaning that Dearborn's Arab American community is both numerically large and historically rich. Most important for our purposes, Dearborn was also the site of an impromptu celebration on 10 April 2003, when footage of the toppling of Saddam Hussein's statue in Baghdad first streamed across U.S. television sets. It would be a few days before reporters proved that the event was staged—it was not an outpouring of anti-Saddam and pro-U.S. Iraqis doing the toppling but Ahmad Chalabi's hired thugs and U.S. troops in street clothes, all working within an area cordoned off by U.S. tanks. Dearborn's Arab Americans did not know this on 10 April, however, and so they took to the streets to celebrate the symbolic fall of Hussein's rotten regime, hence turning the faked spectacle in Baghdad into a genuine show of joy in Michigan. Like the events in Baghdad, the rally in Dearborn had an ominous undertone, as three reporters for the Aljazeera network found themselves surrounded by marchers shouting slogans against Aljazeera. It took seven Dearborn police officers to protect the reporters from the fury of the crowd.[76]

Within eighteen days the president was in town, clearly hoping to use the eruption of anti-Saddam, anti-Aljazeera, pro-U.S. energy as the backdrop for a major address. Delivered before what was expected to be (and was) a rabidly prowar crowd in the final days of the U.S. war on Iraq, the president thus approached the lectern with the confidence and bounce of a man who thought he had just won a war, hence proving his critics wrong and etching his place amid the nation's celebrated war heroes. (In fact, the president's "Top Gun" speech, the occasion for the controversial "Mission Accomplished" banner, was only three days away.) The combination of timing and location meant that the president spoke in Dearborn to an audience thrilled by his policies.

The president delivered his speech in front of a projection screen, with "Renewal in Iraq" written in both English and Arabic over an otherwise blank outline of the shape of Iraq. With no cities, rivers, roads, or surrounding nations in the image, it portrayed Iraq as a blank slate, a *tabula rasa* waiting for the president to fill in the pristine, empty space. This image alone tells us much about the Bush administration's perception of Iraq, where the weight of history, cultural conflicts, or regional and ethnic tensions is insignificant; for the Bush administration and its corporate supporters, Iraq is a vacant space waiting for new content. Thus hearkening back to our comments from chapter 2 about the evangelical impulses driving the *NSSUS*, the image suggests that a benevolent U.S. empire will fill in the empty gaps, bringing meaning to the meaningless, purpose to those who are lost, salvation to the damned.[77]

Nonetheless, the president cautioned his audience that "America has no intention of imposing our form of government or our culture" on Iraq. The bulk of this chapter demonstrates, however, that the United States intends to do just that, via imposing crony capitalism and the CPA's list of rules for governance. In fact, Americans have become so accustomed to hearing the president conflating politics, morals, and economics, with each wrapped tightly in the comforting grandeur of renewed nationalism, that two sentences later an audience member erupts in a chant of "USA! USA! USA!" This is the second time that chant has interrupted the speech, hence making explicit what everyone in the room understands: that the reconstruction of Iraq is an exercise in heroic U.S. empire building. Indeed, as it did the first time the USA! call arose, the giddy audience again applauds the call of USA! USA! USA! So even while the president claims that the reconstruction of Iraq will not be another example of colonial conquest, his audience revels in the nationalist thrill of the moment, hearing the speech less as a statement about the future success of Iraq than about the gigantic power and prowess of the United States. To skeptical viewers or readers, to anyone around the world who doubted the president's claims for waging war on Iraq or who knew that the Dearborn rally was triggered by a fraud, such a moment could not help but seem like orchestrated propaganda, a case study in wartime triumphalism and hypocrisy.[78]

Two passages from this speech merit closer attention. The first concerns the president's portrayal of the role of oil in the reconstruction of Iraq. Speaking of efforts to rebuild Iraq's power grid, the president says that "oil—Iraqi oil, owned by the Iraqi people—is flowing again to fuel Iraq's power plants." The problem with this claim, however, is that the oil in Iraq is owned not by the Iraqi people but by the international consortium of creditors behind the Trade Bank of Iraq (TBI). Managed by the U.S.-based banking giant JP Morgan Chase, which heads a group of thirteen banks, the TBI issues "export guarantees for trade between Iraq and foreign companies and governments." According to Mitch Jeserich of CorpWatch, the TBI has already amassed $2.4 billion to back such guarantees, against which it has already written "$300 million worth of letters of credit." Put simply, no one will do business in Iraq without some certainty that they will be paid for their services, so TBI (working in conjunction with the U.S. Export-Import Bank) functions as a guarantor of payment, an institutional safety net for capitalists doing business in Iraq.[79]

The rebuilding of Iraq cannot move forward without such an institution because Iraq's banking system is shattered, its economy is devastated, and there is little indigenous money to pay for postwar services. But of course there is oil, or at least the promise of oil once the fields are returned to working capacity, meaning Iraq's reconstruction at the hands of U.S. corporations is based not only on the gigantic U.S. outlays discussed here but also on the TBI's credit, which is based on the collateral of Iraqi oil. In short, TBI can only issue credits today on the basis of assumed oil revenues tomorrow. As Jeserich puts it, the U.S.-managed TBI is "mortgaging the national oil revenues." This is a dangerous ploy, however, for according to investment banker Nomi Prins, the still-unstable Iraqi oil fields—the *New York Times* described "the oil industry in the north" as "crippled" by insurgents in November 2004—are a swirl of uncertainty, meaning that the TBI's guarantees to investors and contractors are based on assumed future profits, not confirmed present capacities. And those capacities continue to take a beating, as twenty guerilla strikes against oil facilities were reported for January and February 2005 alone. If and when TBI's credits are called in, and if there is not enough money or oil to cover the loans, then Iraq will dive into both depression and dispossession, for corporations will likely sue TBI for possession of their promised collateral: Iraq's oil. Moreover, the UN-created Compensation Fund will siphon 5 percent of Iraq's future oil sales to pay war reparations for the first Gulf War, while the Development Fund for Iraq—originally created by the CPA—will administer other oil moneys at the discretion of U.S. managers. The network of banking and business regulations at play here is intricate, too labyrinthine to discuss in full detail, but our point is clear: the Iraqi oil does not belong to the Iraqi people, as the president happily claims; rather, it belongs to JP Morgan Chase and the international consortium of bankers behind the TBI, those parties benefiting from the Compensation Fund, and international fossil-fuel elites running the Development Fund for Iraq.[80]

The second moment in the president's speech calling for closer attention deals with the looting of Iraq. The president says, "We're working with the Iraqis to recover artifacts, to find the hoodlums who ravished the National Museum of Antiquities in Baghdad (applause). Like many of you here, we deplore the actions of the citizens who ravished the museum. And we will work with the Iraqi citizens to find out who they were and bring them to justice (applause.)" Given the president's prior comments regarding the use of American-style "justice" to deal with al Qaeda, in almost every instance using justice as a euphemism for killing terrorists, and factoring in President Bush's notorious use of the death penalty while governor of Texas, we suspect many of the members of the audience heard this claim as a restatement, even a celebration, of the president's record as a "get tough on crime" leader. The problem with this bravura claim, however, is that U.S. troops were ordered to stand idly by while most of the "ravishing" took place, instead protecting only the headquarters of the oil ministry. The president may well have ordered U.S. troops to try to "recover artifacts," and he would no doubt not hesitate to hammer the perpetrators of such crimes with the most violent versions of U.S. "justice," but many suggest that U.S. troops were complicit with such acts of cultural theft and destruction in the first place. Thus, as we have demonstrated throughout this book again and again, the president's claims and actions simply do not align.[81]

Whereas the complicated banking arguments offered above may understandably be news to most readers, the looting that took place in Iraq was the subject of nightly news reports. This means that for the president's claims here to ring true, he must count on his audience simply not knowing the facts. Indeed, both moments, the oil and antiquities claims, appear to rely not only on the president twisting the facts but on his knowing he can do so, on his assuming that his audience will respond not with critical questions or informed doubts but with nationalist chants of USA! USA! USA! Jonathan Schell has colorfully described this rhetorical strategy as part of "an active insurgency against facts," as "a preemptive strike against reality itself." Although some Americans may find such fact-starved, reality-bending spectacles endearing, we suspect that many viewers worldwide, like us, find the moment chilling, for it demonstrates orchestrated state propaganda as cheerful spectacle. The president's speech therefore indicates how the reconstruction of Iraq will be discussed by the Bush administration and its supporters not so much as an opportunity to think critically about how to rebuild a devastated nation while respecting its local norms and customs as an occasion for asserting grandiose claims of benevolent nationalism—*USA! USA! USA!*[82]

While the president spun a web of factually challenged nationalist fictions, his CPA was an interim body charged with the frontline work of rebuilding a nation ruined by multiple wars, crippling UN sanctions, and decades of tyranny. To that end the CPA produced an advertising packet meant to lure possible investors and contractors to Iraq; titled *Trade and Foreign Investment Opportunities in Iraq*, the pamphlet is a cheerful, image-laden, outline-style brief portraying Iraq as a capitalist's dreamland of opportunity. We will skip the demographic information (Iraq has "a large indigenous consumer market," "24.6 million people," and so on) and turn to the section of the pamphlet that begins with a headline in bold capital letters claiming that "IRAQ'S ECONOMY WILL BENEFIT FROM REFORMS CURRENTLY UNDERWAY." The "short-term institutional reforms" include "markets opened to international trade and foreign investment"; "legal and judicial reforms instituted"; "access to credit and capital improved"; and "financial systems made more sound." The "long-term institutional reforms" include "establish a stable, sovereign government"; "shrink the public sector"; "reduce energy and food subsidies"; and "change attitudes."[83]

Two of these changes (establishing the rule of law and a sovereign state) are the commonsense transformations needed to help Iraq move from decades of dictatorship to democracy, yet the other six of them are indications that the so-called Washington Consensus will be the driving model of development employed in Iraq. Given the many complications and even outright failures of that model, it is hard to read such claims without cringing. For if the Washington Consensus does to Iraq in 2006 what it did to east Asia in 1997–1998, or what it has done to Mexico, the countries in Central and South America, and India over the past two decades, then the Iraqis are in for more hardship. Indeed, considering the strength of the economies of Israel, Saudi Arabia, Turkey, Kuwait, and Iraq's other regional neighbors, to say nothing of U.S. and European exporters, it is hard to imagine Iraq being able to compete in a Washington Consensus–style free market. Duncan Kennedy has thus argued that forcing Iraq to follow the model of neoliberalism will likely mean that "Iraq will become economically like Palestine in relation to Israel." Duncan argues that the notion that Iraq, smashed into a state of almost prehistoric destruction by the U.S. invasion and the subsequent insurgency, will soon blossom into an independent economic power is ludicrous.[84]

Consider, for example, the market forces involved in supplying the ubiquitous ten-foot blast walls that line Baghdad, turning the city into a tunnel-like warren of protected enclaves hiding behind giant slabs of concrete. Naomi Klein reports that Iraqis have taken to calling the monstrosities "Bremer Walls." Even though Iraq possesses seventeen concrete factories, Klein reports that "not one of these factories has received a single contract to help with the reconstruction." Instead of paying Iraqi firms $100 to make Bremer Walls, the CPA contracted foreign firms to make the walls at $1,000 each. The CPA thus wasted U.S. tax dollars while leaving Iraqi businesses out of work—this is hardly a model for revving up the postwar economy.[85]

Indeed, after examining the CPA's proposed budgets and anticipated growth rates for Iraq, the Iraqi economist and former UN analyst Sabri Zire Al-Saadi concluded that the United States' plan of imposing a Washington Consensus model of economic development on Iraq was "a fantasy vision." Al-Saadi demonstrates that despite the increasing recognition that Iraq's oil production was severely damaged, the CPA's proposed budgets for postwar Iraq were based almost exclusively on revenue from hoped-for oil sales, amounting to 89 percent of the budget for 2004, 97 percent for 2005, and 98 percent for 2006. These figures were based on anticipated sales of $18 billion, $28 billion, and $29 billion respectively for 2004, 2005, and 2006. Yet the *New York Times* was reporting as early as September 2003 that the Bush administration was admitting that oil sales for 2004 would not exceed $12 billion, with sales approaching $20 billion in 2005 and 2006. The CPA's budgets and accompanying statements therefore amounted to a "fantasy vision" for two reasons. First, they indicated not a broadly developing and widely diversified economy but a monolithic kingdom of fossil fuel—this is hardly the stuff of the president's evangelical capitalism. Second, the CPA's numbers did not match up, for the gap between anticipated and real sales will leave the CPA $8–9 billion short, thus forcing Iraq back onto the market for the same kind of debt-trap-producing loans we addressed in chapter 3.[86]

But readers need not wade through the contested terrain of the impacts of the Washington Consensus on developing nations or the adverse effects of pinning national growth to only one sector of the economy to sense that something is amiss in *Trade and Foreign Investment Opportunities in Iraq*. For in a textbook example of telling others to do what you cannot do yourself, the brochure promises a series of changes that would be virtually impossible in the United States. In fact, given the prevalence of crony capitalism among the corporations contracted to bring the Washington Consensus to Iraq, it is difficult to read the "Change attitudes" section of the pamphlet as anything other than a cruel hoax, as a wish list of precisely the neoliberal reforms that crony capitalism makes impossible. For example, three of the four attitude adjustments the CPA hopes to make, with our pointed rejoinders to them inserted here, include "Re-establish trust, particularly toward foreigners"—as seen in the Patriot Act?—"Eliminate environment that rewards relationships instead of competitiveness"—as in the MCI, Halliburton, Boeing, DynCorp, and other crony capitalist deals discussed above?—and "Change expectation that positions of power are opportunities to make money"—as seen in Vice President Cheney's handling of the Energy Task Force and his $13 million golden parachute on leaving Halliburton for the White House? Our questions indicate how *Trade and Foreign Investment Opportunities in Iraq* prophesies modes of capitalism that would be unrecognizable to most Americans; the pamphlet claims the United States will bring reforms to Baghdad that it could not bring to New York City. Written without a hint of self-reflexivity, as if there was no resistance to the U.S. occupation, as if Iraqis and Americans alike were simpletons, as if multinational corporations were law-abiding, upstanding global citizens, the pamphlet amounts to a comic-book version of neoliberal globalization.[87]

This is a surprising conclusion, for the former head of the CPA, Ambassador L. Paul Bremer III, as noted in our introduction, is a sophisticated statesman with considerable experience in the private sector as well. Like his mentor, Henry Kissinger, Bremer is a sharp, figure-spewing, hands-on manager who, even when disliked or distrusted, is respected. For example, in a press conference from Baghdad on 26 September 2003, Bremer offered long, complicated answers full of careful reasoning and thoughtful qualifications—precisely what is lacking in *Trade and Foreign Investment Opportunities in Iraq*. Nonetheless, although Bremer offered realistic assessments of the status of Iraq's reconstruction—even calling for rescinding its international debt, arguing that "debt servicing . . . would bankrupt the country in 2005"—he also fulfilled myth-making functions that correlate nicely with the Bush administration's prewar lies regarding the reasons for invading Iraq. (Bremer's wish was largely fulfilled in November 2004, when wealthy creditors agreed to forgive 80 percent of the $39 billion Iraq owed them; the deal hinges, of course, on Iraq meeting yet-to-be-imposed IMF strictures). In fact, in his opening comments, before taking questions from the press, Bremer claimed that the CPA's chief function is to support "the overall effort to win the war against terrorism in Iraq." Later in the briefing he again claimed that the reconstruction of Iraq was undertaken "to be sure that we can defeat the terrorists in Iraq." Knowing that there were no established links between al Qaeda and Iraq prior to the invasion, a confused reporter asked: "Defeat the terrorists—what do you mean?" Bremer then launched into a long answer describing the different elements of the uprising that has left postwar Iraq a bloody mess. The rhetorical problem here is that Bremer reversed cause and effect: he claimed the CPA (effect) was fighting a war against Iraqi terrorists (cause), when the fact is that the rise of terrorism in Iraq (effect) was a postwar phenomenon launched to rid the nation of what many saw as a U.S. "occupation" carried out through the CPA (cause). Hence, even while offering straight talk about the difficult economics of reconstruction, Bremer's overall message dovetailed with the administration's prewar lies, which claimed that the U.S. invasion was undertaken to rid Iraq of WMDs and to sever Iraq/al Qaeda ties.[88]

Our rhetorical analysis of USAID Administrator Natsios's testimony to Congress, President Bush's Dearborn speech, the CPA's *Trade and Foreign Investment Opportunities in Iraq,* and Ambassador Bremer's press briefing thus demonstrate four related findings. First, Natsios's testimony makes it clear that despite the increasing controversy over U.S. actions in postwar Iraq, the United States is in fact offering massive aid and assistance, in many regards fulfilling the best promises of the United States as a generous and competent world leader. Second, however, as a direct contradiction to the first point, President Bush's speech illustrates how the reconstruction of Iraq will be used not as an occasion for thinking about the economic and cultural needs of the Iraqis but for celebrating the greatness of the United States, for trumpeting renewed U.S. nationalism, for pursuing globalization-through-benevolent-empire. We suspect that Natsios's list of good deeds will appear less and less credible in direct relationship to the increasing boisterousness of the president's triumphant nationalism.

Third, the CPA's *Trade and Foreign Investment Opportunities in Iraq* can only hurt U.S. efforts in Iraq and elsewhere, for by appealing to highly contested Washington Consensus principles in simplistic celebrations of can-do capitalism, the text reveals the profit-driven banality of the CPA's vision of postwar Iraq. Indeed, like the president's blank-slate image of Iraq in his Dearborn speech—or like USAID's dreamy *A Year in Iraq,* a May 2004 report we do not have space to analyze here—the CPA's pamphlet illustrates a crude, uncomplicated view of Iraq. Demonstrating to the world that the U.S. vision for postwar Iraq is based on bootstrap capitalism, such documents can only damage U.S. credibility, proving to the world that the United States knows little about the nation it intends to rebuild. And fourth, whereas the cheeriness of the CPA's advertisement may lead readers to suspect that the CPA is an outfit of simpletons, Ambassador Bremer's press briefing argues for the opposite understanding, demonstrating that its chief officer was capable of offering fact-filled economic analyses in one sentence before switching in the next to myth-making, lie-sustaining, slippery claims. Bremer's insistence that the CPA was fighting against terrorism was particularly important in this regard, for it offered a seamless repetition of the president's prewar lies, turning the onslaught of U.S.-led crony capitalism in Iraq into a necessary move against al Qaeda.[89]

Epilogue: Empire's War on Democracy

In chapter 3 we demonstrated the many ways globalization is hurting U.S. workers by creating unemployment and driving down wages; we have shown in chapter 4 how the reconstruction of Iraq is spreading the Washington Consensus mantras driving neoliberal globalization to that nation as well, hence leading to massive privatization, antilabor laws and practices, dubious banking and accounting norms, insider favoritism, job training too rapid to be credible, and the corruption and malfeasance that mark crony capitalism. Nonetheless, the U.S. war on Iraq has become a boon to some U.S. workers, who even in doing unskilled labor can make hefty tax-free salaries in Iraq. As Russell Gold observes in the *Wall Street Journal*, reconstructing Iraq has become "the largest mobilization of civilians to work in a war zone in U.S. history." DynCorp, for example, pays average salaries of $50,000 plus a "dangerous conditions" bonus to its oversees police officers; Halliburton pays about $80,000 to blue-collar workers from around the country who show up for a two-week training session in an abandoned J.C. Penney store in Houston before shipping out for Iraq. Despite the slogans of the champions of neoliberal free markets, then, military Keynesianism is thriving under the guise of fighting a global war against terrorism and reconstructing Iraq. Given our prior discussion of the many ways globalization harms the U.S. economy, it is hard not to wonder whether this military Keynesianism illustrates how the Bush administration intends to respond to the economic travails of globalization by establishing U.S.-controlled imperial markets. Indeed, if we take the reconstruction of Iraq as a harbinger of things to come, then we may suggest that henceforward the United States will respond to the complexities of globalization by pursuing imperial crony capitalism.[90]

As demonstrated in our analyses of the Bush administration's WMD lies (in chapter 1), the *NSSUS*'s bold principle of unilateral and preemptive warfare (in chapter 2), and the complexities of globalization (in chapter 3), however, such attempts to locate a directly causal relationship between globalization and the United States' actions in Iraq are doomed to simplify a remarkably complicated situation. Nonetheless, the prevalence of crony capitalism makes it look as though the United States is using Iraq for its own self-interest, turning the plight of a devastated nation into an opportunity to extend state-to-corporation welfare to a coterie of administration-friendly and military-industrial complex–linked firms. The bold hopes of Natsios's USAID and Bremer's CPA, then, cannot help but seem naïve, if not intentionally deceptive, in the face of the crushing realization that by relying on crony capitalism to rebuild Iraq, the United States has rendered its promise to bring free markets and democracy to Iraq dubious at best, hypocritical versions of neocolonialism at worst.

As a closing example, one that highlights the ways crony capitalism has dragged the United States ever closer to the twilight of democracy, we turn to Jeffrey Marburg-Goodman's "USAID's Iraq Procurement Contracts: Insider's View." Published in the fall of 2003 in *Procurement Lawyer*, a journal run by the American Bar Association, the essay purports to offer a corrective to the fears about reconstruction contracting raised here. Marburg-Goodman, "a career USAID procurement lawyer," writes that "there is a tremendous tension between the purposely deliberate and unhurried process and the occasional emergency needs of a government agency." War-ravaged nations like Iraq, for example, cannot wait for the United States to plod through its usual assistance contracting cycles, for "the ordinary procurement process could result in the loss of thousands of innocent lives." Because haste in rebuilding Iraq was imperative, USAID triggered "urgency-based regulatory exceptions," thus making open bidding on contracts impossible. From this perspective, the insider favoritism, closed bidding, and ID/IQ contracts that we have cited here as key ingredients of crony capitalism in fact amount to the logistical necessities and commonsense realities of responding to catastrophe. But Marburg-Goodman also reveals that USAID began consulting with prospective postwar reconstruction contractors as early as "fall 2002," many months before the war was launched on 19 March 2003. In fact, Marburg-Goodman admits that "given the fact that the Bush administration was publicly stating that war could be avoided . . . it would have been inadvisable to advertise these reconstruction contracts in the usual manner. Accordingly, we set up a process designed to elicit robust competition, value for money, and timely aid in an environment that required silence as to these plans."[91]

This is a shocking confession, yet another revealing moment of capitalist truth telling, one that admits that from as early as fall 2002 the Bush administration was saying in public that it wanted to avoid war while negotiating behind closed doors with the insider firms who would reap billions of dollars of profit for rebuilding the yet-to-be attacked Iraq. Indeed, this remarkable passage asks readers to understand that practicing the open debates assumed to keep democracy legitimate would have been inconvenient, "inadvisable" for the Bush administration's war plans.

Moreover, if future wars are to be launched, as in the Iraq case, from "an environment that required silence," then Marburg-Goodman is suggesting that future USAID contracts will also have to be assigned under the secrecy entailed by "urgency-based regulatory exceptions." Clearly echoing the neoconservatives driving foreign policy in Washington, Marburg-Goodman thus proposes a blueprint for crony capitalist empire, where the U.S. government wages wars without democratic deliberation, where it awards billion-dollar contracts behind closed doors, where democracy itself becomes an "inadvisable" hindrance to waging imperialist wars. And so the combination of privatizing the empire and crony capitalism drags the United States ever closer to the twilight of democracy while leaving Iraq in bondage to Washington Consensus–chanting free marketeers.

Conclusion

Rhetorical Integrity and the Twilight of Democracy

Stunned by the attacks of 9/11, manipulated by color-coded security threats and dramatic warnings of imminent WMD attacks, misled regarding the status of postinvasion Afghanistan and Iraq, wracked with doubts about an economy plodding through a recession, deeply divided by two hotly contested presidential elections (one of them arguably stolen), and awed through it all by nightly doses of war propaganda, many Americans appear to have responded to post-9/11 life by seeking solace in the militarized grandeur of a violent nationalism that trumps any sense of obligation to open public deliberation or even the slightest trace of factual evidence. Now more than ever, W. H. Auden's lament for a nation sliding toward brutality and alienation rings in our ears:

> Pawed-at and gossiped-over
> By the promiscuous crowd,
> Concocted by editors
> Into spells to befuddle the crowd,
> All words like peace and love,
> All sane affirmative speech,
> Had been soiled, profaned, debased
> To a horrid mechanical screech:
> No civil style survived
> That pandemonium.[1]

Auden is particularly useful for our purposes here, for he came to the United States in January 1939, having witnessed both the rise of fascism in Germany and the terribly bloody war in Spain, where he drove an ambulance for the Republicans in 1937. Disgusted with Europe's decline into madness, Auden, like so many others then and now, sought refuge in

America, yet he eventually became frustrated with American politics as well, as witnessed in this poem, first published in the United States in 1951 and then in London in 1952. Written in another time of entrenched political crisis, when Auden feared for the very soul of America, these disappointed lines point to a nation entering the twilight of democracy, where "civil style" has given way to mass-produced banality, where "sane affirmative speech" has been drowned out by a national security apparatus working in tandem with "editors" to produce the "horrid mechanical screech" of endless fear. Thus recalling our comments on Russell Baker, Wendell Berry, and Joan Didion from our introduction, Auden's poem shows us how fears for the future of the republic are often based on doubts about the rhetorical norms of engagement, about how citizens think and speak and argue with one another and their government. From this perspective, the twilight of democracy is not so much a temporal horizon, an indicator of decline from halcyon better times, as *a constant possibility,* the ever-present threat—as worrisome to Auden in 1951 as to us in 2006—that we may degrade our habits of public deliberation to the point of losing any sense of rhetorical integrity and hence any sense of democracy itself. Nonetheless, like Auden's poem, a literary lament that hopes readers will absorb its message and thus begin the process of renewing the fraying bonds of "civil style," so we attempt in these closing remarks to balance fear and hope, to demonstrate how critical thinking may clear the way for reconstructing a sense of rhetorical integrity. We proceed with the assumption that this delicate balancing act, this ambiguous nestling of contrasting emotions against each other, illustrates how our culture oscillates around divergent, even contradictory impulses.[2]

To think about what losing rhetorical integrity—Auden's "civil style"—can lead to politically, we turn to Hannah Arendt's *The Origins of Totalitarianism.* First published in 1948, while she was "still in grief and sorrow . . . but no longer in speechless outrage and impotent horror" at World War II's carnage, Arendt sought to prove how the rise of imperialism had led to the totalitarian regimes of Hitler's Germany and Stalin's U.S.S.R. Our efforts here to explicate the complicated interweaving of globalization and empire have been inspired in part by Arendt, who tried to illustrate how economic trends dovetailed with political trends, hence providing a historical and interdisciplinary narrative—a scholarly supplement to Auden's poem—that explained the rise of mass-produced barbarism. Although deeply concerned with the material forces that produced first imperialism and then totalitarianism, Arendt also proposed that state-orchestrated violence, whether in the form of wars of expansion or domestic campaigns of extermination, derived much of its legitimacy by responding to the repressed fury of populations who felt that their lives had slipped out of control. Arendt argued that because the revolutionary practices of early to mid-twentieth-century capitalism left increasing segments of the population feeling disempowered, literally bewildered by a strange new world, it produced "apathy and even hostility toward public life." Wrenched from familiar patterns of economic order and political power, the "slumbering majorities" slid into an "unorganized, structureless mass of furious individuals" who, because the leaders of the old order seemed inept, came to believe that "the most respected, articulate, and representative members of the community were fools." Thus unmoored from older norms of deference for traditional intellectual and political elites, enraged by their loss of economic stability, and searching desperately for new ways of making meaning, such populations, according to Arendt—and foreshadowing Didion's line about "bellicose fantasy"—"tended toward an especially violent nationalism." Comparing post-9/11 U.S. politics to Arendt's dreaded totalitarian regimes is of course hyperbolic, yet the comparison is also deeply suggestive, for it shows that then as now, the militarized grandeur of violent nationalism served as solace for those rocked by the disintegration of the familiar.[3]

Moreover, Arendt speculated that because the thrill of imperialist and totalitarian wars satisfied deep psychological needs, the governments launching them had no obligation to adhere to enlightened standards of public discourse or political deliberation. Because waging wars created contexts for experiencing mass heroism and a sense of historical duty and purpose—precisely the values modern capitalism destroys—imperialist and totalitarian regimes understood that they were not beholden to the facts regarding those wars. What mattered were not the consequences of imperialism's and totalitarianism's wars, but the urgent rush of significance they fostered for their participants and spectators. Arendt's most chilling passages therefore revolved around her observation that under imperial and totalitarian regimes "the difference between truth and falsehood may cease to be objective and become a mere matter of power and cleverness, of pressure and infinite repetition." The pleasures of violent nationalism therefore seduced populations to assent to imperial and totalitarian regimes that ruled by producing "an air of mad unreality." Although these words were written almost sixty years ago, they seem to us startlingly accurate regarding post-9/11 American life. Indeed, as suggested by our recalling Auden's lament for the death of "civil style," and as indicated in the case studies offered in chapters 1 through 4, America may well be on the verge of succumbing to the "mad unreality" that Arendt diagnosed as central to totalitarianism.[4]

To consider these provocative thoughts from Auden and Arendt, we conclude our study with four interwoven sets of comments. First, to close our book by returning to the events that triggered the United States' recent wars, hence bringing our thoughts on globalization and empire full circle, we address some of the findings of the *9/11 Commission Report*. A relentlessly detailed critique of the U.S. national security establishment's botched handling of domestic and international terrorism, the report nonetheless says nothing about U.S. foreign and economic policies in their historical or contemporary forms. As a result, the report illustrates precisely how public discourse about globalization and empire has become truncated, compartmentalized, reduced to narrowly focused analyses that do not speak to the larger questions we have addressed herein. Second, as a response to the report's omission of any historical or contextual information regarding the relationships among 9/11, global terrorism, and U.S. economic and foreign policies, we step back from our analysis of post-9/11 U.S. actions to take a longer view of how U.S. empire has affected the world since the end of World War II. In contrast to the report's tightly delineated technocratic language, this second section asks broad political questions about the consequences of U.S. empire. Third, reprising our arguments from chapter 3, we consider how global economics impact these questions about empire and the production of political legitimacy. Although we focus our comments here on recent economic trends, our goal is to demonstrate how the champions of globalization in general and the Washington Consensus version of development in particular view the world through the rose-colored lens of patriotic provincialism. Fourth, returning in our final pages to our driving concern with the norms of democratic deliberation, we explore the possibility that post-9/11 U.S. public culture may be turning away from what we call the rhetorical habits of democracy toward a form of communication and political order more akin to what Arendt diagnosed as totalitarianism.

Taken as a whole, these closing remarks strive not only to conclude our main arguments in this book but also to answer the haunting question of whether the United States has entered the twilight of democracy.

The *9/11 Commission Report* and Bureaucratizing the Imagination

Directed by a bipartisan and tough-minded panel of ten commissioners (five Democrats and five Republicans), completed by a staff of eighty experts, conducted in a manner described as "independent, impartial, thorough, and nonpartisan," and dutifully submitted to the president and the American public "without dissent," the *9/11 Commission Report* may well stand as one of the first major achievements of twenty-first-century U.S. democracy. Indeed, because its research was based on hundreds of at times confrontational interviews with elite officials, the analysis of thousands of internal government documents, and impassioned testimony from hundreds of common citizens (many of whom were directly affected by 9/11), with its preliminary findings presented—much to the chagrin of the Bush administration—before twelve public hearings, the commission in many ways embodied and the report in many ways honors the best aspects of U.S. democracy. Balanced, fair, relentlessly public, showing no special regard for the powerful or the famous, and infused with a sense of pragmatism, the commission functioned and its report now serves as a testament to what democracy could be. Thus modeling the kind of critical patriotism that has fallen out of favor in post-9/11 America, the *9/11 Commission Report* deftly combines painstaking research with pragmatic thinking, and a heart-wrenching love of nation with a blistering critique of the government's botched handling of terrorist threats. There can be few documents in our national literature that so effectively refute our speculations about how the twilight of democracy may be fading into the possible reemergence of totalitarianism.[5]

Like the nation it speaks to and for, however, the report is also fraught with contradictions. For along with its truth-telling and muckraking power, the report functions as a carefully scrubbed whitewash. Indeed, because there is no discussion of U.S. foreign or economic policy in the report, its blockbuster revelations may hide as much as they reveal. Rather than situating 9/11 and its aftermath within the complicated historical, economic, and political contexts we have sought to reconstruct herein, the report instead portrays a benevolent United States under attack by lunatics. When introducing readers to al Qaeda in the report's preface, for example, we are told that "the enemy rallies broad support in the Arab and Muslim world by demanding redress of political grievances, but its hostility toward us and our values is limitless. Its purpose is to rid the world of religious and political pluralism, the plebiscite, and equal rights for women." Thus removing 9/11 from the realm of strategic political action, the report's preface posits the event as something more like the opening cataclysm of an infinite, "limitless" clash of civilizations—*they hate not our actions but our values.* We demonstrated in chapter 2 that this "clash of civilizations" thesis is bankrupt, for it is based on powerful doses of racism, xenophobia, and ahistorical myth, amounting not so much to a careful analysis as a paranoid fantasy. Despite the excellent research that follows, then, the report nonetheless begins by echoing this discredited "clash of civilizations" thesis and, more pointedly, President Bush's and David Brooks's hysterical claims about al Qaeda with which we opened this book.[6]

When coupled with the *9/11 Commission Report*'s omission of any criticism of U.S. economic and foreign policy, its framing 9/11 in this manner suggests that submitting the study "without dissent" entailed a series of delicate evasions. For while the report portrays an innocent United States under attack by madmen, the fact is that the report's authors, as elite insiders with access to the highest levels of economic and military intelligence, are complicit with the economic and foreign policies that led us to this point in the first place. Nonetheless, while the report's authors assail the failures of various intelligence services, they forward a version of 9/11 that isolates it from any discussion of how U.S. economic and foreign policies might have helped to produce the rising tide of international anger and violence toward the United States. In this regard the report reminds us not so much of the glories of twenty-first-century democracy as of the diversionary theater that kept twentieth-century totalitarian regimes afloat. For example, in describing Khrushchev's revelatory June 1956 speech before the Twentieth Party Congress in Moscow, where he admitted the breadth of Stalin's reign of terror and butchery, Arendt notes that "Khrushchev's startling admissions—for the obvious reason that his audience and he himself were totally involved in the true story— concealed considerably more than they revealed" and thus "minimized the gigantic criminality of the Stalin regime." In the same way that Khrushchev's denunciations of Stalin quarantined a systematic problem to a tightly delineated group of wrongdoers, so the report's denunciations of our intelligence failures elide the more challenging questions of if and how post–World War II U.S. economic and foreign policies may have fueled the chain of events leading up to 9/11.[7]

Indeed, the *9/11 Commission Report* is committed to revising some aspects of the U.S. intelligence community while avoiding any discussion of the deeper economic and political dilemmas that have made our age of globalization and empire so dangerous. For example, one of the report's many suggestions for improving U.S. foreign policy in general and counterterrorist intelligence operations in particular is "to find a way of routinizing, even bureaucratizing, the exercise of imagination." In reference to a 1998 Presidential Daily Briefing (PDB) that mentioned the possible use of hijacked planes for terrorist purposes, the report argues that "had the contents of this PDB been brought to the attention of a wider group, including key members of Congress, it might have brought much more attention to the need for permanent changes in domestic airport and airline security procedures." In this example, "the exercise of imagination" is linked to expanding the number of conversants in high-level policy discussions. The problem, of course, is finding a way to make even the most inclusive policy debates more imaginative.[8]

The likelihood of productively bureaucratizing the imagination was addressed in 1937 by Kenneth Burke in *Attitudes toward History*, a sprawling book that sought to provide a "dictionary of pivotal terms" for critical thinking. While Burke understood that modernity inevitably produced a struggle between unfettered imagination and stifling bureaucracy, he also prudently recognized that in combining the two forces "we necessarily come upon the necessity of compromise." The success or failure of such a compromise could be measured for Burke by gauging its output: "A bureaucratic order approaches the stage of alienation in proportion as its unintended by-products become a stronger factor than the original purpose." The notion of unintended by-products swamping original purposes has been popularized via Chalmers Johnson's *Blowback*, where he argues that "blowback means the unintended or unexpected negative consequences of covert special operations that have been kept secret from the American people and, in most cases, from their elected representatives. Blowback does not mean reactions to all historical events but rather to U.S. clandestine operations aimed at overthrowing foreign governments, or engaging 'friendly' foreign police forces to execute people the U.S. government has dubbed 'communists' or 'terrorists,' or helping launch state terrorist operations against target populations."[9]

Johnson's blowback is therefore a historically situated moment of what Burke calls unintended by-products, with the caveat that such by-products are the result not of broad historical trends but of specific covert actions gone wrong. We do not have the space here to dive into the hundreds of possible examples of such blowback; instead we will point readers both to Johnson and to Peter Dale Scott, whose *Drugs, Oil, and War* (2003), *Deep Politics and the Death of JFK* (1993), and *Cocaine Politics* (1991) illustrate the ways the funding networks, mercenary cells, and weapons proliferation produced by covert operations end up boomeranging on the United States. Much like the Taliban, who outlived their "original purpose" to later haunt the United States, the clandestine players involved in the operations described by Johnson and Scott turn up again and again as threats to U.S. interests, as blowback. For Burke, Johnson, and Scott, then, it is clear that bureaucratizing the imagination, especially when undertaken in a secretive manner, amounts to a recipe for both bungled operations and precisely the kinds of unimaginative groupthink that leads to bad decision making, the mass production of alienation, and sometimes deadly blowback.[10]

On one hand, then, the *9/11 Commission Report*'s calling for greater imagination in policy planning makes great sense—and embodies Burke's hope for a productive "compromise" between imagination and bureaucracy —as it demonstrates again and again how more creative thinking could have possibly prevented 9/11 and addressed other pressing foreign policy crises. On the other hand, however, as suggested by our discussion of Johnson and Scott, the report's call for the bureaucratization of the imagination is bizarre for two reasons. First, the report offers this mandate within a study that shows remarkably little imagination regarding the historical, economic, political, and military causes of terrorism in the first place. Second, it offers a scathing indictment of the U.S. intelligence community, especially regarding the ways its massive bureaucracies— including the FBI, CIA, National Security Agency, National Geospatial-Intelligence Agency, National Reconnaissance Office, DIA, INR, and others—function more as competitors than as partners. For example, regarding Zacarias Moussaoui, the suspected "twentieth hijacker" who, if handled differently following his arrest on 16 August 2001, may have enabled the United States to prevent the 9/11 attacks, the report sneers that "the director of central intelligence knew about the FBI's Moussaoui investigation weeks before word of it made its way even to the FBI's own assistant director for counterterrorism." While certain bureaucracies were not sharing useful information, others were stifling fresh thinking. Despite the fact that they include tens of thousands of well-trained personnel and state-of-the-art technological capabilities, are funded each year with multi-billion-dollar budgets, and have access to the world's most sophisticated weaponry, the report concludes that in "look[ing] back" over a decade's worth of counterterrorist planning by the agencies listed above, "we are struck with the narrow and unimaginative menu of options for action offered to both President Clinton and President Bush." The report diagnoses this failure of the imagination as a direct product of the government's labyrinthine bureaucratic structure, which, along with creating the intelligence turf wars addressed in chapter 1, has also created agencies that are "often passive, accepting what are viewed as givens, including that efforts to identify and fix glaring vulnerabilities to dangerous threats would be too costly, too controversial, or too disruptive." Much as argued by Burke, Johnson, and Scott, then, the report illustrates how imagination is devoured by bureaucratic inertia.[11]

Opening up elite policy discussions to a few more members of Congress or select intelligence agencies is therefore, counter to the report's proposal, not likely to expand significantly the range of options offered to the president. Calling for the bureaucratization of imagination therefore seems like a particularly banal, if not cruelly ironic, way of dealing with the crises at hand. In fact, overhauling the bureaucratic structure of U.S. intelligence agencies is little more than a panacea in the face of the United States' rising international legitimacy crisis. For whether the FBI and CIA can work together, or whether the INR and DIA can share information more effectively—as envisioned in the 9/11 Commission–prompted intelligence bill signed into law by President Bush on 17 December 2004—the fact is that the world increasingly sees the United States as a rogue nation. Indeed, although it pains us—both as authors and as Americans—to acknowledge this claim, we demonstrate below that for much of the world the United States is viewed not as an answer to the dilemmas of globalization and empire but as the chief source of the problem.[12]

Afghanistan Abandoned: Why the World Fears the United States as a Rogue Nation

In the opening pages of chapter 1 we invoked the outraged words of Senator Robert Byrd to raise questions about the validity of the Bush administration's claims regarding alleged Iraqi WMDs. We return to Senator Byrd in closing this book as well, for his comments from the floor of the U.S. Senate on 19 March 2003, the day the United States began its invasion of Iraq, point directly to why the United States is increasingly seen as a rogue nation. Byrd lamented that "the image of America has changed. Around the globe, our friends mistrust us, our word is disputed, our intentions are questioned. . . . [For] we flaunt our superpower status with arrogance. We treat UN Security Council members like ingrates who offend our princely dignity by lifting their heads from the carpet." Byrd's angry words were ignored by the U.S. mainstream corporate media, yet his conclusions are supported by a survey conducted by the Pew Research Center for the People and the Press, which shows that people from many nations increasingly see the United States as a dire threat to their safety—*they see the United States as a rogue nation.* On the basis of surveys taken first in the summer and fall of 2002 and then again following the U.S. invasion of Iraq, Pew found that when asked if people thought the United States was a threat, 72 percent of surveyed Nigerians said yes (up from 26 percent before the U.S. invasion of Iraq), 72 percent of Pakistanis said yes (up from 23 percent), 71 percent of Russians said yes (up from 26 percent), 71 percent of Turks said yes (up from 27 percent), 58 percent of Lebanese said yes (up from 41 percent), and so on down the line. As demonstrated in our conclusion to chapter 2, similarly disheartening findings were produced in polls from 2003 and 2004. Rather than dismissing such views as deluded or worse—as we suspect many provincial patriots are likely to do—it may be useful to try to understand them.[13]

Consider, for example, what the Pew interviewees may likely have been thinking about the United States' actions in Afghanistan, where, following its spectacular smashing of the Taliban and its failure to capture bin Laden, the United States now appears uninterested in dedicating the financial clout, policing assistance, and other infrastructural support needed to rebuild that shattered country into a functioning democracy. For as terrorist and guerilla strikes continue to escalate, as disease ravages the countryside, and as political in-fighting among multiple tribes and paramilitary factions stymies the rebuilding process, Afghanistan appears with each day closer to yet another collapse into anarchy. As Scott Baldauf reported from Kabul in April 2003, "Afghanistan is tottering at the edge of civil war. It needs only a nudge." In June 2003 Carlotta Gall echoed this fear, writing from Kabul that "attacks on peacekeepers and workers are increasing. . . . The armed men who rule the districts, regions and whole provinces are becoming more and more entrenched and increasingly powerful." Gall thus concluded that "the country could end up being ruled by a mixture of drug lords and fundamentalist mujahedeen— in other words, people not much different from the Taliban." One year later, Gall reported from Kabul that "more than 321,236 acres of land were planted with poppy in 2004," thus producing $2.8 billion in profit, equaling "about 60 percent of the country's legal gross domestic product." Moreover, Gall observed that "diplomats and Afghan officials acknowledge" that President Hamid Karzai's "administration has included known drug lords" and that "many of his provincial governors, police and army chiefs," including members of the Northern Alliance, are complicit with the drug trade. Writing from the northern province of Balkh in November 2004, Christian Parenti advanced similar charges, arguing that because of the United States abandoning postinvasion Afghanistan, the nation had devolved into "an embryonic narco-mafia state."[14]

Like the Taliban before them, the warlords and drug-running thugs installed by U.S. forces as Afghanistan's new rulers appear not to be concerned with human rights and the rule of law, much less with building democracy. In fact, Human Rights Watch (HRW) concluded in June 2003 that "many Afghans are less secure than they were a year ago." Amnesty International (AI) went further, warning the British government that same week that "by failing to appreciate the gravity of the human rights concerns in relation to Northern Alliance leaders, UK ministers at best perpetuate a culture of impunity for past crimes; at worst they risk being complicit in human rights abuses." The United States defeating the Taliban therefore has not brought democracy and development to Afghanistan—just more misery, more poverty, more feudal infighting, record levels of drug cultivation, and, as witnessed by HRW and AI, more human rights violations by yet another out-of-control U.S. client regime. In addition to its current human rights dilemmas, Afghanistan is a country that has been embroiled in some form of war for almost a quarter of a century; it is a country that has seen more than one million of its people murdered in those wars; it is a country where there is no infrastructure for water, electricity, roads, or phones; it is a country with few functioning banks, a currency that is worthless, and warlords who hoard the little money and goods that manage to filter into the country. Afghanistan is therefore a disaster of unparalleled proportions, a bloodied and battered nation described by the Pulitzer Prize–winning journalist Barry Bearak as "tossing and turning in a benumbing nightmare." Learning even cursory facts about life in Afghanistan thus forces one to marvel at the incomprehensible, almost comic arrogance of U.S. claims to be building democracy there.[15]

Although it would be foolish to lay blame for this "benumbing nightmare" exclusively at the feet of the United States, the fact is that postwar U.S. funding decisions have affected Afghanistan dramatically. As Bearak reports, "America made $649 million available to Afghanistan in fiscal year 2002, which ended in September; in 2003, the amount should exceed $1.2 billion. While a hefty sum, even the latter amount is hardly Marshall Plan size. Indeed, it roughly equals the cost of a single B-2 stealth bomber." In fact, as demonstrated in chapter 4, the United States' 2003 grant of $1.2 billion for all of Afghanistan is but a fraction of the size of the astronomical crony capitalist contracts Bechtel and Halliburton alone have received for reconstruction work in Iraq. Moreover, U.S. expenditures in invading and then occupying Iraq have mushroomed to more than $151 billion for fiscal years 2003–2005 (amounting in one estimate to as much as "$3,415 for every U.S. household"), meaning U.S. efforts to salvage Afghanistan have involved approximately *eight-tenths of one percent* of the money spent on invading Iraq. The international community is equally complicit in abandoning postwar Afghanistan, as Michael Mann reports that whereas "Afghans receive $42 per head [in aid] from the international community, Bosnians get $326, Kosovans $286, and East Timorese $195." These same funding patterns will continue for the foreseeable future, for when President Bush requested $81.9 billion in emergency war spending money in April 2005, Congress responded by stiffing Afghanistan. As reported by the *Washington Post*, the committee debating the president's war package "funded virtually all of the requests for defense but chopped money for foreign assistance from $5.6 billion to $3 billion. Most of the trims came from reconstruction and democracy projects for Afghanistan."[16]

Despite these unsettling facts, Mary C. Andrews, the director of the White House's Office of Global Communications, claimed on 15 October 2004 that the United States was "building peace and stability in Afghanistan." In that same vein, the White House's "Rebuilding Afghanistan" Web page celebrated in late December 2004 the "post-Taliban rebirth of civil society underway in Afghanistan." But as the examples offered above demonstrate, the United States and its allies' claims to be building democracy and fostering economic development in Afghanistan are farcical. Indeed, thinking about the fantastical gap between Bush administration claims and the many reports cited here leads us again to recall Arendt's blistering critique of totalitarianism, which she argued depended for its survival on the production of "an air of mad unreality." If we proceed with the assumption that many of the Pew's respondents know even some of the facts about this mad unreality, then we are forced to see people expressing their rising distrust of the United States not as lunatics or dupes but as rational global citizens who understand that the United States' bold prewar claims do not match its halfhearted postwar actions.[17]

We should be clear that this trust-destroying cycle of invading in the name of democracy only to quickly abandon the cause is not an invention of the Bush administration but a staple of U.S. foreign policy for the past fifty years. In fact, before the invasion and then desertion of Afghanistan, the United States had engaged in *fifty-five* post–World War II military interventions—sometimes overtly, sometimes covertly—in nations that it soon left in various states of anarchy or dictatorship. William Blum's *Killing Hope: U.S. Military and CIA Interventions since World War II* chronicles these fifty-five failures in heartbreaking detail and includes information not only on such well-known interventions as Iran in 1953, Guatemala in 1954, Laos in 1973, Chile in 1973, Zaire in 1975, and Haiti in 1994, but also on lesser-known actions in Syria in 1956, in Haiti in 1959, in Bolivia in 1964, and in Morocco in 1983. In each of these cases national security was invoked to justify military interventions that produced not democracy but ragtag regimes beholden to U.S. economic and geopolitical interests. Patriotic Americans want to believe that their nation is capable of reforming the world, of bringing peace and democracy to those who need it—*we're supposed to be the good guys*—yet historically minded critics like Blum, David Harvey, Johnson, Mann, Scott, Ellen Meiksins Wood, and the many others cited in this study make it clear why so much of the world fears the United States: its grand claims to fight wars in order to build democracy and expedite economic development do not match the harsh realities of postinvasion nations left in various stages of economic bondage, cultural despair, and political disarray.[18]

What makes the current situation so maddening is that while reconstruction efforts in Afghanistan and Iraq flounder, the Bush administration continues to argue, as addressed in chapter 4 and as witnessed in the White House materials cited above, that both countries will become regional "platforms for democracy." Reversing the cold war formula of Communism toppling nations like dominoes, President Bush and his appointees have argued that a democratized Afghanistan and Iraq will encourage the entire region to reject despotism and fundamentalism— Afghanistan and Iraq are thus portrayed as the catalysts in a regionwide democracy-building domino effect. But even the State Department understands that such grand schemes are ridiculous. In fact, the *Los Angeles Times* reported in March 2003 that a classified State Department report from February 2003, titled "Iraq, the Middle East and Change: No Dominoes," found the democracy domino theory "not credible." To appreciate the "mad unreality" of expecting that the United States could rapidly democratize and modernize the region, consider this sobering passage from the *9/11 Commission Report:* "The setting is difficult. The combined GDP of the 22 countries in the Arab League is less than the GDP of Spain. Forty percent of adult Arabs are illiterate, two-thirds of them women. One-third of the broader Middle East lives on less than two dollars a day. Less than 2 percent of the population has access to the Internet." Reflecting the complexities of trying to graft U.S.-style democracy onto this difficult setting, the State Department report cited in the *Los Angeles Times* concluded that the United States would "be lucky to have strong central governments" in the region, "let alone democracy." In fact, the *New York Times* revealed after the war that a "gloomy report" produced by the National Intelligence Council "two months before the war" "predicted that an American invasion would increase support for political Islam and would result in a deeply divided Iraqi society prone to violent internal conflict." Given these glimpses into the consequences of previous interventions, the difficulties facing current U.S. projects, and the damning fact that the Bush White House invaded Iraq despite dire warnings from its own intelligence specialists, the Pew's alarming survey results make clear-eyed sense; they reflect the unpleasant fact that much of the world has learned from firsthand experience to view the United States as a rogue nation.[19]

In response to this escalating crisis in the United States' international legitimacy, the *9/11 Commission Report* recommends that "the U.S. government must define what the message is, what it stands for. We should offer an example of moral leadership in the world." We proved in our introduction, however, that the Abu Ghraib prison abuse scandal has deeply, perhaps permanently, soiled U.S. ambitions to act as a moral leader. And we demonstrated in chapter 1 that the stated reasons for waging war on Iraq were fabrications and that the repeated denials of those fabrications have further fueled what we called "the whole operation of deception"—that is, a pattern of disinformation and propaganda. Likewise, we showed in chapter 2 that the major document defining post-9/11 U.S. foreign policy, the *National Security Strategy of the United States,* offers not a model of moral leadership but a strategy of unchecked unilateralism and unchallenged U.S. military dominance of the globe. We illustrated in chapter 3 how U.S. economic policies have taught much of the world to view globalization as a rigged trade game offering little more than increased poverty and national debt. And we argued in chapter 4 that the United States turning the reconstruction of Iraq into a historically unprecedented display of crony capitalism has convinced much of the world that our supposed wars for democracy and opportunity lead instead to an onslaught of military-industrial complex–fueled corporate favoritism. "Offer[ing] an example of moral leadership" to the world community, then, cannot be solved by defining "the message" more clearly but by changing it in fundamental ways, by addressing how U.S. economic and foreign policy are systematically alienating much of the world. Even the *Report of the Defense Science Board Task Force on Strategic Communication,* the September 2004 study we discussed in our introduction, noted that "good strategic communication cannot build support for policies viewed unfavorably by large populations." As we demonstrate in the following two sections, thinking creatively about how to begin imagining broad changes in "the message" will require two related moves: first, rethinking how patriotic provincialism colors U.S. understandings of globalization, and second, renewing our fraying rhetorical habits of democracy.[20]

Patriotic Provincialism and
Economics without Facts

We close our arguments about globalization by examining how patriotic provincialism colors elite U.S. thinking about the relationships among economic development, national greatness, and the challenge of maintaining intellectual and commercial excellence. To do so, we turn briefly to Carleton Fiorina, the chairman and CEO of Hewlett-Packard (HP). One of the great success stories of the booming 1990s, HP is internationally recognized as a leading technology innovator and provider of topnotch consumer goods, and hence as a shining example of the ways the new post-Fordist economy merges research and development with consumer choice, futuristic genius with real-world applicability, postmodern flexible accumulation with old-fashioned hard work. As one of the most visible stars of the new economy of globalizing technology, HP stands at the center of many of the debates about the ways globalization affects the world; as chairman and CEO of HP, Fiorina in turn stands as a positive example of an empowered woman leading the charge into the future. As part of her ongoing public effort to influence discussions about U.S. economic policy and the impact of globalization, Fiorina wrote a February 2004 *Wall Street Journal* editorial titled "Be Creative, Not Protectionist." Rather than giving in to the impulse for job-saving protectionism, Fiorina argues that HP, its Fortune 500 colleagues, and the U.S. government should embrace the challenges and opportunities of globalization by "focus[ing] on developing [the] next-generation industries and next-generation talent" that will enable the United States to use globalization to its advantage. Although her comments are ostensibly offered as part of the debate about the mechanisms of global neoliberal economics, Fiorina's editorial also conveys a consistent sense of U.S. triumphalism. For example, she boasts that America "has always been the world's most resourceful, productive, and innovative country" and closes her editorial with the claim that "America is the most innovative country on earth." What stands out from the essay, then, is the seamless merging of optimistic, proglobalization economics and robust nationalism, a rhetorical maneuver that drives the popular assumption that the United States is the technological, economic, political, and cultural center and even savior of the universe.[21]

Fiorina's rhetorical strategy is indicative of a trend in U.S. public discourse toward what we call *patriotic provincialism*. That is, whereas we demonstrated in chapters 2 and 3 how globalization is trumpeted by its supporters as opening the world to an empowering cross-cultural mélange of influences, choices, and opportunities, many in the United States appear to think of the United States *as the world*, as if the United States were not one nation among many but a universally accepted model to which the world must inevitably look for guidance. Rather than casting our energies outward to the world in an enthusiastic search for the new and the different, such patriotic provincialism turns comfortably inward, expecting the world to emulate the United States. One of the many problems with this patriotic provincialism is that it serves as a justifying frame of reference, a meaning-making assumption so comforting that it eliminates the need for evidence or counterarguments. In short, patriotic provincialism leads to an "air of mad unreality" in discussions about domestic and international economics.

For example, although the claim that the United States is "the most innovative country on earth" may be reassuring to Americans, it is exceedingly difficult to prove. In fact, since the early 1990s the United States has steadily been losing its place as the world's leader in scientific innovation. In May 2004, the *New York Times* reported that whereas U.S. scientists wrote 61 percent of the papers published in top physics journals in 1983, they wrote merely 29 percent of them in 2003; whereas the United States once dominated the Nobel Prize, its intellectuals have recently received roughly half of them; whereas the United States once led the world in terms of granting science PhDs, it is now surpassed by both the European threesome of Britain, Germany, and France and the Asian combination of Taiwan, South Korea, and Japan. The comparative rise of European and Asian scientists is described by Jack Fritz, a senior officer at the National Academy of Engineering as "all in the ebb and flow of globalization." But that ebb and flow is dramatically influenced by the fact that $66 billion of the United States' 2003 $126 billion research budget was directed to military work. So while the United States has built the world's preeminent war machine, its ability to achieve the kinds of globe-leading scientific excellence trumpeted by Fiorina is declining. Indeed, whereas the nation needs frank discussion of the dilemmas of maintaining economic growth and intellectual excellence in an age of globalization, the rhetoric of patriotic provincialism—veering dangerously close to the production of mad unreality—instead offers the familiar salve of national (and military) greatness.[22]

Via the rhetoric of patriotic provincialism, then, Fiorina, many of her corporate colleagues, and the Bush administration collapse economic cheerleading and nationalist bravado into a worldview that assumes the United States is a godlike yet humble colossus of unchallenged technical genius, moral authority, and economic power. Given these assumptions, Washington Consensus arguments about globalization make perfect sense, for who would refuse the opportunity to follow the United States' noble lead in the race for wealth and excellence? We demonstrated in chapter 3, however, how globalization appears slowly but surely to be sapping the United States of economic vitality. For example, when factored for cost of living, the real minimum wage declined by almost 30 percent between 1974 and 2001; hence, even a full-time job at $8.70 per hour (exceeding the minimum wage of $5.15) was not enough to keep a family of four above the 2001 poverty line of $17,500. These wage difficulties have been compounded by the fact that since President Bush took office the United States has sustained the worst rate of job growth since the Great Depression. The president's tax cuts did nothing to alleviate the downward slide of middle- and working-class Americans, instead putting an average of $65,000 into the pockets of the wealthiest 1 percent. And given the enormous costs of the war on Iraq, the president's proposal to cut the budget deficit in half has been interpreted by many observers as a recipe for the further gutting of social programs. In fact, the 2005 budget already falls $9 billion short of the amount authorized under the No Child Left Behind Act, which was supported as a means of improving schools and training future workers. In addition to these wage, jobs, and education problems, the Center for Community Change reported in January 2003 that 41 million Americans had no health care, 33 million Americans lived in poverty, 9.6 million Americans were unemployed (hovering around 5.8 percent), and more than 3 million people in the United States were homeless. Moreover, in a trend that points toward the future in a frightening way, 82 percent of the jobs created in the United States in April 2004 were in service industries, meaning that workers would be stuck in low-wage, short-term situations without adequate benefits or opportunities for advancement. Naomi Klein thus reports in the *Guardian* that throughout the spring of 2004 "the biggest new employers were temp agencies." Considering that anywhere from 3.3 to 6 million U.S. jobs will likely be lost to "outsourcing" over the next decade, the trend toward low-wage and short-term temping will surely accelerate. Thus standing in stark contrast to Fiorina and others' sunny economic rhetoric of patriotic provincialism, these figures suggest a nation slouching toward long-term economic difficulties if not eventual depression.[23]

These economic difficulties reflect a deeper cultural problem regarding the relationship between twenty-first-century capitalism and the complexities of daily life. As David Callahan argues, "Many Americans already understand that a culture obsessed with money and saturated with envy is a morally perilous place. We understand that people will behave badly in an economy that rewards cutthroat competition and where no one enforces the rules. We fear for our own moral well-being, and even more so for that of our children." Callahan's bleak analysis hints at the many ways globalizing neoliberalism terrifies much of the world, for it offers not only economic uncertainty but also the sense that one's "moral well-being" may come under attack. As we demonstrated in chapter 4, the reconstruction of Iraq via crony capitalism has confirmed such fears, further discrediting both the economic champions of the Washington Consensus and the political champions of a supposedly democracy-expanding U.S. empire. Indeed, if globalization-through-benevolent-empire strikes Callahan—a successful American—as a recipe for accelerating both economic uncertainty and moral peril, then we can only begin to imagine what it brings to mind for impoverished and recently bombed Afghanis and Iraqis.[24]

As we demonstrated in chapters 2, 3, and 4, linking these economic and moral problems to globalization in a causal manner is a complicated affair that requires considerable caution. From a rhetorical perspective, however, it is instructive to observe how Fiorina and other corporate and political elites trumpet an optimistic version of globalization colored by patriotic provincialism even while the United States sinks into a numbing economic morass. Worse yet, we demonstrated in chapters 2 and 4 how the Bush administration consistently speaks of its foreign policy objectives in economic terms, and vice versa, hence collapsing the spread of free-market capitalism with the spread of democracy with the spread of U.S. influence and authority. The Bush administration thus employs the rhetoric of patriotic provincialism to support globalization-through-benevolent-empire, to depict a world where a kind and generous United

States saves the world by bringing U.S. ingenuity and wealth to the scraggly masses. The notion that the United States should couple economic development and the spread of democracy to pursue a missionary role in the world is of course not new. But what makes this post-9/11 version of such thinking so dangerous is that the gap between Washington's triumphant claims and the lived realities of those who suffer at the hands of neoliberalism and empire has become so vast that the American model of democracy—now linked inextricably to globalization by the Bush administration and the sirens of patriotic provincialism—has become discredited in much of the world.[25]

Rhetorical Habits and the Democratic Imagination

Given the dire information presented above—*the world sees us as a rogue nation, our economic indicators are dismal, and the failures of globalization are tarnishing the promises of democracy*—the *9/11 Commission Report*'s suggestion that the United States' crippling crisis in international legitimacy may be fixed by simply "defin[ing] what the message is" sounds alarmingly naïve. The report's refusal to consider broader frameworks for thinking about the causes of violence and slipping U.S. credibility therefore leads us to recall Hannah Arendt's "Civil Disobedience." In this 1969 essay published in *Crises of the Republic*, Arendt argues that "every organization . . . ultimately relies on man's capacity for making promises and keeping them. The only strict moral duty of the citizen is this twofold willingness to give and keep reliable assurance as to his future conduct, which forms the prepolitical condition of all other, specifically political, virtues." Offered alongside her famous essay responding to the public uproar produced by the publication of the Pentagon Papers in June 1971, titled "Lying in Politics," Arendt's claim from "Civil Disobedience" should be read as part of her broad response to a Vietnam- and civil rights–era culture that seemed to be spinning out of control, where "reliable assurance as to future conduct" was dissolving. Indeed, as demonstrated in our reliance on her notion of "the whole operation of deception" in chapter 1, Arendt was deeply attuned to how "the message" can be spun to fit dubious purposes. Arendt accordingly excoriated the Pentagon and White House technocrats who were turning Vietnam into killing fields while blanketing the nation with shameful propaganda. But her fury was not partisan, for she also charged that "what threatens the student movement . . . is not just vandalism, violence, bad temper, and worse manners, but the growing infection of the movement with ideologies (Maoism, Castroism, Stalinism, Marxism-Leninism, and the like)." "And the like" functions here as an offhand dismissal of stultifying groupthink, any set of handy rationalizations, any all-explaining "ideology"—like patriotic provincialism—that enabled its subscribers to take narrow, partisan, one-dimensional views of the problems at hand. This is why the reliable process of making and keeping promises amounts for Arendt to the "prepolitical" manifestation of good manners: because making public claims that stand up to scrutiny and then fulfilling these claims in a fair-minded and nonideological manner embodies the fundamental civic decency of listening, thinking, and responding with care and caution. As seen in her analysis of totalitarianism, Arendt believed that such promise making and fulfilling—all pursued under the glaring spotlight of public scrutiny and fair debate—created the building blocks of civic decency, without which life devolves into systematic lying by elites, knee-jerk opposition by protesters, and alienated withdrawal by vast segments of the population.[26]

One way of thinking about Arendt's concerns so that they seem less like aristocratic blasts of disgust—all that talk of bad manners and such—and more like helpful political wisdom, is to translate her notions of making promises and acting reliably into our vocabulary of rhetorical criticism. That is, when Arendt speaks of the "strict moral duty" of "making promises and keeping them," she is pointing to what we called in our introduction *integrity*. Indeed, by applying public scrutiny to the key ideas of the moment, and hence by fleshing out political proposals or economic strategies via the deliberative give-and-take of fair and broadly inclusive debate, our civic promises are likely to be more sound and less biased, more generous and less likely to fuel crony capitalism, and hence more reliably linked to the public good. Arendt's good manners and our notion of integrity therefore stand at loggerheads with the production of what we described above as the "mad unreality" of a nation awash in propaganda and patriotic provincialism. Envisioning our political hopes as the end product of a deliberative process based in a strong, participatory sense of *rhetorical-criticism-as-the-practice-of-democratic-integrity* therefore encourages us to strive to achieve Arendt's "strict moral duty" by reinvigorating the democratic processes that lead to making public promises in the first place. In this sense, making reliable promises may in large part depend on practicing reliable methods of debate. Pursuing integrity therefore means privileging the means of decision making over the decision. Indeed, in contrast to our comments in the introduction regarding how the Bush administration and its supporters have argued time and time again that ends justify means, our theory of *rhetorical-criticism-as-the-practice-of-democratic-integrity* argues that honoring the means of public deliberation will produce better policy.[27]

One of the central fears expressed in this book, however, is that post-9/11 America is losing the habits of democratic integrity. Bullied into an unnecessary war by President Bush's "operation of deception" regarding alleged Iraqi WMDs and supposed Iraqi links to al Qaeda, vast segments of the U.S. population have been taught to fear demons, to loathe innocents, and to mistake nationalist assertions for reasoned arguments. Awed by nightly video clips of futuristic weapons obliterating unseen enemies with bloodless, godlike precision, Americans have been seduced by the pleasures of what Michael Mann calls "spectator sport militarism." Hammered with wave on wave of economic disinformation, all filtered through the rhetoric of patriotic provincialism, our neighbors have been led to believe that the United States is an economic behemoth, bravely leading the world toward development and equality. Deluged with daily doses of misinformation regarding the postwar status of Iraq and Afghanistan, hundreds of millions of U.S. citizens have been taught to celebrate our nation's heroic humanitarianism despite a mountain of evidence pointing to looming economic, political, and military catastrophes in those occupied territories. Fed a daily diet of shouting television talk-show hosts, hyperventilating radio shock jocks, corporate propagandists, and an ever-more compliant Congress, citizens of the nation that brought free speech to the world have been taught to confuse passionate tirades for informed discussion and to bow dutifully before accepted wisdoms, even those laced with so many obvious factual errors that the rest of the informed world scoffs at our gullibility. It would appear, then, that democratic integrity is giving way to mass-produced banality, to what Auden lamented as "spells" used "to befuddle the crowd." Arendt's *Origins of Totalitarianism* is particularly chilling in this regard, for it reminds us that such transformations in how publics think about life-and-death questions, how they talk about their values and commitments, can never be simply a question of Big Lies snowing the masses. Rather, we must remember that these gradual shifts in rhetorical habits may "correspond to the secret desires and secret complicities of the masses in our time." Indeed, it may be the case that post-9/11 Americans are giving vent to emotions, long held in check but deeply felt, regarding their assumed rightful command of the world.[28]

This book attempts to counter such mass-produced banality, warmongering spells, and pleasurable complicities with empire by offering case studies based on historical research, evidence-based arguments, and detailed rhetorical criticism. We nonetheless fear for the collective loss of democratic integrity. In his careful defense of rhetorical pragmatism in *Contingency, Irony, and Solidarity*, Richard Rorty reminds us that "Europe did not decide to accept the idiom of Romantic poetry, or of socialist politics, or of Galilean mechanics. That sort of shift was no more an act of will than it was a result of argument. Rather, Europe gradually lost the habit of using certain words and gradually acquired the habit of using others." Losing and acquiring the habit of using certain words is another way of saying that the dominant forms of European rhetoric slowly shifted terrain, moving from premodern arguments derived from the thundering commands of God and king to Enlightenment arguments derived from verifiable scientific evidence and public deliberation. No singular moment of revelation or adjudicated point of departure, this cultural shift occurred over many generations, accumulating power as more and more layers of rhetorical revolution piled up into a new common sense, a new set of rhetorical habits that eventually displaced other ways of thinking. Assuming that Rorty is correct about the ways social transformations are driven largely by changing rhetorical habits, we fear that post-9/11 America is engaged in yet another of these epochal shifts of rhetorical terrain, one where dissent is no longer a cherished term of obligation but a pejorative term suggesting treason; where any argument that takes longer than thirty seconds is too high-minded for airing on the corporate-controlled mass media; where thinking about the historical causes of violence is considered evidence of sympathy for terrorists; and so on in a numbing process that seems to have sapped Americans of any sense of their historical roots as some of the world's most creative and cantankerous practitioners of democratic integrity. In short, what if America is losing the rhetorical habits of democracy?[29]

Although we are persuaded by Rorty's theory that social change unfolds via gradual transformations in rhetorical habits, we are also troubled by the fact that his model elides the question of who makes such transformations happen. For surely the process of losing one idiom and acquiring another is at least partially the result of concerted political action. This is certainly true in post-9/11 America, where, as we have shown in our case studies, the Bush administration and its supporters have embarked on a massive campaign to change the ways Americans think about democracy, globalization, and empire. For example, in another revealing moment of what we have called capitalist truth telling, Robert Kaplan states as clearly as we have ever seen it stated the ultimate political function of the post-9/11 corporate mass media. "The best information strategy," he claims, "is to avoid attention-getting confrontations in the first place and to *keep the public's attention as divided as possible.*" Kaplan therefore functions as a cheerleader for the dilemma addressed in Guy Debord's *Society of the Spectacle,* where, as noted in chapter 3, he feared that political states, capitalist elites, and the mass media were combining forces to produce a world of "*limitless artificiality*" driven by the mass-produced "*falsification of life.*" Thus righteously calling in 2003 for the same dynamic that Debord feared in 1967 would lead to totalitarianism, Kaplan understands that the society of the spectacle is an omnivorous diversion seducing citizens to engage in the frivolous and the vulgar rather than studying the causes of violence and building routes of collective empowerment. Offered by one of the handful of neoconservatives who have guided the Bush administration's policies, Kaplan's call for mass-produced stupidity announces the death knell of democratic integrity. No gradual cultural shift due to accumulating rhetorical patterns, Kaplan's essay illustrates how the post-9/11 assault on democratic integrity via the cheerful falsification of life is part of a carefully orchestrated campaign.[30]

In fact, in the weeks following 9/11, White House Press Secretary Ari Fleischer warned that "all Americans need to watch what they say, watch what they do," thus making it clear that political criticism was unwelcome in a time of crisis. Speaking before the Senate Judiciary Committee in December 2001, Attorney General John Ashcroft argued that those who dare criticize the government "only aid terrorists, for they erode our national unity and diminish our resolve." In November 2001 the American Council of Trustees and Alumni (ACTA) released *Defending Civilization,* a hysterical report charging academics who questioned either the causes of or U.S. responses to 9/11 with undermining the nation's universities and the nationalist cause they are presumed to serve. Fleischer,

Ashcroft, and the provincial patriots behind the ACTA report not only rallied in an unconditional manner to support the U.S. government, but charged that those who do not share their commitments are traitors. The list of such post-9/11 assaults on free speech and imaginative thinking could be extended ad nauseam, with a raft of additional examples culled from the months leading up to the invasion of Iraq, but these three examples make our point: Americans are not only losing the rhetorical habits of democratic integrity but are being systematically bullied into doing so by the Bush administration and its allies.[31]

Democracy both in America and around the world has always been hotly contested, with every generation fighting its own battles over specific policies and the cultural norms that frame beliefs and actions. As we have shown throughout this book, and as we catalogue in our appendix, the rise of globalization and empire has thus been met with an outpouring of brave and creative voices. Indeed, the global economy of information producers and activists is wonderfully diverse: newspapers, magazines, Web sites, think tanks, action groups, watchdog services, Independent Media Centers, alternative publishers, and NGOs are proliferating like wildfire, meaning both that information free from corporate constraint and government spin is available to those who choose to look for it and that activist opportunities spanning an infinite array of positions and perspectives await those with the commitment and courage to act. Moreover, the remarkable outpouring of opposition to the U.S. invasion of Iraq suggests that millions of Americans and tens of millions of our international neighbors are indeed thinking critically about how U.S. economic and foreign policies need to change. Thus, although the corporate consolidation of mass media foreshadows a coming age of oligopolistic commodity fetishism, and although the reelection of President Bush in November 2004 illustrates the power of the pleasures of complicity with empire, the sources used here suggest that we may also be entering a golden age of democratic information, where Big Lies unravel under the weight of investigative reporting, activist pressure, and politically committed scholarship. To revive and celebrate our endangered rhetorical habits of democracy, and hence to reinvent the ways we argue about the fate of the nation and the world, we will need to rely on these alternative sources for our information, empowerment, and community.[32]

We will not attempt to proscribe the forms such responses might take; instead, the analyses forwarded in our cases studies and the materials conveyed in our appendix are offered as opening moves in a process of rhetorical invention that will surely evolve in unexpected yet productive ways. For although our generation's responses to globalization and empire will pursue political and aesthetic forms dramatically different from those envisioned by Auden when he lamented the passing of civil style, or by Arendt when she chastised Vietnam-era Americans in a tone of high aristocratic contempt, we are confident that our neighbors' responses will strive for the same goal Auden and Arendt and the many other figures cited here share: to make the promises of American democracy more real and the possibilities of global economic development more fair. We have offered more than enough harrowing examples in this book to suggest that the twilight of democracy may fade into an age of totalitarianism, where civil style shrinks beneath the weight of propaganda and banality; we have also demonstrated, however, that our current moment may, if we so choose, be reclaimed as the dawn of a new enlightenment fueled by the multifaceted rhetorical habits of democratic integrity. As ever, then, the fate of the republic is an open question.[33]

Appendix

Sources of Information for Scholars and Empowerment for Activists

Recognizing the complicated nature of activism in our era of globalization and empire as both a compelling crisis in our political imagination and an exciting space for rhetorical invention, we encourage readers, scholars, and activists to use the resources listed below to help inform and enrich their local actions. Covering a remarkably broad range of topics and perspectives, these resources present readers with a cornucopia of options and opportunities. We have arranged our resources alphabetically within thematic subsets, which are as follows:

- Globalization and Its Critics
- War and Its Impact on Democracy
- Civil Liberties and Human Rights
- U.S. Government and Elite IGOs
- Alternatives to Corporate Mainstream Media
- Print Sources
- Think Tanks and Advocacy Groups
- Activism
- Databases

Globalization and Its Critics

The Center for Economic and Policy Research (www.cepr.net) strives to make the complicated economic issues that drive globalization accessible to the public by offering workshops, seminars, panels, and other educational forums.

50 Years Is Enough (www.50years.org) focuses on the role of the IMF and the World Bank, calls for cancelling third-world debt, and agitates for

making the deliberative processes of the IMF and World Bank conform to democratic practices.

Free Trade Area of the Americas (www.alca-ftaa.org) contains full-text copies of all ministerial declarations and includes a useful hemispheric trade database.

Global Exchange (www.globalexchange.org) provides information about globalization, offers extensive analyses of the WTO and the IMF, and provides both reports on and strategies for democratizing the impact of globalization on people around the world.

The Institute for Policy Studies (www.ips-dc.org) calls itself "the nation's oldest progressive think tank"; its Global Justice Cluster initiative offers a remarkable array of information and activist ideas.

The Inter-American Development Bank (www.iadb.org) offers primary documents regarding hemispheric lending practices; this is a good source of primary documents chronicling the Washington Consensus.

International Labor Organization (www.ilo.org) was founded as part of the Treaty of Versailles in 1919 and became the UN's first specialized agency in 1946; it monitors worldwide working conditions and sets international labor standards.

International Monetary Fund (www.imf.org) issues biannual *World Economic Outlook* and *Global Financial Stability* reports. Use the IMF site to see how the organization works but do not expect to find many details.

NAFTA (www.nafta-sec-alena.org) offers laws, contracts, hearings, press briefings and other primary documents pertaining to the U.S./Canada/Mexico FTA.

Office of the U.S. Trade Representative (www.ustr.gov) includes former representative Robert Zoellick's statements and speeches. Sections on the FTAA, NAFTA, and the United States' role in the WTO negotiations offer useful links to primary documents and other government sites.

Sustainable Energy and Economy Network (www.seen.org), partially supported by the Institute for Policy Studies, contains a searchable database of world lending institutions, the projects they fund, and the human and environmental consequences.

World Bank Group (www.worldbank.org) is surprisingly transparent and has a fantastic collection of detailed statistics on world poverty and development projects.

World Trade Organization (www.wto.org) offers a fair number of primary documents, including ministerial proceedings and dispute settlements. The section on trade topics is particularly useful for understanding how the WTO addresses some of the detailed issues in world trade.

War and Its Impact on Democracy

Contract Watch (www.contractwatch.org) was created by Taxpayers for Common Sense, a nonprofit watchdog group that monitors wasteful government spending. Contract Watch collects information related to rebuilding projects in Iraq and seeks transparency in and better public scrutiny of the contracting process.

CorpWatch (www.corpwatch.org) is a watchdog group monitoring the difference between proglobalization rhetoric and the reality of globalization's trail of havoc and poverty; they are especially helpful regarding the actions taking place under the rubric of reconstruction in Afghanistan and Iraq.

Iraq Body Count (www.iraqbodycount.net); based on comprehensive surveys of international news accounts, this group counters the Bush administration's disinformation on the costs of empire by offering daily updates of the death and injury toll in Iraq.

Iraq Coalition Casualty Count (www.icasualties.org/oif); like Iraq Body Count, this group offers tabulations of the violence in Iraq, complete with references to the news story corroborating each claim.

Iraq War Debate (www.lib.umich.edu/govdocs/iraqwar.html#iraqthreat) offers a remarkable collection of links to think tanks, government documents, scholarly reports, and other war-related materials.

Occupation Watch (www.occupationwatch.org), based in Baghdad, publishes articles on the American occupation of Iraq gathered from a variety of news sources. Founded as a collaboration between several peace groups that have stayed in Iraq throughout the war and ensuing violence, this site is an essential starting point for daily information about Iraq.

Open Democracy (www.opendemocracy.net) offers a broad-ranging archive of information on globalization and empire; their "Iraq—The War & After" section is especially helpful.

WarProfiteers (www.warprofiteers.com), sponsored by CorpWatch, monitors and profiles the private corporations awarded contracts for security, reconstruction, and military logistics in Iraq, as well as weapons production in the war on terror.

Civil Liberties and Human Rights

American Civil Liberties Union (ACLU, www.aclu.org); founded in the dark days of World War I, the ACLU is among the oldest and most noble of our civic institutions; its defense of civil liberties in these Patriot Act days has been brave, and its offering of information on civil liberties is invaluable.

American Library Association (www.ala.org) has a section called "issues and advocacy" where it outlines how the Patriot Act affects library patrons' privacy and freedom of information.

Amnesty International (www.amnesty.org) is an international, member-driven campaign against human rights abuses that issues reports about human rights violations in all regions of the globe, makes recommendations to the UN and other international institutions, and supports the 1948 Universal Declaration of Human Rights.

Center for Constitutional Rights (www.ccr-ny.org) is a nonprofit legal organization that represents victims of human rights and civil liberties violations, vowing to uphold the Constitution and the International Declaration of Human Rights. Its statements and reports are timely, thorough, and influential in the justice system.

Electronic Frontier Foundation (www.eff.org) brings together citizens concerned with protecting digital freedom; this site has a remarkable amount of information on copyright and trade law, censorship, surveillance, and the Patriot Act.

Federation of American Scientists (www.fas.org), founded by atomic scientists working on the A-bomb in 1945 for the Manhattan Project, investigates biological, chemical, and nuclear weapons and is committed to ending the global arms trade.

First Amendment Center (www.firstamendmentcenter.org) monitors cases where free speech and expression has been limited, educates the public on First Amendment issues, and makes policy recommendations.

Human Rights Watch (www.hrw.org) is another international group that monitors human rights issues around the globe, issuing recommendations and opinions as well as detailed reports.

International Red Cross (www.icrc.org), the organization catapulted to the center of humanitarian questions in Iraq, Afghanistan, and Guantánamo Bay, publishes a quarterly journal, the *International Review*, and operates in eighty countries worldwide.

The Reporter's Committee for Freedom of the Press (www.rcfp.org), like the ACLU, is one of the crucial groups monitoring freedom of speech; it is particularly good on the dangers of the Patriot Act and how wars cramp independent reporting.

Union of Concerned Scientists (www.ucsusa.org) is a group of scientists and experts that conducts research on a wide range of environmental and policy issues, combating the problem of scientific censorship.

U.S. Government and Elite IGOs

As important as it is to seek alternative news services, global activism also requires being familiar with the inner workings of mainstream media, the U.S. government, and the international governmental and elite institutions driving neoliberal globalization. If you can ignore the spin, then, these sites are remarkably useful.

Bureau of Labor Statistics (www.bls.gov) contains all of the relevant figures on employment, wages, demographics, and consumer and producer price indexes.

Census Bureau (www.census.gov), like the Bureau of Labor Statistics, contains basic demographic and income information; it also contains highly accessible national, state, and county population figures.

The Central Intelligence Agency (www.cia.gov) offers information in the form of studies on the war on terrorism, CIA press releases and congressional testimonies, and the invaluable *World Factbook*.

Government Printing Office (www.gpo.gov) is a searchable collection of all federal documents available to the public, including the *Congressional Record* and errata from the *Weekly Compilation of Presidential Documents* from 1993 to present.

National Security Agency (www.nsa.gov) monitors U.S. and foreign information systems using complex numeric and alphabetic codes; although its Web site offers limited specific information, it offers insight into the role of code breaking in national security.

The National Security Archive (www.gwu.edu/~nsarchiv/) is *the* site to obtain declassified government documents, recordings, and videotapes.

United Nations (www.un.org) contains a wealth of information about current projects, reports, "Millennium Goals," and all of the UN divisions (UNCTAD, UNESCO, UNSCOM, and so on); it also has four UNTV channels and recordings of live and archived meetings and events.

U.S. Congress (http://thomas.loc.gov) uses the Library of Congress to organize its clearinghouse of information, documents, and links. Use this site to find bills and committee reports.

U.S. Department of Defense (www.defenselink.mil), a portal to the military-industrial complex, is updated regularly with news and press releases; it also contains the daily schedules of top officials, as well as basic background information on officials and the Department of Defense.

U.S. Department of Energy (www.energy.gov) is charged with developing nuclear weapons and disposing of the U.S. military's toxic waste; it is another portal to the military-industrial complex.

U.S. Embassy, Baghdad, Iraq (www.iraq.usembassy.gov), took the place of the Coalition Provisional Authority on the official transfer of sovereignty from the United States to Iraq on 28 June 2004. The embassy site includes links to Iraqi government agencies and to the Iraq Project and Contracting Office, where readers can find information on the reconstruction of Iraq.

U.S. State Department (www.state.gov) archives all of its press briefings and releases, its extensive country and region reports, and its useful studies on terrorism, poverty, and international relations.

USAID (www.usaid.gov) lists all of its contracts with corporations purporting to aid in the economic and political development of struggling countries.

The White House (www.whitehouse.gov) contains extensive information, including copies of all presidential and cabinet member speeches, transcripts of White House press conferences, and printer-friendly versions of many of the key government documents, including the *National Security Strategy of the United States*.

Alternatives to Corporate Mainstream Media
(Available Online)

The U.S. media is owned by a small number of oligopolists who, if not working alongside the Bush administration, are seemingly uninterested in providing balanced coverage or supporting investigative journalism, instead opting for programming that will rake in money from advertisers and cost as little as possible to produce. Although it is impossible to escape totally the stranglehold of corporate media, the following sources offer fresh perspectives on relevant topics.

The Agonist (www.agonist.org) collects news from a variety of sources and provides an eclectic list of blogs that encourage discussion and participation.

Aljazeera (www.aljazeera.net) has become the leading Arab news service, offering perspectives on Iraq, the Middle East, and America that one will not find in U.S. corporate media.

BBC News (British Broadcasting Corporation, www.news.bbc.co.uk) is where the United Kingdom gets its news; BBC's *World Service* is broadcast on some U.S. public radio stations and is available in streaming audio from this Web site.

Center for Public Integrity (www.publicintegrity.org) is a Washington-based collaboration of investigative journalists who report on international, national, and state issues.

Christian Science Monitor (www.csmonitor.com) originated in 1908 at the First Church of Christ, Scientist, in Boston and was founded by activist Mary Baker Eddy; it has grown into a major daily international newspaper that, despite being supported by the church, is focused on news rather than religion.

CommonDreams (www.commondreams.org) collects information and news for America's progressive community, featuring articles by top progressive writers published in other news venues or exclusively for CommonDreams.

CounterPunch (www.counterpunch.org) is a radical newsletter published twice monthly and edited by Alexander Cockburn and Jeffrey St. Clair; it offers substantive articles of opinion and analysis.

Democracy Now! (www.democracynow.org) is a daily radio program hosted by Amy Goodman and syndicated nationally by Pacifica Radio (www.pacifica.org); it embodies the bravery, intelligence, and independent reporting that keep free speech alive.

FAIR (Fairness & Accuracy in Reporting, www.fair.org) is a watchdog group that analyzes mass media. Along with its radio show, *Counterspin*, FAIR offers excellent information on how empire and globalization are marketed by corporate media.

Focus on the Global South (www.focusweb.org) is primarily concerned with the Asia-Pacific region but offers a range of opinion papers and bulletins on how globalization affects the impoverished South.

Free Speech Radio News (www.fsrn.org) spawned from the Pacifica Radio project, one of the nation's first social justice–driven attempts to produce media. Pacifica has a daily half-hour broadcast that includes reports by a growing number of independent radio journalists in more than fifty countries and most states.

The *Guardian* (www.guardian.co.uk) is England's best newspaper and an important source for news on both globalization and empire; free from the corporate constraints choking U.S. media, the *Guardian* frequently covers stories blacked out in the United States.

In These Times (www.inthesetimes.com) is a Chicago-based progressive magazine published twice monthly.

Le Monde Diplomatique (www.mondediplo.com) is a monthly French journal with limited access to current and archived articles in English, focusing on world politics.

Middle East Report Online (www.merip.org) publishes a monthly journal of news and perspectives on the Middle East, offering information that is not found in mainstream sources. It is nonpartisan, not religiously affiliated, and based in Washington, D.C.

Monthly Review (www.monthlyreview.org) is a monthly Marxist-socialist journal and book publisher, founded in 1949 in New York City in the midst of the Red Scare.

Mother Jones (www.motherjones.com), named for the famous American muckraker and champion of the working class Mary "Mother" Jones, comes out of San Francisco and is published every other month.

The *Nation* (www.thenation.com) has been providing progressive news since 1865 and is an invaluable weekly source of information, ideas, and inspiration.

National Public Radio (www.npr.org), although increasingly underwritten by major corporations, is not the cacophony of commercial advertising heard on most talk radio; segment clips and entire shows may be downloaded from this site.

The *Progressive* (www.progressive.org) is another long-standing voice in American progressive politics, founded in 1909, published monthly, and distributed widely and cheaply.

Salon (www.salon.com), an online daily magazine of politics and culture, produces original content, in-depth investigations, and straightforward commentaries.

Slate (www.slate.com) is a daily general-interest magazine run by Microsoft Network that has surprisingly interesting, fast-breaking, and original content.

Tom Paine. Common Sense (www.tompaine.com), named for the champion of liberty and democracy Thomas Paine, publishes critical articles that are of public interest and invites submissions.

Z-Net (www.zmag.org) is an exhaustive collection of activist resources, including online blogs and links to other sites as well as to the monthly independent social justice magazine *Z-Mag.*

Print Sources

Many of the sources listed above existed in print before they launched an online presence; this is a list of publications that either have limited Web access or that we prefer to see in the old-fashioned form in which they originally began.

Boston Review (www.bostonreview.net) is a bimonthly literary magazine that promotes political conversation by hosting an online forum and publishing reviews and responses.

The *Economist* (www.economist.com) originated in Scotland in 1843; it is a weekly political and economic news journal with anonymously written articles that often lean both right and left, for the *Economist* describes itself as "radically centrist."

Foreign Affairs (www.foreignaffairs.org) is the key publication of the Council on Foreign Relations, which is made up of America's elite past and present government leaders; *Foreign Affairs* has influenced conversations on international issues since 1922.

Harper's (www.harpers.com), a general-interest magazine edited by Lewis Lapham, was founded in 1850 and offers a healthy dose of entertainment and literature alongside insightful political essays.

International Affairs (www.riaa.org), a quarterly European journal published by Britain's Royal Institute of International Affairs, is a place for serious scholarship on foreign policy, strategy, the military, and world economics.

London Review of Books (www.lrb.co.uk) is a literary journal that began as part of the *New York Review of Books* and became autonomous in 1980; like the *New York Review of Books*, it offers radical, critical analyses of important issues.

Los Angeles Times (www.latimes.com) is the leading daily paper of the West Coast.

New Left Review (www.newleftreview.net) features leading international thinkers and scholars on various topics related to globalization and empire, published in a substantive journal every other month.

The *New Yorker* (www.newyorker.com), although aimed at urban literati, contains some of the best groundbreaking reports about the government, military, and Iraq war by investigative journalist Seymour Hersh.

The *New York Review of Books* (www.nybooks.com) is published twice monthly; more than a list of suggested reading, it is an intellectually vibrant space for engaging current events and the place to find Mark Danner's frontline reporting.

The *New York Times* (www.nytimes.com) is essential reading; although the online version is not the same as having it on your doorstep, "all the news that's fit to print" is accessible on the Web, with interactive and video features.

The *Wall Street Journal* (www.wsj.com) is the daily newspaper for those interested in getting their news from an economic and financial perspective; it is a key resource for finding moments of capitalist truth telling.

The *Washington Post* (www.washpost.com) requires a subscription for full services and online registration; it is Washington D.C.'s daily paper of national and international interest and has been strong in its coverage of rising U.S. empire.

Think Tanks and Advocacy Groups

The Brookings Institution (www.brookings.edu) is a Washington powerhouse, a think tank with a huge endowment that funds researchers, supports scholars, trains executives in philanthropy, and publishes materials on foreign policy and economics.

Carnegie Endowment for International Peace (www.ceip.org) has a special Global Policy Program that publishes well-researched reports on the main issues in our era of globalization; the CEIP has been privately funded since it was founded in 1910 by robber baron Andrew Carnegie.

CATO Institute (www.cato.org) is a multi-million-dollar nonprofit group of libertarians concerned that contemporary liberals have corrupted the American Revolution, free markets, and the unfettered neoliberalism they support.

Center for American Progress (www.americanprogress.org) is a group committed to progressive politics that seeks to educate the public by providing fellowship opportunities for top scholars who publish on this site and in other venues.

Center for Defense Information (www.cdi.org), founded in the late days of the cold war by retired military officers, works with Foreign Policy in Focus and accepts no government or military funding; it researches security and military spending and publishes the *Defense Monitor.*

Center for Strategic and International Studies (www.csis.org) is a good place to see what is on the minds of foreign strategists and those who influence U.S. foreign policy. It has a regularly updated "what's new" list and an impressive collection of publications.

Center on Budget and Policy Priorities (www.cbpp.org) researches the federal budget and U.S. fiscal policy, focusing on how state and federal decisions impact the lives of low-income citizens.

Economic Policy Institute (www.epinet.org) is a useful place to find sound research on how global economics affects working people. EPI issues policy briefs that often inform public policy.

Foreign Policy in Focus (www.fpif.org), sponsored by the Institute for Policy Studies, releases reports and policy briefs on key domestic and global issues.

Heritage Foundation (www.heritage.org), a conservative think tank with its own experts and researchers, offers recommendations on domestic and international issues.

Institute for Science and International Security (www.isis-online.org) works on nonproliferation and world peace, publishing detailed reports of weapons caches in strategically important countries.

Open Secrets (www.opensecrets.org), sponsored by the Center for Responsive Politics, is a wonderful source of information dedicated to revealing the ways corporate and war-related money drives politics in Washington—this is an invaluable muckraking tool.

OxFam (www.oxfam.org) works with several organizations that have humanitarian workers in hundreds of countries; it seeks to alleviate world poverty by supporting these workers and by issuing briefing papers and reports on timely policy issues.

Program on International Policy Attitudes (www.pipa.org) is a collaborative effort of academics interested in public opinion in matters of international affairs; it publishes extensive reports on American attitudes toward globalization and war.

Project for the New American Century (www.newamericancentury.org) is the key neoconservative organization promoting U.S. dominance on all world fronts.

Activism

The information revolution has made it possible not only to access all of the resources listed above but also to participate in them and communicate with others around the world in a newly emerging electronic democracy. These organizations encourage hands-on participation in justice-driven projects, whether it be participating in local demonstrations, signing electronic petitions, or finding your favorite blogosphere.

AlterNet (www.alternet.org) offers a wide sampling of reports and editorials regarding empire and globalization; their "War on Iraq" page is especially useful.

Fellowship of Reconciliation (www.forusa.org) is an interfaith organization that advocates world peace through nonviolence.

Free Press (www.mediareform.net) is the crucial activist group working for media reform and the organizing force behind the biennial National Media Reform conferences; its home page contains a searchable database with innumerable links for activists.

Indymedia (www.indymedia.org, and www.ucimc.org for our local Independent Media Center) is a grassroots, nonprofit, open-publishing Web activism group that provides alternative news; each Independent Media Center has links to other Independent Media Centers around the world, enabling activists to bypass the corporate mass media to receive local perspectives from fellow activists.

MoveOn (www.moveon.org) is a crucial site of Web activism; they have been flooding Congress with Web-instigated petitions, phone calls, and e-mails. In addition to offering materials on globalization and empire, Move On is reinvigorating the election process.

People for the American Way (www.pfaw.org) is an activist network with members in all fifty states; it works in collaboration with other groups and maintains a strong presence on Capitol Hill.

Rethinking Schools Online (www.rethinkingschools.org) offers "Teaching about the War," which contains suggestions for lesson plans, readings, background materials, and maps; although built for teachers, the site is a wonderful tool for activists as well.

Traprock Peace Center (www.traprockpeace.org) offers an extensive collection of reports (some audio), editorials, and news of activist events—it is an invaluable source of both information and inspiration.

United for Peace and Justice (www.unitedforpeace.org) is reinventing activism as an online endeavor; this group's Web page offers ready-to-print posters, announcements of events, and endless information on the links between globalization and empire.

Databases

Much of our research was done by daily monitoring of news and Web sources, but many of those sources offer either limited or pay-only access to archives and back issues. In such cases, we used our library at the University of Illinois to page through print holdings or to search electronic archives by date or keyword. The following list includes helpful databases available through most college libraries and many public libraries.

EBSCO is host to several databases including *Newspaper Source*, which allows access to general newspapers, magazines, and journals for a broad readership.

Google Scholar (www.scholar.google.com) searches the Web for peer-reviewed, scholarly publications from all disciplines; it provides links not only to full-text and .pdf versions of books, articles, and abstracts but also to citations within publications.

J-Stor (Journal Storage) contains the full text of hundreds of academic journals; although there are some gaps in the availability of archived journals because of permission problems and technology changes, J-Stor is an invaluable tool for academic research.

Legal Trac, one of the Gale Group's databases (InfoTrac/Expanded Academic is another popular database supported by the Gale Group), can be used to search for legal information in major law journals, including U.S. and international sources.

Lexis Nexis is a research tool for academic, legal, and business publications; its database contains full-text access to most major U.S. newspapers and worldwide news journals.

Project MUSE, like J-Stor, allows full-text access to academic journals; it is useful for finding recent journal articles rather than older materials.

WorldCat is an incredibly useful tool for academic research; it includes databases of general and specific interest as well as access to library holdings worldwide.

Notes

Note: (1) We provide page numbers for all documents consulted in paper form; (2) Web-based documents that print in universal .pdf formats are also given with page numbers; (3) Web-based documents that may print with different formats on different computers and printers do not have page numbers; (4) instead of page numbers for those documents, for materials posted by Web-based groups or sources included in our appendix, see the appendix for their home address, where the specific source may be found using the site's search function; and (5) Web sources not included in the appendix but cited in our notes include Web addresses.

Introduction

1. George Bush, "State of the Union Address" (29 January 2002), available from the White House; David Brooks, "The Cult of Death," *New York Times* (7 September 2004), A27.

2. Herbert Marcuse, *One-Dimensional Man* (Boston: Beacon Press, 1964), 7.

3. Susan Sontag, "The Talk of the Town," *New Yorker* (24 September 2001 but accessed online 17 September 2004).

4. "A Clean Break: A New Strategy for Securing the Realm" is archived at www.israeleconomy.org/strat1.htm; Rashid Khalidi, *Resurrecting Empire: Western Footprints and America's Perilous Path in the Middle East* (Boston: Beacon Press, 2004), 52; the PNAC letter of 26 January 1998 is archived at www.newamericancentury.org/iraqclinton-letter.htm; Robert Kagan, "Bombing Iraq Isn't Enough," *New York Times* (30 January 1998); on the neoconservatives' long push for regime change in Iraq, see Todd S. Purdum and the staff of the *New York Times*, *A Time of Our Choosing: America's War in Iraq* (New York: Times Books, 2003), 9–20; more broadly, see James Mann, *Rise of the Vulcans: The History of Bush's War Cabinet* (New York: Viking, 2004); on the Iraq Liberation Act, see Dilip Hiro, *Secrets and Lies: Operation "Iraqi Freedom" and After* (New York: Nation Books, 2004), 20–22.

5. Seymour Hersh, *Chain of Command: The Road from 9/11 to Abu Ghraib* (New York: HarperCollins, 2004), 258; Bob Woodward, *Plan of Attack* (New York: Simon and Schuster, 2004), 24; Ron Suskind, *The Price of Loyalty: George W. Bush, the White House, and the Education of Paul O'Neill* (New York: Simon and Schuster, 2004), 184; Richard Clarke, *Against All Enemies: Inside America's War on Terror* (New York: Free Press, 2004), 30; for further confirmation of Woodward's, Suskind's, and Clarke's re-

ports, see *9/11 Commission Report: Final Report of the National Commission on Terrorist Attacks upon the United States* (New York: W. W. Norton, 2003), 334–336; for an overview of post-9/11 calls for war by these PNAC figures, see Scott Sherman, "Kristol's War," *Nation* (30 August 2004), 6–8.

6. John Updike, "The Talk of the Town," *New Yorker* (24 September 2001).

7. J. A. Hobson, *Imperialism: A Study* (New York: James Pott and Company, 1902), 51.

8. Hobson, *Imperialism*, 53, 100; Eric Hobsbawm, *The Age of Empire, 1875–1914* (New York: Vintage, 1987), 163.

9. Peter Linebaugh and Marcus Rediker, *The Many-Headed Hydra: Sailors, Slaves, Commoners, and the Hidden History of the Revolutionary Atlantic* (Boston: Beacon Press, 2000); for an article linking eighteenth-century piracy, nineteenth-century anticolonial violence, and twenty-first-century terrorism, see Stephen Hartnett, "Subjects, Slaves, and Patriots: Rhetorics of Belonging and the Democratic Imagination," *Rhetoric and Public Affairs* 6, no. 1 (Spring 2003): 161–178.

10. Italicized quotation (emphasis added) is from David Armitage's unpublished dissertation, as quoted in Linda Colley, *Captives: Britain, Empire, and the World, 1600–1850* (New York: Random House, 2004), 155; Colley quotation from ibid., 155; and see ibid., 208–212 on the global implications of the American Revolution; P. J. Cain, *Economic Foundations of British Overseas Expansion, 1815–1914* (London: Macmillan, 1980), 19, 20; on the entwined histories of unfolding versions of capitalism and empire, including those practiced by the Dutch and British, see Ellen Meiksins Wood, *Empire of Capital* (London: Verso, 2003); for introductions to the notion of globalization, complete with wildly differing arguments, see Malcolm Waters, *Globalization*, 2nd ed. (London: Routledge, 2001); Fredric Jameson and Masao Miyoshi, eds., *The Cultures of Globalization* (Durham, NC: Duke University Press, 1998); and Benjamin Barber, *Jihad vs. McWorld: How Globalism and Tribalism Are Reshaping the World* (New York: Ballantine, 1995); for a rhetorical history of "free trade" from a U.S. perspective, see James Arnt Aune, *Selling the Free Market: The Rhetoric of Economic Correctness* (New York: Guilford, 2001).

11. Harry Magdoff, "Imperialism without Colonies," in *Studies in the Theory of Imperialism*, ed. Roger Owen and Bob Sutcliffe (New York: Longman, 1972), 144–170; for a concise history of these issues see Leo Panitch and Sam Gindin, "Global Capitalism and American Empire, in *The New Imperial Challenge*, ed. Leo Panitch and Colin Leys, 1–42 (London: Palgrave, 2003).

12. Chalmers Johnson, *Blowback: The Costs and Consequences of American Empire* (New York: Metropolitan, 2000), eight hundred bases from p. 4, and see 34–64 and 95–118 on how Okinawa and South Korea respectively have experienced the "footprint" left by U.S. military bases; Cynthia Enloe, *Bananas, Beaches, and Bases: Making Feminist Sense of International Politics* (Berkeley and Los Angeles: University of California Press, 1989); Chalmers Johnson, *The Sorrows of Empire: Militarism, Secrecy, and the End of the Republic* (New York: Metropolitan Books, 2004), 32, 23; Aijaz Ahmad, "Imperialism of Our Time," *New Imperial Challenge* (see preceding note 11), 43–62, quotation from 44.

13. *National Security Strategy of the United States* (Washington, DC: White

House, September 2002), iii, iv, 2; for a colorful account of the reasons Europeans have cringed for the past two hundred years at such American arrogance, see Simon Schama, "The Unloved American," *New Yorker* (posted online, 3 March 2003).

14. Theodor Adorno, *Minima Moralia: Reflections from Damaged Life,* trans. E. F. N. Jephcott (London: Verso, 1984), 108–109—this passage comes from part two, written in 1945; for scathing reviews of the media failures leading up to war, see Michael Massing, "Now They Tell Us," *New York Review of Books* (26 February 2004), 43–49 and "Unfit to Print?" *New York Review of Books* (24 June 2004), 6–10; more generally, see Robert McChesney, Russell Newman, and Ben Scott, eds., *The Future of Media: Resistance and Reform in the Twenty-first Century* (New York: Seven Stories, 2005).

15. Thomas Farrell, *Norms of Rhetorical Culture* (New Haven, CT: Yale University Press, 1993), 304–305; for extended versions of this thesis, see Stephen Hartnett, *Democratic Dissent and the Cultural Fictions of Antebellum America* (Champaign: University of Illinois Press, 2002); Thomas Nilsen, "Free Speech, Persuasion, and the Democratic Process," *Quarterly Journal of Speech* 44, no. 3 (October 1958): 235–243; and Richard Rorty, *Contingency, Irony, and Solidarity* (Cambridge: Cambridge University Press, 1989).

16. Gerard Hauser, "Rhetorical Democracy and Civic Engagement," in *Rhetorical Democracy: Discursive Practices of Civic Engagement,* ed. Gerard Hauser and Amy Grim, 1–14 (Mahwah, NJ: Lawrence Erlbaum, 2004), quotation from 12; the closing phrases of the last sentence of this paragraph were suggested in an October 2004 letter from Robert Hariman—for his contribution to these issues, see *Political Style: The Artistry of Power* (Chicago: University of Chicago Press, 1995).

17. On the degraded status of post-9/11 public deliberation in general and the corporate news in particular, see Michael Massing's essays cited in note 14 above, and Douglas Kellner, *From 9/11 to Terror War: The Dangers of the Bush Legacy* (New York: Rowman and Littlefield, 2003), 49–70; Sheldon Rampton and John Stauber, *Weapons of Mass Deception: The Uses of Propaganda in Bush's War on Iraq* (New York: Tarcher, 2003); Steven Kull, *Misperceptions, the Media, and the Iraq War* (University of Maryland, Program on International Policy Attitudes, October 2003); and Robert McChesney, *The Problem of the Media: U.S. Communication Politics in the Twenty-First Century* (New York: Monthly Review Press, 2004); for one of the many examples of what critics are now referring to as "media culpas," after-the-fact apologies from media that blew their coverage of the events leading up to war, see "From the Editors, The Times and Iraq," *New York Times* (26 May 2004), A10.

18. On DeLay's situation, see Carl Huse, "House G.O.P. Acts to Protect Its Chief," *New York Times* (18 November 2004), A1, 20, and Mike Allen, "House Ethics Standstill Stalls DeLay Decision," *Washington Post* (9 June 2005), A1; Goss quotations from Douglas Jehl, "Chief of C.I.A. Tells His Staff to Back Bush," *New York Times* (17 November 2004), A1, 23; Thomas Powers, "Secret Intelligence and the 'War on Terror,'" *New York Review of Books* (16 December 2004), 50–54, quotation from 54; Office of the Under Secretary of Defense (William Schneider, Jr., DSB Chairman), *Report of the Defense Science Board Task Force on Strategic Communication* (Washington, DC: GPO, 2004), 2, 15, 11, 99; on the institutionalized corruption underlying the

charges raised here, see Elizabeth Drew, "Selling Washington," *New York Review of Books* (23 June 2005), 24–27.

19. Russell Baker, "In Bush's Washington," *New York Review of Books* (13 May 2004), 25; Wendell Berry, "A Citizen's Response to the National Security Strategy of the United States," in *Citizens Dissent: Security, Morality, and Leadership in an Age of Terror*, ed. Wendell Berry (Barrington, MA: Orion Society, 2003), 2–3; Joan Didion, "Politics in the 'New Normal' America," *New York Review of Books* (21 October 2004), 64–73, quotation from 63; for a damning report of how the processes discussed here have politicized and degraded science, turning it into little more than administration propaganda, see the Union of Concerned Scientists, *Scientific Integrity in Policymaking: An Investigation into the Bush Administration's Misuse of Science* (Boston: Union of Concerned Scientists, 2004).

20. David Harvey, *The Condition of Postmodernity* (London: Blackwell, 1990), 350.

21. The images described here have been distributed widely on the Web; the first two were printed in the *New Yorker* (10 May 2003), 42–43, and the third was printed in the *New York Times* (7 May 2004), A11; many more are available online via the *Washington Post;* and see the graphic textual descriptions in Seymour Hersh, "Chain of Command," *New Yorker* (17 May 2004), 37–43; quotations from Staff Sergeant Ivan Frederick's diary in James Risen and David Johnston, "Photos of Dead Show the Horrors of Abuse," *New York Times* (7 May 2004), A11; "ghost detainees" quotation from Douglass Jehl and Eric Schmitt, "CIA Bid to Keep Some Detainees Off Abu Ghraib Roll Worries Officials," *New York Times* (25 May 2004), A13; for an introduction to the scandal, see Mark Danner, "Torture and Truth," *New York Review of Books* (10 June 2004), 46–50.

22. International Committee of the Red Cross (ICRC), *Report on the Treatment by the Coalition Forces of Prisoners of War and Other Protected Persons by the Geneva Conventions in Iraq during Arrest, Internment and Interrogation* (Geneva: ICRC, November 2004), page 8 of the printout downloaded from the *Guardian*; James R. Schlesinger, *Final Report of the Independent Panel to Review DOD Detention Operations* (Washington, DC: Department of Defense, August 2004), 61, 29 (emphasis added); for analyses of the Schlesinger report, see Eric Schmitt, "Rules on Inmates Need Overhaul, Abuse Panel Says," *New York Times* (25 August 2004), A1, 10, and Mark Danner, "Abu Ghraib: The Hidden Story," *New York Review of Books* (7 October 2004), 44–50; for further evidence of the innocence of many of the Iraqi prisoners, consider the fact that U.S. forces have begun emptying Abu Ghraib, releasing 624 wrongfully arrested Iraqis on 28 May 2004 alone (see Christine Hauser, "To Frenzied Scenes, Abu Ghraib Frees 624 Prisoners," *New York Times* [29 May 2004], A8); for a grueling account of how the disappearance squads whisked innocents into months of wrongful imprisonment, see Luke Harding, "After Abu Ghraib," *Guardian* (22 September 2004), where he recounts the story of Huda Alazawi, one of the first Iraqi women to discuss her treatment in Abu Ghraib.

23. Salah Edine Sallat's mural is reproduced in Mark Danner, "The Logic of Torture," *New York Review of Books* (24 June 2004), 70–74, image on 70, and in Lisa Hajjar, "Our Heart of Darkness," *Amnesty Now* (publication of Amnesty International, Summer 2004), 4–7, 15, image on 7; listed only as "River," the blog entry is

part of *Baghdad Burning: Girl Blog from Iraq* (Feminist Press, 2005), as excerpted in "Baghdad Burning," posted to AlterNet on 20 April 2005; Klose quoted in Julio Godoy, "Prison Abuse Making Europeans Uneasy over Ties with U.S.," Inter Press Service (13 May 2004), available from Global NewsBank at http://infoweb. newsbank.com.

24. Hamby quotation from Ann Scott Tyson, "Lessons from Abu Ghraib," *Christian Science Monitor* (5 May 2004); Inhofe quotation from Maura Reynolds, "Some Republicans Vent 'Outrage at the Outrage,'" *Los Angeles Times* (12 May 2004), A8; William Safire, "Hold Fast, Idealists," *New York Times* (12 May 2004), A23; first Rumsfeld quotation from the abridged transcript of his testimony before the Senate Armed Services Committee, printed as "'My Deepest Apology' from Rumsfeld," *New York Times* (8 May 2004), A6; second Rumsfeld quotation from Eric Schmitt, "Rumsfeld Aide and a General Clash on Abuse," *New York Times* (12 May 2004), A1, 10; and see Thom Shanker and Eric Schmitt, "Rumsfeld Accepts Blame and Offers Apology in Abuse," *New York Times* (8 May 2004), A1, 6; Limbaugh quotation from David Remnick, "Hearts and Minds," *New Yorker* (17 May 2004), 30.

25. George Bush, "Remarks by the President to the American Conservative Union 40th Anniversary Gala" (13 May 2004), available from the White House; Rumsfeld's denials quoted in Eric Schmitt, "Rumsfeld Denies Details of Abuses at Interrogations," *New York Times* (28 August 2004), A1, 6.

26. Al Gore, speech, 26 May 2004, transcript available from Move On; Susan Sontag, "Regarding the Torture of Others," *New York Times Magazine* (23 May 2004), 24–29, 42, quotation from 26, emphasis added; and see Bonnie Kerness, "This Is the America We Know," *Vision* (publication of the American Friends Service Committee's Criminal Justice Program) (Summer 2004): 2; for a visual corollary to this argument, see the cover of the *New Yorker* (18 October 2004), where the first image described above is inscribed lightly over a U.S. flag, hence showing how Abu Ghraib casts a shadow over the United States.

27. Antonio Taguba, *Article 15-6: Investigation of the 800th Military Police Brigade* (the Taguba Report, as printed in Mark Danner, *Torture and Truth: America, Abu Ghraib, and the War on Terror* [New York: New York Review Books, 2004], 279–328, quotation from 326, list of abuses on 292–293); for analysis of the Taguba report, see Seymour Hersh, "Torture at Abu Ghraib," *New Yorker* (10 May 2004), 42–47, and "Excerpts from Prison Inquiry," *Los Angeles Times* (3 May 2004), A8; for additional documentation of these abuses, see George R. Fay, *AR 15-6: Investigation of the Abu Ghraib Detention Facility and 205th Military Intelligence Brigade* (August 2004, downloaded from www.findlaw.com), 68–95; "twisted joviality" from Kate Zernike, "Accused Soldier Paints Scene of Eager Mayhem," *New York Times* (14 May 2004), A1, 10; for damning reports on abuses in U.S. prisons, see American Civil Liberties Union, *Human Rights Violations in the United States* (Washington, DC: ACLU, 1993); The Coalition against Indiana Control Units, *Human Rights Violations and Torture on the Rise at the Maximum Control Complex at Westville* (Chicago: CAICU, 1994); Bruce Porter, "Is Solitary Confinement Driving Charlie Chase Crazy?" *New York Times Magazine* (8 November 1998), 55–56; Page Bierma, "Torture behind Bars," *Progressive* (July 1994), 21–27; Rick Bragg, "Prison Chief Encouraged Brutality, Wit-

nesses Report," *New York Times* (1 July 1997), A12; Bob Herbert, "Brutality behind Bars," *New York Times* (7 July 1997), A17; Pamela Podger, "Lawmakers Demand End to Abuse of Inmates at Prisons," *San Francisco Chronicle* (22 October 1998), A20; Mark Arax and Mark Gladstone, "State Thwarted Brutality Probe at Corcoran, Investigation Says," *Los Angeles Times* (5 July 1998); Corey Weinstein, "Brutality at Corcoran," *California Prison Focus* (Winter 1997): 4; and Stephen Hartnett, "Behavior Modification or Rights Violation?" *Nuvo Newsweekly* (1 June 1994), 10—these reports are central to the arguments in Stephen Hartnett, *Incarceration Nation: Investigative Prison Poems of Hope and Terror* (Walnut Creek, CA: AltaMira, 2003).

28. Information on Frederick from Hersh, "Torture at Abu Ghraib," and Edward Wong, "Sergeant Is Sentenced to 8 Years in Abuse Case," *New York Times* (22 October 2004), A8; McCotter information from Dan Frosch, "Exporting America's Prison Problems," *Nation* (12 May 2004); on Graner's prison experience, see David Finkel and Christian Davenport, "Records Paint Dark Picture of Guard," *Washington Post* (5 June 2004), A1, and Naomi Klein, "Children of Bush's America," *Guardian* (18 May 2004), 21; on Armstrong, Stewart, and Ryan, see Dan Frosch, "Uncle Sam Wants You Anyway," posted to AlterNet (24 May 2004).

29. Stephen Grey, "America's Gulag," *New Statesman* (17 May 2004), accessed at www.newstatesman.com; Jason Burke, "Secret World of U.S. Jails," *Observer* (13 June 2004); Tom Engelhardt, "Welcome to Guantánamo World," AlterNet (5 April 2004); on the intrigue surrounding these practices, see Dana Priest, "Memo Lets CIA Take Detainees Out of Iraq," *Washington Post* (24 October 2004), A1; on rendition, see Scott Shane, Stephen Grey, and Ford Fessenden, "Detainee's Suit Gains Support from Jet's Log," *New York Times* (30 March 2005), A1, 9; in addition to the sources cited above regarding the U.S. prison-industrial complex, see Nils Christie, *Crime Control as Industry: Towards Gulags, Western Style*, 2nd ed. (London: Routledge, 1994); Joel Dyer, *The Perpetual Prisoner Machine: How America Profits from Crime* (Boulder, CO: Westview, 2000); and *Invisible Punishment: The Collateral Consequences of Mass Imprisonment*, ed. Marc Mauer and Meda Chesney-Lind (New York: New Press, 2002).

30. Whereas twenty-five prison deaths were reported in Ian Fisher, "Brutal Images Buttress Anger of Ex-Prisoners," *New York Times* (10 May 2004), A1, 10, two weeks later U.S. officials admitted that the number had risen to thirty-seven (see Douglass Jehl, Steven Lee Myers, and Eric Schmitt, "G.I.'s Prison Abuse More Widespread, Says Army Survey," *New York Times* [26 May 2004], A1, 11, and Steven Lee Myers, "Military Completed Death Certificates for 20 Prisoners Only after Months Passed," *New York Times* [31 May 2004], A8).

31. Rumsfeld, "My Deepest Apology"; "The Vietnam" from John Barry, Michael Hirsh, and Michael Isikoff, "The Roots of Torture," *Newsweek*, accessed at www.msnbc.com on 19 May 2004, emphasis added; Schlesinger, *Report*, 70; and see Josh White and Scott Higham, "Sergeant Says Intelligence Directed Abuse," *Washington Post* (20 May 2004), A1.

32. Seymour Hersh, "The Gray Zone: How a Secret Pentagon Program Came to Abu Ghraib," *New Yorker* (24 May 2004), 38–44, quotations from 38 and 39; Anthony R. Jones, *AR 15–6: Investigation of the Abu Ghraib Prison and 205th Military*

Intelligence Brigade (August 2004, downloaded from www.findlaw.com), 10–11; Jehl, Myers, and Schmitt, "G.I.'s Prison Abuse More Widespread"; "The Horror of Abu Ghraib," *Nation* (24 May 2004), 3.

33. White House memo reproduced as Appendix C in the Schlesinger report; Anthony Lewis, "Making Torture Legal," *New York Review of Books* (15 July 2004), 4–8, quotation from 4; and see Dana Priest and Jeffrey Smith, "Memo Offered Justification for Use of Torture," *Washington Post* (8 June 2004), A1, where they quote Tom Malinowski of Human Rights Watch arguing that the memos reveal how the Bush administration was "contemplating the commission of war crimes and looking for ways to avoid legal accountability"; Francis Boyle, "The Democrats Are Caving on Gonzalez; War Criminal as Attorney General?" posted to *CounterPunch* (18 November 2004); on the State Department's opposition to the president's strategy, see R. Jeffrey Smith, "Lawyer for State Dept. Disputed Detainee Memo," *Washington Post* (24 June 2004), A7, and Human Rights Watch (HRW), *The Road to Abu Ghraib* (New York: Human Rights Watch, 2004), 6–7.

34. "[M]igrated" from Schlesinger, *Report*, 37; "imported" from Fay, *Investigation*, 87; for a timeline of the migration see Douglas Jehl and Eric Schmitt, "Army's Report Faults General in Prison Abuse," *New York Times* (27 August 2004), A1, 10.

35. Information on CACI and Titan from Joel Brinkley and James Glanz, "Contract Workers Implicated in February Army Report on Prison Abuse Remain on the Job," *New York Times* (4 May 2004), A6; note that CACI has denied any wrongdoing (see John Cushman, "Private Company Finds No Evidence Its Interrogators Took Part in Prison Abuse," *New York Times* [13 August 2004], A8), even while other reports implicate the company (see Renae Merle and Ellen McCarthy, "6 Employees from CACI International, Titan Referred for Prosecution," *Washington Post* [26 August 2004], A18); Nelson quoted in Julian Borger, "Iraq Conflict: Cooks and Drivers Working as Interrogators," *Guardian* [7 May 2004], 4; Schlesinger, *Report*, 69; Klein, "Children of Bush's America"; regarding CACI's posttorture contracts, see Ellen McCarthy, "CACI Gets New Interrogation Contract," *Washington Post* (5 August 2004), E5; André Verloy and Daniel Politi, "Contracting Intelligence: Department of Defense Releases Abu Ghraib Contract" (28 July 2004), available from Windfalls of War/Center for Public Integrity; and Tim Shorrock, "CACI and Its Friends," *Nation* (21 June 2004), 6–7.

36. Screen saver story from HRW, *Road to Abu Ghraib*, 34; Sontag, "Regarding the Torture of Others," 28–29; for a grueling overview of torture, its causes and effects, and its many apologists, see *A Glimpse of Hell: Reports on Torture Worldwide*, ed. Duncan Forrest (New York: Amnesty International, 1996).

37. Robert Kaplan, "Supremacy by Stealth," *Atlantic Monthly* (July/August 2003), accessed at www.theatlantic.com.

38. Robert Kaplan interview with Elizabeth Shelburne, "The Hard Edge of American Values," *Atlantic Monthly Online/Atlantic Unbound* (18 June 2003), accessed at www.theatlantic.com.

39. Michael Ignatieff, "The American Empire; The Burden," *New York Times Magazine* (5 January 2003), accessed at www.query.nytimes.com; George Bush, "President Outlines Steps to Help Iraq Achieve Democracy and Freedom" (24 May

2004), available from the White House; Hannah Arendt, *The Origins of Totalitarianism* (1948; New York: Harcourt Brace, 1976), xviii; for a blistering critique of Ignatieff's reluctant imperialism and military humanism, see Amy Bartholomew and Jennifer Breakspear, "Human Rights as Swords of Empire," *New Imperial Challenge,* 125–145.

40. For a profile of Bremer see James Dao, "At the Helm in Shattered Iraq: Lewis Paul Bremer III," *New York Times* (8 May 2003), A14; on the post-9/11 Kissinger nomination uproar, see Eric Schmitt, "Democrats Seeking Kissinger Disclosures," *New York Times* (12 December 2002); Amy Goodman, "9/11 Families Protest Selection of Henry Kissinger to Head September 11 Investigation," *Democracy Now!* (2 December 2002); and David Firestone, "Kissinger Pulls Out as Chief of Inquiry into 9/11 Attacks," *New York Times* (14 December 2002), A1, 12; for scalding reviews of Kissinger's activities, see Christopher Hitchens, *The Trial of Henry Kissinger* (London: Verso, 2001), and Seymour Hersh, *The Price of Power: Kissinger in the Nixon White House* (New York: Summit, 1983).

41. The quotation describing Marsh and McLennan's Crisis Consulting Practice is from their Web site, www.mmc.com; "Marsh Forms Crisis-Consulting Practice," *Insurance Journal* (15 October 2001), accessed at www.insurancejournal.com; and see "Marsh Forms Crisis Consulting Practice under Ambassador L. Paul Bremer," *Business Wire* (11 October 2001); for additional elite sources of information on the question of how to manage global crises, see the International Monetary Fund's annual *Global Financial Stability Report,* available from the IMF.

42. L. Paul Bremer III, "New Risks in International Business," *MMC Views* (2001), accessed at www.mmc.com.

43. Naomi Klein, "Downsizing in Disguise," *Nation* (23 June 2003), 10; for a sound-bite version of Bremer's thesis, see the transcript of his conversation with David Haffenreffer on CNNFN's *Before Hours* morning show (8 November 2001).

44. Thomas Friedman, *The Lexus and the Olive Tree: Understanding Globalization* (New York: Farrar, Straus, Giroux, 1999), 195–196; this Golden Arches Theory informs Thomas Frank's claim in *One Market under God: Extreme Capitalism, Market Populism, and the End of Economic Democracy* (New York: Doubleday, 2000) that "what makes his [Friedman's] writing such a touchstone for our times was the way he mixed an enthusiasm for markets and the smashing of wages with passionate cheers for democracy and statements of deep concern for the workers of the (rest of the) world. The equation of democracy and laissez-faire principles was so automatic for him that it seems whatever the market touched, it liberated" (p. 65).

45. Friedman, *Lexus and Olive Tree,* 196; United Nations Development Programme, *Human Development Report 2002* (New York: Oxford University Press, 2002), 16, hereafter *HDR;* Friedman, *Lexus and Olive Tree,* 373.

46. Editorial, "The Rigged Trade Game," *New York Times* (20 July 2003); for general support of the *Times*'s claims tempered with a sharp counterargument about the role of agricultural subsidies, see Dean Baker and Mark Weisbrot, "False Promises on Trade," a 24 July 2003 editorial posted by the Center for Economic and Policy Research (CEPR); on the WTO-negotiated cuts in subsidies, see Elizabeth Becker, "Looming Battle over Cotton Subsidies," *New York Times* (24 January 2004), B1, 3,

and "U.S. Will Cut Farm Subsidies in Trade Deal," *New York Times* (31 July 2004), B1, 3.

47. William Finnegan, "The Economics of Empire," *Harper's Magazine* (May 2003), 41–54, quotation from 49; Robert Scott, "Trade Picture," Economic Policy Institute (13 February 2004); see the related arguments in Jan Nederveen Pieterse, *Globalization or Empire?* (New York: Routledge, 2004), where he argues that "neoliberal globalization, shaped by the Wall-Street-Treasury-IMF complex and convergence with WTO, is unilateralism with a multilateral face" (p. 21); Joyce Kolko goes further in *Restructuring the World Economy* (New York: Pantheon, 1988), where she argues that neoliberal globalization would more accurately be described as a "neomercantilist" system of imperial protectionism (p 232).

48. Amy Waldman, "Low-Tech or High, Jobs Are Scarce in India's Boom," *New York Times* (6 May 2004), A3; United Nations Development Programme, *HDR*, 13; for a scathing version of this thesis, which we address below in chapters 2 and 3, see Amy Chua, *World on Fire: How Exporting Free Market Democracy Breeds Ethnic Hatred and Global Instability* (New York: Anchor Books, 2004); for a powerful counterargument to these charges, one celebrating globalization's impact on India, see Katherine Wood, "The Best Job in Town: The Americanization of Chennai," *New Yorker* (5 July 2004), 55–69.

49. Hugo Chávez, "Speech by President Hugo Chávez, at the Opening of XII G-15 Summit," 1 March 2004, p. 7 of the transcript available from Venezuelanalysis.com at *www.venezuelanalysis.com*; for a summary of an even more pointed speech by Chávez, see Cleto Sojo, "Venezuela's Chávez Closes World Social Forum with Call to Transcend Capitalism," posted to Venezuelanalysis on 31 January 2005.

50. Arundhati Roy, *Power Politics*, 2nd ed. (Cambridge, MA: South End Press, 2001), 2, emphasis added; Fredric Jameson, *Postmodernism; or, The Cultural Logic of Late Capitalism* (Durham, NC: Duke University Press, 1991), 25–31; for a concise statement of these issues, see Benjamin Barber, "Jihad vs. McWorld: On Terrorism and the New Democratic Realism," *Nation* (21 January 2002), 11–18.

51. Arjun Appadurai, *Modernity at Large: Cultural Dimensions of Globalization* (Minneapolis: University of Minnesota Press, 1996), 48; and see Zygmunt Bauman, *Globalization: The Human Consequences* (New York: Columbia University Press, 1998), and Anthony Giddens, *Runaway World: How Globalization Is Reshaping Our Lives* (New York: Routledge, 2000).

Chapter 1

1. Dead and wounded figures as of 9 June 2005 from Iraq Coalition Casualty Count, available at http://www.icasualties.org/oif (this group's figures are based on reports by the U.S. Defense Department), and Phyllis Bennis and the IPS Task Force, *A Failed Transition: The Mounting Costs of the Iraq War* (Washington, DC: Institute for Policy Studies, 2004), 5–7.

2. For reporting on and estimates about Iraqi deaths and injuries see Iraq Body Count; Simon Jeffery, "War May Have Killed 10,000 Civilians," *Guardian* (13 June 2003), 18; Laura King, "Baghdad's Death Toll Assessed," *Los Angeles Times* (18 May

2003), A1; Peter Ford, "Surveys Pointing to High Civilian Death Toll in Iraq," *Christian Science Monitor* (22 May 2003), 1; and see the grueling MedAct report, *Continuing Collateral Damage: The Health and Environmental Costs of War on Iraq, 2003* (London: Medact, 2003; note that Medact is the UK affiliate of Physicians for the Prevention of Nuclear War); Les Roberts, Riyadh Lafta, Richard Garfield, Jamal Khudhairi, and Gilbert Burnham, "Mortality Before and After the 2003 Invasion of Iraq: Cluster Sample Survey," *Lancet* 364 (2004): 1857–1864. For a visual account of 202 deaths and injuries among Iraqi civilians and police, U.S. military, and coalition forces in Iraq within a two-week period at the beginning of 2005, see Adriana Lins de Albuquerque and Alicia Cheng, "14 Days in Iraq," *New York Times* (16 January 2005), A11. For a review of media disinformation on this subject, see "Many Deaths Left Out of Iraq Story," a 19 August 2003 Action Alert posted by FAIR.

3. On Dana's murder, see Orville Schell, "Another Tribe without a State," *New York Times Magazine* (7 September 2003), 20; Patrick Barrett, "Al-Jazeera Man Killed in Iraq," *Guardian* (21 May 2004); forty-four media deaths from Bennis, *Failed Transition*, 7, and see the online information from the Reporter's Committee for Freedom of the Press.

4. Whereas Christian Parenti reported an average of thirteen attacks per day in early autumn (see "The Progress of Disaster," AlterNet [11 September 2003]), thirty-three attacks per day were reported by the close of October 2003 (see Susan Sachs, "Postwar G.I. Death Toll Exceeds Wartime Total," *New York Times* (30 October 2003), A12), and a stunning eighty-seven attacks per day were reported by September 2004 (see Dexter Filkins, "General Says Less Coercion of Captives Yields Better Data," *New York Times* (7 September 2004), A10). Accounts of mayhem from "36 Dead in Baghdad Suicide Bombing," *Guardian* (11 February 2004); Sebastian Rotella and Patrick J. McDonnell, "Death Toll in Twin Strikes on Iraqi Shiites Rises to 143," *Los Angeles Times* (3 March 2004), A1; and "68 Dead in Basra Blasts," *Guardian* (21 April 2004). George Packer describes the Baghdad morgue following the Ashura bombings as "a charnel house filled with bodies, heads, limbs, and buckets of flesh" (in "Letter from Baghdad: Caught in the Crossfire," *New Yorker* [17 May 2004]). For two riveting accounts of the disaster of postwar Iraq, see Peter Davis, "Ignited Iraq: A Baghdad Journal," *Nation* (15 September 2003), 9–22, and George Packer, "War after the War: Letter from Baghdad," *New Yorker* (24 November 2003), 58–85.

For additional stories depicting "postwar" Iraq as sliding toward chaos, see: on the UN bombing, Dexter Filkins and Richard Oppel, Jr., "Scene of Carnage," *New York Times* (20 August 2003), A1, 8; Thom Shanker, "Chaos as Strategy against the U.S.," *New York Times* (20 August 2003), A1, 9; and Patrick McDonnell and Tracy Wilkerson, "Baghdad Bomb Had the Mark of Experts," *Los Angeles Times* (21 August 2003), A1. On the Najaf bombing, see Neil MacFarquhar and Richard Oppel, Jr., "Car Bomb in Iraq Kills 95 at Shiite Mosque," *New York Times* (30 August 2003), A1, 6; Dexter Filkins, "Death and Hesitation," *New York Times* (30 August 2003), A1, 6; and Patrick McDonnell and Tracy Wilkerson, "Blast Kills Scores at Iraq Mosque," *Los Angeles Times* (30 August 2003), A1. On the Jordanian hospital battle, see Alex Berenson, "Iraqis Charge G.I.'s Killed 8 Policemen in Chaotic Battle," *New York*

Times (13 September 2003), A1, 7. On the suicide bombings of 27 October, see Dexter Filkins and Alex Berenson, "34 Killed in 5 Suicide Bombings in Baghdad," *New York Times* (28 October 2003), A1, 8, and Alissa Rubin and David Lamb, "4 Suicide Bombings Kill 35 in Baghdad," *Los Angeles Times* (28 October 2003), 1. On the helicopter downing, see Alex Berenson, "16 G.I.'s Are Killed, 20 Hurt as Missile Downs U.S. Copter," *New York Times* (3 November 2003), A1, 8; Alissa Rubin, "Missile Downs U.S. Copter in Iraq, Killing 16 Soldiers," *Los Angeles Times* (3 November 2003), 1; Theola Labbe and Rajiv Chandrasekaran, "Missile Hits U.S. Copter in Iraq," *Washington Post* (3 November 2003), A1; and Thomas E. Ricks, "New Attacks Intensify Pressure on Bush," *Washington Post* (3 November 2003), A1. On the Khan Bani Saad bombings, see Ian Fisher and Dexter Filkins, "Bombers Kill 14 in Iraq; Missile Hits Civilian Plane," *New York Times* (23 November 2003), A14; John Hendren, "2 Suicide Bombers Kill at Least 14 in Iraq," *Los Angeles Times* (23 November 2003), 1; and Daniel Williams, "17 Killed in Attacks on Police in Iraq," *Washington Post* (23 November 2003), A 23. On the wedding massacre, see Rory McCarthy, "Wedding Party Massacre," *Guardian* (20 May 2004).

5. Eric Schmitt, "Test in a Tinderbox," *New York Times* (28 April 2004), A1; Christine Hauser, "Siege Defined on Stones Set in Haste in the Dirt," *New York Times* (28 April 2004), A8.

6. Robert Byrd, speaking in the Senate, 21 May 2003, page 3 of the transcript available from CommonDreams.

7. Although written in schematic, nonnarrative form, Sam Gardiner's *Truth from These Podia: Summary of Study of Strategic Influence, Perception Management, Strategic Information Warfare, and Strategic Psychological Operations in Gulf War II* (n.p., October 2003) offers a suggestive compendium of the "pattern of lies" cited here. Gardiner is a retired U.S. Air Force colonel; he can be reached at SamGard@aol.com.

8. Wayne Booth's notion of "rhetrickery," meant to distinguish between the noble arts of rhetoric and the political spinning practiced by President Bush, comes from his lecture, "The Rhetoric of RHETORIC, and Its Sad Neglect," delivered 7 July 2003 at "Rhetoric's Road Trips: Histories and Horizons," a conference organized by Rosa Eberly for Penn State University. For a pre-9/11 attempt to make sense of President Bush's rhetoric, see Mark Crispin Miller, *The Bush Dyslexicon: Observations on a National Disorder* (New York: W. W. Norton, 2001); for a compendium of Bushisms, see the archives at www.bushwatch.com and www.thetruthaboutgeorge.com.

9. Among the many exposés of both the Bush administration and its conservative allies' penchant for lying, see Al Franken, *Lies and the Lying Liars Who Tell Them: A Fair and Balanced Look at the Right* (New York: E. P. Dutton, 2003); Joe Conason, *Big Lies: The Right-Wing Propaganda Machine and How It Distorts the Truth* (New York: St. Martin's, 2003); David Corn, *The Lies of George W. Bush: Mastering the Politics of Deception* (New York: Crown, 2003); and Robert and Christopher Scheer, *The Five Biggest Lies Bush Told Us about Iraq* (New York: Seven Stories, 2003).

10. *National Security Strategy of the United States* (Washington, DC: White House, September 2002), 5, hereafter cited in the text as *NSSUS;* Hannah Arendt, "Lying in Politics; Reflections on the Pentagon Papers," in *Crises of the Republic* (New York: Harcourt Brace Jovanovich, 1969), 31.

11. Charles Krauthammer, "What Makes the Bush Haters So Mad?" *Time* (22 September 2003), 84.

12. Central Intelligence Agency, *Iraq's Weapons of Mass Destruction Programs* (October 2002)—we should note that the CIA's Web page is an invaluable source of information that includes, no kidding, a link "for kids"; chemical weapons deaths on 8; nukes claim on 1; *probably* on 2; *capable* on 2; bolded claim on 5; list of violated UN resolutions on 4; for an overview of the pertinent UN resolutions, see David Cortwright, "The Legal Basis for UN Weapons Inspections," in *Iraq: A New Approach,* ed. Joseph Cirincione and Jessica T. Mathews, 55–61 (Washington, DC: Carnegie Endowment for International Peace, August 2002).

13. CIA, *Iraq's Weapons of Mass Destruction,* 5; Thomas Powers, "The Vanishing Case for War," *New York Review of Books* (4 December 2003).

14. Bob Woodward, *Plan of Attack* (New York: Simon and Schuster, 2004), 247–250 on the meeting, quotations from 249; on the terrifying implications of Tenet's performance in particular and the politicization of intelligence in general, see Thomas Powers, "The Failure," *New York Review of Books* (29 April 2004), 4–6, and "How Bush Got It Wrong," *New York Review of Books* (23 September 2004), 87–93.

15. Quotation from the March draft of the report from Dilip Hiro, *Secrets and Lies: Operation "Iraqi Freedom" and After* (New York: Nation Books, 2004), 62, and see 62–71 on the revising process; [British] Joint Intelligence Committee, *Iraq's Weapons of Mass Destruction: The Assessment of the British Government* (24 September 2002)—along with all of Prime Minster Blair's speeches, this document is available at www.pm.gov.uk; the identical photograph is on page 23 of the British dossier and page 23 of the CIA's report.

16. This second British dossier, dated January 2003 and titled *Iraq—Its Infrastructure of Concealment, Deception and Intimidation,* bears no trace of authorship; it may be found by searching under "concealment" at www.number10.gov.uk. Colin L. Powell, "Remarks to the United Nations Security Council," 5 February 2003, page 6 of the transcript available from the U.S. State Department, hereafter cited in the text as "RUN." On the dossier's plagiarism, see Gaby Hinsliff, Martin Bright, Peter Beaumont, and Ed Vulliamy, "First Casualties in the Propaganda Firefight," *Observer* (9 February 2003), 16, and Brian Whitaker, "UK Dossier Lifted Evidence," *Guardian* (7 February 2003), 5. On the botched forty-five-minute claim, see Warren Hoge, "British Spy Chief Stands behind Disputed Iraq Dossier at Inquiry," *New York Times* (16 September 2003), A16.

17. Warren Hoge, "Parliamentary Panel Faults British Government on Iraq but Clears It of Falsifying Information," *New York Times* (12 September 2003), A12; "trust" quotation from "The Danger of Doubt," *London Times* (28 July 2003), 17; on British responses to the scandals surrounding the production of both dossiers, see Glenn Frankel, "British Experts Protested Iraq Dossier," *Washington Post* (2 September 2003), A10, and Hoge, "Parliamentary Panel," A12.

18. "Iraq: Nuclear, Biological, Chemical, and Missile Capabilities and Programs," a brief posted under "Weapons of Mass Destruction in the Middle East" on the home page of the Center for Nonproliferation Studies at the Monterey Institute

of International Studies, written in 1998 and updated in 2001, available at http://cns. miis.edu/, quotations from pages 1, 2, 3, emphasis added.

19. Joseph Cirincione, for the Carnegie Endowment for International Peace, "Iraq Biological and Chemical Weapons Fact Sheet"; we are quoting here from the updated version of April 2003, but prior fact sheets made these same arguments—readers may access these documents at www.ProliferationNews.org.

20. Anthony Cordesman, *If We Fight Iraq: Iraq and Its Weapons of Mass Destruction* (Washington, DC: Center for Strategic and International Studies, June 2002), 2, 18, 21; and see Cordesman's comments as part of the Committee on Foreign Relations' 31 July and 1 August 2002 *Hearings to Examine Threats, Responses, and Regional Considerations Surrounding Iraq,* available online at www.access.gpo.gov.

21. Kenneth Katzman, *Iraq: U.S. Efforts to Change the Regime; Report for Congress* (Washington, DC: Congressional Research Service, 3 October 2002), 10–11, emphasis added.

22. Thomas Powers, "Choosing a Strategy for World War III," *Atlantic Monthly* (November 1982), 82–110, quotation from 103—thanks for this lead to David Corn, "W.M.D.? MIA," *Nation* (2 June 2003), 4–5.

23. William Odom, *Fixing Intelligence: For a More Secure America* (New Haven, CT: Yale University Press, 2003), 48–50; for a blistering critique of the intelligence community, see James Bamford, *Body of Secrets: Anatomy of the Ultra-Secret National Security Agency, from the Cold War through the Dawn of a New Century* (New York: Doubleday, 2002); for analysis of the politicization of intelligence, see Bamford, *A Pretext for War: 9/11, Iraq, and the Abuse of America's Intelligence Agencies* (New York: Doubleday, 2004); for a list of suggestions for restructuring the intelligence community, see the *9/11 Commission Report: Final Report of the National Commission on Terrorist Attacks upon the United States* (New York: W. W. Norton, 2003), 407–419.

24. Hans Blix, *Disarming Iraq* (New York: Pantheon, 2004), 259; and see Blix's comments in Warren Hoge, "Ex-U.N. Inspector Has Harsh Words for Bush," *New York Times* (16 March 2004), A3; George Bush, "President Delivers State of the Union Address," (29 January 2002), available from the White House. Woodward reports in *Plan of Attack* that "axis of evil" was originally drafted by White House speechwriters as "axis of hatred" but that the phrase was switched from "hatred" to "evil" in order to "broaden the notion, making it more sinister, even wicked . . . as if Saddam was an agent of the devil" (p. 87).

25. George Bush, "President Bush Outlines Iraqi Threat," Cincinnati Museum Center (7 October 2002), 1, 2, 2, 3, available from the White House; considering the dubious evidence on which these claims were based, media coverage of the Cincinnati speech amounts to little more than cheerleading; see Karen DeYoung, "Bush Cites Urgent Threat," *Washington Post* (8 October 2003), 1, and David Sanger, "Bush Sees 'Urgent Duty' to Pre-empt Attack by Iraq," *New York Times* (8 October 2003), 1.

26. House Joint Resolution 114, as posted by the White House and dated 2 October 2002; the president signed the bill into law on 16 October 2002; see the president's comments on that occasion under "Statement by the President"; for coverage of the debates surrounding the bill, see Howard LaFranchi, "Bush Faces Crucial

Week in Forging Unity on Iraq," *Christian Science Monitor* (7 October 2002), 1; Jim VandeHei and Juliet Eilperin, "Congress Passes Iraq Resolution," *Washington Post* (11 October 2002), A1; Edward Epstein, "Congress Debates Giving Bush War Power," *San Francisco Chronicle* (9 October 2002), A3; and Andrew Grice, "Clinton Urges Caution over Iraq as Bush Is Granted War Powers," *Independent* (3 October 2002), 1.

27. George Bush, "President Delivers State of the Union," (28 January 2003), available from the White House, all quotations from p. 6.

28. George Bush, "President Says Saddam Hussein Must Leave Iraq within 48 Hours" (17 March 2003), available from the White House; for a point-by-point refutation of the president's claims in this speech, see Stephen Zunes, "An Annotated Critique of President George W. Bush's March 17 Address Preparing the Nation for War," *Foreign Policy in Focus Report* (March 2003).

29. Richard Lanham, *A Handlist of Rhetorical Terms,* 2nd ed. (Berkeley and Los Angeles: University of California Press, 1991), 77; Douglas Walton, *A Pragmatic Theory of Fallacy* (Tuscaloosa: University of Alabama Press, 1995), 44.

30. Scott McClellan is the featured protagonist in the remarkably long and testy White House press briefing of 18 July 2003; the reporters asking questions are unnamed in the transcript used here; quotation from p. 24—see the transcript at www.usinfo.state.gov.

31. Dick Cheney, speaking before the national convention of the Veterans of Foreign Wars, Nashville, 26 August 2002, pages 3 and 4 of the transcript available from the White House.

32. Ari Fleischer, daily press briefing of 9 January 2003, Washington, DC, pages 2 and 3 of the transcript available from the White House.

33. Ari Fleischer, daily press briefing of 21 March 2003, Washington, DC, page 5 of the transcript available from the White House.

34. Vince Brooks, daily press briefing of 22 March 2003, Central Command in Doha, Qatar, page 2 of the transcript available at www.usinfo.state.gov.

35. Tommy Franks, daily press briefing of 22 March 2003, Central Command in Doha, Qatar, page 8 of the transcript available at www.centcom.mil/CENTCOMnews/Transcripts.

36. Kenneth Adelman, quoted in Mike Allen and Dana Milbank, "Question of the Day Dogs Administration Officials: Where Are Iraq's Weapons of Mass Destruction?" *Washington Post* (23 March 2003), A27.

37. Colin Powell, *Meet the Press,* 4 May 2003, page 2 of transcript available from the Department of State.

38. On prolepsis, see Lanham, *Rhetorical Handlist,* 120–121.

39. Ibid., 86. Iraqi military expenditures from U.S. General Accounting Office (GAO), *Weapons of Mass Destruction: UN Confronts Significant Challenges in Implementing Sanctions against Iraq* (Washington, DC: GAO, May 2002), 14–15, and Steven Miller, "Gambling on War: Force, Order, and the Implications of Attacking Iraq," in *War with Iraq: Costs, Consequences, and Alternatives,* ed. Carl Kaysen et al. (Cambridge, MA: American Academy of Arts and Sciences, 2002), 43.

40. On "position-to-know" fallacies, see Walton, *Pragmatic Theory*, 149–152, and note that Powell uses the phrase "position-to-know" to describe the anonymous Iraqi exiles from whom he draws his evidence (see "RUN," 9). First Blair quotation from *Iraq's Weapons of Mass Destruction* (the first dossier), 3; second Blair quotation and commentary on it from Gaby Hinsliff, Nick Paton Walsh, and Peter Beaumont, "Blair: I Have Secret Proof of Weapons," *Observer* (1 June 2003), 2; Sarah Left, "W.M.D. in Iraq: Who Said What, and When," *Guardian* (29 May 2003); Ben Russell and Andy McSmith, "The Case for War Is Blown Apart," *Independent* (29 May 2003), 1; and Warren Hoge, "Blair Accused of Distorting Intelligence on Iraqi Arms," *New York Times* (5 June 2003), A17. For essays arguing that Blair did not lie but rather was the victim of organizational miscommunication between agencies, see Daniel Soar, "At the Hutton Inquiry," and Peter Clarke, "Peter Clarke Explains Why He Once Supported Tony Blair and Now Believes He Should Go," both in *London Review of Books* (11 September 2003), 10 and 9–10; and see Conor Gearty, "A Misreading of the Law," *London Review of Books* (19 February 2004), 3–7.

41. Barton Gellman and Walter Pincus, "Depiction of Threat Outgrew Supporting Evidence," *Washington Post* (10 August 2003); Kenneth Katzman, *Iraq: Weapons Programs, UN Requirements, and U.S. Policy* (issue brief of the Foreign Affairs, Defense, and Trade Division of the Congressional Research Service of the Library of Congress) (Washington, DC: Library of Congress, 16 April 2003), 5; Blix, *Disarming Iraq*, 28–29; and see Stephen Black, "The UNSCOM Record," in *Iraq: A New Approach*, 37–39, and Garry Dillon, "The IAEA Iraq Action Team Record: Activities and Findings," in ibid., 41–44; also see the powerful commentaries by weapons experts in Robert Greenwald's 2003 documentary film, *Uncovered: The Whole Truth about the Iraq War*.

42. Stockholm International Peace Research Institute, "Iraq: The UNSCOM Experience," fact sheet (October 1998), available at http://www.sipri.org; regarding the longevity of VX and the impossibility of Iraq using it in long-range rockets, see John Prados, "Iraq: A Necessary War? Not According to UN Monitors—or to U.S. Intelligence," *Bulletin of the Atomic Scientists* 59, no. 3 (May/June 2003); Jafar quoted in Seymour Hersh, "The Stovepipe: How Conflicts between the Bush Administration and the Intelligence Community Marred the Reporting on Iraq's Weapons," *New Yorker* (27 October 2003), 87; Duelfer report summarized in Douglas Jehl, "U.S. Report Finds Iraqis Eliminated Illicit Arms in 90s," *New York Times* (7 October 2004); the full report, titled *Comprehensive Report of the Special Advisor to the DCI on Iraq's WMD* (30 September 2004), is available from the CIA.

43. Goss and Harman's angry letter quoted from Dana Priest, "House Probers Conclude Iraq War Data Was Weak," *Washington Post* (28 September 2003), A1; and see Priest, "Democrat Disputes Rice on Iraq Claims," *Washington Post* (30 September 2003), A13; on Goss's nomination, see David Sanger, "President Picks House Intelligence Chief to Lead CIA," *New York Times* (11 August 2004), A1, 13.

44. For an overview of how the press granted Powell's speech a free pass, see Eric Alterman, "Colin Powell and the Power of Audacity," *Nation* (22 September 2003), 10, and "A Failure of Skepticism in Powell Coverage," press release, FAIR, 10 Febru-

ary 2003; for a point-by-point refutation of Powell's claims, see Hiro, *Secrets and Lies*, 123–135. Despite Alterman's claim that Powell's speech received little to no critical commentary, some reporters did excellent work. For example, in a brave illustration of the press fulfilling its function of debunking propaganda, the *New York Times* ran an article on 15 February detailing Powell's lying; to enhance the point visually the *Times* printed a sidebar in two columns, with the left side featuring quotations from Powell's testimony and the right side offering refutations of Powell's claims from Blix and Elbaradei; see "Verbatim, Weighing the Evidence," *New York Times* (15 February 2003), A6. For other critical reviews of Powell's UN testimony see Bob Drogin, "Inspectors Challenge Washington over Weapons Evidence," *Los Angeles Times* (15 February 2003), 18; Maggie Farley, "Inspection Report Firms Up Council's Opposition to War," *Los Angeles Times* (15 February 2003), 1; Duncan Campbell, "Blix's Underlying Message: Give Us More Time," *Guardian* (15 February 2003), 4; Jonathan Steele, "U.S. Claims on Iraq Called into Question," *Guardian* (15 February 2003), 4; and Joby Warrick, "Despite Defector's Accounts, Evidence Remains Anecdotal," *Washington Post* (6 February 2003), A28.

45. The evidence regarding Hussein's brutality is overwhelming: for a report summarizing this evidence, see the White House's 12 September 2002 white paper, *A Decade of Deception and Defiance: Saddam Hussein's Defiance of the United Nations*, 11–17, available from the White House; equally damning evidence—although the numbers are still uncorroborated—is offered in Andrew Natsios, "Iraq: From Mass Graves to a Better Life," 17 March 2004 speech before the Washington Foreign Press Center, available online from USAID.

46. William Safire, "Irrefutable and Undeniable," *New York Times* (7 February 2003), A39; for a reprised attempt by Safire to link al Qaeda and Hussein, see "Missing Link Found," *New York Times* (24 November 2003), A25—the titles of these essays alone demonstrate that Safire, following the Bush administration's lead, systematically speaks of conditional circumstances and possible leads as if proven true.

47. On Zarqawi and Powell's and others' attempt to turn him into the smoking gun linking Iraq and al Qaeda, and the counterevidence, see Ed Vulliamy, Martin Bright, and Nick Pelham, "The Truth about Iraq's Al Qaeda Connection," *Observer* (2 February 2003), 16; Ian Johnson, David Crawford, and Gary Fields, "The Case against Iraq: Germans Call Link between Zarqawi, Al Qaeda Unclear," *Wall Street Journal* (7 February 2003), A6; Walter Pincus, "Alleged Al Qaeda Ties Questioned; Experts Scrutinize Details of Accusations against Iraqi Government," *Washington Post* (7 February 2003), A21; Don Van Natta and David Johnston, "A Terror Lieutenant with a Deadly Past," *New York Times* (9 February 2003), A1; and Jeffrey Gettleman, "Zarqawi's Journey: From Dropout to Prisoner to an Insurgent Leader in Iraq," *New York Times* (13 July 2004), A8. For an excellent summary of these refutations of Powell's and others' claims regarding alleged Zarqawi/al Qaeda/Iraq links, see David Cortwright, Alistair Millar, George Lopez, and Linda Gerber, *Unproven: The Flawed Case for War in Iraq* (South Bend, IN: Fourth Freedom Forum/Notre Dame Institute for International Peace Studies, June 2003), 9–12.

48. Hans Blix, "Briefing of the Security Council" (14 February 2003), 6, available from the UN; Blix, *Disarming Iraq*, 155; for a postwar revelation of just how far Pow-

ell's testimony was from the truth, see Luke Harding, "Germans Accuse US over Iraq Weapons Claim," *Guardian* (2 April 2004).

49. The fire truck claim is one among many critiques of Powell's testimony offered by former intelligence officials in Greenwald, *Uncovered*.

50. Regarding Powell's testimony before the Senate Foreign Relations Committee, see Seymour Hersh, "Who Lied to Whom?" *New Yorker* (31 March 2003); for a detailed debunking of the aluminum-tubes argument, see David Barstow, William Broad, and Jeff Gerth, "Skewed Intelligence Data in March to War in Iraq," *New York Times* (3 October 2004), A1, 16, 18.

51. Mohamed ElBaradei, "The Status of Nuclear Inspections in Iraq: 14 February 2003 Update; Statement to the United Nations Security Council," 4, 1, 4 (emphasis added), available at www.iaea.org/worldatom; for an earlier version of these comments, see "The Status of Nuclear Inspections in Iraq; Statement to the United Nations Security Council," 27 January 2003; for a comprehensive refutation of the administration's lies regarding Iraq's nuclear weapons program, see "Claims and Evaluations of Iraq's Proscribed Weapons, Nuclear," posted by the Traprock Peace Center.

52. Scott McClellan speaking at White House press briefing of 18 July 2003, quotations from 5 and 4; David Albright, "The CIA's Aluminum Tubes Assessment: Is the Nuclear Case Going Down the Tubes?" (10 March 2003), 2, article posted by the Institute for Science and International Security; Gellman and Pincus, "Depiction of Threat Outgrew Supporting Evidence"; for a blistering refutation of the aluminum-tubes argument see Linda Rothstein, "You Call That Evidence?" *Bulletin of Atomic Scientists* (12 September 2002), available at www.thebulletin.org; on the negotiating processes involved in producing *NIE*s, see Odom, *Fixing Intelligence*, 80–81.

53. George Bush, "2003 State of the Union Address," 6; Rice quoted in James Risen, "Bush Aides Now Say Claim on Uranium Was Accurate," *New York Times* (14 July 2003), A7; and see Adam Nagourney, "Shifting Gears, White House Shoves Back on Bush Claims," *New York Times* (15 July 2003), A1, 12.

54. ElBaradei quoted in Jeff Sallot, "Documents Linking Iraq to Uranium Were Forged," *Globe and Mail* (Canada) (8 March 2003), available at www.globeandmail.com; details of the forgeries from Dana Priest and Karen DeYoung, "CIA Questioned Documents Linking Iraq, Uranium Ore," *Washington Post* (22 March 2003), A30, and Hersh, "Who Lied to Whom?"

55. CIA quotation from Hersh, "Stovepipe," 84; for a remarkable interview in which he suggests that the forgeries were actually made by disgruntled CIA agents, who hoped the crude documents would reveal the shabby nature of the intelligence work driving the White House's push for war, see "Behind the Mushroom Cloud," an interview of Seymour Hersh by Amy Davidson, available from the *New Yorker On-line Only* (3 December 2003).

56. Nicholas Kristof, "White House in Denial," *New York Times* (13 June 2003), A33; Dana Priest, "Uranium Claim Was Known for Months to Be Weak," *Washington Post* (20 July 2003), A22; and see Kristof, "16 Words and Counting," *New York Times* (15 July 2003), A25.

57. Joseph Wilson, "What I Didn't Find in Africa," *New York Times* (6 July 2003), sec. 4, p. 9; Joseph Wilson, *The Politics of Truth: Inside the Lies That Led to War and Betrayed My Wife's CIA Identity—A Diplomat's Memoir* (New York: Carroll and Graf, 2004), 21, and see 17–29 on his trip to Niamey; also see Andrew Buncombe, "Iraq, the Niger Connection: The CIA Briefing—Diplomat Who Blew the Whistle on Falsified Evidence," *Independent* (UK) (9 July 2003).

58. Wilson's *Meet the Press* quotation as replayed on NPR's *Weekend All Things Considered*, 8 p.m. edition (6 July 2003); Wilson has subsequently been awarded the Fertel Foundation and Nation Institute's Ron Ridenhour Prize for Truth Telling (see *Nation* [13 October 2003], 21).

59. The leak was made public in Robert Novak, "Mission to Niger," *Washington Post* (14 July 2003), A21; "Nixonian" quotation from Eric Alterman, "Abrams and Novak and Rove? Oh My!" *Nation* (3 November 2003), 10; on the ensuing scandal see Jonathan Kaplan, "Lawmakers Demand Probe into Outing of Undercover CIA Agent," *Hill* (29 July 2003), 3; Kim Sengputa, "Whistleblower on Niger Uranium Claim Accuses White House of Launching Dirty Tricks Campaign," *Independent* (UK) (4 August 2003), 4; and David Cole, "Nigergate Thuggery," *Nation* (4/11 August 2003), 5–6; for a blistering profile of Novak, see Amy Sullivan, "Little Big Man," AlterNet (6 December 2004).

60. Wilson, *Politics of Truth,* 427; Tom Brune, "Air Force One Records Subpoenaed," *Newsday* (5 March 2004), A2; on the political gaming surrounding the Justice Department's investigation, see Mike Allen and Dana Priest, "Bush Administration Is Focus of Inquiry," *Washington Post* (28 September 2003), A1; Eric Lichtblau and Richard Stevenson, "A Top Bush Aide Didn't Identify CIA Agent, White House Says," *New York Times* (30 September 2003), A1, 11; Richard Stevenson and Eric Lichtblau, "White House Looks to Manage Fallout over CIA Leak Inquiry," *New York Times* (2 October 2003), A22; and Adam Liptak, "Reporters Put under Scrutiny in CIA Leak," *New York Times* (28 September 2004), A1, 21.

61. Woodward, *Plan of Attack,* 201; further discussion of memos and phone calls in Dana Milbank and Walter Pincus, "Bush Aides Disclose Warnings from CIA," *Washington Post* (23 July 2002), A1; Henry Waxman letter to the president, 17 March 2003, available at www.house.gov; note that the Senate Select Committee on Intelligence demanded that the White House send it copies of the memos discussed here to aid its investigation, but that the committee announced that no findings would be published until after the November 2004 presidential election (see Walter Pincus, "Panel to See Prewar CIA Memos on Iraq," *Washington Post* [5 November 2003], A24).

62. Official quoted in Richard Stevenson, "White House Tells How Bush Came to Talk of Iraq Uranium," *New York Times* (19 July 2003), A6; Senator Durbin quoted in James Risen and David Sanger, "After the War: CIA Uproar; New Details Emerge on Uranium Claim and Bush's Speech," *New York Times* (18 July 2003), A1.

63. "Negotiations" from Greg Miller, "CIA Names Bush Aide in Speech Scandal," *Los Angeles Times* (18 July 2002), A10; and see Dana Millbank and Dana Priest, "Warning in Iraq Unread; Bush, Rice, Did Not See State's Objection," *Washington*

Post (19 July 2003), A1; McClellan quoted from transcript of 18 July 2003 White House press briefing cited above; for a timeline of the deception, see Warren Hoge and Don Van Natta, "Tracing a Disputed Claim," *New York Times* (17 July 2003), A8; for an overview see the FAIR media advisory of 18 July 2003, "Bush Uranium Lie Is Tip of Iceberg."

64. George Tenet, "Press Release and Statements," 11 July 2003, available from the CIA; while he misses the irony of the moment, see Richard Stevenson, "President Asserts He Still Has Faith in Tenet and CIA," *New York Times* (13 July 2003), A1, 8; Tenet resigned on 3 June 2004.

65. On Hadley's performance see Maura Reynolds, "White House Admits CIA Warned It before Speech," *Los Angeles Times* (23 July 2003), A6, and David Sanger and Judith Miller, "National Security Aide Says He's to Blame for Speech Error," *New York Times* (23 July 2003), A11; when Rice was promoted to secretary of state in November 2004, Hadley was rewarded for being a good soldier with a promotion to national security adviser (for a cheerleading account see Scott Shane, "A Picture of Sturdy Loyalty: Stephen John Hadley," *New York Times* [17 November 2004], A 21).

66. On the vote not to convene an independent commission, see Carl Hulse, "Senate Rejects Panel on Prewar Iraq Data," *New York Times* (17 July 2003), A10; on the workings of the Senate Select Committee on Intelligence, see Douglas Jehl, "Senate Panel Demands CIA Data Leading Up to War by Friday Noon," *New York Times* (30 October 2003), A12; Dana Priest, "Inquiry Faults Intelligence on Iraq," *Washington Post* (24 October 2003), A1; and Douglas Jehl, "CIA Disputes Accusations That Its Prewar Conclusions on Iraq Arms Were Flawed," *New York Times* (25 October 2003), A8; on the committee's findings, see Douglas Jehl, "Senators Assail CIA Judgments on Iraq's Arms as Deeply Flawed," *New York Times* (10 July 2004), A1, 6.

67. Robert Dreyfuss, "The Pentagon Muzzles the CIA," *American Prospect* 13, no. 22 (16 December 2002): 1, available at www.prospect.org.

68. Hersh, "Stovepipe," 77; and see Hiro, *Secrets and Lies,* 83–84; for evidence of the White House's attempt to sweep the work of the OSP under the rug (an effort with which he is complicit), see Woodward, *Plan of Attack,* 288–289; at this same time Feith was also running another stovepiping operation, this one called the Counter-Terrorism Evaluation Group (see James Risen, "How Pair's Findings on Terror Led to Clash on Shaping Intelligence," *New York Times* [28 April 2004], A1, 19).

69. Hinsliff, Bright, Beaumont, and Vulliamy, "First Casualties in the Propaganda Firefight," 16; Douglas Jehl, "Agency Belittles Information Given by Iraqi Defectors," *New York Times* (29 September 2003), A1, 8 (Jehl notes that milking Chalabi-linked defectors for bogus intelligence cost the government "more than $1 million in taxpayers' money"); Gordon Mitchell, "The Difference between Pre-Emptive and Preventive War" *University Times (University of Pittsburgh)* (19 February 2004), archived at www.umc.pitt.edu; *Telegraph* quotation cited from Isabel Hilton, "Need to Build a Case for War? Step Forward Mr. Chalabi," *Guardian* (6 March 2004), emphasis added.

70. Chalabi information from Jane Mayer, "The Manipulator," *New Yorker* (7

June 2004), 58–72, quotation from 63; Seymour Hersh, *Chain of Command: The Road from 9/11 to Abu Ghraib* (New York: Simon and Schuster, 2004), 163–189; and Hiro, *Secrets and Lies*, 239–241.

71. Background information and Powell quotation from Bruce Auster, Mark Mazzetti, and Edward Pound, "Truth and Consequences: New Questions about US Intelligence Regarding Iraq's Weapons of Mass Terror," *US News and World Report* (2 June 2003), accessed online; and see Suzanne Goldenberg and Richard Norton-Taylor, "Powell's Doubts over CIA Intelligence on Iraq Prompted Him to Set Up Secret Review," *Guardian* (2 June 2003), 3; Odom, *Fixing Intelligence*, 39.

72. Eric Schmitt, "Aide Denies Shaping Data to Justify War," *New York Times* (5 June 2003), A17; James Risen and David Sanger, "New Details Emerge on Uranium Claim and Bush's Speech," *New York Times* (18 July 2003), A1, 8; William Safire, "Tribal Warfare in Iraq," *New York Times* (24 May 2004), A27; Karen Kwiatkowski, "The New Pentagon Papers," *Salon.com* (10 March 2004); Senator Levin quoted in Douglas Jehl, "Pentagon Reportedly Skewed CIA's View of Qaeda Tie," *New York Times* (22 October 2004), A10.

73. Seymour Hersh, "Selective Intelligence," *New Yorker* (9 July 2003); Steering Group (Richard Beske, Kathleen McGrath, William Christison, Raymond McGovern) of Veteran Intelligence Professionals for Sanity, "Memorandum for the President" (1 May 2003), emphasis added, available at *Tom Paine.Common Sense*.

74. Arendt, "Lying in Politics," 31.

75. Paul Krugman, "Things to Come," *New York Times* (18 March 2003), A31. On the media's role in this scenario, see Douglas Kellner, *From 9/11 to Terror War: The Dangers of the Bush Legacy* (New York: Rowman and Littlefield, 2003), 49–70; Sheldon Rampton and John Stauber, *Weapons of Mass Deception: The Uses of Propaganda in Bush's War on Iraq* (New York: Tarcher, 2003); and Steven Kull, *Misperceptions, the Media, and the Iraq War* (University of Maryland, Program on International Policy Attitudes, October 2003); for the *Times*'s confession see the editors, "The Times and Iraq," *New York Times* (26 May 2004), A10.

76. On Kay's findings see Douglas Jehl, "Draft Report Said to Cite No Success in Iraq Arms Hunt," *New York Times* (25 September 2003), A1, 10; James Risen and Judith Miller, "No Illicit Arms Found in Iraq, U.S. Inspector Tells Congress," *New York Times* (3 October 2003), A1, 12; and David Sanger and James Risen, "President Says Report on Arms Vindicates War," *New York Times* (4 October 2003), A1, 6; Powers, "Vanishing Case for War," 7. After resigning his post, Kay made even more damning remarks about the Bush administration's faulty WMD arguments; see Richard Stevenson, "Iraq Illicit Arms Gone before War, Inspector Insists," *New York Times* (24 January 2004), A1, 7, and James Risen, "CIA Lacked Iraq Arms Data, Ex-Inspector Says," *New York Times* (26 January 2004), A1, 10. Duelfer report cited in Jehl, "U.S. Report Finds Iraqis Eliminated Illicit Arms in 90s" and "Iraq Study Finds Desire for Arms, but not Capacity," *New York Times* (17 September 2004), A1, 11; for a comprehensive postwar summary of these issues, see Joseph Cirincione, Jessica Mathews, George Perkovich, and Alexis Orton, *WMD in Iraq: Evidence and Implications* (Washington, DC: Carnegie Endowment for International Peace, 2004).

77. Rycroft memo quoted as it appears reprinted in Mark Danner, "The Secret Way to War," *New York Review of Books* (9 June 2005), 70–74, memo on p. 71, emphases added; also see Ray McGovern, "Proof Bush Fixed the Facts," posted to AlterNet, 5 May 2005.

78. Dillon, "IAEA Iraq Action Team Record," 43; Katzman, *Iraq: U.S. Efforts to Change the Regime,* 15; CIA revelations noted in Douglas Jehl and David Sanger, "CIA Admits It Didn't Give Weapon Data to the UN," *New York Times* (21 February 2004), A7.

79. Chalmers Johnson, *Blowback: The Costs and Consequences of American Empire* (New York: Henry and Holt, 2000), 88ff.; Peter Dale Scott, *Drugs, Oil, and War: The United States in Afghanistan, Colombia, and Indochina* (New York: Rowman and Littlefield, 2003), 29; for case studies of this thesis, see Scott, *Deep Politics and the Death of JFK* (Berkeley and Los Angeles: University of California Press, 1993), and Scott and Jonathan Marshall, *Cocaine Politics: Drugs, Armies, and the CIA in Central America* (Berkeley and Los Angeles: University of California Press, 1991).

80. Richard Butler, *The Greatest Threat: Iraq, Weapons of Mass Destruction, and the Crisis of Global Security* (New York: Public Affairs, 2000), xv, 8, xv, 3; for an equally insipid version of this genre of hysterical WMD discourse (that reads, it must be said, as an exciting spy novel), see Khidhir Hamza, *Saddam's Bombmaker: The Terrifying Inside Story of the Iraqi Nuclear and Biological Weapons Agenda* (New York: Scribner, 2000)—originally titled *Fizzle: Iraq and the Atomic Bomb,* Hamza was apparently persuaded by publishers to turn his factual account of Iraq's nuclear failures into a fictional account of its alleged success (see Hersh, *Chain of Command,* 213); for a critique of such WMD hysteria, see Owen Cote, Jr., "Weapons of Mass Confusion," *Boston Review* 28, no. 2 (2003); for a sober analysis see Scott Ritter, *Endgame: Solving the Iraq Crisis* (New York: Simon and Schuster, 1999).

81. Dilip Hiro, *Iraq: In the Eye of the Storm* (New York: Thunder's Mouth/Nation, 2002), 39.

82. John Muller and Karl Muller, "Sanctions of Mass Destruction, *Foreign Affairs* 78, no. 3 (1999): 43–53; James Fine, "The Iraq Sanctions Catastrophe," *Middle East Report* (January/February 1992), 36; and see *Iraq Sanctions: Humanitarian Implications and Options for the Future,* report for the UN Security Council (6 August 2002); and David Reiff, "Were the Sanctions Right?" *New York Times Magazine* (27 July 2003), 41–46.

83. *The World Health Report* (Geneva, Switzerland: World Health Organization, 2002), 8, 9; Jolly quoted in "Price of Safe Water for All: $10 Billion and the Will to Provide It," *New York Times* (23 November 2000), A10; UNICEF immunization figures and quotation from Bennis, *Failed Transition,* 54; U.S. military budget figures from 2002, as posted under "Last of the Big Time Spenders," by the Center for Defense Information; war costs from www.costofwar.com, where they note that the figure of $5.46 billion includes their calculation of interest on these expenditures at 4 percent over ten years; for the minutia of military spending see *The National Defense Authorization Act for Fiscal Year 2004* (H.R. 1588, signed by the president on 24 November 2003), available from the Congressional Budget Office.

84. Richard Bernstein, "Foreign Views of U.S. Darken after Sept. 11," *New York*

Times (11 September 2003), A1, 18; U.S. Advisory Group quoted in Steven Weisman, "Bush-Appointed Panel Finds U.S. Image Abroad Is in Peril," *New York Times* (1 October 2003), A1, 8; and see the BBC's damning poll, released 20 January 2005, which carried the header "In 18 of 21 Countries Polled, Most See Bush's Reelection as Negative for World Security."

Chapter 2

1. Boxer's and Rice's comments from the transcript of the Senate Foreign Relations Committee hearing of 18 January 2005, available from the *New York Times* at www.nytimes.com/international; for coverage of the day's exchanges, see Steven Weisman and Joel Brinkley, "At Hearing, Rice Claims Progress in Iraq Training," *New York Times* (19 January 2005), A1, 10.

2. Quotations from "Transcript: Day Two of Rice Testimony" (19 January 2005), downloaded from the *Washington Post*; for praise for Boxer's efforts, see Carl Hulse, "Boxer Is Loudest Voice of Opposition to Rice Nomination," *New York Times* (20 January 2005), A6.

3. *National Security Strategy of the United States* (Washington, DC: White House, September 2002), hereafter cited in the text as *NSSUS*.

4. *Pax Americana* is a phrase peppered throughout many of the critical evaluations of the *NSSUS* cited herein; for example, see the bitter use of the phrase in Peter Beaumont, "Now for the Bush Doctrine," *Observer* (22 September 2002), available online through *Guardian;* and see Max Boot, *The Savage Wars of Peace* (New York: Basic Books, 2002), 336–352.

5. John M. Murphy, "'Our Mission and Our Moment': George W. Bush and September 11th," *Rhetoric and Public Affairs* 6, no. 4 (2003): 607–632, quotations from 609, 610; and see Murphy, "Epideictic and Deliberative Strategies in Opposition to War: The Paradox of Honor and Expediency," *Communication Studies* 43 (1992): 65–78; for his confusing attempt to define the genre, see Aristotle, *On Rhetoric,* trans. George Kennedy (New York: Oxford University Press, 1991), 78–87.

6. George Bush, "President Bush Outlines Iraqi Threat," Cincinnati Museum Center (7 October 2002), available from the White House; House Joint Resolution 114 (dated 2 October 2002, the president signed the bill into law on 16 October 2002); and "President Bush to Send Iraq Resolution to Congress Today" (19 September 2002), all available from the White House.

7. "Dr. Condoleezza Rice Discusses President's National Security Strategy" (1 October 2002), available from the White House, hereafter cited in the text as "Rice."

8. For a case study of how to analyze jointly authored documents, in this case the Office of the National Drug Control Policy's annual drug war reports, see Stephen Hartnett, "A Rhetorical Critique of the Drug War and 'the Nauseous Pendulum' of Reason and Violence," *Journal of Contemporary Criminal Justice* 16, no. 3 (August 2000): 247–271.

9. Carl Kaysen, John Steinbruner, and Martin Malin, "U.S. National Security Policy: In Search of Balance," in *War with Iraq: Costs, Consequence, and Alternatives,*

ed. Carl Kaysen et al. (Cambridge, MA: American Academy of Arts and Sciences, 2002), 4; Foreign Policy in Focus Advisory Committee, "Our Fateful Choice: Global Leader or Global Cop," originally signed on 11 December 2002.

10. George Bush, "Statement by the President" (11 September 2001), available from the White House.

11. Robert Hariman, "Speaking of Evil," *Rhetoric and Public Affairs* 6, no. 3 (Fall 2003): 511–517, quotation from 511. The literature on state-sponsored terrorism is overwhelming; for an introduction to this genre, see Robert Merrill, "Simulations and Terrors of Our Time," and Edward Herman, "Terrorism: Misrepresentations of Power," both in *Violent Persuasions: The Politics and Imagery of Terrorism,* ed. David Brown and Robert Merrill (Seattle: Bay Press, 1993), 27–46 and 47–66 respectively; Noam Chomsky, *The Culture of Terrorism* (Boston: South End Press, 1998); Chalmers Johnson, *Blowback: The Costs and Consequences of American Empire* (New York: Holt, 2000), 65–94; Peter Dale Scott and Jonathan Marshall, *Cocaine Politics: Drugs, Armies, and the CIA in Central America* (Berkeley and Los Angeles: University of California Press, 1991); and Edward Herman, *The Real Terror Network: Terrorism in Fact and Propaganda* (Boston: South End Press, 1987).

12. Michael Mann, *Incoherent Empire* (London: Verso, 2003), 159–193 in general, quotation from 178–179; for additional critiques, see Douglas Kellner, *From 9/11 to Terror War* (New York: Rowman and Littlefield, 2003); Richard Falk, *The Great Terror War* (New York: Olive Branch, 2003); and Lewis Lapham, *Theater of War* (New York: New Press, 2002).

13. Richard Norton-Taylor, "This Marks the Death of Deterrence," *Guardian* (9 October 2002); 18; "Vigilante-Orchestrated War a Dangerous Precedent," *Statesman* (India) (8 October 2002); Jay Bookman, "Bush's Real Goal in Iraq: The Global Cop's Beat," *Edmonton (Alberta) Journal* (6 October 2002), E5; "Is the U.S. a Threat to World Peace?" *Daily Inquirer* (Philippines) (22 September 2002), section 10; and see the blistering editorial by Allison Hall, *Montreal Gazette* (25 September 2002), A30; for a cheerful neoconservative precursor to the imperial ideas questioned here, see Robert Kagan, "The Benevolent Empire," *Foreign Policy* (Summer 1998), available online at www.ceip.org/people/kagbenev.htm.

14. George Bush, "President Bush to Send Iraq Resolution to Congress Today" (19 September 2002), available from the White House.

15. Sarah Anderson, Phyllis Bennis, and John Cavanagh, *Coalition of the Willing or Coalition of the Coerced? How the Bush Administration Influences Allies in Its War on Iraq* (Washington, DC: Institute for Policy Studies, 2003), 3 on Bulgaria, 4 on Guinea and Cameroon; and see William Hartung and Michelle Ciarrocca, "Buying a Coalition," *Nation* (17 March 2003), 4–5; Paul Richter, "Bulgaria, Romania Pin Hopes on U.S.," *Los Angeles Times* (11 March 2003), A11; and Bob Herbert, "With Ears and Eyes Closed," *New York Times* (17 March 2003), A25.

16. These Central American states feared that a recession in the United States due to the Iraq war would have dire implications on their economies, hence making membership in CAFTA even more important. Indeed, Central America exports $11.7 billion annually to the United States, three-fourths of which enters our country duty-free, meaning that any retaliatory U.S. sanctions against states that chose not to

support the war could have devastated these nations. Along with their supporting the war, Honduras, El Salvador, and Nicaragua (and Guatemala, which refused to join the war) finished negotiations for CAFTA on 17 December, 2003; Costa Rica walked out of the December negotiations due to protests in San Juan against the telecommunications and insurance industries aspects of CAFTA, but it became the fifth Central American country to join CAFTA on 25 January 2004; the Dominican Republic eventually signed on as well. See Nfer Muoz, "Central America: Experts, Citizens Fear Economic Fallout of Iraq War," CorpWatch (21 March 2003); Mark Engler, *The Trouble with CAFTA* (Washington, DC: Foreign Policy in Focus, 3 February 2004); Elizabeth Becker, "Costa Rica to Be 5th Country in New Trade Pact with U.S.," *New York Times* (25 January 2004), A6.

17. Colombia's surprise is recounted in Dan Balz and Mike Allen, "U.S. Names 30 Countries Supporting War Effort," *Washington Post* (19 March 2003), A1; information on other coalition nations from Sarah Anderson, Phyllis Bennis, John Cavanagh, and Erik Leaver, *Coalition of the Willing or Coalition of the Coerced? Part II* (Washington, DC: Institute for Policy Studies, 2003), 3; for early lists of coalition troop deployments, see Felicity Barringer, "U.S. Is Struggling to Make New Iraq Resolution Matter," *New York Times* (20 September 2003), A5, and "The Other Troops in Iraq," *New York Times* (21 November 2004), A16; November 2004 coalition numbers from Phyllis Bennis and the IPS Task Force, *A Failed Transition: The Mounting Costs of the Iraq War* (Washington, DC: Institute for Policy Studies, 2004), 13; 2005 figures from Ian Fisher, "Italy Planning to Start Pullout of Iraq Troops," *New York Times* (16 March 2005), A1, 8.

18. State Department report summarized in Anderson, Bennis, Cavanagh, and Leaver, *Coalition of the Willing, Part II*, 2; on the dubious political systems of many of the coalition members, see Erik Leaver and Sara Johnson, "A Coalition of Weakness," downloaded from *Asia Times* (www.atimes.com) on 18 April 2003; for a list of coalition members and their respective payoffs, see Sarah Boyer, "Meet the Coalition!" *Public-i* (May 2003), 6–7 (available online at www.publici.ucimc.org); Schroeder's comments were published initially in "Iraq: The Case against Preemptive War," *American Conservative* (21 October 2002), but we first heard these words delivered by Schroeder on 30 January 2003, when he participated in our University of Illinois Teachers for Peace and Justice Teach-In titled "A Town Meeting: Is War Necessary?"

19. For an extended version of these claims, see Clyde Prestowitz, *Rogue Nation: American Unilateralism and the Failure of Good Intentions* (New York: Basic Books, 2003).

20. "A Strategy of Hubris," *Boston Globe* (6 October 2002), H10; and see Robert Wright, "Contradictions of a Superpower," *New York Times* (29 September 2002), sec. 4, p. 13.

21. For comments along these lines, see James Der Derian, "Decoding the *National Security Strategy of the United States of America*," *boundary 2* 30, no. 3 (2003): 19–27.

22. This thesis is elucidated in Eric Hobsbawm, *The Age of Empire, 1875–1914* (New York: Vintage, 1987), 302–340; for concise definitions of key terms, including

balance of power, see Tom Barry, *The U.S. Power Complex: What's New*, Special Report No. 20 (Washington, DC: Foreign Policy in Focus, 2002).

23. George Bush, "President Signs Iraq Resolution" (16 October 2002), available from the White House.

24. Lewis Lapham, *Theater of War* (New York: New Press, 2002), 32; for recent examples of scholarship that addresses the relationship between presidential rhetoric and deep religious traditions, see Murphy, "Our Mission and Our Moment"; John Angus Campbell, "Evil as the Allure of Perfection," and James McDaniel, "Figures of Evil: A Triad of Rhetorical Strategies for Theo Politics," both in *Rhetoric and Public Affairs* 6, no. 3 (Fall 2003): 523–530 and 539–550; Denise Bostdorff, "George W. Bush's Post-September 11 Rhetoric of Covenant Renewal: Upholding the Faith of the Greatest Generation," *Quarterly Journal of Speech* 89, no. 4 (November 2003): 293–319; and Mark Crispin Miller, *The Bush Dyslexicon: Observations on a National Disorder* (New York: Norton, 2001), 147–154.

25. George Bush, "Remarks on Arrival at the White House and an Exchange with Reporters" (16 September 2001), pages 2 and 3 of the transcript downloaded from *Weekly Compilation of Presidential Documents*, available through the Government Printing Office.

26. Ibid.; for glowing responses to the president's "Islam Is Peace" speech, see "Wartime Rhetoric," *New York Times* (19 September 2001), A26, which praised the president's "high eloquence," and Dana Milbank and Emily Wax, "Bush Visits Mosque to Forestall Hate Crimes," *Washington Post* (18 September 2001), A1; for a more sober analysis, see Peter Waldman, "Some Muslims Fear War on Terrorism Is Really a War on Them," *Wall Street Journal* (21 September 2001), A1.

27. Hywel Williams, "Crusade Is a Dirty Word," *Guardian* (18 September 2001); all other quotations from Peter Ford, "Europe Cringes at Bush 'Crusade' against Terrorists," *Christian Science Monitor* (19 September 2001); and see Rahul Mahajan, *The New Crusade: America's War on Terrorism* (New York: Monthly Review, 2002), 16–19.

28. William Safire, "On Language: Words at War," *New York Times* (30 September 2001), accessed through LexisNexis; for two examples of articles that cite the crusade slipup but do not analyze it, see John F. Harris, "Bush Gets More International Support for U.S. 'Crusade' against Terrorism," *Washington Post* (17 September 2001), A1, and Todd Purdum, "Bush Warns of a Wrathful, Shadowy and Inventive War," *New York Times* (17 September 2001), A2.

29. Sigmund Freud, *The Psychopathology of Everyday Life*, trans. Alan Tyson (1901; New York: Norton, 1965), 64, 61.

30. George Bush, "President's Remarks at National Day of Prayer and Remembrance" (14 September 2001), emphasis added, available from the White House; for a similarly expansive use of such terms, see David Frum and Richard Perle, *An End to Evil: How to Win the War on Terror* (New York: Random House, 2004).

31. Bostdorff, "Bush's Post-September 11 Rhetoric of Covenant Renewal," 297 (note that for purposes of prose flow we have changed her original past-tense claim to present); Brick Church covenant and following quotation from Paul E. Johnson, *A Shopkeeper's Millennium: Society and Revivals in Rochester, New York, 1815–1837* (New

York: Hill and Wang, 1978), 110–111 and 110; and see Nathan Hatch, *The Democratization of American Christianity* (New Haven, CT: Yale University Press, 1989).

32. Bush, "President's Remarks at National Day of Prayer and Remembrance" (14 September 2001); Peter Yoonsuk Paik, "Smart Bombs, Serial Killings, and the Rapture: The Vanishing Bodies of Imperial Apoclypticism," *Postmodern Culture* 14, no. 1 (2003), paragraph 20 of the version accessed at Project Muse; on the deep cultural resonance of the religious arguments explored here, see Sacvan Bercovitch, *The American Jeremiad* (Madison: University of Wisconsin Press, 1978) and Perry Miller, *Errand into the Wilderness* (1956; Cambridge, MA: Harvard University Press, 1993); for a study examining the connections among religious thought, nationalism, and the psychology of group identification, see Carolyn Marvin, *Blood Sacrifice and the Nation: Totem Rituals and the American Flag* (Cambridge: Cambridge University Press, 1999).

33. George Bush, "President's Remarks to the Nation: Spirit of Freedom Tribute" (11 September 2002), available from the White House; for a blistering attack on how the president's religious rhetoric masks deceit, see Jack Beatty, "The Faith-Based Presidency," *Atlantic On-line* (25 March 2004), accessed at www.theatlantic.com; for an insider's account of this process, see Ron Suskind, "What Makes Bush's Presidency So Radical—Even for Some Republicans—Is His Preternatural, Faith-Infused Certainty in Uncertain Times," *New York Times Magazine* (17 October 2004), 44–51, 64, 102, 106.

34. The presidential speeches referred to here are collected in *The President and the Public: Rhetoric and National Leadership*, ed. Craig Allen Smith and Kathy B. Smith (New York: University Press of America, 1985), 269–282; we should note that each of these speeches poses its own rhetorical problems—we point here, then, not so much to successful speeches as simply to deliberative political speeches that eschew the religious and epideictic moves employed by President Bush.

35. George Bush, "President Bush Announces Combat Operations in Iraq Have Ended" (1 May 2003), available from the White House; the "Top Gun" moment was so overwhelming a propaganda stunt that even the president's usual critics missed the speech's religious overtones: see John Prados, "Open Ending" (2 May 2003), posted at *Tom Paine.Common Sense,* and Julian Borger and Oliver Burkman, "Bush Makes Carrier Landing for TV Address," *Guardian* (2 May 2003).

36. Michael Coogan, ed., *The New Oxford Annotated Bible,* 3rd ed. (Oxford: Oxford University Press, 2001), historical information from 974–975, quotation from page 978 of the Hebrew Bible (HB), hereafter cited in the text by chapter, verse, and page number.

37. For examples of nineteenth-century U.S. peace activists using the book of Isaiah to their advantage, see the early issues of the Boston-based journal *Advocate of Peace;* by the late twentieth century the term "ploughshares" was used by literary journals, peace groups, and even "socially conscious" investment funds.

38. George Bush, "President Delivers 'State of the Union'" (28 January 2003), available from the White House; Martin Marty, "The Sin of Pride," *Newsweek* (10 March 2003), 32; for a scathing and often comic portrayal of President Bush's courting of the religious right, a group they call "Shiite Republicans" (83), see Molly

Ivins and Lou Dubose, *Shrub: The Short but Happy Political Life of George W. Bush* (New York: Random House, 2000), 57–83; on Michael Gerson, the evangelical Episcopalian widely believed to have written the president's speeches, see Mike Allen, "For Bush's Speechwriter, Job Grows beyond Words," *Washington Post* (11 October 2002), A35.

39. See the mission statement of Bush Country at www.Bushcountry.org; Rapture Index available at www.raptureready.com; this latter Web site is run by Tim LaHaye and Jerry Jenkins, the authors of the mega-best-selling *Armageddon* series, which in various installments over the past years has topped the *New York Times* best-seller list for weeks at a time; for analysis of these books, see Paik, "Smart Bombs, Serial Killings, and the Rapture."

40. "Born again" statistics from Melani McAlister, "An Empire of Their Own: How Born Again Christians Turned Biblical Prophecy into Big-Time Profit," *Nation* (22 September 2003), 31; James Arnt Aune, "The Argument from Evil in the Rhetoric of Reaction," *Rhetoric and Public Affairs* 6, no. 3 (Fall 2003): 521; Howard Fineman, "Bush and God," *Newsweek* (10 March 2003), pages 2, 6, and 2 of the printout available on LexisNexis; John Sutherland, "Be Rapture Ready! The End Times Are Nigh!" *London Review of Books* (5 June 2003), 33.

41. Editorial, "For Religious Bigotry," *New York Times* (26 August 2004), A26.

42. Joseph Stiglitz, *Globalization and Its Discontents* (New York: Norton, 2002), 40, and see his comments on neocolonialism on 41, 44–45, 51, and 72.

43. Tony Blair, "Tony Blair's Speech to the U.S. Congress," *Guardian* (18 July 2003), emphasis added.

44. Hobsbawm, *Age of Empire*, 20, 30, emphasis added.

45. MedAct, *Continuing Collateral Damage: The Health and Environmental Costs of War on Iraq* (London: MedAct, 2003) is available at www.medact.org, quotation from p. 7; *Trade and Foreign Investment Opportunities in Iraq*, created by the Coalition Provisional Authority, available online; for commentary on Friedman's "Golden Arches Theory of Conflict Resolution," see our introduction.

46. Ann Simons, "Free Expression Has Costs," *Los Angeles Times* (5 January 2004), A5; and see David Reiff, "The Shiite Surge," *New York Times* (1 February 2004), sec. 6, p. 34; for analyses of the significance of McDonald's to the questions addressed here, see George Ritzer, *The McDonaldization of Society: An Investigation into the Changing Character of Contemporary Social Life* (London: Sage, 2000) and Benjamin Barber, *Jihad vs. McWorld: How the Planet Is Both Falling Apart and Coming Together—And What This Means for Democracy* (New York: Times Books, 1995).

47. Edmund Andrews and Thom Shanker, "U.S. Military Chief Cows More Troops to Quell Iraqi Looting," *New York Times* (18 May 2003), A15; quotation from Ewen MacAskill, "Marines Accuse Baghdad Museum of Hampering Hunt of Treasures," *Guardian* (5 May 2003), 12; Ewen MacAskill, "Fake Artifacts for Sale on a Side Street," *Guardian* (6 May 2003), 12; Eleanor Robson, "The Collection Lies in Ruins, Objects from a Long, Rich Past in Smithereens," *Observer* (13 April 2003), 5, which Robson refuted in "Iraq Museums: What Really Happened," *Guardian* (18 June 2003), 19; Robert Fisk, "Library Books, Letters and Priceless Documents Are Set Ablaze in Final Chapter of the Sacking of Baghdad," *Independent* (15 April

2003), available at www.argument.independent.co.uk, and see Amy Goodman's interview with Fisk on *Democracy Now!* (22 April 2003).

48. "[B]ollocks" from David Aaronovitch, "Lost from the Baghdad Museum: Truth," *Guardian* (9 June 2003), 5; Jennie Matthew, "Baghdad Museum Too Afraid to Reopen," *Middle East Online* (5 February 2004), available from Occupation Watch; and see Barry Beir, "Most Iraqi Treasures Are Said to Be Kept Safe," *New York Times* (6 May 2003), A12; Alan Riding, "Loss Estimates Are Cut on Iraqi Artifacts," *New York Times* (1 May 2003), A1, 19; Philip Shenon, "U.S. Says It Has Recovered Hundreds of Artifacts and Thousands of Manuscripts in Iraq," *New York Times* (8 May 2003), A12; and Yaroslav Trofimov and Farnaz Fassihi, "In This Library's Tale, Seeds of Mistrust and Hope in Iraq," *Wall Street Journal* (28 April 2003), 1.

49. Mark Danner, "Delusions in Baghdad," *New York Review of Books* (18 December 2003); and see Andrew Lawler, "Mayhem in Mesopotamia," *Science* (1 August 2003), 582–588, and Polly Curtis, "Priceless Artifacts Still Missing in Iraq," *Guardian* (13 April 2004).

50. Ed Vuillamy, "US Troops Vandalize Ancient City of Ur," *Observer* (18 May 2003), 2.

51. Edmund Andrews, "Iraqi Looters Tearing Up Archeological Sites," *New York Times* (23 May 2003), A1; history and collection information from Roger Matthews, untitled editorial, *Guardian* (31 January 2003); and see Martin Gottlieb, "Looters Swarm over Remote Sites, Study Finds," *New York Times* (12 June 2003), A14; and Lawler, "Mayhem in Mesopotamia."

52. Edmund Andrews, "Global Network Aids Theft of Iraqi Artifacts," *New York Times* (28 May 2003), A12; Henry Wright et al., "The National Geographic Society's Cultural Assessment of Iraq," *National Geographic* (May 2003), available at www.nationalgeographic.com.

53. Joanne Mariner, "Looting Antiquity: The Legal Implications for the Pentagon," posted to *CounterPunch* (17 April 2003); the 1956 UN law and the September 2003 UNESCO statement are both archived online by those agencies.

54. *Iraq Cultural Heritage Act,* HR 2009, 108th Cong. (7 May 2003); UNESCO, *Iraq—Heritage in Danger* (13 March 2003), available at www.portal.unesco.org; Interpol, *Cultural Property: Stolen Iraqi Art* (n.d.), available at www.interpol/int/Public/WorkOfArt-/Iraq/Gallery.asp.

55. UN Resolution 1483 is available from the UN; and see Martin Gottleib, "Campaign Starts to Help Iraq Rebuild Cultural Institutions," *New York Times* (30 April 2003), A15.

56. Max Rodenbeck, "Bohemia in Baghdad," *New York Review of Books* (3 July 2003), 20–23; Christian Parenti, *The Freedom: Shadows and Hallucinations in Occupied Iraq* (New York: New Press, 2004), 111; Rory McCarthy, "Where There's Muck There's Dinars," *Guardian* (30 January 2004); and see Jo Wilding, "The Unbelievable Sadness in This Place" *Guardian* (30 March 2003).

57. Neil MacFarquar, "Humiliation and Rage Stalk the Arab World," *New York Times* (13 April 2003), A1, 5; on the status of shrines in the face of ongoing battles, see Dexter Filkins, "Two Shrines Intact, but U.S. Reputation Is Marred after Clashes

with Rebels," *New York Times* (27 May 2004), A10; John F. Burns, "At Least 143 Die in Attacks at Two Sacred Sites in Iraq," *New York Times* (3 March 2004), A1; Jane Little, "US Dilemma over Iraq's Mosques," *BBC News* (29 April 2004), accessed from Occupation Watch; and Rory McCarthy, "US Troops in Fierce Clashes in Holy Cities," *Guardian* (22 May 2004).

58. John Tomlinson, *Globalization and Culture* (Chicago: University of Chicago Press, 1999), 24, 31; for additional studies of the importance of culture in an age of globalization and empire, see Tyler Cowen, *Creative Destruction* (Princeton, NJ: Princeton University Press, 2002); Arjun Appadurai, *Modernity at Large: Cultural Dimensions of Globalization* (Minneapolis: University of Minnesota Press, 1996), 89–135; Paul Hirst and Grahame Thompson, *Globalization in Question*, 2nd ed. (Malden, MA: Polity Press, 1999), 256–280; and David Held, "Cosmopolitanism: Ideas, Realities and Deficits," in *Governing Globalization: Power, Authority and Global Governance*, ed. David Held and Anthony McGrew (Malden, MA: Polity Press, 2002), 305–324.

59. Ellen Meiksins Wood, *Empire of Capital* (London: Verso, 2003)—the term "commercial imperialism" is used throughout her study, to which we turn in detail in chapters 3 and 4; for a rhetorical history of the trope of free markets, see James Arnt Aune, *Selling the Free Market: The Rhetoric of Economic Correctness* (New York: Guilford, 2001); and see Gordon Bigelow, "Let There Be Markets: The Evangelical Roots of Economics," *Harper's Magazine* (May 2005), 33–38.

60. George Bush, "President Proposes $5 Billion Plan to Help Developing Nations" (14 March 2002), available from the White House; for more of the president's thoughts on globalizing free markets see "President Outlines U.S. Plan to Help World's Poor," Cintermex Convention Center, Monterrey, Mexico (22 March 2002); for his thoughts on corruption see "President Bush Taking Action to Strengthen America's Economy," Chicago (7 January 2003), all available from the White House.

61. Stiglitz, *Globalization and Its Discontents*, 83; on the crisis of U.S. poverty, see David Shipler, *The Working Poor: Invisible in America* (New York: Knopf, 2004); Tamar Levin, "Study Finds That Youngest U.S. Children Are Poorest," *New York Times* (15 March 1998), sec. Y, p. 18, and Robert Pear, "Number of People Living in Poverty Increases in U.S.," *New York Times* (25 September 2002), A1, 19.

62. Amy Chua, *World on Fire: How Exporting Free Market Democracy Breeds Ethnic Hatred and Global Instability* (New York: Anchor Books, 2004), 245.

63. Elizabeth Becker, "Bush Scaling Back Dollars for Third World," *New York Times* (29 January 2004), A15; note that the president's claim was to submit $5 billion over three years—the 2004 figure was scheduled to be $3.3 billion, not the $2.5 billion actually offered; David Harvey, *The New Imperialism* (Oxford: Oxford University Press, 2003), 130; see the White House's claims regarding the Millennium Challenge Account at its home page, under the heading "Helping Developing Nations"; and see Christopher Marquis, "Overhaul by U.S. Will Reroute Aid for Poor Nations," *New York Times* (22 February 2004), A1, 6; 2005 figures from Celia Dugger, "Bush Initiative for Poor Nations Faces Sharp Budget Cuts and Criticism of Slow Pace," *New York Times* (17 June 2005), A8.

64. United Nations Development Programme, *HDR*, 30, emphasis added; for an

example of how U.S. foreign policy and financial clout actually enforce corruption, see Peter Waldman, "Washington's Tilt to Business Stirs a Backlash in Indonesia," *Wall Street Journal* (11 February 2004).

65. Jennie Cummings, "Wal-Mart Opens for Business in Tough Market: Washington," *Wall Street Journal* (24 March 2004), A1; Glen Ford and Peter Gamble, "No 'Choice': Wal-Mart Prepares to Bury the Left under a Mountain of Money," *In These Times* (31 March 2004); insurance information from Steven Greenhouse, "Wal-Mart, a Nation unto Itself," *New York Times* (17 April 2004); sales numbers from "Special Report: Wal-Mart," *Economist* (17 April 2004), 67–69 and "Learning to Love Wal-Mart," *Economist* (17 April 2004), 9; regarding the company's international assault on worker's rights, see Oxfam International, *Trading Away Our Rights: Women Working in Global Supply Chains* (Oxford: Oxfam International, 2004); regarding its recent $3.1 million fine for violating environmental laws, see Michael Janofsky, "U.S. Discloses Wal-Mart Fine of $3.1 Million," *New York Times* (13 May 2004), A21; and see Stan Cox, "Wal-Mart Wages Don't Support Wal-Mart Workers," AlterNet (10 June 2003), and Steven Greenhouse, "Wal-Mart to Pay U.S. $11 Million in Lawsuit on Immigrant Workers," *New York Times* (14 March 2005), A1, 10.

66. Aaron Bernstein, "Waking Up from the American Dream," *Business Week* (1 December 2003), 54; Paul Krugman, "The Death of Horatio Alger," *Nation* (5 January 2004), 16–17; quotation from the editorial "Harvesting Poverty: The Unkept Promise," *New York Times* (30 December 2003), A20.

67. Chua, *World on Fire*, 75.

68. For two classic exposés of the military-industrial complex, see Richard Kaufman, *The War Profiteers* (New York: Anchor, 1972) and Anthony Sampson, *The Arms Bazaar* (New York: Viking, 1977); on the U.S. military's standing as the world's most egregious polluter, see William Thomas, *Scorched Earth: The Military's Assault on the Environment* (Philadelphia: New Society, 1995); on its damaging effects on the areas surrounding U.S. bases, see Cynthia Enloe, *Bananas, Beaches, and Bases: Making Feminist Sense of International Politics* (Berkeley and Los Angeles: University of California Press, 1989) and Johnson, *Blowback*, 34–64 on the colonial status of Okinawa; for further revelations of excess and waste in the military-industrial complex, see Griff Witte, "Pentagon Wasted Supplies, GAO Finds," *Washington Post* (8 June 2005), D1; for an overview see Bryan Taylor and Stephen Hartnett, "National Security and All That It Implies: Communication and (Post-) Cold War Culture," *Quarterly Journal of Speech* 86, no. 4 (2000): 465–491.

69. "GAO Finds Defense Firms Owe Billions in Back Taxes," *Wall Street Journal* (12 February 2004); Jonathan Karp, "Lockheed, Raytheon Post Profits," *Wall Street Journal* (27 January 2004); Robert Hershey, Jr., "Tax Questions for Military's Contractors," *New York Times* (12 February 2004), C3.

70. A. R. Lacey, *A Dictionary of Philosophy* (New York: Scribner, 1976), 128; on "weak ontology" see Stephen White, *The Strengths of Weak Ontology in Political Theory* (Princeton, NJ: Princeton University Press, 2000); Allen Scult, "Aristotle's *Rhetoric* as Ontology: A Heideggerian Reading," *Philosophy and Rhetoric* 32, no. 2 (1999): 146–159, quoted questions from 148; and see Jamie Morgan, "Addressing Hu-

man Wrongs: A Philosophy-of-Ontology Perspective," *Philosophy East and West* 53, no. 4 (2003): 575–587.

71. George Bush, "The President's News Conference" (11 October 2001), available from *Weekly Compilation of Presidential Documents* at www.frwebgate.access.gpo. gov; George Bush, "Address to the Nation on Homeland Security from Atlanta" (9 November 2001), ibid.; George Bush, "President Delivers the State of the Union Address" (28 January 2002), "President Bush Thanks Germany for Support against Terrorism" (23 May 2002), and "President Bush Signs Homeland Security Act" (25 November 2002), all available from the White House; Robert Ivie, *Democracy and America's War on Terror* (Tuscaloosa: University of Alabama Press, 2005), 10, 15, 149.

72. George Bush, "President Bush Delivers Graduation Speech at West Point" (1 June 2002), emphases added, available from the White House.

73. Samuel Huntington, "The Clash of Civilizations," *Foreign Affairs* 72, no. 3 (Summer 1993): 22–50, cited hereafter by page numbers as they appear in the downloaded version available at www.alamut.com/-subj/economics/misc/clash.html; regarding Bernard Lewis, the precursor to Huntington's argument, see Peter Waldman, "A Historian's Take on Islam Steers U.S. in Terrorism Fight," *Wall Street Journal* (3 February 2004).

74. The book version appeared as *The Clash of Civilizations and the Remaking of the World* (New York: Simon and Schuster, 1996); for a blistering left-wing critique, see Tariq Ali, *The Clash of Fundamentalisms: Crusades, Jihads, and Modernity* (London: Verso, 2002), 297–310; for a representative right-wing response, see Roger Sandall, "The Politics of Oxymoron," *New Criterion: A Web Special* (Summer 2003), available at www.newcriterion.com; for more moderate treatments, see Michael Elliott, "When Worlds Collide," *Washington Post Book World* (1 December 1996), 4, and Richard Rosecrance, review of *The Clash of Civilizations* in *American Political Science Review* (December 1998), available at www.findarticles.com.

75. Michael Ignatieff, "Fault Lines," *New York Times* (1 December 1996), sec. 7, p. 13; for a similar critique of Huntington's civilizational categories, see John Gray, *False Dawn: The Delusions of Global Capitalism* (New York: New Press, 1998), 121–130.

76. Chua, *World on Fire*, 6, 43–44.

77. Information and Heryanto quotation from Johnson, *Blowback*, 81–82; for an intriguing analysis of the role of U.S. capital in destabilizing Indonesia, in this case via the crony capitalism driving the 1994 Paiton One energy deal between Suharto family members and Edison International and General Electric, see Peter Waldman, "Washington's Tilt to Business Stirs a Backlash in Indonesia," *Wall Street Journal* (11 February 2004); for a grueling portrayal of exploitation in Indonesia, see John Pilger, *The New Rulers of the World* (London: Verso, 2002), 15–44; for a similar critique of Chua's work, see Greg Grandin, "What's a Neoliberal To Do?" *Nation* (10 March 2004), 25–29.

78. Edward Said, "The Clash of Ignorance," *Nation* (22 October 2001).

79. Office of the Under Secretary of Defense (William Schneider, Jr., DSB Chairman), *Report of the Defense Science Board Task Force on Strategic Communication* (Washington, DC:GPO, 2004), findings on 45, quotations from 46, 35, 46; for equally

damaging information, see Robin Wright, "Iraq Occupation Erodes Bush Doctrine," *Washington Post* (28 June 2004), A1; regarding Morocco, see Andrew Higgins, "Morocco's Fragile Democracy Tests U.S. Prescriptions for World," *Wall Street Journal* (29 January 2004).

Chapter 3

1. See Susannah Nesmith, "Security Boosted for FTAA Talks," *Miami Herald* (10 November 2003), and Douglas Hanks, "Miami Secures Money to Run Americas Free Trade Talks," *Miami Herald* (6 November 2003), both accessed at www.miami. com/mld/miamiherald/.

2. On the arrests and for from-the-street perspectives, see Tom Hayden, "Miami Vice," AlterNet (20 November 2003), and Steven Greenhouse, "Demonstration Turns Violent at Trade Talks in Miami," *New York Times* (21 November 2003), A28; for our firsthand observations and photographs from the march, and for extensive links to additional coverage of the FTAA protests, see Laura Stengrim and Stephen Hartnett, "The FTAA, Globalization, and the Future of Democracy," *Public-i* 4, no. 1 (February 2004): 8–9, available online at www.publici.ucimc.org.

3. Korean linguistic practice refers to Lee Kyung Hae as Lee; for a reprint of his letter see Laura Carlson, "WTO Kills Farmers: In Memory of Lee Kyung Hae," *CounterCurrents* (16 September 2003), available at www.countercurrents.org; see also Tom Hayden, "Cancún Files: Remembering Lee Kyung Hae," AlterNet (12 September 2003), and John Ross, "WTO Collapses in Cancún: Autopsy of a Fiasco Foretold," *CounterPunch* (20 September 2003); on suicide among farmers, see Luis Hernandez Navarro, "Mr. Lee Kyung Hae," *Food First* (23 September 2003), available at www.foodfirst.org.

4. Quang Duc and Biggs quotations and historical information on self-immolation from Michael Biggs, "Protest by Self-Immolation, 1963–2002," in *Making Sense of Suicide Missions,* ed. Diego Gambetta (Oxford: Oxford University Press, 2005), quotations from 25 and 8 of the manuscript version; for an overview of global suicides, see Sheryl Gay Stolberg, "War, Murder and Suicide: A Year's Toll Is 1.6 Million," *New York Times* (3 October 2002), A12.

5. Stephen Lucas, *Portents of Rebellion: Rhetoric and Revolution in Philadelphia, 1765–1776* (Philadelphia: Temple University Press, 1976), 32.

6. Kurt Campbell, "Globalization at War," *Washington Post* (22 October 2001); Steven Staples, "How Globalization Promotes War," available in poster form from United for Peace and Justice.

7. Thomas Barnett, excerpt from *The Pentagon's New Map* (New York: Putnam's Sons, 2004) in *Esquire* (March 2003), pages 2 and 4 of the printout from www.esquire.com.

8. See Benjamin Barber, *Jihad vs. McWorld: How Globalism and Tribalism Are Reshaping the World* (New York: Ballantine, 1995), and M. Lane Bruner, "Global Governance and the Critical Public," *Rhetoric and Public Affairs* 6, no. 4 (2003): 687–708, quotation from 698; Timothy Mitchell, "McJihad: Islam in the U.S. Global Order," *Social Text* 20, no. 4 (Winter 2002): 1–18; *National Security Strategy of the United States*

(Washington, DC: White House, September 2002), 31, emphasis added, hereafter cited in the text as *NSSUS.*

9. Walden Bello and Aileen Kwa, "The Stalemate in the WTO, An Update on Global Trends," CorpWatch (11 June 2003).

10. William Greider, *One World, Ready or Not: The Manic Logic of Global Capitalism* (New York: Simon and Schuster, 1997), 11.

11. Malcolm Waters, *Globalization,* 2nd ed. (London: Routledge, 2001), 125–126; Ernest Mandel, *Late Capitalism,* trans. Joris De Bres (1972; London: Verso, 1987); and Fredric Jameson, *Postmodernism: or, The Cultural Logic of Late Capitalism* (Durham, NC: Duke University Press, 1991); we turn to Debord below.

12. Karl Marx, *The Communist Manifesto* (1848; New York: Norton, 1988), 58, 61; and see Mandel, *Late Capitalism,* 44–74.

13. Monthly cost of $3.9 billion cited in David Firestone and Thom Shanker, "War's Cost Brings Democratic Anger," *New York Times* (11 July 2003), A1, 8; five-year estimate cited in Sue Pleming, "U.S. Senators Say Five Years in Iraq Likely," Reuters (30 June 2003), downloaded from the Information Clearing House at www.informationclearinghouse.info; Andrew Natsios, "Iraq: From Mass Graves to Better Life," speech, Washington Foreign Press Center (17 March 2004), downloaded from USAID.

14. The figure of sixteen million starving Iraqis is from James Meek and Rory McCarthy, "Invading Troops Will Have to Feed 16M Iraqis, Warn Aid Agencies," *Guardian* (20 March 2003); UN and malnutrition information from Michael Slackman, "Aid Agencies Fear a Humanitarian Disaster in Iraq," *Los Angeles Times* (18 March 2003), A4; the overall cost estimate from "The Price We Pay," *New York Times* (15 February 2003), A31; reparations figures from Kenneth Katzman, *Iraq: Weapons Programs, U.N. Requirements, and U.S. Policy* (issue brief for Congress prepared by the Foreign Affairs, Defense, and Trade Division of the Congressional Research Service) (Washington, DC: Library of Congress, 16 April 2003), 10, and David Teather, "Jobs for the Boys: The Reconstruction Billions," *Guardian* (15 April 2003).

15. For the overarching figure of $675 billion, see the calculations, including the cost of interest on all borrowed monies, at www.costofwar.com; other estimated costs from "Price We Pay"; for specific reconstruction figures, see chapter 4; "Iraq and Beyond," *Nation* (7 April 2003), 3.

16. Budgetary figures from Firestone and Shanker, "War's Cost Brings Democratic Anger," A8; by comparison, see the military expenses detailed in the *National Defense Authorization Act for Fiscal Year 2004,* HR 1588 (signed by the president 24 November 2004), available online at www.cbo.gov; Jennifer Beeson and Deborah Weinstein, *The President's Fiscal Year 2005 Budget: Slamming the Door Shut on Opportunity for All Americans* (Washington, DC: Coalition on Human Needs, March 2004), 5.

17. Patrick Tyler, "Panel Faults Bush on War Costs and Risks," *New York Times* (12 March 2003), A11; CBO cited and Hagel quoted in Jim Lobe, "Bush Faces Rising Skepticism about 'Morning After' Plans," *Inter Press Service* (13 March 2003), downloaded from CommonDreams; Edmund L. Andrews, "Bush Aides Say Budget Deficit Will Rise Again," *New York Times* (26 January 2005), A1, 12; for more war cost

information see Richard Stevenson, "Delaying Talk about the Cost of War," *New York Times* (23 March 2003), A24, and Carl Hulse, "Democrats Step up Attacks on Iraq War," *New York Times* (25 September 2003), A10.

18. Lawrence Lindsey's estimate quoted in Bob Davis, "Bush Economic Aide Says Cost of Iraq War May Top $100 Billion," *Wall Street Journal* (16 September 2002), A1; William Nordhaus, "The Economic Consequences of a War with Iraq," in *War with Iraq: Costs, Consequences, and Alternatives,* ed. Carl Kaysen, Steven Miller, Martin Malin, William Nordhaus, and John Steinbruner (Cambridge, MA: American Academy of Arts and Letters, 2002), table 2, p. 55, and table 7, p. 77.

19. McClellan's shuffling comments from the White House daily press briefing of 16 September 2002 are available from the White House.

20. Ellen Meiksins Wood, *Empire of Capital* (London: Verso, 2003), 134.

21. David Harvey, *The New Imperialism* (Oxford: Oxford University Press, 2003), 27, 29, 48; and see Peter Gowan, *The Global Gamble: Washington's Faustian Bid for World Dominance* (London: Verso, 1999), 60–100.

22. Chalmers Johnson, *Blowback: The Costs and Consequences of American Empire* (New York: Owl, 2000), 27; for a devastating analysis of how this trade-off ruins local economies and local cultures, see ibid., 34–64.

23. Harvey, *New Imperialism,* 41; for a concise history of some of these economic and political trajectories, see David Harvey, *The Condition of Postmodernity* (London: Blackwell, 1990), 121–200.

24. Wood, *Empire of Capital,* 139.

25. Eric Hobsbawm, *The Age of Empire, 1875–1914* (1987; New York: Vintage, 1989), 54, 67; Greider, *One World Ready or Not,* 363–365; for analyses of fascism from the fusing-of-economic-and-state perspective offered here, see Stephen Hartnett, "The Ideologies and Semiotics of Fascism: Analyzing Pound's *Cantos* 12–15," *boundary 2* 20, no. 1 (Spring 1993): 65–93, and Nicos Poulantzas, *Fascism and Dictatorship: The Third International and the Problem of Fascism* (London: New Left, 1974); on the possible relationships among states and globalization, see Waters, *Globalization,* 123–159.

26. Harvey, *New Imperialism,* 59; for a chilling rendering of this thesis, see Peter Dale Scott, *Drugs, Oil, and War: The U.S. in Afghanistan, Colombia, and Indochina* (New York: Rowman and Littlefield, 2003).

27. Harvey, *New Imperialism,* 74.

28. We are condensing a vast amount of historical material here; for an overview of the fifteenth through eighteenth centuries, see Fernand Braudel, *Civilization and Capitalism, 15th–18th Century, Vol. 1, The Structures of Everyday Life,* trans. Sian Reynolds (1979; New York: Harper, 1981) and *Civilization and Capitalism, 15th–18th Century, Vol. 2, The Wheels of Commerce,* trans. Sian Reynolds (1979; New York: Harper, 1981)—quotation from vol. 2, p. 544; on Grotius, see Wood, *Empire of Capital,* 68–72; for the nineteenth century see Eric Hobsbawm, *The Age of Capital, 1848–1875* (1975; New York: Vintage, 1996) and *Age of Empire;* for a case study of our claims regarding the roles of modernity and race as explanations for economic and state expansion see Stephen Hartnett, *Democratic Dissent and the Cultural Fictions of Antebellum America* (Champaign: University of Illinois Press, 2002), 40–131.

29. Karl Marx, *Capital, A Critique of Political Economy*, vol. 1, trans. Ben Fowkes (1867; New York: Vintage, 1977), 165.

30. Guy Debord, *The Society of the Spectacle*, trans. Donald Nicholson-Smith (1967; New York: Zone, 2004), no. 68, pp. 44–45.

31. Debord, *Spectacle*, no. 5, p. 13, no. 64, p. 42; for a magisterial attempt to prove this claim via case studies of contemporary art, film, architecture, and literature, see Jameson, *Postmodernism*.

32. Emory H. Woodard IV and Natalia Gridina, *Media in the Home: The Fifth Annual Survey of Parents and Children* (Washington, DC: Annenberg Public Policy Center, 2000), available at www.annenbergpublicpolicycenter.org, statistics on pages 16, 19, 17 of the printout; *Trade and Foreign Investment Opportunities in Iraq*, created by the Coalition Provisional Authority, no date and no page numbers, archived online at www.cpa-iraq/economy/investment_roadshow.pdf.

33. Ibid., n.p.

34. Ralph Waldo Emerson, "The American Scholar" (1837), in *Selected Essays* (New York: Penguin, 1985), 84; for more detailed explanations of the transformations noted here, see Stuart Blumin, *The Emergence of the Middle Class: Social Experience in the American City, 1760–1900* (Cambridge: Cambridge University Press, 1989); Richard Brown, *Modernization: The Transformation of American Life, 1600–1865* (New York: Hill and Wang, 1976); Christopher Clark, "Household Economy, Market Exchange, and the Rise of Capitalism in the Connecticut Valley, 1800–1860," *Journal of Social History* 13, no. 2 (Winter 1979): 169–189; Jonathan Prude, *The Coming of Industrial Order: Town and Factory Life in Rural Massachusetts, 1810–1860* (Cambridge: Cambridge University Press, 1983); and Winifred Rothenberg, "The Emergence of a Capital Market in Rural Massachusetts, 1730–1838," *Journal of Economic History* 45, no. 4 (December 1985): 781–808.

35. Marx, *Communist Manifesto*, 61, 70—note that these two paragraphs are modified from Hartnett, *Democratic Dissent*, 134.

36. Debord, *Society of the Spectacle*, no. 12, p. 15; on the use of television as a political weapon during the 1991 Gulf War, what he calls "the first war ever orchestrated for television," see Douglas Kellner, *The Persian Gulf TV War* (Boulder, CO: Westview Press, 1992), quotation from 110.

37. Waters, *Globalization*, 44; Eric Hobsbawm, *The Age of Revolution, 1789–1848* (1962; New York: Vintage, 1996), 202, 204; Hobsbawm, *Age of Empire*, 15.

38. Braudel, *Wheels of Commerce*, 493; Joseph Stiglitz, *Globalization and Its Discontents* (New York: Norton, 2002), 5.

39. Benjamin Friedman, "Globalization: Stiglitz's Case," *New York Review of Books* (15 August 2002), pages 1 and 2 of the printout available online.

40. Peter Singer, *One World: The Ethics of Globalization* (New Haven, CT: Yale University Press, 2002), 77–105, quotation from 85.

41. Xavier Sala-i-Martin, "The Disturbing 'Rise' of Global Income Inequality," *National Bureau of Economic Research*, Working Paper No. 8904 (April 2002), 33, 32, 300–500 million less poor from his abstract; Sala-i-Martin and his Columbia colleagues' documents are available at www.socialanalysis.org; for more on globalization and AIDS see United Nations Development Programme, *HDR*, 27–28.

42. Branko Milanovic, "It Won't Fit on a Bumper Sticker: Determining the Benefits of Globalization Is a Complex Story," Center for American Progress (27 February 2004); World Bank, "Key Indicators: Regional Data from the *2004 World Development Indicators* database" (13 April 2004), available online; World Bank, *World Development Report 2004: Making Services Work for Poor People* (Washington, DC: World Bank, 2004).

43. Mike Davis, "Planet of Slums," *New Left Review* 26 (March/April 2004): 5–34, cited passages from 6, 9, 13; headline from Amy Waldman, "Low-Tech or High, Jobs Are Scarce in India's Boom," *New York Times* (6 May 2004), A3.

44. Davis, "Planet of Slums," 17–18, 21, 22.

45. United Nations Development Programme, *HDR*, 13, 16.

46. Ibid., 9, 34–35.

47. Tony Blair, "Tony Blair's Speech to the U.S. Congress," reprinted in *Guardian* (18 July 2003).

48. Waters, *Globalization*, 217; note that our definition attempts to circumvent much confusion in the literature regarding these terms; Greider's *One World Ready or Not* and Mandel's *Late Capitalism*, for example, both use multinational to describe— eloquently and impressively—what we are calling here TNCs; other critics use the terms interchangeably.

49. Along these lines, see Mahmood Monshipouri, Claude Welch, Jr., and Evan Kennedy, "Multinational Corporations and the Ethics of Global Responsibility: Problems and Possibilities," *Human Rights Quarterly* 25, no. 4 (2003): 965–989.

50. Dates of nineteenth-century U.S. troop landings from Howard Zinn, *A People's History of the United States* (New York: Perennial, 1980), 291; sales figures from ibid., 293; for a concise history of the rise of U.S. capitalism to global dimensions during the periods addressed herein, see Alfred E. Eckes, Jr., and Thomas W. Zeiler, *Globalization and the American Century* (Cambridge: Cambridge University Press, 2003); for the European side, see Hobsbawm, *Age of Empire*, 34–83; for essays considering the histories of U.S. imperialism, see *Cultures of United States Imperialism*, ed. Amy Kaplan and Donald Pease (Durham, NC: Duke University Press, 1993).

51. Figures from Rolfe and Danim's *The Multi-National Corporations in the World Economy* (1970) and quotation from Simmonds and Brown's *World Business* (1969) both from Mandel, *Late Capitalism*, 321–322.

52. Most quotations here from Waters, *Globalization*, 47; but also see Joshua Karliner, *The Corporate Planet: Ecology and Politics in an Age of Globalization* (Sierra Club, 1997), as quoted here from excerpts printed by CorpWatch as "Globalization 101."

53. Greider, *One World Ready or Not*, 21, 22; Joseph Nye, *The Paradox of American Power: Why The World's Only Superpower Can't Go It Alone* (Oxford: Oxford University Press, 2002), 34; and see Mandel, *Late Capitalism*, 343–376; Jan Nederveen Pieterse, "Globalization and Emancipation: From Local Empowerment to Global Reform," in *Globalization and the Politics of Resistance*, ed. Barry K. Gills (London: Palgrave, 2001), 189–206, quotation from 190.

54. Trade figures from U.S. Census Bureau, "Foreign Trade Statistics," last accessed 22 April 2004.

55. Walden Bello, *The Future in the Balance: Essays on Globalization and Resistance* (Oakland, CA: Food First Books, 2001), 4; and see the special edition on the World Bank and IMF, "More World Less Bank," *New Internationalist* 365 (March 2004); for a history of the World Bank, see Catherine Caufield, *Masters of Illusion: The World Bank and the Poverty of Nations* (New York: Holt, 1996).

56. Michael Moore, *World without Walls: Freedom, Development, Free Trade, and Global Governance* (London: Cambridge University Press, 2003), 26–27, 42; there is a vast literature describing both these original intentions and their ultimate betrayal—for introductions, see Stiglitz, *Globalization and Its Discontents*, the special edition of *New Internationalist* and Caufield's *Masters of Illusion* (both cited above in note 55), and the materials offered by 50 Years Is Enough; for a critique of Moore's arguments, see Robert Wade, "The Ringmaster of Doha," *New Left Review* 25 (January/February 2004): 146–152.

57. Fred Block, *The Origins of International Economic Disorder: A Study of United States International Monetary Policy from World War II to the Present* (Berkeley and Los Angeles: University of California Press, 1977), 37, 90.

58. Leo Panitch, "The New Imperial State," *New Left Review* (April 2000): 5–20, quotation from 7; World Bank, *World Development Report 2004;* for two glowing accounts of recent World Bank achievements see Elizabeth Becker, "A World Bank Mission to Bring Help to the Poor," *New York Times* (22 April 2004), W1, 7, and "World Bank Meetings to Focus on Poverty," *New York Times* (24 April 2004), B2.

59. Stiglitz, *Globalization and Its Discontents,* 47, loan amount from 148; on the ways such development projects harm local communities in India, see Arundhati Roy, *War Talk* (Cambridge, MA: South End Press, 2003), 9–15; on the IMF's ongoing difficulties in Argentina, see "Which Is the Victim?" *Economist* (6 March 2004), 63–64.

60. Quotation from Global Exchange, "World Bank/IMF Questions"; and see the materials available from 50 Years Is Enough and Cheryl Payer, *The Debt Trap: The IMF and Third World* (Markham, Ontario: Penguin Books, 1974).

61. For a history of Bretton Woods, see Caufield, *Masters of Illusion,* 39–54; for the WTO's own history and an overview of it procedures, see World Trade Organization, *Understanding the WTO,* 3rd ed. (Geneva, Switzerland: World Trade Organization, Sept. 2003), available online; Moore, *World without Walls,* 55; for the IMF's history and its key figures from Bretton Woods onward, see Paul Blustein, *The Chastening: Inside the Crisis That Rocked the Global Financial System and Humbled the IMF* (New York: PublicAffairs, 2001), 36–50.

62. Moore, *World without Walls,* 157, 128; Singer, *One World,* 51–105 on the WTO, quotation from 75.

63. Bello, *Future in the Balance,* 45.

64. For an overview of the Washington Consensus, see Stiglitz, *Globalization and Its Discontents,* 53–88, and Davis, "Planet of Slums," 17–23.

65. George Bush, "President Outlines U.S. Plan to Help World's Poor" (22 March 2002) and "President Proposes $5 Billion Plan to Help Developing Nations" (14 March 2002), both available from the White House.

66. Stiglitz, *Globalization and Its Discontents,* 22; voting numbers from Global

Exchange, "World Bank/IMF Questions"; on the relationships between these global institutions and their host nations, see "How the IMF and the World Bank Undermine Democracy and Erode Human Rights" (September 2001), available from Global Exchange; note that the G-7 became the G-8 when Russia was invited to join.

67. The WTO's day-by-day rendering of the Cancún meeting is available from its Web site.

68. Editorial, "The Cancún Failure," *New York Times* (19 September 2003), A24; Elizabeth Becker, "Brazil Stands Firm Amid Criticism on Trade Talks," *New York Times* (26 September 2003), A1; editorial, "Trade Talks: The Right Next Step," *Business Week* (29 September 2003), 152; Mark Weisbrot and Todd Tucker, "The Cancún Ministerial and the U.S.: Public Perception, Reality, and Implications," Center for Economic and Policy Research (6 February 2004); also see Walden Bello and Aileen Kwa, "The Stalemate in the WTO: An Update on Global Trends," CorpWatch (14 April 2003).

69. Dean Baker and Mark Weisbrot, "False Promises on Trade," Center for Economic and Policy Research (24 July 2003); on President Lula's leadership of the G-20, see Perry Anderson, "The Cardoso Legacy," *London Review of Books* (12 December 2002), 18–22; and see "Sour Subsidies," *Economist* (17 April 2004), 11.

70. For an extended version of this thesis, see Paulo S. Wrobel, "A Free Trade Area of the Americas in 2005?" *International Affairs* 74, no. 3 (July 1998): 547–561.

71. Council of Economic Advisers, *Economic Report of the President* (Washington, DC: GPO, 2004), 21, 14.

72. On congressional approval of NAFTA see Helen Dewar, "NAFTA Wins Final Congressional Test," *Washington Post* (21 November 1993), A1, and Anthony DePalma, "World Markets: Mexico, Post-NAFTA, Gets More Respect," *New York Times* (21 November 1993), Sec. 3, p. 15; on its signing into law see Bill Clinton, "Remarks on Signing the North American Free Trade Agreement Implementation Act" (8 December 1993), downloaded from *Weekly Compilation of Presidential Documents,* available through the GPO at www.frwebgate.access.gpo.gov; quotation from Celia Dugger, "Report Finds Fewer Benefits for Mexico in NAFTA," *New York Times* (18 November 2003), A9.

73. Office of the United States Trade Representative, *NAFTA: A Decade of Strengthening Dynamic Relationships* (2004), available on-line from the USTR.

74. Robert Zoellick's speech of 26 July 2001 is available from the USTR; on the utopian impulses behind such neoliberalism, see John Gray, *False Dawn: The Delusions of Global Capitalism* (New York: New Press, 1998), 100–132; following President Bush's reelection in November 2004, Zoellick was promoted to deputy secretary of state; for one account of his actions in that capacity, see Joel Binkley, "A Closer Look at Falluja Finds Rebuilding Is Slow, *New York Times* (14 April 2005), A10.

75. Historical trajectory of Mexico's slide from Martin Hart-Landsberg, "Challenging the Neo-Liberal Myths: A Critical Look at the Mexican Experience," *Monthly Review* (December 2002), and "How the IMF and the World Bank Undermine Democracy and Erode Human Rights" (September 2001), available from Global Exchange; banking information from John Lyons, "Mexico's Foreign Banks Grow Uneasy," *Wall Street Journal* (17 March 2004), A15.

76. Gray, *False Dawn*, 50; for a Mexican success story see David Luhnow, "As Jobs Move East, Plants in Mexico Retool to Compete," *Wall Street Journal* (5 March 2004); as a counterpoint, see Joel Millman, "Latin America Grows Poorer Despite Boom," *Wall Street Journal* (12 April 2004).

77. Information and statistics on NAFTA from Bello, *Future in the Balance*, 137; Public Citizen's Global Trade Watch (2001), available at www.citizen.org; Robert Scott, "The High Price of 'Free' Trade," Economic Policy Institute, briefing paper 147 (November 2003); Sarah Anderson and John Cavanagh, "Factsheet on the NAFTA Record: A 10th Anniversary Assessment," report from the Institute of Policy Studies (18 December 2003); Jeff Faux et al., *NAFTA at Seven: Its Impact on Workers in All Three Nations* (Washington, DC: Economic Policy Institute, April 2001); and Sarah Anderson and John Cavanagh, "Rethinking the NAFTA Record," Institute for Policy Studies (August 2002); Bernie Sanders, "The View from Mexico," *Nation* (2 February 2004), 13.

78. For examples of these provisions, see articles 1126-2A and 1121-2B, both subsets of Chapter 11, available in the full text version of the NAFTA bylaws posted at the NAFTA Web site; Echeverria quoted in Adam Liptak, "NAFTA Tribunals Stir U.S. Worries," *New York Times* (18 April 2004), A1, 19; on Chapter 11 suits, see the September 2001 report by Public Citizen's Global Trade Watch, *NAFTA Chapter 11 Investor-to-State Cases: Bankrupting Democracy* (Washington, DC: Public Citizen, 2001); and see Tamara Straus, "Trading Democracy" (15 January 2002), posted to AlterNet.

79. Christian Weller, "Ignore at Your Own Peril: The Manufacturing Crisis in Perspective," Center for American Progress (6 February 2004), available at www.americanprogress.org; on the NAFTA/deficit relationship, see Robert Scott, "The High Price of Free Trade," *EPI Briefing Paper* (Washington, DC: Economic Policy Institute, November 2003), and Scott, "Trade Picture," Economic Policy Institute (13 February 2004).

80. Maquiladora quotation from Hart-Landsberg, "Challenging the Neo-Liberal Myths"; on the wider phenomenon of how women bear the brunt of globalization, see Oxfam's *Trading Away Our Rights: Women Working in Global Supply Chains* (Oxford: Oxfam International, 2004).

81. The information in this paragraph comes from the IADB Web site.

82. Nadia Martinez, "Destabilizing Investments in the Americas II: The Inter-American Development Bank's Fossil Fuel Financing: 1992–2004," Sustainable Energy and Economy Network (March 2004).

83. See ibid.; World Bank energy funding figure from Joshua Karliner, "The World Bank and Corporations Fact Sheet" (1 December 1997), downloaded from CorpWatch; Jim Valette and Steve Kretzmann, *The Energy Tug of War: The Winners and Losers of World Bank Fossil Fuel Finance* (Washington, DC: Sustainable Energy and Economy Network/Institute for Policy Studies, April 2004); and Steve Kretzmann, "Extractive Industries Rarely Alleviate Poverty: Calls for End to Support for Coal and Oil," *Economic Justice News* 7.1 (January 2004), 1–14.

84. Ecuador example from Kenny Bruno, "Indigenous Struggle in Ecuador Becomes a 'Cause beyond Control,'" *Earth Rights International* (13 March 2003), available from CorpWatch; Exxon-Mobil story from Jane Perlez, "Indonesia's Guerrilla

War Puts Exxon under Seige," *New York Times* (14 July 2003), A3; Shell information from Mahmood Monshipouri, Claude E. Welch, Jr., and Evan T. Kennedy, "Multinational Corporations and the Ethics of Global Responsibility: Problems and Possibilities," *Human Rights Quarterly* 25, no. 4 (2003): 965–989; and see Arvind Ganesan and Alex Vines, "Engine of War: Resources, Greed, and the Predatory State," Human Rights Watch (January 2004).

85. The thirty-four countries included in the FTAA are Antigua and Barbuda, Argentina, Bahamas, Barbados, Belize, Bolivia, Brazil, Canada, Chile, Colombia, Costa Rica, Dominica, Dominican Republic, Ecuador, El Salvador, Grenada, Guatemala, Guyana, Haiti, Honduras, Jamaica, Mexico, Nicaragua, Panama, Paraguay, Peru, St. Kitts and Nevis, St. Lucia, St. Vincent and the Grenadines, Surinam, Trinidad and Tobago, United States, Uruguay, and Venezuela (see "Countries" at the FTAA Web site); Latin America facts from a UN report cited in Oxfam International, "From Cancún to Miami: The FTAA Threat to Development in the Hemisphere," Oxfam Briefing Note (November 2003); U.S. figures from Beeson and Weinstein, *President's Fiscal Year 2005 Budget.*

86. Ministerial Declaration of Denver, *Summit of the Americas Trade Ministerial Joint Declaration* (30 June 1995), available from the FTAA Web site; and see Global Exchange, "Frequently Asked Questions about the Free Trade Area of the Americas" (no date), available at www.tradewatch.org, and the "Global Trade Watch" division of Public Citizen.

87. The NAFTA Web site contains some documents on this case; ADM information from NAFTA Tribunal, *First Partial Award of August 7, 2002* (Washington, DC: International Centre For Settlement of Investment Suits, 2002), 74, available by following the State Department's links to Methanex documents at www.state.gov; for a catalogue of MTBE statistics and testimonials gathered by the Illinois Corn Collective, see the materials at www.ilcorn.org; for a revealing analysis of the political machinations driving ADM and assorted California and Bush administration officials in this case, see "'The Nature of Things to Come': ADM and Bush Administration Unite in Ethanol and High Fructose Corn Syrup Scam," *Agribusiness Examiner* 123 (July 2001), available at www.electricarrow.com; and see William Greider, "The Right and U.S. Trade Law: Invalidating the 20th Century," *Nation* (15 October 2001).

88. "Looking South, North, or Both?" *Economist* (7 February 2004), 35, 36; Public Citizen, "The Little Known Threat to U.S. Wheat, Soy, Beef, Produce Growers of President Bush's Request for Fast Track for FTAA/NAFTA Expansion" (n.d.); quotation on fudging from Paul Blustein, "Trade Talks End in Vague Accord," *Washington Post* (21 November 2003), E1; and see the Oxfam Briefing Note, *From Cancún to Miami: The FTAA Threat to Development in the Hemisphere* (London: Oxfam, 2003).

89. Sarah Anderson and John Cavanagh, "From Seattle to Miami," *Nation* (1 December 2003), accessed online; Anderson, "Cardoso Legacy," 20; see also William Greider and Kenneth Rapoza, "Lula Raises the Stakes," *Nation* (1 December 2003), 11–17; poll figures from Steven Kull, *Americans on Globalization, Trade, and Farm Subsidies,* Program on International Policy Attitudes (22 January 2004), available at www.pipa.org, page 11 on our printout.

90. Elizabeth Becker, "Bush Signs Trade Pact with Singapore, A Wartime Ally," *New York Times* (7 May 2003), C4; Thomas Carothers, "Punishing Democracy," *Washington Post* (19 May 2003), A19; on proposed FTAs with Bahrain, Morocco, Chile, and others, see the materials posted at the home page of the USTR; for a critique of these bilateral FTAs, see Jagdish Bhagwati, *Free Trade Today* (Princeton, NJ: Princeton University Press, 2002), 107ff.

91. Helen Dewar, "Senate Approves Chile, Singapore Trade Pacts: U.S. Hopes to Create Global Network," *Washington Post* (2 August 2003), E2; Dan Morgan, "House GOP Clears Way for Free-Trade Deals," *Washington Post* (24 July, 2003), A5; President Bush, "Remarks by the President in Signing Ceremony for Chile and Singapore Free Trade Agreements" (3 September 2003), available from the White House.

92. On Nixon's economic warfare against Chile, see Seymour Hersh, *The Price of Power: Kissinger in the Nixon White House* (New York: Summit, 1983), 294–295; Caufield, *Masters of Illusion,* 203–207; and Payer, *Debt Trap,* 184–199.

93. On the pending FTAs with Bahrain, Morocco, and other Middle Eastern states, see the materials at the USTR Web page.

94. Michael Hardt and Antonio Negri, *Empire* (Cambridge, MA: Harvard University Press, 2000), 283; on the underdevelopment thesis, see Immanuel Wallerstein, *The Capitalist World Economy* (Cambridge: Cambridge University Press, 1979), and Andre Gunder Frank, *Capitalism and Underdevelopment in Latin America* (New York: Monthly Review, 1967).

95. Jesse Gordon, "The Sweat behind the Shirt," *Nation* (3–10 September 2001), 14; for a blistering firsthand account of the terrible working conditions fueling such circuitous production processes, including in an Indonesian sweatshop making clothes for the Gap, see John Pilger, *The New Rulers of the World* (London: Verso, 2002), 15–44.

96. Gap Inc., *Social Responsibility Report* (2003), p. 40 of the printout available online at www.gapinc.com.

97. "Gap's Code of Conduct vs. Carmencita Abad's Reality" is available online from Global Exchange; Naomi Klein, *No Logo* (New York: Picador, 2002), 211, 434.

98. Giovanni Arrighi, "Hegemony Unravelling—I," *New Left Review* 32 (March/April 2005): 23–80, quotation from 39–40.

99. Public Citizen's Global Trade Watch, *Down on the Farm: NAFTA's Seven-Years War on Farmers and Ranchers in Alabama* (Washington, DC: Public Citizen, 2001), 1, 2, 3.

100. On peanut butter tariffs see William Finnegan, "The Economics of Empire," *Harper's Magazine* (May 2003), 41–54, 50–51 in particular.

101. Greider, *One World,* 202. Consider the case of Trenton, New Jersey, which features many bridges spanning the Delaware River linking New Jersey to Pennsylvania. An old railroad bridge proclaims in large letters welded to its girding that what "Trenton Makes, the World Takes"—once true in the heady manufacturing days of a post–World War II boom, that claim is now false. For a grueling representation of this thesis, see Global Trade Watch, *What Really Happened at the WTO Qatar Ministerial: U.S. Concedes Everything and Gets What?* (Washington, DC: Public Citizen, 2002).

102. Harvey, *Condition of Postmodernity*, 163, 297, 332; for a report on the effects of this new economy, see Sarah Anderson and John Cavanagh, *Bearing the Burden: The Impact of Global Financial Crisis on Workers* (Washington, DC: Institute for Policy Studies, 2000).

103. Harvey, *New Imperialism*, 61, and see 168–169 on bank failures as a result of these processes; Don DeLillo, *Underworld* (New York: Scribner, 1997), 786.

104. Mandel, *Late Capitalism*, 372; and see Harvey, *Postmodernity*, 164, figure 2.12.

105. Caufield, *Masters of Illusion*, 134; Forbes quoted in Eduardo Porter, "Good Times Roll On for Developing World, for Now," *New York Times* (17 February 2004); UN, *HDR*, table 1.4, p. 31; Joyce Kolko, *Restructuring the World Economy* (New York: Pantheon, 1988), 201–213 and 263–277 on debt, quotation from 267.

106. Amin quoted in Mandel, *Late Capitalism*, 346; second quotation from ibid., 66; details of this process are offered in Frank, *Capitalism and Underdevelopment*.

107. See John Nolan, "Emerging Market Debt and Vulture Hedge Funds" (29 September 2001), Special Policy Report 3 of the Financial Policy Forum Derivatives Study Center, available at www.financial-policy.org; Randall Dodd, "Sovereign Debt Restructuring," *Financier* 9 (2002), 1–5.

108. European Network on Debt and Development, "Investors Twist Debt Laws, Exploit Impoverished Countries," *Economic Justice News* 4, no. 4 (January 2002), available from 50 Years Is Enough; and see Nolan, "Emerging Market Debt," and Dodd, "Sovereign Debt Restructuring."

109. Information in this paragraph from the sources in notes 107 and 108 above.

110. Panama figures from Nolan, "Emerging Market Debt," 11; list of nations from "Vulture Fund Investors Make Millions out of Third World Debt Crisis," posted by the Jubilee 2000 Coalition at www.jubilee2000uk.org, accessed 22 May 2003, and Matthew Cookson, "Hedge Funds Push Peru to Brink," *Socialist Worker* (n.d.), accessed at www.socialistworker.co.uk.

111. Harvey, *New Imperialism*, 118, 87, 122, 66–67, 73, 122, 134, and see 181 and 185.

112. Stiglitz, *Globalization and Its Discontents*, 99, 148, 153, 150, 171.

113. Genoa Summit participants (including G-8 nations and representatives from the African Development Bank, Asian Development Bank, European Bank for Reconstruction and Development, IADB, IMF, and World Bank), *A Globalized Market—Opportunities and Risks for the Poor: Global Poverty Report 2001* (Genoa, Italy: G8 Genoa Summit, July 2001): quotation from p. 8 on the printout available via the World Bank; for newspaper coverage of the Genoa Summit and protests surrounding it, see Michael R. Gordon, "Genoa Summit Meeting: News Analysis," *New York Times* (23 July 2001), A1; David E. Sanger, "Genoa Summit Meeting: The Overview," *New York Times* (23 July 2001), A1; Sarah Delaney, "One Man's Mission to Genoa," *Washington Post* (22 July 2001), A1; Michael M. Phillips, "As G-8 Leaders Meet, US Has Pivotal Role in Leading Recovery," *Wall Street Journal* (20 July 2001), A1.

114. For enthusiastic "how to" articles advising investors to strike while the vulture fund market is hot, see Phyllis Berman, "The Life of a Vulture," *Forbes* (30 September 2002), accessed online at www.forbes.com; Lewis Branham, "Vulture Investing," *Business Week* (27 August 2001), and Emily Thornton and Roger Crockett,

"Bonds: The Day of the Vulture," *Business Week* (3 June 2002), both accessed at www.businessweek.com; on vulture funds at play in Argentina, see Pamela Drucker-man, "Frustrated Argentine Bond Holders Try Suing," *Wall Street Journal* (23 March 2003), accessed at www.bradynet.com.

115. Greider, *One World*, 23 (emphasis added), locations of the twenty biggest multinationals in note 9, p. 475.

116. UN report cited in Warren Hoge, "Latin America Losing Hope in Democracy, Report Says," *New York Times* (22 April 2004), A3; for an extended version of this thesis see Amy Chua, *World on Fire: How Exporting Free Market Democracy Breeds Ethnic Hatred and Global Instability* (New York: Anchor Books, 2004), and see our comments on Chua in chapter 2.

117. Kevin Bales, *Disposable People: New Slavery in the Global Economy* (Berkeley and Los Angeles: University of California Press, 1999), 236.

118. DeLillo, *Underworld*, 63.

119. See Greider, *One World*, 105–106, 111; although he treats the subject of auto manufacturing more as symbol than as economic dilemma, see Thomas Friedman, *The Lexus and the Olive Tree: Understanding Globalization* (New York: Farrar, Straus, Giroux, 1999).

120. Figures from Danny Hakim, "U.S. Automakers Improve Efficiency, but Some Troubling Figures Remain," *New York Times* (19 June 2003), C1, 5, and "G.M.'s Net Income Declined 30% in Second Quarter," *New York Times* (18 July 2003), C2.

121. Greider, *One World*, 12.

122. No alarms from "Thai Factory Fire's 200 Victims Were Locked Inside, Guard Says," *New York Times* (12 May 1993), A2; blocked exits from "Arson or Neglect Suspected in Thai Fire That Killed 209," *New York Times* (14 May 1993), A5; wages from Haider Rizvi, "Toying with Workers," *Multinational Monitor* 17, no. 4 (April 1996): 1; code fines from "A Decade of Scandalous Neglect," *Human Rights for Workers* 8, no. 5 (May 2003): 1; for a shamefully happy profile of Dennis H. S. Ting, the chairman of Kader, see Rone Tempest, "For Asian Tycoons, Success Is a Matter of Seizing Initiative," *Los Angeles Times* (7 June 1994), 14; and see the comments in Greider, *One World*, 337–338.

123. "Are Global Companies Too Mobile for Workers' Good?" *Economist* (27 March 2004), 77.

124. David Miller, "That Fire Wasn't Fault of U.S. Toy Makers," *New York Times* (31 December 1994), A24.

125. Mitchell Koss, "Why Attack Iraq? Because We Can," *Los Angeles Times* (30 March 2003), M3.

Chapter 4

1. Andrew Natsios, "Iraq and Afghanistan: Accomplishments and Next Steps," 30 September 2003 testimony before the House Appropriations Foreign Operations Subcommittee, available from the home page of USAID by following the links to "testimony."

2. Weekly CPA "Reports," USAID "Updates," and U.S. Embassy documents all

available online; quotation from unnamed military report in Seymour Hersh, "The Gray Zone," *New Yorker* (24 May 2004), 41.

3. Tariq Ali, "Re-Colonizing Iraq," *New Left Review* 21 (May/June 2003): 5–19, quotation from 9; David Harvey, *The New Imperialism* (London: Verso, 2003), 41; and see Pratap Chatterjee, "The Thief of Baghdad," AlterNet (23 August 2004).

4. Conversation recorded in Mark Danner, "Torture and Truth," *New York Review of Books* (10 June 2004), 46–50, quotation from 46.

5. J. A. Hobson, *Imperialism: A Study* (New York: James Pott and Company, 1902), 51; Antonia Juhasz, "Capitalism Gone Wild," *Tikkun* 19, no. 1 (2004): 19–22; Adams quoted in Jeff Gerth and Don Van Natta, Jr., "Halliburton Contracts in Iraq: The Struggle to Manage Costs," *New York Times* (29 December 2003), A1; Parenti, *Freedom*, 50.

6. Robert D. Kaplan, "A Post-Saddam Scenario," *Atlantic Monthly* (November 2002), accessed at www.theatlantic.com.

7. Ayad Allawi, "A New Beginning," *Washington Post* (27 June 2004), B7; President Bush and Prime Minister Blair, speaking in Istanbul, Turkey (28 June 2004), transcript available from the White House.

8. See James Glanz and Erik Eckholm, "Reality Intrudes on Promises in Rebuilding of Iraq," *New York Times* (30 June 2004), A1.

9. Coalition Provisional Authority, Program Management Office, "PMO Name Change, but Business as Usual," press release (28 June 2004), available at www. rebuilding-iraq.net; Ellen McCarthy, "Immunity Provision Extended for U.S. Firms with Reconstruction Contracts," *Washington Post* (29 June 2004), A18; "ludicrous" from "A Secretive Transfer in Iraq," *New York Times* (29 June 2004), A26; closing quotation from Antonia Juhasz, "The Handover That Wasn't," Foreign Policy in Focus (20 July 2004); on Allawi, see Peter W. Galbraith, "Iraq: The Bungled Transition," *New York Review of Books* (23 September 2004), 70–74, and Jon Lee Anderson, "A Man of Shadows: Can Iyad Allawi Hold Iraq Together?" *New Yorker* (24/31 January 2005), 56–69; on Bremer's one hundred orders, see Rajiv Chandrasekaran and Walter Pincus, "U.S. Edicts Curb Power of Iraq's Leadership," *Washington Post* (27 June 2004), A1.

10. Secretary Powell's remarks from "Negroponte Sworn In as Ambassador to Iraq" (23 June 2004), available under "Speeches" at the U.S. Embassy's Web site, www.iraq.usembassy.gov; quotations from Stephen Kinzer, "Our Man in Honduras," *New York Review of Books* (20 September, 2001); biographical details from "Biography of Ambassador John D. Negroponte," available online from the U.S. embassy, and Serge Schmemann, "After a Delay, U.S. Envoy Starts in Post at the U.N.," *New York Times* (20 September 2001), A7.

11. Wil Haygood, "Ambassador with Big Portfolio," *Washington Post* (21 June 2004), C1; Ben Ehrenreich, "Other Officials' Profiles," Foreign Policy in Focus (9 November 2001); for a stunning analysis of the patterns of denial and deception marshaled in the 1987 congressional hearings regarding the Iran-Contra scandal, see Michael Lynch and David Bogen, *The Spectacle of History: Speech, Text, and Memory at the Iran-Contra Hearings* (Durham, NC: Duke University Press, 1995).

12. See Gary Cohn and Ginger Thompson, "Unearthed: Fatal Secrets," *Balti-*

more Sun (11 June 1995), A1; Ginger Thompson and Gary Cohn, "Torturers' Confessions," *Baltimore Sun* (13 June 1995), A1; Thompson and Cohn, "A Carefully Crafted Deception," *Baltimore Sun* (18 June 1995), A1; and Cohn and Thompson, "A Survivor Tells Her Story," *Baltimore Sun* (15 June 1995), A1.

13. Quotation from Michael Dobbs, "Papers Illustrate Negroponte's Contra Role," *Washington Post* (12 April 2005), A4; also see Walter Pincus, "Nominations of Negroponte, Deputy Backed," *Washington Post* (15 April 2005), A6; Scott Shane, "Negroponte Confirmed as Director of National Intelligence," *New York Times* (22 April 2005); A19, and Julian Borger, "Rough Ride for Bush Nominee: Negroponte Tried to Undermine Central America Peace Process," *Guardian* (13 April 2005), 15; on the challenges facing Negroponte in his new role, see Walter Pincus, "Rumsfeld Memo on Intelligence Criticized," *Washington Post* (8 April 2005), A4.

14. NIE information from Douglas Jehl, "U.S. Intelligence Shows Pessimism on Iraq's Future," *New York Times* (16 September 2004), A1, 13; Dana Priest and Thomas Ricks, "Growing Pessimism on Iraq," *Washington Post* (29 September 2004), A1.

15. See Khalid Al-Ansary and Ian Fisher, "70 Are Killed by Car Bomber in an Iraqi City," *New York Times* (29 July 2004), A1, 6; Edward Wong, "Bombing Kills 47 at Police Station in Iraqi Capital," *New York Times* (15 September 2004), A1, 12; Edward Wong, "Ambush Kills 50 Iraq Soldiers Execution Style," *New York Times* (25 October 2004), A1, 11; and Karl Vick, "Insurgents Massacre 49 Iraqi Recruits," *Washington Post* (25 October 2004), A1.

16. Adriana Lins de Albuquerque, Michael O'Hanlon, and Amy Unikewicz, "The State of Iraq: An Update," *New York Times* (10 August 2004), A23; Eric Schmitt and Thom Shanker, "Estimates by U.S. See More Rebels with More Funds," *New York Times* (22 October 2004), A1, 8; see also Jeffrey Gettleman, "Anti-U.S. Outrage Unites a Growing Iraqi Resistance," *New York Times* (11 April 2004), A11.

17. Robert Burns and Erik Eckholm, "In Western Iraq, Fundamentalists Hold U.S. at Bay," *New York Times* (29 August 2004), A1, 8; Eric Schmitt and Steven Weisman, "U.S. Conceding Rebels Control Regions of Iraq," *New York Times* (8 September 2004), A1, 12; "triangle of death" from James Glanz and Edward Wong, "U.S. Is Expanding Iraqi Offensive in Violent Area," *New York Times* (24 November 2004), A1, 12; and see Edward Wong, "U.S. Airstrikes Kill Dozens as Guerilla Attacks Rage," *New York Times* (18 September 2004), A5; on U.S. strikes along the Iraq/Syria border, see James Glanz, "U.S. Troops Begin New Offensive in Iraqi Desert near Syrian Border," *New York Times* (18 June 2005), A6.

18. Center for Strategic and International Studies, *Progress or Peril? Measuring Iraq's Reconstruction* (Washington, DC: CSIS, 2004); on the escalation of postwar violent crime in Baghdad, see Phyllis Bennis and the IPS Task Force, *A Failed Transition: The Mounting Costs of the Iraq War* (Washington, DC: Institute for Policy Studies, 2004), 36; higher figure from Christian Parenti, "The Rough Guide to Baghdad," *Nation* (19 July 2004), 13–18, "at least six hundred" from 14; David Remnick, "Comment: Escalation," *New Yorker* (19 April 2004), 63–64, quotation from 64.

19. See Les Roberts, Riyadh Lafta, Richard Garfield, Jamal Khudhairi, and Gilbert Burnham, "Mortality Before and After the 2003 Invasion of Iraq: Cluster Sample Survey," *Lancet* 364 (2004): 1857–1864; Elisabeth Rosenthal, "Study Puts Iraqi

Deaths of Civilians at 100,000," *New York Times* (28 October 2004), A8; and see Lila Guterman, "Researchers Who Rushed into Print a Study of Iraqi Civilian Deaths Now Wonder Why It Was Ignored," *Chronicle of Higher Education* (27 January 2005), accessed online.

20. Thom Shanker, "Iraq Commanders Warn That Delays in Civil Projects Undermine Military Mission," *New York Times* (17 October 2004), A13; James Glanz, "In Iraq Chaos, Uphill Struggle to Bring Power," *New York Times* (17 October 2004), A1, 13; Sabrina Tavernise, "Scores Are Dead after Violence Spreads in Iraq," *New York Times* (23 September 2004), A1, 10; James Glanz and Thom Shanker, "Reports in Iraq Show Attacks in Most Areas," *New York Times* (29 September 2004), A1, 10; Dexter Filkins, "2 Car Bombings in Iraq Kill 41, Many Children," *New York Times* (1 October 2004), A1, 6; Edward Wong, "At Least 26 Dead as 3 Car Bombs Explode in Iraq," *New York Times* (5 October 2004), A1, 10; Parenti, "Rough Guide to Baghdad," 13; and see George Packer, "Letter from Baghdad: Caught in the Crossfire," *New Yorker* (17 May 2004).

21. Rahul Mahajan, "Witnessing Fallujah's 'Ceasefire,'" AlterNet (12 April 2004); Dahr Jamail, "Sarajevo on the Euphrates: An Eyewitness Account from Inside the US Siege of Falluja," *Nation* (12 April 2004, online only); Mahajan's and Jamail's accounts have been corroborated in Parenti, *Freedom,* 138; quotation from Jeffrey Gettleman, "Marines Use Low-Tech Skill to Kill 100 in Urban Battle," *New York Times* (15 April 2004), A8; Edward Wong, "Provincial Capital near Falluja Is Rapidly Slipping into Chaos," *New York Times* (28 October 2004), A1, 12; on the battles in Najaf, see Dexter Filkins, "Agreement by U.S. and Rebels to End Fighting in Najaf," *New York Times* (28 May 2004), A1, 10; John F. Burns, "Marines Pushing Deeper into City Held By Shiites," *New York Times* (8 August, 2004), A1, 6; and Alex Berenson, "After the Siege, A City of Ruins, Its Dead Rotting," *New York Times* (28 August, 2004), A1, 7; James Glanz, "Roadside Bomb Kills 5 Marines," *New York Times* (11 June 2005), A7.

22. Information on Allawi's speech from Dana Milbank and Mike Allen, "U.S. Effort Aims to Improve Opinions about Iraq Conflict," *Washington Post* (30 September 2004), A20; Susan Watkins, "Vichy on the Tigris," *New Left Review* 28 (July/ August 2004).

23. Quotation from Dexter Filkins, "Defying Threats, Millions of Iraqis Flock to Polls," *New York Times* (31 January 2005), A1; the front page of this issue also included stories on the elections by David Sanger, John F. Burns, and Thom Shanker and Eric Schmitt; stories covered all of pages A8–A11; for a sobering commentary, see Bob Herbert, "Acts of Bravery," ibid., A25; Mark Danner, "Iraq: The Real Election," *New York Review of Books* (28 April 2005), 41–44, quotation and 260 attacks from p. 44; for a profile of al-Jaafari, see Robert Worth, "Shiite Leader Named Premier to End 2 Months of Wrangling," *New York Times* (8 April 2005), A1, 6; on the delayed constitution, see Jonathan Finer and Salih Saif Aldin, "Bush Urges End to Impasse over Writing of Iraq Constitution," *Washington Post* (14 June 2005), A16.

24. Elisabeth Bumiller, "Canadians to Bid on Iraq Projects," *New York Times* (14 January 2004), A1, 11; Mark Tran, "UK Firm Wins Big Iraq Contract," *Guardian* (12 March 2004); see also Terry Macalister, "Leak Reveals Ministers' Fears over Iraqi

Contracts," *Guardian* (13 February 2004); "China Wins Contract in Iraq," Al Jazeera (10 February 2004); Mary Fitzgerald, "U.S. Contracts to British Firm Sparks Irish American Protest," *Washington Post* (9 August 2004), A13; Douglas Jehl, "Pentagon Bars Three Nations from Iraq Bids," *New York Times* (10 December 2003), A1, 12; and Erin E. Arvedlund, "Allies Angered at Exclusion from Bidding," *New York Times* (11 December 2003), A20; for updates on Iraq reconstruction contracts, see www. ContractWatch.org and the materials posted by the U.S. Program Management Office at www.rebuilding-iraq.net and by USAID at www.usaid.gov/iraq/activities. html#contracts.

25. General Accounting Office, *Rebuilding Iraq: Fiscal Year 2003 Contract Award Procedures and Management Challenges,* report number GAO-04-605 (June 2004), available at www.gao.gov/cgi-bin/getrpt?gao-04-605; David M. Walker, "Testimony before the Committee on Government Reform" (15 June 2004), available at www.gao.gov/news.items/d04869t.pdf; Reuters, "U.S. Audit Finds Fraud in Iraq," *New York Times* (31 July 2004), A6.

26. NBS information from Douglas Jehl, "Insiders' New Firm Consults on Iraq," *New York Times* (30 September 2003), A1, 11; see NBS's materials at www. newbridgestrategies.com.

27. Figures from Leslie Wayne, "Pentagon Spends without Bids, a Study Finds," *New York Times* (30 September 2004), C1, 6.

28. Libyan penalties reported in Laura Peterson, "Kellogg, Brown and Root (Halliburton)," an April 2004 Windfalls of War report posted by the Center for Public Integrity; Jane Mayer, "Contract Sport: What Did the Vice-President Do for Halliburton?" *New Yorker* (16/23 February 2004), 80–91; Dan Baum, "Nation Builders for Hire," *New York Times Magazine* (22 June 2003), 32ff., quotation from 35.

29. Pratap Chatterjee, "Halliburton Makes a Killing on Iraq War," downloaded from CorpWatch on 31 March 2003; Haiti and Somalia figures from George Anders and Susan Warren, "Military Service: For Halliburton, Uncle Sam Brings Lumps, Steady Profits," *Wall Street Journal* (19 January 2004); Balkans figure from Peterson, "Kellogg, Brown and Root (Halliburton)"; and see Terry Jones, "Welcome Aboard the Iraqi Gravy Train," *Observer* (13 April 2003); Don Van Natta, Jr., "High Payments to Halliburton for Fuel in Iraq," *New York Times* (10 December 2003), A1, 12; Erik Eckholm, "Halliburton May Have Been Pressured by U.S. Diplomats to Disregard High Fuel Prices," *New York Times* (11 November 2004), A14; and Erik Eckholm, "Pentagon Auditor Urges Army to Withhold Some Payments to Halliburton," *New York Times* (25 November 2004), A14.

30. Mayer, "Contract Sport," 84; Erik Eckholm, "White House Officials and Cheney Aide Approved Halliburton Contract in Iraq, Pentagon Says," *New York Times* (14 June 2004), A6; Waxman's letter is available through the House Committee on Government Reform Minority Office, http://www.house.gov/reform/min/index.htm; on Halliburton's history of doing studies for the Pentagon, starting when Cheney was secretary of defense during the first Bush administration, see Kevin Phillips, *American Dynasty: Aristocracy, Fortune, and the Politics of Deceit in the House of Bush* (New York: Viking/Penguin, 2004), 171–177.

31. Jeff Danziger, political cartoon from the Tribune Media Services, printed in

"Views: A Portfolio from Around the Nation," *New York Times* (13 April 2003), sec. 4, p. 4; and see the wonderful collections of such cartoons compiled each month by the *Funny Times,* available at www.funnytimes.com.

32. Fiscal year 2003 figure from World Policy Institute, "Iraq: Contractors Are Cashing in on the War on Terror" (24 February 2004); contract estimate from Russell Gold, "Halliburton Sustains a Loss on $1.1 Billion Asbestos Charge," *Wall Street Journal* (30 January 2004), A2; ID/IQ from Laura Peterson, "Outsourcing Government" (30 October 2003), posted by the Center for Public Integrity; on the relationship between the Bush administration and the contractors, see Edmund L. Andrews and Elizabeth Becker, "Bush Got $500,000 from Companies That Got Contracts, Study Finds," *New York Times* (31 October 2003), A8.

33. Lesar quoted in Anders and Warren, "Military Service," and see "Rebuilding Iraq—The Contractors" (28 April 2003), posted by Open Secrets, the Center for Responsive Politics; on the accusation that Halliburton was overcharging for fuel, see Douglas Jehl, "Evidence Is Cited of Overcharging in Iraq Contract," *New York Times* (12 December 2003), A1, 16; Richard Stevenson, "Bush Sees Need for Repayment if Fee Was High," *New York Times* (13 December 2003), A1, 8.

34. See Elizabeth Becker and Richard Oppel, Jr., "U.S. Gives Bechtel a Major Contract in Rebuilding Iraq," *New York Times* (18 April 2003), A1, B7; David Baker, "USA: Bechtel to Rebuild Iraq," *San Francisco Chronicle* (18 April 2003), posted at CorpWatch; cost overruns from Andrew Gumbel, "Well-Connected and Wealthy: Bechtel Wins from Saddam's Demise," *Independent* (UK) (24 May 2003), available at CommonDreams; San Onofre information from Pratap Chatterjee, "Bechtel's Nuclear Nightmare," CorpWatch (1 May 2003) and "Bechtel's Friends in High Places," CorpWatch (24 April 2003); water information from "About Bechtel—A Letter to the Iraqi People from Representatives of Cochabamba, Bolivia" (30 May 2003), available at Occupation Watch; for film footage of the struggle in Cochabamba, see the award-winning documentary *The Corporation* (Big Media, 2004).

35. See "Public Citizen Calls for Investigation of Bechtel's Failure to Provide Adequate Water Services to Iraqi Citizens" (5 April 2004), posted by Occupation Watch; Natsios, "Iraq and Afghanistan: Accomplishments and Next Steps," 4; school investigations reported in Pratap Chatterjee and Herbert Docena, "Iraq: Occupation, Inc." (4 February 2004), a CorpWatch report posted at WarProfiteers; and see Laura Peterson, "Bechtel Group, Inc.," an April 2004 Windfalls of War report posted at the Center for Public Integrity, and Becker and Oppel, "U.S. Gives Bechtel a Major Contract."

36. Teaching claims made in USAID's "Iraq Reconstruction and Humanitarian Relief" Weekly Update #30, 4 May 2004, page 7 of the printout available from USAID; we suspect that readers with expertise in the update's other areas of alleged accomplishment, including medicine, electricity, and sewage, will find similarly dubious claims.

37. Creative Associates information from Neela Banerjee, "Poverty and Turmoil Cripple Iraq Schools, Driving Students from Learning to Labor," *New York Times* (14 March 2004), sec. 1, p. 8; on the difficulty of reconstructing schools and hospitals,

see Joel Brinkley, "American Companies Rebuilding Iraq Find They Are Having to Start from the Ground Up," *New York Times* (22 February 2004), A10.

38. Figures in this bulleted list from the 29 April 2004 Windfalls of War report, "Contractors: Iraq," posted by the Center for Public Integrity; for up-to-date contract information go to the Web page of USAID and follow the links to "Assistance for Iraq"; also see the Coalition Provisional Authority's Program Management Office, "Another Contract in Place to Continue Construction in Iraq," press release (2 April 2004); USAID, "Financial Summary FY 2003–2005," *Iraq Reconstruction Weekly Update* (28 October 2004), available at www.usaid.gov/iraq; Center for Public Integrity, "Post-War Contractors Ranked by Total Contract Value in Iraq and Afghanistan," Windfalls of War (4 November 2004); and see Diana Henriques, "The Catch-22 of Iraq Contracts," *New York Times* (12 April 2003), C1, 3; Stephen Pizzo, "Divvying up the Iraq Pie," posted to AlterNet on 3 October 2003; and Edmund L. Andrews and Neela Banerjee, "Companies Get Few Days to Offer Bids on Iraq Work," *New York Times* (19 October 2003), A12.

39. See Becker and Oppel, "U.S. Gives Bechtel a Major Contract in Rebuilding Iraq."

40. James Glanz, "Western Ways Force Iraq to Trim Water Projects," *New York Times* (26 July 2004), A8; Erik Eckholm, "Winning Hearts of Iraqis with a Sewage Pipeline," *New York Times* (5 September 2004), A12; Glanz and Eckholm, "Reality Intrudes on Promises in Rebuilding of Iraq"; Reuters, "A Plan to Switch Money to Make Iraq Safer," *New York Times* (14 September 2004), A12; 30 percent for security from James Glanz, "Iraqis Warn That U.S. Plan to Divert Billions to Security Could Cut Off Crucial Services," *New York Times* (21 September 2004), A10.

41. Christian Parenti, "Fables of Reconstruction," *Nation* (18 August 2004); Erik Eckholm, "Rebuilding of Basra Progresses, But It's Harder Than Expected," *New York Times* (19 January 2005), A1, 8; on the outbreak of water-borne health threats, including hepatitis E and diarrhea, see James Glanz, "Hepatitis Outbreak Laid to Water and Sewage Failures," *New York Times* (25 September 2004), A6; and see Pratap Chatterjee, "Democracy by the Dollars," CorpWatch (19 July 2004); on the gap between contract allocations and projects completed, including notice that as of October 2004 only $2 million has been spent on health care (compared to $22 million on "administrative expenses," $34 million on "private sector employment development," $623 on "security and law enforcement," and so on), see Erik Eckholm, "U.S. Is Pressing Donors to Speed Aid for Iraq," *New York Times* (12 October 2004), A12.

42. Cook quoted in Elizabeth Becker, "U.S. Business Will Get Role in Rebuilding Occupied Iraq," *New York Times* (18 March 2003), A16; Yaseen quoted in Arianna Eunjung Cha, "$1.9 Billion of Iraq's Money Goes to U.S. Contractors," *Washington Post* (4 August 2004), A1.

43. Naomi Klein, "Bomb before You Buy: What Is Being Proposed in Iraq Is Not Reconstruction but Robbery," *Guardian* (14 April 2003) (also available as "Privatization in Disguise," *Nation* [28 April 2003], 14).

44. On Nour's disputed contract see Christopher Cooper, "Pentagon Delays

Iraq Contracts Amid Protests," *Wall Street Journal* (2 March 2004), and Mary Pat Flaherty and Jackie Spinner, "Missteps Led to Canceled Iraq Contract," *Washington Post* (11 March 2004), A22.

45. Bribery figure from Neil King, Jr., "Halliburton Tells the Pentagon Workers Took Iraq-Deal Kickbacks," *Wall Street Journal* (23 January 2004); Michael Janofsky, "Halliburton Turns Over $6.3 Million to Government," *New York Times* (24 January 2004), A9; Greenhouse information from Erik Eckholm, "A Top U.S. Contracting Official for the Army Calls for an Inquiry in the Halliburton Case," *New York Times* (25 October 2004), A11, and "A Watchdog Follows the Money in Iraq," *New York Times* (15 November 2004), A6.

46. Tamimi information from Neil King, Jr. "Halliburton Hits Snafu on Billing in Kuwait," *Wall Street Journal* (2 February 2004); $700 million contract "discrepancy" from T. Christian Miller, "Contract Flaws in Iraq Cited," *Los Angeles Times* (11 March 2004), A1; Waxman quotation from Susan Warren, "Leading the News: Halliburton Wins New Iraq Contract Amid U.S. Probe," *Wall Street Journal* (19 January 2004); and see Gerth and Van Natta, "Halliburton Contracts in Iraq," A1, 8, and Eric Schmitt, "Halliburton Stops Billing U.S. for Meals Served to Troops," *New York Times* (17 February 2004), A8.

47. On Halliburton's recommendation to hire Altanmia, see Mayer, "Contract Sport"; statistics on Altanmia from Glenn R. Simpson and Chip Cummins, "At Center of Halliburton Uproar, Little-Known Kuwaiti Company," *Wall Street Journal* (14 April 2004), A1; and see King, "Halliburton Hits Snafu on Billing in Kuwait."

48. Andrew Higgins, "As It Wields Power Abroad, U.S. Outsources Law and Order Work," *Wall Street Journal* (2 February 2004); and see Andre Verloy, "DynCorp (Computer Sciences Corp.)," an April 2004 Windfalls of War report posted at the Center for Public Integrity; for a report claiming that such outsourcing extends to international mercenaries and "former commandos" trained in Augusto Pinochet's Chilean military and hired by the U.S. firm Blackwater, see Jonathan Franklin, "US Contractor Recruits Guards for Iraq in Chile," *Guardian* (5 March 2004).

49. On Executive Order 12600 and its abuse by U.S. contractors in Iraq, see Daniel Politi, "Cutting through the Fog of War" (30 October 2003), posted by the Center for Public Integrity; for a startling visual example of how this law enables MNCs to shield their practices from full scrutiny by redacting damaging information, see Erik Eckholm, "Now You See It: An Audit of KBR," *New York Times* (20 March 2005), sec. 4, p. 4.

50. On SSA's contract see "Contractors: Iraq"; on its antilabor history and the CPA's law banning unions, see David Bacon, "Umm Qasr—From National Pride to War Booty," a 15 December 2003 CorpWatch Report, available at WarProfiteers; for more on the notion of privatizing the empire, see Peterson, "Outsourcing Government," and Juhasz, "Capitalism Gone Wild"; on union busting and wage controls in occupied Iraq, see Pratap Chatterjee, *Iraq, Inc.: A Profitable Occupation* (New York: Seven Stories, 2004), 16–19.

51. Chalmers Johnson, *The Sorrows of Empire: Militarism, Secrecy, and the End of the Republic* (New York: Metropolitan Books, 2004), 58, 118, 285.

52. William Greider, *Fortress America: The American Military and the Consequences of Peace* (New York: Public Affairs, 1998), 11–12.

53. See Tim Weiner, "Air Superiority at $258 Million a Pop," *New York Times* (27 October 2004), C1, 8; Johnson reports in *Sorrows of Empire* (p. 57) that as much as 25 percent of annual Pentagon weapons expenditures land in California, making that state by far the largest recipient of MIC largesse; *9/11 Commission Report: Final Report of the National Commission on Terrorist Attacks upon the United States* (New York: W. W. Norton, 2003), 95; on Lockheed's military contracts generally, see Geoffrey Gray, "Inside Lockheed's $250 Billion Pentagon Connection," CorpWatch (19 March 2003); Leslie Wayne, "A Well-Kept Military Secret," *New York Times* (16 February 2003), Sec. 3, p. 1; Anne Marie Squeo, "Dollars for the Defense," *Wall Street Journal* (14 October 2002), R6.

54. John Tirman, *Spoils of War: The Human Costs of America's Arms Trade* (New York: Free Press, 1997), 281; Center for Defense Information, "Post Sept. 11 Arms Sales and Military Aid Demonstrate Dangerous Trend" (18 June 2003), available at www.cdi.org.

55. P. W. Singer, *Corporate Warriors: The Rise of the Privatized Military Industry* (Ithaca, NY: Cornell University Press, 2003), see 171–174 and 230–233 on PMFs as destabilizing forces, quotation from 13; similar concerns are raised in Greider, *Fortress America*, 108–110; Lord Camden quotation from his 5 March 1776 speech in Parliament, as reprinted in *The Spirit of 'Seventy-Six: The Story of the American Revolution as Told by Participants*, ed. Henry Steele Commager and Richard B. Morris (1958; New York: Da Capo, 1995), 267—and see Ben Franklin's typically brilliant satire on the subject in ibid., 269–270; Tom Barry, "The U.S. Power Complex: What's New," *Foreign Policy in Focus Special Report #20* (Washington, DC: Foreign Policy in Focus, November 2002), 7, 8.

56. Singer, *Corporate Warriors*, 145.

57. See Louis Uchitelle and John Markoff, "Terrorbusters, Inc.: The Rise of the Homeland Security-Industrial-Complex," *New York Times* (17 October 2004), sec. 3, pp. 1, 8; Christopher Lee, "Northrop Grumman Gets $175 Million Pact," *Washington Post* (8 July 2004), A15.

58. Enron's shady tax dealings from David Cay Johnston, "Wall St. Banks Said to Help Enron Devise Tax Shelters," *New York Times* (14 February 2002), C1, 6; for an overview of the problem, see "Pigs, Pay, and Power," *Economist* (28 June 2003), 7–9; on the dilemmas of accounting in a postmodern age, see Michael J. Shapiro, "Globalization and the Politics of Discourse," *Social Text* 17, no. 3 (1999): 111–129, especially 115–116; and see Vijay Prashad, *Fat Cats and Running Dogs: The Enron Stage of Capitalism* (Monroe, ME: Common Courage Press, 2003) and Robin Blackburn, "The Enron Debacle and the Pension Crisis," *New Left Review* 14 (2002): 26–51.

59. Cheney's Cayman Islands subterfuge reported in Peterson, "Kellogg, Brown and Root (Halliburton)"; Carrie Johnson, "Halliburton to Pay $7.5 Million to Settle Probe," *Wall Street Journal* (4 August 2004), E1; Elizabeth Becker, "Halliburton Is Faulted by Pentagon Accounts," *New York Times* (12 August 2004), A10; on what he calls the "Enron-Halliburton Administration," see Phillips, *American Dynasty*, 149–

177; and see Bob Herbert, "The Halliburton Shuffle," *New York Times* (30 Jan. 2004), A21, where he reports that in addition to the Cayman Islands, Halliburton subsidiaries use Bermuda, Trinidad and Tobago, Panama, Liechtenstein, and Vanuatu as tax shelters.

60. For a list of the crony capitalists listed here, see "The Scandal Sheet," *Economist* (28 June 2003), 7—stories on them can be found on an almost daily basis in the business pages of any credible newspaper; MCI information from Anne Marie Squeo, "Inquiry into Boeing Raises the Question of Corporation Size in Federal Discipline," *Wall Street Journal* (10 June 2003); on the Adelphia case and other trials, see Andrew Ross Sorkin, "Adelphia Is Next in Parade of Fraud Trials," *New York Times* (23 February 2004), C1, 6; and Roger Lowenstein, "The Company They Kept," *New York Times Magazine* (1 February 2004), 21.

61. Boeing information from Squeo, "Inquiry into Boeing"; Arianna Huffington, "The Enronization of Public Policy," *Tom Paine.Common Sense* (12 June 2003); World Policy Institute, "Iraq: Contractors Are Cashing in on the War on Terror" (24 February 2004), posted at WarProfiteers; Leslie Wayne, "Defense Dept. Delays Action on Boeing Jets Till November," *New York Times* (26 May 2004), C1, 4; idem., "Documents Show Extent of Lobbying by Boeing," *New York Times* (2 September 2003), C1, 7; Richard Oppel, Jr., "Pentagon Says Changes Are Needed in Boeing Jet Deal," *New York Times* (10 April 2004), A9; Leslie Wayne, "Ex-Pentagon Official Gets 9 Months for Conspiring to Favor Boeing," *New York Times* (20 October 2004), B1, 13; Pentagon e-mail quoted in R. Jeffrey Smith, "E-Mails Detail Air Force Push for Boeing Deal," *Washington Post* (7 June 2005), A1.

62. Matt Kelley, "Ten U.S. Contractors in Iraq Penalized $300 Million in Past Four Years" (26 April 2004), Associated Press/*Newsday*, posted by Occupation Watch.

63. William D. Hartung, "Making Money on Terrorism," *Nation* (23 February 2004), 19.

64. On CB see Erik Eckholm, "Memos Warned of Billing Fraud by Firm in Iraq," *New York Times* (23 October 2004), A1, 8; regarding the court battle over CB and its alleged improprieties, see *United States ex Rel. DRC, Inc., et al., v. Custer Battles, LLC, et al.*, CV-04-199-A, U.S. District Court, Eastern District of Virginia, downloaded from ContractWatch.

65. Secretary of Defense Rumsfeld, speaking 15 November 2002, quoted in "Rumsfeld: It Would Be a Short War," downloaded from CBS News, available at www.cbsnews.com.

66. On the court cases, see "Bush Administration Ramping Up Secrecy Fight; In Unprecedented Move, Solicitor General to Defend Cheney in GAO Lawsuit over Energy Task Force Records," press release from the National Resource Defense Council (16 September 2002), downloaded from CommonDreams.

67. On the futile appeal see "Judges Question Bid to Halt Lawsuit on Cheney," *New York Times* (18 April 2003), A12; vacation and recusal information from Sharon Little, "Scalia's Flippant Refusal Prompts Petition for Recusal," *Public Citizen News* (March/April 2004), 1, 13, and Stephen Gillers, "Scalia's Flawed Judgment," *Nation* (19 April 2004), 21; excerpt from Michael Janofsky, "Scalia Refusing to Take Himself

off Cheney Case," *New York Times* (19 March 2004), A1, 15; verbal jousting from Adam Liptak, "In Re Scalia the Outspoken v. Scalia the Reserved," *New York Times* (2 May 2004), A1, 27.

68. William Safire, "Behind Closed Doors," *New York Times* (17 December 2003), A35.

69. Light quoted in Peterson, "Outsourcing Government."

70. Larry Makinson, "Outsourcing the Pentagon: Who Benefits from the Politics and Economics of National Security?" Center for Public Integrity (29 September 2004); on contractors in the Iraq war, see Dan Guttman, "The Shadow Pentagon: Private Contractors Play a Huge Role in Basic Government Work—Mostly Out of Public View," Center for Public Integrity (29 September 2004); for the case of mistaken identity, see Alex Knott, "The Pentagon's $200 Million Shingle: Defense Data Shows Billions in Mistakes and Mislabeled Contracts," Center for Public Integrity (29 September 2004).

71. The bulk of information in this paragraph is from Jim Vallette, Steve Kretzmann, and Daphne Wysham, *Crude Vision: How Oil Interests Obscured U.S. Government Focus on Chemical Weapons Use by Saddam Hussein* (Washington, DC: Institute for Policy Studies, 2003); quotation from Richard Oppel, Jr., "Company Has Ties in Washington, and to Iraq," *New York Times* (18 April 2003), B7; and see Frida Berrigan, "Oil and Democracy Don't Mix," *In These Times* (2 February 2004).

72. For copies of recently declassified exchanges between Bechtel representatives and Iraqi officials regarding the proposed pipeline, follow the links at the Sustainable Energy and Economy Network; see also the "Saddam Hussein Sourcebook: Declassified Secrets from the U.S.-Iraq Relationship," a collection of documents available online from the National Security Archive.

73. Lutz Kleveman, "Oil and the New 'Great Game,'" *Nation* (16 February 2004), 11–14, quotation from 13; on the U.S. push for control of Caspian oil reserves, see Johnson, *Sorrows of Empire*, 167–185; on one recent blockbuster oil deal in the region, see Heather Timmons, "Oil Majors Agree to Develop a Big Kazakh Field," *New York Times* (26 February 2004), W1, 7; on the links between oil and authoritarian regimes, see Marina Ottaway, "Tyranny's Full Tank," *New York Times* (31 March 2005), A27.

74. Greg Palast, "Secret U.S. Plans for Iraq Oil," posted to AlterNet on 17 March 2005; Aijaz Ahmad, "Imperialism of Our Time," in *The New Imperial Challenge*, ed. Leo Panitch and Colin Leys, 43–62, quotation from 58 (London: Palgrave, 2003); Michael Klare, "Blood for Oil: The Bush-Cheney Energy Strategy," *New Imperial Challenge*, 166–185, quotations from 169, 175; and see the claims along these lines in Michael Ruppert, *Crossing the Rubicon: The Decline of the American Empire and the End of the Age of Oil* (Gabiola Islands, British Columbia, Canada: New Society, 2004), and Peter Dale Scott, *Drugs, Oil, and War: The United States in Afghanistan, Colombia, and Indochina* (New York: Rowman and Littlefield, 2003).

75. HRW quotations from "Uzbekistan: Rights Defenders Targeted after Massacre," 9 June 2005 press release, and "Uzbekistan: Andijan Crisis Aftermath," undated "Background Document," both posted at www.hrw.org; and see C. J. Chivers, "Rights Group Calls Deadly Uzbek Crackdown a 'Massacre,'" *New York Times* (8 June 2005), A4.

76. The 300,000 figure from ABC News 12/Associated Press, "Residents Take to the Streets" (14 December 2003), available at http://ablocal.go.com/wjrt/news/print_121403_AP_r2_arabamerican_celebrate.html; Gary Younge, "Under the Veil, Who's for Kerry?" *Nation* (8 November 2004), 15; Steven Gold, "Arab Americans in Detroit" (January 2001), downloaded from http://www.commurb.org/features-/sgold/detroit. html; CNN, "Arab-Americans Rally after Saddam Statue Toppled" (10 April 2003), downloaded from http://www.cnn.com/2003/US/midwest/04/09/sprj.irq.dearbon.rally.

77. For newspaper coverage of the Dearborn speech, see Amy Goldstein, "Bush Seeks Support of U.S. Arabs," *Washington Post* (29 April 2003), A12; Richard W. Stevenson, "Bush, Visiting Michigan, Promises All Iraqis a Voice in a New Government," *New York Times* (29 April 2003), A19.

78. George Bush, "President Discusses the Future of Iraq" (28 April 2003), Dearborn, Michigan, available from the White House.

79. Mitch Jeserich, "Banking on Empire" (4 February 2004), a CorpWatch report posted by WarProfiteers.

80. Jeserich quotation and Prins comments from ibid.; for more on the TBI see Kevin Baron, Neil Gordon, and Laura Peterson, "Contracts with Provisional Authorities," a 30 October 2003 Windfalls of War report posted at the Center for Public Integrity, and Chatterjee, *Iraq, Inc.,* 92–95; attacks on oil facilities for January and February 2005 from "Iraqi Oil Disaster," posted by TBRNews.org at www.tbrnews.org; on the Compensation Fund and the Development Fund for Iraq, see Abbas Alnasrawi, "Iraq's Odious Debt: Where Do We Go from Here?" *Middle East Economic Survey* 47, no. 13 (March 2004), posted by Occupation Watch; "crippled" from Edward Wong, "Showing Their Resolve, Rebels Mount Attacks in Northern and Central Iraq," *New York Times* (18 November 2004), A12; and see Wong, "Insurgents Blow Up an Iraqi Oil Pipeline," *New York Times* (3 November 2004), A6.

81. Bush, "President Discusses the Future of Iraq"; regarding the looting of Baghdad, see our comments in chapter 2.

82. Jonathan Schell, "Potemkin Government," *Nation* (25 October 2004), 10.

83. Quotations from unnumbered pages of *Trade and Foreign Investment Opportunities in Iraq,* produced by the CPA (n.d.) and posted at www.cpa-iraq.org/economy/investment_roadshow.pdf.

84. Duncan Kennedy, "Shock and Awe Meets Market Shock," *Boston Review* (October/November 2003), available at http://bostonreview.net.

85. Naomi Klein, "Baghdad Year Zero: Pillaging Iraq in Pursuit of Neocon Utopia," *Harper's* (September 2004).

86. Budget analysis from page 3 of the printout version of Sabri Zire Al-Saadi, "Iraq's Post-War Economy: A Critical Review" (5 April 2004), an article written for *Middle East Economic Survey* and available as posted by Occupation Watch; oil sales figures from Richard Stevenson, "The Struggle for Iraq: The Money; War Budget Request More Realistic but Still Uncertain," *New York Times* (9 September 2003), A10.

87. *Trade and Foreign Investment Opportunities in Iraq;* Cheney's "retirement

package" figure from Anders and Warren, "Military Service"; and note that the figure for Cheney's golden parachute is listed at $35 million in Peterson, "Kellogg, Brown and Root (Halliburton)."

88. L. Paul Bremer III, "Iraq Reconstruction Update Briefing with Ambassador Bremer" (26 September 2003), debt claim on 10, terror on 1, and exchange on 7–8 of the transcript downloaded from U.S. Department of Defense at www.defenselink.mil; for press coverage of Bremer's activities that day, see Dana Milbank, "Bremer Says Some Iraq Rebuilding Will Wait," *Washington Post* (27 September 2003), A18, Douglas Jehl, "Bremer Says 19 Qaeda Fighters Are in U.S. Custody in Iraq," *New York Times* (27 September 2003), A6, and Patrick E. Tyler, "Iraq Leaders Seek Greater Role Now in Running Nation," *New York Times* (27 September 2003), A1; on the status of Iraq's international debt, see Naomi Klein, "The Double Life of James Baker," *Nation* (1 November 2004), 13–20; 80 percent and IMF requirements from Craig S. Smith, "Major Creditors Agree to Cancel 80% of Iraq Debt," *New York Times* (22 November 2004), A1, 7.

89. See USAID, *A Year in Iraq* (Washington, DC: USAID, 2004)—among its many stunning rhetorical moves, this glossy propaganda pamphlet divides Iraqi history into the U.S.-driven present and "pre-liberation" times (p. 15).

90. Quotation from Russell Gold, "The Temps of War—Blue Collar Workers Ship Out for Iraq," *Wall Street Journal* (5 February 2004); DynCorp information from Higgins, "As It Wields Power Abroad, U.S. Outsources Law and Order Work"; Halliburton information from Simon Romero, "Halliburton, in Iraq for the Long Haul, Recruits Employees Eager for Work," *New York Times* (24 April 2004), B1, 14; note that the J. C. Penney store referred to here has alternately been called "a defunct Montgomery War store" (in Chatterjee, *Iraq, Inc.*, 25).

91. Jeffrey Marburg-Goodman, "USAID's Iraq Procurement Contracts: Insider's View," *Procurement Lawyer* 39, no. 1 (Fall 2003): 10–12, quotations from 10, 11.

Conclusion

1. W. H. Auden, "To Reinhold and Ursula Niebuhr," in *Nones* (London: Faber and Faber, 1952), unnumbered dedication page; like so many of his cold war compatriots, Auden lived in fear of "a crater whose blazing fury could not be fixed" ("In Praise of Limestone," p. 11)—that is, nuclear war; the bulk of the claims in our opening sentence are substantiated throughout this book; regarding the 2004 elections, which we have not addressed here, see Michael Powell and Peter Slevin, "Several Factors Contributed to 'Lost' Voters in Ohio," *Washington Post* (15 December 2004), A1.

2. Jed Esty observes in *A Shrinking Island: Modernism and National Culture in England* (Princeton, NJ: Princeton University Press, 2004) that Auden was among a group of writers who were committed to "existential male antiheroism in a world of corrupt politics and culture" and who forwarded a "historical sense of pervasive national decline" (p. 9).

3. Hannah Arendt, *The Origins of Totalitarianism* (1948; New York: Harcourt

Brace, 1976), xxiii, 313, 315, 317; Joan Didion, "Politics in the 'New Normal' America," *New York Review of Books* (21 October 2004), 64–73, quotation from 63; as Eric Hobsbawm argued in *The Age of Empire, 1875–1914* (New York: Vintage, 1987), "nationalism lent itself exceptionally well to expressing the collective resentments of people who could not explain their discontents precisely" (160); along these lines see Stephen Hartnett, "Ideologies and Semiotics of Fascism: Analyzing Pound's *Cantos* 12–15," *boundary 2* 20, no. 1 (1993): 65–93; for further analysis of the rise of mass-produced barbarism, see Max Horkheimer and Theodor Adorno, *Dialectic of Enlightenment,* trans. John Cumming (1944; New York: Continuum, 1999).

4. Arendt, *Origins of Totalitarianism,* 333, 445; for a U.S. version of this thesis, see Bertram Gross, *Friendly Fascism: The New Face of Power in America* (Boston: South End Press, 1980); for another echo between post-9/11 U.S. culture and prior modes of authoritarianism, consider the troubling rise of the notion of "homeland" to describe the nation (see Amy Kaplan, "Violent Belongings and the Question of Empire Today," *American Quarterly* 56, no. 1 [2004]: 1–18, 8–10 for her read of why "homeland" is a dangerous phrase).

5. *9/11 Commission Report: Final Report of the National Commission on Terrorist Attacks upon the United States* (New York: W. W. Norton, 2003), xv, and see 439–447 for details on the hearings; for a representative story of how the commission's open hearings aggravated Washington insiders, see Jim Rutenberg, "9/11 Panel Comments Freely (Some Critics Say Too Freely)," *New York Times* (15 April 2004), A1, 21; for a celebration of the panel's work, see Elizabeth Drew, "Pinning the Blame," *New York Review of Books* (23 September 2004), 6–12.

6. *9/11 Commission Report,* xvi; see our comments on President Bush and David Brooks from page 1.

7. Arendt, *Origins of Totalitarianism,* xxix, and see 310, 343; among its many staggering confessions, Khrushchev's speech (available online at www.trussel.com/hf/1956nk.htm) reveals that "of the 139 members and candidates of the party's Central Committee who were elected at the Seventeenth Congress, . . . 70 percent were arrested and shot!!"

8. *9/11 Commission Report,* 344.

9. Kenneth Burke, *Attitudes toward History,* 3rd ed. (1937; Berkeley and Los Angeles: University of California Press, 1989), 216, 225, 226; Chalmers Johnson, *Blowback: The Costs and Consequences of American Empire* (2000; New York: Metropolitan Books, 2001), xiii.

10. Peter Dale Scott, *Drugs, Oil, and War: The United States in Afghanistan, Colombia, and Indochina* (New York: Rowman and Littlefield, 2003); *Deep Politics and the Death of JFK* (Berkeley and Los Angeles: University of California Press, 1993); and, coauthored with Jonathan Marshall, *Cocaine Politics: Drugs, Armies, and the CIA in Central America* (Berkeley and Los Angeles: University of California Press, 1991); for appraisals of Scott's remarkable work, see Stephen John Hartnett, "Imperial Ideologies," *Journal of Communication* 45, no. 4 (Autumn 1995): 161–169, and "Four Meditations on the Search for Grace amidst Terror," *Text and Performance Quarterly* 19, no. 3 (Summer 1999): 196–216.

11. See the list of agencies in *9/11 Commission Report,* 407–408; quotations from

ibid., 350, 352; and see 335–336 for further evidence of similar bungling of information that may have led, if handled differently, to preventing 9/11; for more on Moussaoui, see Seymour Hersh, *Chain of Command: The Road from 9/11 to Abu Ghraib* (New York: Simon and Schuster, 2004), 103–120.

12. For coverage of the much-debated intelligence bill, see Nedra Pickler (Associated Press), "Bush Signs Intelligence Bill into Law," posted 17 December 2004 by www.washingtonpost.com.

13. Senator Robert Byrd, "Today I Weep for My Country," Senate speech of 19 March 2003, available from CommonDreams; Pew report cited in Christopher Marquis, "World's View of U.S. Sours after Iraq War, Poll Finds," *New York Times* (4 June 2003), A19; and see Richard Bernstein, "Foreign Views of U.S. Darken after Sept. 11," *New York Times* (11 September 2003), A1, 18; Steven Weisman, "Bush-Appointed Panel Finds U.S. Image Abroad Is in Peril," *New York Times* (1 October 2003), A1, 8; and Susan Sachs, "Poll Finds Hostility Hardening toward U.S. Policies," *New York Times* (17 March 2004), A3; for an overview of the causes of the United States' declining status in the world, see Clyde Prestowitz, *Rogue Nation: American Unilateralism and the Failure of Good Intentions* (New York: Basic Books, 2003).

14. Scott Baldauf, "Letter from Afghanistan," *Nation* (28 April 2003), 24; Carlotta Gall, "In Warlord Land, Democracy Tries Baby Steps," *New York Times* (11 June 2003), A3—Gall has produced an array of brave reports from around the disintegrating region, including: "In Afghanistan, Violence Stalls Renewal Effort," *New York Times* (26 April 2003), A1, 12; "In Pakistan Border Towns, Taliban Has a Resurgence," *New York Times* (6 May 2003), A14; and "Kabul Bombing Kills 4 German Soldiers and Wounds 29," *New York Times* (8 June 2003), A17; 2004 opium cultivation figures from Gall, "Afghan Poppy Growing Reaches Record Level, U.N. Says," *New York Times* (19 November 2004), A3; Christian Parenti, "Who Rules Afghanistan?" *Nation* (15 November 2004), 13–18, quotation from 14; and see Hersh, *Chain of Command*, 145–161, and Eric Schmitt and David Rhode, "Afghan Rebels Widen Attack," *New York Times* (1 August 2004), A1, 11.

15. Human Rights Watch report quoted in John Sifton and Sam Zia Zarifi, "Peacekeeping in Iraq: The Lessons of Afghanistan," *International Herald Tribune* (20 May 2003); Amnesty International quoted in John Pilger, "The War of Lies Goes On," *Mirror* (UK) (16 November 2001); these dire reports are confirmed in Parenti, "Who Rules Afghanistan?"; Barry Bearak, "Unreconstructed: Scenes from the New Afghanistan," *New York Times Sunday Magazine* (1 June 2003), 40–47, 62, 96, 101, quotation from 42; and see the grim report filed by Charles Glass, "You Can Have Patience or You Can Have Carnage," *London Review of Books* (18 November 2004), 11–14.

16. Bearak, "Unreconstructed," 45; $151 billion total from Phyllis Bennis and the IPS Task Force, *A Failed Transition: The Mounting Costs of the Iraq War* (Washington, DC: Institute for Policy Studies/Foreign Policy in Focus, 2004), 22; cost to every U.S. household calculated by Doug Henwood and cited in ibid., 16; Michael Mann, *Incoherent Empire* (London: Verso, 2003), 154; Mike Allen, "Emergency War Funding Wins Backing," *Washington Post* (4 March 2005), A19.

17. Andrews's comments from the 15 October 2004 round of online "Ask the

White House" questions and answers; "Rebuilding Afghanistan" materials from the White House; Arendt, *Origins of Totalitarianism,* 445; and see Jon Henley, "'We Have Been Promised So Much, Billions of Dollars, But Where Has It Gone?'" *Guardian* (28 May 2003); Carlotta Gall, "Afghan Economic Reconstruction Still Sputters," *New York Times* (8 June 2003), A3; and Ahmed Rashid, "The Mess in Afghanistan," *New York Review of Books* (12 February 2004), 24–27.

18. William Blum, *Killing Hope: U.S. Military and CIA Interventions since World War II* (Monroe, ME: Common Courage, 1995); Chalmers Johnson, *Blowback* and *The Sorrows of Empire: Militarism, Secrecy, and the End of the Republic* (New York: Metropolitan, 2004); Scott, *Drugs, Oil, and War;* David Harvey, *The New Imperialism* (Oxford: Oxford University Press, 2003); Mann, *Incoherent Empire;* Ellen Meiksins Wood, *Empire of Capital* (London: Verso, 2003); for analyses of the causes behind some of the actions noted here and their being spun into propaganda, see Noam Chomsky, *The Culture of Terrorism* (Boston: South End Press, 1988), and David Brown and Robert Merrill, eds., *Violent Persuasions: The Politics and Imagery of Terrorism* (Seattle: Bay Press, 1993).

19. For an example of the administration's claims regarding imminent democracy in Iraq, see George Bush, "President Outlines Steps to Help Iraq Achieve Democracy and Freedom" (24 May 2004), available from the White House; State Department report cited in Greg Miller, "Democracy Domino Theory 'Not Credible,'" *Los Angeles Times* (14 March 2003), A1; *9/11 Commission Report,* 376; intelligence report quoted in Douglas Jehl and David Sanger, "Prewar Assessment on Iraq Saw Chance of Strong Divisions," *New York Times* (28 September 2004), A1, 11; on similar postwar assessments, see Douglas Jehl, "U.S. Intelligence Shows Pessimism on Iraq's Future," *New York Times* (16 September 2004), A1, 13.

20. *9/11 Commission Report,* 376; Office of the Under Secretary of Defense (William Schneider, Jr., DSB Chairman), *Report of the Defense Science Board Task Force on Strategic Communication* (Washington, DC: GPO, 2004), 11; for further evidence of how the military-industrial complex's crony capitalism sullies democratic practices at home, see Leslie Wayne, "The Flawed Plane Congress Loves," *New York Times* (24 March 2005), C1, 2, where she uncovers the cronyism driving congressional support for the C130-J, a $66.5 million plane that "cannot fly its intended combat missions."

21. Carleton (Carly) Fiorina, "Be Creative, Not Protectionist," *Wall Street Journal* (13 February 2004); the HP home page, www.hp.com, offers links to many of her speeches; on her status as a media darling, see Evelyn Nussenbaum, "Technology and Show Business Kiss and Make Up," *New York Times* (26 April 2004), C1, 3.

22. William Broad, "U.S. Is Losing Its Dominance in the Sciences," *New York Times* (3 May 2004), A1, 19.

23. Eileen Appelbaum, Annette Bernhardt, and Richard J. Murnane, "Low-Wage America: An Overview," in *Low-Wage America: How Employers Are Reshaping Opportunity in the Workplace,* ed. Appelbaum, Bernhardt, and Murnane (New York: Sage, 2003), 1–29; Jared Bernstein and Lee Price, "Tax Cuts for the Wealthy Haven't Created Confidence for U.S. Households or Employers," *Insight* (2 February 2004), available from the EPI; Paul Krugman, "The Tax-Cut Con," *New York Times Maga-*

zine (14 September 2003), 54–62; Jennifer Beeson and Deborah Weinstein, *The President's Fiscal Year 2005 Budget: Slamming the Door Shut on Opportunity for All Americans* (Washington, DC: Coalition on Human Needs, March 2004), 4, 6–7, 5; Center for Community Change, "Embrace Peace and Prosperity, Not War, Recession, and Poverty," *New York Times* (7 January 2003), A9; Naomi Klein, "Children of Bush's America," *Guardian* (18 May 2004), 21; job loss estimates from "Outsourcing Statistics in Perspective," a 16 March 2004 bulletin from the Center for American Progress, www.americanprogress.org; for additional overviews of the jobs crunch, see Beth Shulman, "Working and Poor in the USA," *Nation* (9 February 2004), 20–22; Cathy Davidson, "Economy Sails Away from Workers," *Newsday* (13 February 2004), available from CommonDreams; and Daniel McGinn, "Help Not Wanted," *Newsweek* (1 March 2004), 31–33; on rising poverty, see David Leonhardt, "More Americans Were Uninsured and Poor in 2003, Census Finds," *New York Times* (27 August 2004), A1, 18; for an overview of U.S. economic difficulties in light of globalization, see Jan Nederveen Pieterse, *Globalization or Empire?* (New York: Routledge, 2004).

24. David Callahan, "Take Back Values," *Nation* (9 February 2004), 17–20, quotation from 19; to hear the voices of those confronted with globalizing neoliberalism's challenges, see the materials collected under "Voices of the Poor," available from the World Bank's PovertyNet at www1.worldbank.org/prem/poverty/voices/index.htm; as noted in chapters 2 and 3, one of the many ironies of our current moment is the way the Bush administration has both orchestrated the economic crises discussed here *and* capitalized on them as occasions for forwarding a "moral" vision of neoliberalism.

25. Regarding such efforts to link domestic economics to international politics, see Anuradha Mittal's powerful "Open Fire and Open Markets: Strategy of an Empire," *Backgrounder* 9, no. 3 (Summer 2003), available from Food First Institute for Food and Development Policy at www.foodfirst.org; for historical accounts of earlier attempts by the United States to couple economic development, the spread of democracy, and missionary zeal, see Stephen Hartnett, *Democratic Dissent and the Cultural Fictions of Antebellum America* (Champaign: University of Illinois press, 2002), 93–131, and the essays collected in *Cultures of United States Imperialism*, ed. Amy Kaplan and Donald Pease (Durham, NC: Duke University Press, 1993).

26. Hannah Arendt, "Civil Disobedience," in *Crises of the Republic* (1969; New York: Harcourt Brace Jovanovich, 1972), 92, 98; for her thoughts on ideology, see *Origins of Totalitarianism*, 468–471.

27. As Gerard Hauser argues in his preface to *Rhetorical Democracy: Discursive Practices of Civic Engagement*, ed. Hauser and Amy Grim (Mahwah, NJ: Lawrence Erlbaum, 2004), "tending to the business of democracy means tending to its rhetorical practices" (xi); for an argument shifting the terrain from ideological critique to rhetorical norms of debate, see Hartnett, *Democratic Dissent*, 17–25.

28. Mann, *Incoherent Empire*, 101; Arendt, *Origins of Totalitarianism*, 437; for further thoughts on the notion of complicity, see Stephen John Hartnett "9/11 and the Poetics of Complicity: A Love Poem for a Hurt Nation," *Cultural Studies <=> Critical Methodologies* 2, no. 3 (August 2002): 315–326; for a brilliant analysis of the ways spectator-sport militarism was produced during the first Gulf War, see Gordon R.

Mitchell, "Placebo Defense: Operation Desert Mirage? The Rhetoric of Patriot Missile Accuracy in the 1991 Persian Gulf War," *Quarterly Journal of Speech* 86, no. 2 (May 2000): 121–145.

29. Richard Rorty, *Contingency, Irony, and Solidarity* (Cambridge: Cambridge University Press, 1989), 6; for a collection of primary documents illustrating the historical transformations noted in the first half of the paragraph, see *The Portable Enlightenment Reader,* ed. Isaac Kramnick (New York: Penguin, 1995).

30. Robert Kaplan, "Supremacy by Stealth," *Atlantic Monthly* (July/August 2003), accessed at www.theatlantic.com; Guy Debord, *The Society of the Spectacle,* trans. Donald Nicholson-Smith (1967; New York: Zone, 2004), passage no. 68, pp. 44–45.

31. Ashcroft quotation from "Excerpts from Attorney General's Testimony before the Senate Judicial Committee," *New York Times* (7 December 2001), B6; Ari Fleischer's comments from his 26 September 2001 press conference, available from the White House; the ACTA report (by Jerry Martin and Anne Neal), *Defending Civilization: How Our Universities Are Failing America and What Can Be Done about It* (Washington, DC: ACTA, 2001), can be ordered at *www.goacta.org;* for overviews of these issues, see Stephen John Hartnett, "A Review of Civil Liberties One Year after 9/11," *Public-i* 2, no. 10 (November 2002): 4–5, and David Cole and James X. Dempsey, *Terrorism and the Constitution: Sacrificing Civil Liberties in the Name of National Security* (New York: New Press, 2002).

32. For extended versions of this claim, see Stephen John Hartnett, "'You are Fit for Something Better': Communicating Hope in Anti-War Activism," in *Communication Activism,* ed. Larry Frey (Mahwah, NJ: Lawrence Erlbaum, forthcoming 2006); Laura Ann Stengrim, "Negotiating Postmodern Democracy, Political Activism, and Knowledge Production: Indymedia's Grassroots and E-savvy Answer to Media Oligopoly," *Communication and Critical Cultural Studies* (forthcoming 2005); and the essays collected in *Globalization and the Politics of Resistance,* ed Barry K. Gills (London: Palgrave, 2000).

33. For a provocative study arguing that "civil style" should now be understood in expansive and mediated terms, see Kevin Michael DeLuca and Jennifer Peeples, "From Public Sphere to Public Screen: Democracy, Activism, and the 'Violence' of Seattle," *Critical Studies in Mass Communication* 19 (2002): 125–151.

Index

IMF loan to, 177; sweatshop labor, 195; view of *NSSUS* doctrine of preemption, 96
Russian Mafia, 132
Rwanda, 96
Ryan, Chuck, 23, 24
Rycroft, Matthew, 79

Sadik, Ahmad, 4
Sadr City, 233
Safire, William: attack on U.N. inspection process, 63, 64; "Behind Closed Doors," 250; defense of Abu Ghraib abuses, 20; defense of Bush's use of term "crusade," 101–02; on intelligence turf wars, 76
Said, Edward, 136
St. Clair, Jeffrey, 299
Saipan, 196
Sala-i-Martin, Xavier, 165, 167
Sallat, Salah Edine, mural in Sadr City, Baghdad, 19–20
"Sanctions of Mass Destruction," 81
Sanders, Bernie, 185
San Onofre (CA) nuclear reactor, 230
Saudi Arabia: PMF support, 242; televisions in, 160; United States' relationship with, 253
Scalia, Antonio, friendship with Dick Cheney, 249–50
Scarlett, John, 78
Schell, Jonathan, 259
schizophrenia of globalization, 38–39, 141
Schlesinger, James R., 19, 150
Schlesinger report, 24, 25, 26, 27
Schroeder, Paul, 96
Schumer, Charles, 70
scientific innovation, U.S. decline in, 283
Scott, Peter Dale, 80, 274, 279
Second Great Awakening, 103
security-consulting firms, free from international law and congressional oversight, 29
selective protectionism, 174
Senate Finance Committee, Joint Committee on Taxation (JCT), 244, 245
Senate Foreign Relations Committee: refusal to confront questions about U.S. policy in Iraq, 85; Tenet's testimony before, 65
Senate Select Committee on Intelligence,

shielding of president in African uranium claim, 71, 73, 324n61
Senor, Dan, 224
Seven Years' War, 8
Shaw Group, 233
Shell, 188
Shiites, 224
Shulsky, Abram, 73
Shultz, George, 252
Sierra Club, 249
Simmonds, Kenneth, 172
Simons, Ann, 112
Singapore, 95, 182
Singer, P. W., 241–42
Singer, Peter, 165, 178
slavery, 157, 207
slum populations, 166–67
social transformations, driven by changing rhetorical habits, 289–90
society of the spectacle, 147, 159–60, 161, 162, 290
Solomon Islands, 95
Sontag, Susan: on brutality in American life, 27–28; post 9/11 comments, 3, 5, 7; "Regarding the Torture of Others," 22
South Korea, 95
Spain, 95
Spanish-American War, 171
Spanish conquistadores, 155
"Special Access Programs," 240
"spectator sport militarism," 288
Stalin, Joseph, 268, 272, 273
Staples, Steven, 142
State Department, U.S.: African Affairs Bureau, 69; Bureau of Intelligence and Research (INR), 65, 66, 274; Human Rights report, 96; "Iraq, the Middle East and Change: No Dominoes," 280
stealth imperialism, 136
Steering Group of Veteran Intelligence Professionals for Sanity, 77
Steinbruner, John, 91
Stevedoring Services of America (SSA Marine), 239
Stevenson, Adlai, 63
Stewart, Terry, 24